Spanish

FOR ATTORNEYS
& PARALEGALS

William C. Harvey, M.S.

BARRON'S

Special thanks to Jeffrey Hummel, Attorney at Law.

All inquiries should be addressed to:
Barron's Educational Series, Inc.
250 Wireless Boulevard
Hauppauge, NY 11788
www.barronseduc.com

ISBN-13: 978-0-7641-4236-9 (book only)
ISBN-10: 0-7641-4236-4 (book only)
ISBN-13: 978-0-7641-9611-9 (book and CD set)
ISBN-10: 0-7641-9611-1 (book and CD set)

Library of Congress Control Number 2009019971

Library of Congress Cataloging-in-Publication Data
Harvey, William C.
   Spanish for attorneys and paralegals / William C. Harvey.
      p. cm.
   ISBN-13: 978-0-7641-4236-9 (book only)
   ISBN-10: 0-7641-4236-4 (book only)
   ISBN-13: 978-0-7641-9611-9 (book and CD set)
   ISBN-10: 0-7641-9611-1 (book and CD set)
  1. Spanish language—Conversation and phrase books (for lawyers).
 2. Spanish language—Conversation and phrase books—English. I. Title.
   PC4120.L38H37   2009
   468′.342102434—dc22
                                                    2009019971

PRINTED IN THE UNITED STATES OF AMERICA

9 8 7 6 5 4 3 2 1

CONTENTS

INTRODUCTION

A NOTE FROM THE AUTHOR

Not everyone is contented with speaking English in the courtroom today. From initial conversations with a plaintiff in a civil case to fighting for a defendant in criminal court, more and more lawyers and paralegals are attempting to communicate in Spanish with the people they serve. Moreover, legal professionals are now realizing the value of Hispanic cultural understanding in the complicated field of law and litigation. And it is obvious that, once those language and cultural barriers are removed, one's relationship with the entire community improves. So, the verdict is in—learn Spanish now, and you'll be on your way to more personal satisfaction and greater professional success!

¡Buena suerte! (*'bweh-nah 'swehr-teh*, Good luck!)

Bill Harvey

HOW TO USE THE GUIDEBOOK AND AUDIO CDs

Spanish for Attorneys and Paralegals teaches English-speaking professionals how to communicate effectively with the Spanish-speaking community. This book provides readers with the Spanish vocabulary and phrases that are needed to question, instruct, counsel, and assist Latino clients in a variety of job-related scenarios, as well as to converse about life and everyday activities. To accelerate the process, all Spanish language skills are taught gradually, and reinforced systematically through practice and review.

Every Spanish word or sentence is followed by its phonetic pronunciation. Please note that the stress is indicated by an apostrophe ('), so that in **oficina** (*oh-fee-'see-nah* office) you pronounce SEE louder that the other syllables. In addition, two audio CDs are included with this book. They provide valuable help with pronunciation, and you can listen to them whenever you find the time.

To get the most out of this book, either use the convenient specialized glossary in the back, or try focusing on the icons provided below. They can be helpful when you are working on a specific skill or topic of interest. Simply scan the pages for the corresponding icon, and read up on whatever you need.

- **NOTICE!—¡Fíjese!** (*'fee-heh-seh*): Extra information and tips on how to use language skills

- **CULTURAL COMMENT—Comentario cultural** (*koh-mehn-'tah-ree-oh kool-too-'rahl*): Insights on Latino cultural awareness

- **VERBS IN ACTION!—¡Verbos activos!** (*'vehr-bohs ahk-'tee-vohs*): Spanish infinitives and verbal phrases

- **THE SENTENCE!—¡La frase!** (*lah 'frah-seh*): New verb tenses in complete sentences

- **PRIVATE PRACTICE—Práctica privada** (*'prahk-tee-kah pree-'vah-dah*): Review practice exercises

Chapter One

Capítulo Uno
(kah-'pee-too-loh 'oo-noh)

Necessary Skills
Habilidades necesarias
(lahs ah-bee-lee-'dah-dehs neh-seh-'sah-ree-ahs)

PRONUNCIATION
La pronunciación *(lah proh-noon-see-ah-see-'ohn)*

Here's the only thing you need to know about Spanish pronunciation:
ALMOST ALL SPANISH LETTERS HAVE ONLY <u>ONE</u> SOUND.
Start by repeating the five Spanish vowels:

a *(ah)*	like yacht	**cha-cha-cha**
e *(eh)*	like met	**excelente**
i *(ee)*	like keep	**Cecilia**
o *(oh)*	like open	**loco**
u *(oo)*	like spoon	**burro***

Keep going. These are the consonant sounds you'll need to know. Again, don't forget—Spanish sounds are pronounced the way they're written:

c (after an **e** or **i**)	**s** as in Sam (**cigarro,** *see-'gahr-roh*)
g (after an **e** or **i**)	**h** as in Harry (**general,** *heh-neh-'rahl*)
h	silent, like the **k** in knife (**hola,** *'oh-lah*)
j	**h** as in hot (**Juan,** *hoo-'ahn*)
ll	**y** as in yes (**llama,** *'yah-mah*)
qu	**k** as in kit (**tequila,** *teh-'kee-lah*)
rr	the rolled **r** sound (**carro,** *'kahr-roh*)
v	**b** as in blue (**vino,** *'vee-noh*)
z	**s** as in sun (**cerveza,** *sehr-'veh-sah*)

The rest of the letters in Spanish are very similar to their equivalents in English, so reviewing them isn't necessary. To practice these sounds, read the English pronunciation that follows every Spanish word. And to review the secrets on how to sound like a native speaker, follow the pronunciation tips below:

---

*When the letter **u** is preceded by a **g**, it doesn't make the *oo* sound (**guitarra** *[ghee-'tahr-rah]*, **guerra** *['gehr-rah]*).

— Remember that your poor pronunciation won't really hurt communication. People generally *are* forgiving, and most will understand you anyway.
— Just tell yourself: Spanish is pronounced the way it's spelled, and vice versa. So pronounce each sound the same way every time the corresponding letter appears.
— Spanish sounds are usually made toward the front of the mouth instead of back, with little or no air coming out. And, short, choppy sounds are better than long stretched-out ones.
— Accented (´) parts of words should always be pronounced LOUDER and with more emphasis (**olé**). If there's no accent mark, say the last part of the word LOUDER and with more emphasis (**español**). For words ending in a vowel, or in **n** or **s**, the next to the last part of the word is stressed (**importante**).

  NOTICE!   ¡Fíjese!

Go look at yourself in the mirror. Now hold up your right hand and make this pledge:

"I will ruin Spanish."

Did you say it ... aloud? Good. Your language skills are limited at best, and your chances of acquiring native-like pronunciation are almost zero. Feel better? So the next time you feel uncomfortable about speaking Spanish, just remember your pledge!

THE SPANISH ALPHABET
El abecedario
(ehl ah-beh-seh-'dah-ree-oh)

Take a few moments to review the alphabet. It can be helpful either when you're on the phone or when you haven't a clue what someone is saying. The key question to ask is:

How do you spell it? **¿Cómo se deletrea?** *('koh-moh seh deh-leh-'treh-ah)*
To practice, say each letter aloud:

a *(ah)*	**h** *('ah-cheh)*	**ñ** *('ehn-yeh)**	**u** *(oo)*
b *(beh)*	**i** *(ee)*	**o** *(oh)*	**v** *(veh)*
c *(seh)*	**j** *('hoh-tah)*	**p** *(peh)*	**w** *('doh-bleh veh)*
ch *(cheh)**	**k** *(kah)*	**q** *(koo)*	**x** *('eh-kees)*
d *(deh)*	**l** *('eh-leh)*	**r** *('eh-reh)*	**y** *(ee-gree-'eh-gah)*
e *(eh)*	**ll** *('eh-yeh)**	**rr** *('ehr-reh)*	**z** *('seh-tah)*
f *('eh-feh)*	**m** *('eh-meh)*	**s** *('eh-seh)*	
g *(heh)*	**n** *('eh-neh)*	**t** *(teh)*	

*These letters have been removed from the official Spanish alphabet. However, people still refer to them when spelling out a word.

THE SENTENCE!   ¡La frase!

This next question will also come in handy:

How do you write it?   **¿Cómo se escribe?** *('koh-moh seh ehs-'kree-beh)*
How do you write your name? **¿Cómo se escribe su nombre?**
                             ('koh-moh seh ehs-'kree-beh soo 'nohm-breh)

PRIVATE PRACTICE   **Práctica privada**

Pronounce these words and then spell them in Spanish. Remember to sound out each letter:

amigo	**excelente**	**macho**	**trabajo**
amor	**dinero**	**enchilada**	**nada**
carro	**grande**	**pollo**	**señor**
español	**hombre**	**chiquita**	**vino**

GREETINGS AND EXPRESSIONS
Los saludos y las expresiones
(lohs sah-'loo-dohs ee lahs ex-preh-see-'oh-nehs)

Look over these popular exchanges, and highlight the ones you'll need right away. Note the upside-down marks: questions start with ¿ and exclamations start with ¡:

Hi!   **¡Hola!** *('oh-lah)*
How are you?   **¿Cómo está?** *('koh-moh ehs-'tah)*
How's it going?   **¿Qué tal?** *(keh tahl)*
Real well.   **Muy bien.** *(mwee bee-'ehn)*
And you?   **¿Y usted?** *(ee oos-'tehd)*
Not bad.   **Más o menos.** *(mahs oh 'meh-nohs)*
What's happening?   **¿Qué pasa?** *(keh 'pah-sah)*
Nothing much!   **¡Sin novedad!** *(seen noh-veh-'dahd)*
Good morning.   **Buenos días.** *('bweh-nohs 'dee-ahs)*
Good afternoon.   **Buenas tardes.** *('bweh-nahs 'tahr-dehs)*
Good evening, good night.   **Buenas noches.** *('bweh-nahs 'noh-chehs)*
Good-bye.   **Adiós.** *(ah-dee-'ohs)*
Take it easy.   **Cúidese bien.** *('kwee-deh-seh bee-'ehn)*
See you tomorrow.   **Hasta mañana.** *('ahs-tah mahn-'yah-nah)*

Here are some more.

I'm sorry.   **Lo siento.** *(loh see-'ehn-toh)*
Come in.   **Adelante.** *(ah-deh-'lahn-teh)*
Go ahead.   **Pase.** *('pah-seh)*

These groups of words can be used separately:

What's your name?	**¿Cómo se llama?** (*'koh-moh seh 'yah-mah*)
My name is...	**Me llamo...** (*meh 'yah-moh*)
Nice to meet you!	**¡Mucho gusto!** (*'moo-choh 'goos-toh*)
Same to you.	**Igualmente.** (*ee-gwahl-'mehn-teh*)
I'd like to introduce...	**Quiero presentarle a...** (*kee-'eh-roh preh-sehn-'tahr-leh ah*)
Please.	**Por favor.** (*pohr fah-'vohr*)
Thanks a lot.	**Muchas gracias.** (*'moo-chahs 'grah-see-ahs*)
You're welcome.	**De nada.** (*deh 'nah-dah*)
Wait a moment.	**Espere un momento.** (*ehs-'peh-reh oon moh-'mehn-toh*)
Pay attention.	**Preste atención.** (*'prehs-teh ah-tehn-see-'ohn*)
Be careful.	**Tenga cuidado.** (*'tehn-gah kwee-'dah-doh*)

The following words mean the same thing in English, but are used differently in Spanish. Picture saying them while on the job:

Excuse me! (*if you are moving through a crowd*)	**¡Con permiso!** (*kohn pehr-'mee-soh*)
Excuse me! (*if you need someone's attention*)	**¡Disculpe!** (*dees-'kool-peh*)
Excuse me! (*if you cough, belch, or sneeze*)	**¡Perdón!** (*pehr-'dohn*)

And here are some of my favorites:

Do you understand?	**¿Entiende usted?** (*ehn-tee-'ehn-deh oos-'tehd*)
I don't understand.	**No entiendo.** (*noh ehn-tee-'ehn-doh*)
Do you know?	**¿Sabe?** (*'sah-beh*)
I don't know.	**No sé.** (*noh seh*)
Do you speak English?	**¿Habla inglés?** (*'ah-blah een-'glehs*)
I speak a little Spanish.	**Hablo poquito español.**
	(*'ah-bloh poh-'kee-toh ehs-pahn-'yohl*)
I'm learning Spanish.	**Estoy aprendiendo español.**
	(*ehs-'toh-ee ah-prehn-dee-'ehn-doh ehs-pahn-'yohl*)
More slowly.	**Más despacio.** (*mahs dehs-'pah-see-oh*)
Thanks for your patience.	**Gracias por su paciencia.**
	(*'grah-see-ahs pohr soo pah-see-'ehn-see-ah*)
What does it mean?	**¿Qué significa?** (*keh seeg-nee-'fee-kah*)

And throw in *and* (**y**), *or* (**o**), and *but* (**pero**) as often as possible:

¡No sé y no entiendo! (*noh seh ee noh ehn-tee-'ehn-doh*)

NOTICE!   ¡Fíjese!

Start a specialized list of expressions on your own:

Bless you!	**¡Salud!** *(sah-'lood)*
Welcome!	**¡Bienvenidos!** *(bee-ehn-veh-'nee-dohs)*
Good luck!	**¡Buena suerte!** *('bweh-nah 'swehr-teh)*
Congratulations!	**¡Felicitaciones!** *(feh-lee-see-tah-see-'oh-nehs)*
Merry Christmas!	**¡Feliz navidad!** *(feh-'lees nah-vee-'dahd)*
Happy birthday!	**¡Feliz cumpleaños!** *(feh-'lees koom-pleh-'ahn-yohs)*

CULTURAL COMMENT   Comentario cultural

The word **tú** *(too)* is the informal way of saying *you* in Spanish. This casual form is generally exchanged between family and friends, or you use it when you address children. Here are some examples:

You are my friend.	**Tú eres mi amigo.** *(too 'eh-rehs mee ah-'mee-goh)*
Do you speak Spanish?	**¿Tú hablas español?** *(too 'ah-blahs ehs-pahn-'yohl)*
You have an excellent case.	**Tú tienes un caso excelente.**
	(too tee-'eh-nehs oon 'kah-soh ex-seh-'lehn-teh)

The informal word for *your* is **tu** as well, which is the same as *you* but without the accent:

Where's your family?	**¿Dónde está tu familia?**
	('dohn-deh ehs-'tah too fah-'mee-lee-ah)

YOU, FORMAL AND INFORMAL
El *tú* y el *usted*
(ehl too ee ehl oos-'tehd)

And then we arrive at the formal *you* word: **usted** *(oos-'tehd)*. The problem is that **tú** and **usted** require the application of different grammar rules, including different verb conjugations, which significantly complicates matters. The solution? We will drop the informal **tú** form from this book, because if you use **usted** with *anybody,* you will never make a mistake. To be formal is to be safe. Use **usted** with your clients, with your superiors, your employees, and even children, and nobody will ever get upset.

PRIVATE PRACTICE   **Práctica privada**

Practice reading these conversations without looking up the translations:

A. **¡Qué tal!**
B. **Muy bien, gracias. ¿Y usted?**
A. **Más o menos.**

A. **¡Ahh-choo! Perdón.**
B. **¡Salud!**
A. **Muchas gracias.**

A. **¿Cómo se llama?**
B. **Me llamo Felipe. ¿Y usted?**
A. **Me llamo Jason.**
B. **Mucho gusto.**
A. **Igualmente.**

NOTICE!   **¡Fíjese!**

The names for people, places, and things are either masculine or feminine, and have either **el** or **la** in front. Generally, if the word ends in the letter **o** there's an **el** in front (e.g., **el carro**, **el niño**). Conversely, if the word ends in an **a** there should be a **la** in front (e.g., **la tortilla**, **la persona**). There are very few exceptions, such as **el agua**, **la mano**, **el sofá**.

Words not ending in either **o** or **a** need to be memorized (e.g., paper, **el papel**; light, **la luz**). In the case of single objects, use **el** and **la** much like the word *the* in English: The office is big: **La oficina es grande**.

Remember too, that **el** and **la** are used in Spanish to indicate a person's sex. **El abogado** is a male lawyer, whereas **la abogada** is a female. Here's how we change words to refer to the female gender:

baby	**el bebé** *(ehl beh-'beh)*	**la bebé** *(lah beh-'beh)*
child	**el niño** *(ehl 'neen-yoh)*	**la niña** *(lah 'neen-yah)*
teenager	**el muchacho** *(ehl moo-'chah-choh)*	**la muchacha** *(lah moo-'chah-chah)*

To form the plural, words ending in a vowel end in **-s**, while words ending in a consonant end in **-es**. Notice how **el** becomes **los** and **la** becomes **las**:

man	**el hombre** *(ehl 'ohm-breh)*
men	**los hombres** *(lohs 'ohm-brehs)*
woman	**la mujer** *(lah moo-'hehr)*
women	**las mujeres** *(lahs moo-'heh-rehs)*

PRONOUNS
Los pronombres
(lohs proh-'nohm-brehs)

This group of words is used to identify everyone:

I	**Yo** *(yoh)*
You	**Usted (Ud.)** *(oos-'tehd)*
He	**Él** *(ehl)*
She	**Ella** *('eh-yah)*
We	**Nosotros** *(noh-'soh-trohs)*
You guys	**Ustedes (Uds.)** *(oos-'teh-dehs)*
They	**Ellos/Ellas** *('eh-yohs, 'eh-yahs)*

And these words indicate possession. They *replace* **el** and **la**:

my	**mi** *(mee)*	**mi amigo** *(mee ah-'mee-goh)*
your, his, her, their	**su** *(soo)*	**su casa** *(soo 'kah-sah)*
our	**nuestro** *('nwehs-troh)*	**nuestro carro** *('nwehs-troh 'kahr-roh)*

PRIVATE PRACTICE   Práctica privada

Practice pronouns by inserting your name and the name of a friend:

¿Yo? <u>Mi</u> nombre es <u>Roberto</u>.
¿Él? <u>Su</u> nombre es <u>Francisco</u>.
¿Nosotros? ¡<u>Nuestros</u> nombres son <u>Roberto</u> y <u>Francisco</u>!

EVERYDAY QUESTIONS
Preguntas de todos los días
(preh-'goon-tahs deh 'toh-dohs lohs 'dee-ahs)

One of the first questions you should memorize is the following. It will prevent you from having to repeat yourself in Spanish or English:

Do you have a question? **¿Tiene una pregunta?** *(tee-'eh-neh 'oo-nah preh-'goon-tah)*

Now prepare to answer by studying the ten most common question words in Spanish:

What?	**¿Qué?**	*(keh)*
How?	**¿Cómo?**	*('koh-moh)*
Where?	**¿Dónde?**	*('dohn-deh)*
When?	**¿Cuándo?**	*('kwahn-doh)*
Which?	**¿Cuál?**	*(kwahl)*
Who?	**¿Quién?**	*(kee-'ehn)*
Whose?	**¿De quién?**	*(deh kee-'ehn)*
How much?	**¿Cuánto?**	*('kwahn-toh)*
How many?	**¿Cuántos?**	*('kwahn-tohs)*
Why?	**¿Por qué?**	*(pohr keh)*

Here's how they work in every day conversations:

What?	**¿Qué?**	*(keh)*
What's happening?	**¿Qué pasa?**	*(keh 'pah-sah)*
How?	**¿Cómo?**	*('koh-moh)*
How are you?	**¿Cómo está?**	*('koh-moh ehs-'tah)*
Where?	**¿Dónde?**	*('dohn-deh)*
Where is it?	**¿Dónde está?**	*('dohn-deh ehs-'tah)*
When?	**¿Cuándo?**	*('kwahn-doh)*
When is it?	**¿Cuándo es?**	*('kwahn-doh ehs)*
Which?	**¿Cuál?**	*(kwahl)*
Which is it?	**¿Cuál es?**	*(kwahl ehs)*
Who?	**¿Quién?**	*(kee-'ehn)*
Who is it?	**¿Quién es?**	*(kee-'ehn ehs)*
Whose?	**¿De quién?**	*(deh kee-'ehn)*
Whose is it?	**¿De quién es?**	*(deh kee-'ehn ehs)*
How much?	**¿Cuánto?**	*('kwahn-toh)*
How much does it cost?	**¿Cuánto cuesta?**	*('kwahn-toh 'kwehs-tah)*

How many?	**¿Cuántos?** *('kwahn-tohs)*
How old are you?	**¿Cuántos años tiene?** *('kwahn-tohs 'ahn-yohs tee-'eh-neh)*
Why?	**¿Por qué?** *(pohr keh)*
Why not?	**¿Por qué no?** *(pohr keh noh)*

By the way, the word **porque** *('pohr-keh)* means *because*, and it sounds and looks a lot like **¿Por qué?** *(Why?)*:

Why doesn't he have a car?	**¿Por qué no tiene carro?** *(pohr keh noh tee-'eh-neh 'kahr-roh)*
Because he doesn't have a license.	**Porque no tiene licencia.** *('pohr-keh noh tee-'eh-neh lee-'sehn-see-ah)*

Obviously, not all interrogative phrases can be translated literally, so use them as one-liners whenever you can. For example, notice how *you* and *your* are implied, but not included:

What's your name?	**¿Cómo se llama?** *('koh-moh seh 'yah-mah)*
How old are you?	**¿Cuántos años tiene?** *('kwahn-tohs 'ahn-yohs tee-'eh-neh)*
What's your address?	**¿Cuál es su dirección?** *(kwahl ehs soo dee-rehk-see-'ohn)*

Here are some of the most common phrases that include question words:

How can I help you?	**¿Cómo puedo ayudarle?** *('koh-moh 'pweh-doh ah-yoo-'dahr-leh)*
What's the matter?	**¿Qué pasó?** *(keh pah-'soh)*
Who's calling?	**¿Quién habla?** *(kee-'ehn 'ah-blah)*

This popular series of questions can be used with the phrase, **¿Cuál es su...?** *(kwahl ehs soo)*. We'll look at it in more detail in Chapter Two:

What's your...?	**¿Cuál es su...?** *(kwahl ehs soo)*
address	**dirección** *(dee-rehk-see-'ohn)*
age	**edad** *(eh-'dahd)*
date of birth	**fecha de nacimiento** *('feh-chah deh nah-see-mee-'ehn-toh)*
driver's license number	**número de licencia de manejar** *('noo-meh-roh deh lee-'sehn-see-ah deh mah-neh-'hahr)*
e-mail address	**correo electrónico** *(kohr-'reh-oh eh-lehk-'troh-nee-koh)*
full name	**nombre completo** *('nohm-breh kohm-'pleh-toh)*
phone number	**número de teléfono** *('noo-meh-roh deh teh-'leh-foh-noh)*
place of birth	**lugar de nacimiento** *(loo-'gahr deh nah-see-mee-'ehn-toh)*
social security number	**número de seguro social** *('noo-meh-roh deh seh-'goo-roh soh-see-'ahl)*

NOTICE! ¡Fíjese!

To change a question word to refer to more than one thing, simply add **-es** to the question word:

Which one ?   **¿Cuál?** *(kwahl)*
Which ones?   **¿Cuáles?** *('kwah-lehs)*

But always be aware of the masculine-feminine business:

How many men?   **¿Cuántos hombres?** *('kwahn-tohs 'ohm-brehs)*
How many women?   **¿Cuántas mujeres?** *('kwahn-tahs moo-'heh-rehs)*

CULTURAL COMMENT Comentario cultural

When referring to others by name, it helps to pronounce the names correctly, as it makes people feel much more at ease. Also, it's not uncommon for someone in Latin America to have no middle name and two last names. Don't get confused. Here's the order for males and unmarried females:

José Antonio García Sánchez

First name   **José Antonio** *(hoh-'seh ahn-'toh-nee-oh)*
primer nombre *(pree-'mehr 'nohm-breh)*

Father's last name   **García** *(gahr-'see-ah)*
apellido paterno *(ah-peh-'yee-doh pah-'tehr-noh)*

Mother's last name   **Sánchez** *('sahn-chehs)*
apellido materno *(ah-peh-'yee-doh mah-'tehr-noh)*

And here's the order for married females:

María Lourdes García Sánchez Meza

First name   **María Lourdes** *(mah-'ree-ah 'loor-dehs)*
primer nombre *(pree-'mehr 'nohm-breh)*

Father's last name   **García** *(gahr-'see-ah)*
apellido paterno *(ah-peh-'yee-doh pah-'tehr-noh)*

Mother's last name   **Sánchez** *('sahn-chehs)*
apellido materno *(ah-peh-'yee-doh mah-'tehr-noh)*

Husband's last name   **Meza** *('meh-sah)*
apellido del esposo *(ah-peh-'yee-doh dehl ehs-'poh-soh)*

PRIVATE PRACTICE **Práctica privada**

Answer these questions about yourself aloud:

¿Cómo se llama? *('koh-moh seh 'yah-mah)* _____

¿Cuál es su dirección? *(kwahl ehs soo dee-rehk-see-'ohn)* _____

¿Cuántos años tiene? *('kwahn-tohs 'ahn-yohs tee-'eh-neh)* _____

¿Quién es su amigo? *(kee-'ehn ehs soo ah-'mee-goh)* _____

¿Qué pasa? *(keh 'pah-sah)* _____

PEOPLE AND THINGS
La gente y las cosas
(lah 'hehn-teh ee lahs 'koh-sahs)

The first thing to do is identify everyone around you:

baby	**el/la bebé** *(ehl/lah beh-'beh)*
boy	**el niño** *(ehl 'neen-yoh)*
child	**el niño/la niña** *(ehl 'neen-yoh/lah 'neen-yah)*
elderly person	**la persona mayor** *(lah pehr-'soh-nah mah-'yohr)*
friend	**el amigo/la amiga** *(ehl ah-'mee-goh/lah ah-'mee-gah)*
girl	**la niña** *(lah 'neen-yah)*
man	**el hombre** *(ehl 'ohm-breh)*
neighbor	**el vecino/la vecina** *(ehl veh-'see-noh/lah veh-'see-nah)*
person	**la persona** *(lah pehr-'soh-nah)*
relative	**el/la pariente** *(ehl/lah pah-ree-'ehn-teh)*
roommate	**el compañero/la compañera** *(ehl kohm-pahn-'yeh-roh/lah kohm-pahn-'yeh-rah)*
woman	**la mujer** *(lah moo-'hehr)*
young person	**el muchacho/la muchacha** *(ehl moo-'chah-cho/lah moo-'chah-chah)*
How's (the)...?	**¿Cómo está...?** *('koh-moh ehs-'tah)*

When referring to others, utilize these words when appropriate:

Mr. or a man	**Señor (Sr.)** *(sehn-'yohr)*
Mrs. or a lady	**Señora (Sra.)** *(sehn-'yoh-rah)*
Miss or a young lady	**Señorita (Srta.)** *(sehn-yoh-'ree-tah)*

Now name the following common objects, if they're within view:

Where's (the)...?	**¿Dónde está...?** *('dohn-deh ehs-'tah)*
armchair	**el sillón** *(ehl see-'yohn)*
book	**el libro** *(ehl 'lee-broh)*

car	**el carro** *(ehl 'kahr-roh)*
chair	**la silla** *(lah 'see-yah)*
clothing	**la ropa** *(lah 'roh-pah)*
computer	**la computadora** *(lah kohm-poo-tah-'doh-rah)*
couch	**el sofá** *(ehl soh-'fah)*
desk	**el escritorio** *(ehl ehs-kree-'toh-ree-oh)*
door	**la puerta** *(lah 'pwehr-tah)*
floor	**el piso** *(ehl 'pee-soh)*
food	**la comida** *(lah koh-'mee-dah)*
furniture	**el mueble** *(ehl 'mweh-bleh)*
house	**la casa** *(lah 'kah-sah)*
lamp	**la lámpara** *(lah 'lahm-pah-rah)*
money	**el dinero** *(ehl dee-'neh-roh)*
notebook	**el cuaderno** *(ehl kwah-'dehr-noh)*
office	**la oficina** *(lah oh-fee-'see-nah)*
paper	**el papel** *(ehl pah-'pehl)*
pen	**el lapicero** *(ehl lah-pee-'seh-roh)*
pencil	**el lápiz** *(ehl 'lah-pees)*
room	**el cuarto** *(ehl 'kwahr-toh)*
table	**la mesa** *(lah 'meh-sah)*
telephone	**el teléfono** *(ehl teh-'leh-foh-noh)*
tool	**la herramienta** *(lah ehr-rah-mee-'ehn-tah)*
window	**la ventana** *(lah vehn-'tah-nah)*

LEGAL TERMINOLOGY
La terminología jurídica
(lah tehr-mee-noh-loh-'hee-ah hoo-'ree-dee-kah)

No matter what you do in the legal field, you'll have to know these survival words:

case	**el caso** *(ehl 'kah-soh)*
charge	**el cargo** *(ehl 'kahr-goh)*
consultation	**la consulta** *(lah kohn-'sool-tah)*
court	**el tribunal, la corte** *(ehl tree-boo-'nahl, lah 'kohr-teh)*
courtroom	**la sala de tribunal** *(la 'sah-lah deh tree-boo-'nahl)*
crime	**el delito, el crimen** *(ehl deh-'lee-toh, ehl 'kree-mehn)*
defense	**la defense** *(lah deh-'fehn-sah)*
judge	**el juez/la jueza** *(ehl hwehs/lah 'hweh-sah)*
jurisdiction	**la jurisdicción** *(lah hoo-rees-deek-see-'ohn)*
jury	**el jurado** *(ehl hoo-'rah-doh)*
law	**la ley** *(lah 'leh-hee)*
lawsuit	**el pleito** *(ehl 'pleh-ee-toh)*
legal action	**la querella** *(lah keh-'reh-yah)*
prosecution	**la acusación** *(lah ah-koo-sah-see-'ohn)*
representation	**la representación** *(lah reh-preh-sehn-tah-see-'ohn)*
settlement	**el convenio** *(ehl kohn-'veh-nee-oh)*
trial	**el juicio** *(ehl hoo-'ee-see-oh)*
verdict	**el veredicto** *(ehl veh-reh-'deek-toh)*

And these basic words refer to those involved in legal matters:

client	**el/la cliente** *(ehl/lah klee-'ehn-teh)*
defendant (civil)	**el demandado/la demandada** *(ehl deh-mahn-'dah-doh/lah deh-mahn-dah-dah)*
defendant (criminal)	**el acusado/la acusada** *(ehl ah-koo-'sah-doh/lah ah-koo-'sah-dah)*
lawyer	**el abogado/la abogada** *(ehl ah-boh-'gah-doh/lah ah-boh-'gah-dah)*
legal representative	**el/la representante legal** *(ehl/lah reh-preh-sehn-'tahn-teh leh-'gahl)*
paralegal	**el/la ayudante** *(ehl/lah ah-yoo-'dahn-teh)*
party	**la parte interesada** *(lah 'pahr-teh een-teh-reh-'sah-dah)*
plaintiff	**el/la demandante** *(ehl/lah deh-mahn-'dahn-teh)*
suspect	**el sospechoso/la sospechosa** *(ehl sohs-peh-'choh-soh/lah sohs-peh-'choh-sah)*
victim	**la víctima** *(lah 'veek-tee-mah)*
witness	**el testigo/la testiga** *(ehl tehs-'tee-goh/lah tehs-'tee-gah)*

PRIVATE PRACTICE **Práctica privada**

Read these sample sentences aloud:

The lawyer has many cases.	**El abogado tiene muchos casos.** *(ehl ah-boh-'gah-doh tee-'eh-neh 'moo-chohs 'kah-sohs)*
There's a trial in the courtroom.	**Hay un juicio en la sala de tribunal.** *('ah-ee oon hoo-'ee-see-oh ehn lah 'sah-lah deh tree-boo-'nahl)*
I want to speak with the defendant.	**Quiero hablar con la acusada.** *(kee-'eh-roh ah-'blahr kohn lah ah-'koo-'sah-dah)*

KEY COMMANDS
Las órdenes principales
(lahs 'ohr-deh-nehs preen-see-'pah-lehs)

Another powerful way to memorize Spanish is through the use of commands. The command form of verbs can be practiced all day, especially when you're telling others what to do. Be sure to add the word, *please.*

Por favor... *(pohr fah-'vohr)*

Answer!	**¡Conteste!** *(kohn-'tehs-teh)*
Call!	**¡Llame!** *('yah-meh)*
Check!	**¡Revise!** *(reh-'vee-seh)*
Come!	**¡Venga!** *('vehn-gah)*
Continue!	**¡Siga!** *('see-gah)*

Drive!	**¡Maneje!** *(mah-'neh-heh)*
Enter!	**¡Entre!** *('ehn-treh)*
Explain!	**¡Explique!** *(ex-'plee-keh)*
Finish!	**¡Termine!** *(tehr-'mee-neh)*
Go!	**¡Vaya!** *('vah-yah)*
Leave!	**¡Salga!** *('sahl-gah)*
Listen!	**¡Escuche!** *(ehs-'koo-cheh)*
Look!	**¡Mire!** *('mee-reh)*
Read!	**¡Lea!** *('leh-ah)*
Sign!	**¡Firme!** *('feer-meh)*
Speak!	**¡Hable!** *('ah-bleh)*
Return!	**¡Regrese!** *(reh-'greh-seh)*
Study!	**¡Estudie!** *(ehs-'too-dee-eh)*
Walk!	**¡Camine!** *(kah-'mee-neh)*
Write!	**¡Escriba!** *(ehs-'kree-bah)*

These commands are expressions and a little harder to pronounce:

Hurry up!	**¡Apúrese!** *(ah-'poo-reh-seh)*
Sit down!	**¡Siéntese!** *(see-'ehn-teh-seh)*
Stand up!	**¡Levántese!** *(leh-'vahn-teh-seh)*
Stay!	**¡Quédese!** *('keh-deh-seh)*
Wait!	**¡Espere!** *(ehs-'peh-reh)*

Most commands can be used with an object. For example, *Bring the information* is
Traiga la información *('trah-ee-gah lah een-fohr-mah-see-'ohn)*.

Bring...	**Traiga...** *('trah-ee-gah)*
Buy...	**Compre...** *('kohm-preh)*
Change...	**Cambie...** *('kahm-bee-eh)*
Clean...	**Limpie...** *('leem-pee-eh)*
Close...	**Cierre...** *(see-'ehr-reh)*
Fill out...	**Llene...** *('yeh-neh)*
Give...	**Dé...** *(deh)*
Look for...	**Busque...** *('boos-keh)*
Open...	**Abra...** *('ah-brah)*
Park...	**Estacione...** *(ehs-tah-see-'oh-neh)*
Pick up...	**Recoja...** *(reh-'koh-hah)*
Put inside...	**Meta...** *('meh-tah)*
Put...	**Ponga...** *('pohn-gah)*
Remove...	**Saque...** *('sah-keh)*
Set up...	**Prepare...** *(preh-'pah-reh)*
Take...	**Tome...** *('toh-meh)*
Tell...	**Diga...** *('dee-gah)*
Throw out...	**Tire...** *('tee-reh)*
Use...	**Use...** *('oo-seh)*

NOTICE! ¡Fíjese!

To give an order to more than one person, simply add the letter **n** to the singular verb form:

¡Apúrense! *(ah-'poo-rehn-seh)*   Hurry up, you guys!
¡Lean! *('leh-ahn)*   Read, you guys!

PRIVATE PRACTICE   Práctica privada

Have a Spanish speaker command you to touch, look at, or point to things nearby:

Touch...	**Toque.** *('toh-keh)*
Touch the paper.	**Toque el papel.** *('toh-keh ehl pah-'pehl)*
Look at...	**Mire.** *('mee-reh)*
Look at the car.	**Mire el carro.** *('mee-reh ehl 'kahr-roh)*
Point to...	**Señale.** *(sehn-'yah-leh)*
Point to the house.	**Señale la casa.** *(sehn-'yah-leh lah 'kah-sah)*

COLORS
Los colores
(lohs koh-'loh-rehs)

The best way to practice these words is to call out the colors of things around you:

It's...	**Es...** *(ehs)*
black	**negro** *('neh-groh)*
blue	**azul** *(ah-'sool)*
brown	**café** *(kah-'feh)*
gray	**gris** *(grees)*
green	**verde** *('vehr-deh)*
orange	**anaranjado** *(ah-nah-rahn-'hah-doh)*
pink	**rosado** *(roh-'sah-doh)*
purple	**morado** *(moh-'rah-doh)*
red	**rojo** *('roh-hoh)*
white	**blanco** *('blahn-koh)*
yellow	**amarillo** *(ah-mah-'ree-yoh)*

NOTICE!   ¡Fíjese!

The "reversal rule" is usually applied when you give a description in Spanish. The descriptive word generally goes <u>after</u> the word being described. Study these examples:

The big house	**La casa grande** (*lah 'kah-sah 'grahn-deh*)
The green car	**El carro verde** (*ehl 'kahr-roh 'vehr-deh*)
The important man	**El hombre importante** (*ehl 'ohm-breh eem-pohr-'tahn-teh*)

To make a description plural, not only do all the nouns and adjectives need to end in **-s** or **-es**, but when they are used together, the genders (the **o** and **a**) must match as well:

Two white doors	**Dos puertas blancas** (*dohs 'pwehr-tahs 'blahn-kahs*)
Three black books	**Tres libros negros** (*trehs 'leeb-rohs 'neh-grohs*)

 PRIVATE PRACTICE   **Práctica privada**

(1) **(Number in a circle: Check the answers at the end of the book.)**
Change these sentences to plural:

1. **el carro rojo**   los _____

2. **una casa grande**   tres _____

3. **la mesa negra**   las _____

NUMBERS
Los números
(lohs 'noo-meh-rohs)

You can't say much in Spanish without knowing your numbers:

0	**cero** (*'seh-roh*)	14	**catorce** (*kah-'tohr-seh*)
1	**uno** (*'oo-noh*)	15	**quince** (*'keen-seh*)
2	**dos** (*dohs*)	16	**dieciséis** (*dee-eh-see-'seh-ees*)
3	**tres** (*trehs*)	17	**diecisiete** (*dee-eh-see-see-'eh-teh*)
4	**cuatro** (*'kwah-troh*)	18	**dieciocho** (*dee-eh-see-'oh-choh*)
5	**cinco** (*'seen-koh*)	19	**diecinueve** (*dee-eh-see-'nweh-veh*)
6	**seis** (*'seh-ees*)	20	**veinte** (*'veh-een-teh*)
7	**siete** (*see-'eh-teh*)	30	**treinta** (*'treh-een-tah*)
8	**ocho** (*'oh-choh*)	40	**cuarenta** (*kwah-'rehn-tah*)
9	**nueve** (*'nweh-veh*)	50	**cincuenta** (*seen-'kwehn-tah*)
10	**diez** (*dee-'ehs*)	60	**sesenta** (*seh-'sehn-tah*)
11	**once** (*'ohn-seh*)	70	**setenta** (*seh-'tehn-tah*)
12	**doce** (*'doh-seh*)	80	**ochenta** (*oh-'chehn-tah*)
13	**trece** (*'treh-seh*)	90	**noventa** (*noh-'vehn-tah*)

For all the numbers in-between, just add **y** (ee), which means *and*:

21	**veinte y uno** *('veh-een-teh ee 'oo-noh)*
22	**veinte y dos** *('veh-een-teh ee dohs)*
23	**veinte y** _____ (your turn...)
34	_____
55	_____
87	_____

You'll also need to know how to say the larger numbers in Spanish. They aren't that difficult, so practice aloud:

100	**cien**	*(see-'ehn)*
200	**doscientos**	*(dohs-see-'ehn-tohs)*
300	**trescientos**	*(trehs-see-'ehn-tohs)*
400	**cuatrocientos**	*('kwah-troh-see-'ehn-tohs)*
500	**quinientos**	*(kee-nee-'ehn-tohs)*
600	**seiscientos**	*(seh-ees-see-'ehn-tohs)*
700	**setecientos**	*(seh-teh-see-'ehn-tohs)*
800	**ochocientos**	*(oh-choh-see-'ehn-tohs)*
900	**novecientos**	*(noh-veh-see-'ehn-tohs)*
1000	**mil**	*(meel)*
million	**millón**	*(mee-'yohn)*

And everyone on the job needs the ordinal numbers, too:

first	**primero**	*(pree-'meh-roh)*
second	**segundo**	*(seh-'goon-doh)*
third	**tercero**	*(tehr-'seh-roh)*
fourth	**cuarto**	*('kwahr-toh)*
fifth	**quinto**	*('keen-toh)*
sixth	**sexto**	*('sex-toh)*
seventh	**séptimo**	*('sehp-tee-moh)*
eighth	**octavo**	*(ohk-'tah-voh)*
ninth	**noveno**	*(noh-'veh-noh)*
tenth	**décimo**	*('deh-see-moh)*
eleventh	**undécimo**	*(oon-'deh-see-moh)*
twelfth	**duodecimo**	*(doo-oh-'deh-see-moh)*

☞   NOTICE!   ¡Fíjese!

To say *a* or *an* in Spanish, use **un** *(oon)* for masculine words or **una** *('oo-nah)* for feminine words:

A phone	**Un teléfono** *(oon teh-'leh-foh-noh)*
A white phone	**Un teléfono blanco** *(oon teh-'leh-foh-noh 'blahn-koh)*
An office	**Una oficina** *('oo-nah oh-fee-'see-nah)*
A yellow office	**Una oficina amarilla** *('oo-nah oh-fee-'see-nah ah-mah-'ree-yah)*

And to say *some*, use **unos** (*'oo-nohs*) or **unas** (*'oo-nahs*), and don't forget the rule about plurals:

Some folders	**Unos cuadernos** (*'oo-nohs kwah-'dehr-nohs*)
Some red folders	**Unos cuadernos rojos** (*'oo-nohs kwah-'dehr-nohs 'roh-hohs*)
Some tables	**Unas mesas** (*'oo-nahs 'meh-sahs*)
Some black tables	**Unas mesas negras** (*'oo-nahs 'meh-sahs 'neh-grahs*)

PRIVATE PRACTICE   **Práctica privada**

2 A. Change these ordinal numbers to cardinals:

1. **quinto** _____

2. **octavo** _____

3. **primero** _____

B. Say these numbers aloud in Spanish:

1. 5,000
2. 300
3. 67

TIME AND PLACE
El tiempo y el lugar
(ehl tee-'ehm-poh ee ehl loo-'gahr)

In the legal profession, you consistently need to mention time-referenced and place-referenced vocabulary. These will do for now:

When ?	**¿Cuándo?** (*'kwahn-doh*)
after	**después** (*dehs-'pwehs*)
already	**ya** (*yah*)
always	**siempre** (*see-'ehm-preh*)
before	**antes** (*'ahn-tehs*)
during	**durante** (*doo-'rahn-teh*)
early	**temprano** (*tehm-'prah-noh*)
late	**tarde** (*'tahr-deh*)
later	**luego** (*'lweh-goh*)
never	**nunca** (*'noon-kah*)
right now	**ahora** (*ah-'oh-rah*)
since	**desde** (*'dehs-deh*)
sometimes	**a veces** (*ah 'veh-sehs*)
soon	**pronto** (*'prohn-toh*)
then	**entonces** (*ehn-'tohn-sehs*)

today	**hoy** (ˈoh-ee)
tomorrow	**mañana** (mahn-ˈyah-nah)
until	**hasta** (ˈahs-tah)
while	**mientras** (mee-ˈehn-trahs)
yesterday	**ayer** (ah-ˈyehr)

When it comes to locating people or things, you may respond briefly:

Where?	**¿Dónde?** (ˈdohn-deh)
above	**encima** (ehn-ˈsee-mah)
along	**a lo largo** (ah loh ˈlahr-goh)
around	**alrededor** (ahl-reh-deh-ˈdohr)
at the bottom	**en el fondo** (ehn ehl ˈfohn-doh)
back	**atrás** (ah-ˈtrahs)
behind	**detrás** (deh-ˈtrahs)
between	**entre** (ˈehn-treh)
down	**abajo** (ah-ˈbah-hoh)
far	**lejos** (ˈleh-hohs)
forward	**adelante** (ah-deh-ˈlahn-teh)
here	**aquí** (ah-ˈkee)
in front	**enfrente** (ehn-ˈfrehn-teh)
in the middle	**en medio** (ehn ˈmeh-dee-oh)
inside	**adentro** (ah-ˈdehn-troh)
near	**cerca** (ˈsehr-kah)
next to	**al lado** (ahl ˈlah-doh)
outside	**afuera** (ah-ˈfweh-rah)
over	**sobre** (ˈsoh-breh)
straight ahead	**adelante** (ah-deh-ˈlahn-teh)
there	**allí** (ah-ˈyee)
to the left	**a la izquierda** (ah lah ees-kee-ˈehr-dah)
to the right	**a la derecha** (ah lah deh-ˈreh-chah)
toward	**hacia** (ˈah-see-ah)
under	**debajo** (deh-ˈbah-hoh)
up	**arriba** (ahr-ˈree-bah)
way over there	**allá** (ah-ˈyah)

NOTICE! ¡Fíjese!

Collect your own set of expressions dealing with time and location, and use them every day. Once they're mastered, start all over again with a different set:

not yet	**todavía no** (toh-dah-ˈvee-ah noh)
as soon as	**tan pronto como** (tahn ˈprohn-toh ˈkoh-moh)
two years ago	**hace dos años** (ˈah-seh dohs ˈahn-yohs)
backwards	**al revés** (ahl reh-ˈvehs)
upside down	**boca abajo** (ˈboh-kah ah-ˈbah-hoh)
the other side	**el otro lado** (ehl ˈoh-troh ˈlah-doh)

PRIVATE PRACTICE **Práctica privada**

(3) Match the opposites:

1. **ayer**	**detrás**
2. **arriba**	**temprano**
3. **siempre**	**abajo**
4. **enfrente**	**nunca**
5. **tarde**	**mañana**

MORE KEY WORDS
Más palabras claves
(mahs pah-'lah-brahs 'klah-vehs)

Visualize a scenario where one of the following can be used effectively, and get creative:

with	**con** *(kohn)*	**Jaime está con sus amigos.**
without	**sin** *(seen)*	**La oficina está sin teléfono.**
alone	**solo** *('soh-loh)*	_____
with me	**conmigo** *(kohn-'mee-goh)*	_____
almost	**casi** *('kah-see)*	_____
enough	**bastante** *(bahs-'tahn-teh)*	_____
none	**ninguno** *(neen-'goo-noh)*	_____
not yet	**todavía no** *(toh-dah-'vee-ah noh)*	_____
only one	**solamente uno** *(soh-lah-'mehn-teh 'oo-noh)*	_____
too much	**demasiado** *(deh-mah-see-'ah-doh)*	_____
most of it	**la mayor parte** *(lah mah-'yohr 'pahr-teh)*	_____
the rest of it	**lo demás** *(loh deh-'mahs)*	_____

This list provides lawyers with vocabulary to create more simple sentences, along with quick, generic one-word responses:

anyone	**cualquier persona** *(kwahl-kee-'ehr pehr-'soh-nah)*
anything	**cualquier cosa** *(kwahl-kee-'ehr 'koh-sah)*
anywhere	**en cualquier sitio** *(ehn kwahl-kee-'ehr 'see-tee-oh)*
everyone	**todos** *('toh-dohs)*
everything	**todo** *('toh-doh)*
everywhere	**por todas partes** *(pohr 'toh-dahs 'pahr-tehs)*
no one	**nadie** *('nah-dee-eh)*

nothing	**nada** *('nah-dah)*
no where	**en ningún sitio** *(ehn neen-'goon 'see-tee-oh)*
someone	**alguien** *('ahl-gee-ehn)*
something	**algo** *('ahl-goh)*
somewhere	**en algún sitio** *(ehl ahl-'goon 'see-tee-oh)*

PRIVATE PRACTICE   Práctica privada

 Read these dialogues aloud and translate them:

1. **¿Quién trabaja el domingo?**   **Nadie.**
2. **¿Cuánto chocolate quiere usted?**   **Lo demás.**
3. **¿Dónde están las computadoras?**   **Por todas partes.**

TELLING TIME
Decir la hora
(deh-'seer lah 'oh-rah)

In Spanish, *time in general* is **el tiempo** *(ehl tee-'ehm-poh)*. The *specific time* is **la hora** *(lah 'oh-rah)*. *Time* in reference to *an occurrence* is **la vez** *(lah vehs)*.

What time is it?   **¿Qué hora es?** *(keh 'oh-rah ehs)*

To answer in Spanish, simply give the hour, followed by the word **y** (*and*), and the minutes. For example, 6:15 is **seis y quince**. To give a specific hour, there is no need for *o'clock*:

It's...	**Son las...** *(sohn lahs)*
8:00	**ocho** *('oh-choh)*
3:40	**tres y cuarenta** *(trehs ee kwah-'rehn-tah)*
10:30	**diez y treinta** *(dee-'ehs ee 'treh-een-tah)*
5:00	**cinco** *('seen-koh)*
12:05	**doce y cinco** *('doh-seh ee 'seen-koh)*

To express *at* a certain time, use this phrase:

At...	**A las...** *(ah lahs)*
2:35	**dos y treinta y cinco** *(dohs ee 'treh-een-tah ee 'seen-koh)*
11:00	**once** *('ohn-seh)*
7:10	**siete y diez** *(see-'eh-teh ee dee-'ehs)*

A.M. is **de la mañana** *(deh lah mahn-'yah-nah)* and *P.M.* is **de la tarde** *(deh lah 'tahr-deh)* or **de la noche** *(deh lah 'noh-cheh)*:

It's 6:20 A.M.	**Son las seis de la mañana.**
	(sohn lahs 'seh-ees deh lah mahn-'yah-nah)

At 9:00 P.M.	**A las nueve de la tarde.**
	(ah lahs 'nweh-veh deh lah 'tahr-deh)

For 1:00–1:59, use **Es la ...** *(ehs lah)* instead of **Son las...**

It's one o'clock.	**Es la una.** *(ehs lah 'oo-nah)*
It's one-thirty.	**Es la una y treinta.** *(ehs lah 'oo-nah ee 'treh-een-tah)*

NOTICE!   ¡Fíjese!

Learn these other expressions when you find the time:

a quarter till	**un cuarto para** *(oon 'kwahr-toh 'pah-rah)*
half past	**y media** *(ee 'meh-dee-ah)*
midnight	**medianoche** *(meh-dee-ah-'noh-cheh)*
noon	**mediodía** *(meh-dee-oh-'dee-ah)*
on the dot	**en punto** *(ehn 'poon-toh)*

PRIVATE PRACTICE   Práctica privada

(5) A. Translate into Spanish:

1. What time is it? _____

2. At 8:45 A.M. _____

3. It's nine o'clock. _____

DAYS AND MONTHS
Los días y los meses
(lohs 'dee-ahs ee lohs 'meh-sehs)

Check out the basic questions and answers related to the date (**la fecha**—*lah 'feh-chah*):

What's the <u>date</u>?	**¿Cuál es la <u>fecha</u>?** *(kwahl ehs lah 'feh-chah)*
On what <u>date</u>?	**¿En qué <u>fecha</u>?** *(ehn keh 'feh-chah)*

Days of the Week	Los días de la semana
	(lohs 'dee-ahs deh lah seh-'mah-nah
Monday	**lunes** *('loo-nehs)*
Tuesday	**martes** *('mahr-tehs)*
Wednesday	**miércoles** *(mee-'ehr-koh-lehs)*
Thursday	**jueves** *('hweh-vehs)*
Friday	**viernes** *(vee-'ehr-nehs)*
Saturday	**sábado** *('sah-bah-doh)*
Sunday	**domingo** *(doh-'meen-goh)*

Months of the Year	Los meses del año
	(lohs 'meh-sehs dehl 'ahn-yoh)
January	**enero** *(eh-'neh-roh)*
February	**febrero** *(feh-'breh-roh)*
March	**marzo** *('mahr-soh)*
April	**abril** *(ah-'breel)*
May	**mayo** *('mah-yoh)*
June	**junio** *('hoo-nee-oh)*
July	**julio** *('hoo-lee-oh)*
August	**agosto** *(ah-'gohs-toh)*
September	**septiembre** *(sehp-tee-'ehm-breh)*
October	**octubre** *(ohk-'too-breh)*
November	**noviembre** *(noh-vee-'ehm-breh)*
December	**diciembre** *(dee-see-'ehm-breh)*

To give the date in Spanish, just reverse the word order:

May 5th	**el cinco de mayo** *(ehl 'seen-koh deh 'mah-yoh)*
June 3rd	**el tres de junio** *(ehl trehs deh 'hoo-nee-oh)*
February 15th	**el quince de febrero** *(ehl 'keen-seh deh feh-'breh-roh)*

The word *year* is **el año** *(ehl 'ahn-yoh)*. Just read it as one large number:

2010	**dos mil diez** *(dohs meel dee-'ehs)*

The only anomaly in the established order is the first of every month:

October 1st	**el primero de octubre** *(ehl pree-'meh-roh deh ohk-'too-breh)*
	(not **el uno de octubre**).

By the way, *on Monday* is **el lunes**, while *on Mondays* is **los lunes**:

When?	**¿Cuándo?** *('kwahn-doh)*
On Tuesday.	**El martes** *(ehl 'mahr-tehs)*

NOTICE!   ¡Fíjese!

Memorize these other "timely" one-liners:

last night	**anoche** *(ah-'noh-cheh)*
last week	**la semana pasada** *(lah seh-'mah-nah pah-'sah-dah)*
the next day	**el día siguiente** *(ehl 'dee-ah see-ghee-'ehn-teh)*
next month	**el próximo mes** *(ehl 'prohk-see-moh mehs)*
the weekend	**el fin de semana** *(ehl feen deh seh-'mah-nah)*
the day after tomorrow	**pasado mañana** *(pah-'sah-doh mahn-'yah-nah)*
the day before yesterday	**anteayer** *(ahn-teh-ah-'yehr)*

PRIVATE PRACTICE   **Práctica privada**

(6) Fill in the blanks with the missing words:

1. lunes, _____, miércoles, jueves, _____, sábado, _____

2. _____, febrero, marzo, _____, mayo, _____

3. julio, agosto, septiembre, _____, _____, diciembre

THE WEATHER
El tiempo
(ehl tee-'ehm-poh)

What? Wasn't **el tiempo**, *time*? Yes it was, but, strangely enough, **tiempo** also means *weather* in Spanish. Here's another common exchange in daily conversation:

How's the weather?	**¿Qué tiempo hace?** *(keh tee-'ehm-poh 'ah-seh)*

It's going to...	**Va a...** *(vah ah)*
rain	**llover** *(yoh-'vehr)*
snow	**nevar** *(neh-'vahr)*

It's...	**Hace...** *('ah-seh)*
cold	**frío** *('free-oh)*
hot	**calor** *(kah-'lohr)*
nice weather	**buen tiempo** *(bwehn tee-'ehm-poh)*
sunny	**sol** *(sohl)*
windy	**viento** *(vee-'ehn-toh)*

It's...	**Está...** *(ehs-'tah)*
clear	**despejado** *(dehs-peh-'hah-doh)*
cloudy	**nublado** *(noo-'blah-doh)*
drizzling	**lloviznando** *(yoh-vees-'nahn-doh)*
raining	**lloviendo** *(yoh-vee-'ehn-doh)*
snowing	**nevando** *(neh-'vahn-doh)*

There's...	**Hay...** *('ah-ee)*
ice	**hielo** *(ee-'eh-loh)*
frost	**escarcha** *(ehs-'kahr-chah)*
fog	**neblina** *(neh-'blee-nah)*
a storm	**una tormenta** *('oo-nah tohr-'mehn-tah)*
a tornado	**un tornado** *(oon tohr-'nah-doh)*
a hurricane	**un huracán** *(oon oo-rah-'kahn)*

These are great words to use with the time and weather:

It's...	**Es...** *(ehs)*
spring	**la primavera** *(lah pree-mah-'veh-rah)*
summer	**el verano** *(ehl veh-'rah-noh)*
fall	**el otoño** *(ehl oh-'ton-yoh)*
winter	**el invierno** *(ehl een-vee-'ehr-noh)*

PRIVATE PRACTICE   **Práctica privada**

(7) Translate these phrases about the weather into Spanish:

1. It's cold.

2. It's summer.

3. There's a storm.

4. How's the weather?

5. It's sunny and windy.

CULTURAL COMMENT   **Comentario cultural**

Not all folks panic when it comes to tardiness—some cultures put less emphasis on beating the clock than others. Be direct, and explain the importance of punctuality in the U.S. legal system. But also be sensitive to those who believe that personal or family issues are valid reasons for being a little late. To play it safe, inform your client of the concern:

You have to arrive early.
Tiene que llegar temprano.
(tee-'eh-neh keh yeh-'gahr tehm-'prah-noh)

Don't be late!
¡No llegue tarde!
(noh 'yeh-gheh 'tahr-deh)

If you're late again, we will have a problem.
Si llega tarde otra vez, tendremos un problema.
(see 'yeh-gah 'tahr-deh 'oh-trah vehs, tehn-'dreh-mohs oon proh-'bleh-mah)

DESCRIPTIONS
Las descripciones
(lahs dehs-kreep-see-'oh-nehs)

Descriptive words for legal work will fill the following chapters, but for now, let's learn the basics:

bad	**malo** (*'mah-loh*)
big	**grande** (*'grahn-deh*)
good	**bueno** (*'bweh-noh*)
handsome	**guapo** (*'gwah-poh*)
long	**largo** (*'lahr-goh*)
new	**nuevo** (*noo-'eh-voh*)
old	**viejo** (*vee-'eh-hoh*)
pretty	**bonito** (*boh-'nee-toh*)
short (in height)	**bajo** (*'bah-hoh*)
short (in length)	**corto** (*'kohr-toh*)
small	**chico** (*'chee-koh*)
tall	**alto** (*'ahl-toh*)
ugly	**feo** (*'feh-oh*)
young	**joven** (*'hoh-vehn*)

Here are more descriptions everyone should know.

fat	**gordo** (*'gohr-doh*)
thin	**delgado** (*dehl-'gah-doh*)
strong	**fuerte** (*foo-'ehr-teh*)
weak	**débil** (*'deh-beel*)
dirty	**sucio** (*'soo-see-oh*)
clean	**limpio** (*'leem-pee-oh*)
slow	**lento** (*'lehn-toh*)
fast	**rápido** (*'rah-pee-doh*)
easy	**fácil** (*'fah-seel*)
difficult	**difícil** (*dee-'fee-seel*)
cold	**frío** (*'free-oh*)
hot	**caliente** (*kah-lee-'ehn-teh*)
rich	**rico** (*'ree-koh*)
poor	**pobre** (*'poh-breh*)
inexpensive	**barato** (*bah-'rah-toh*)
expensive	**caro** (*'kah-roh*)

NOTICE! ¡Fíjese!

Add these words to elaborate:

más grande *(mahs 'grahn-deh)*	bigger
lo más grande *(loh mahs 'grahn-deh)*	biggest
tan grande como *(tahn 'grahn-deh 'koh-moh)*	as big as
un poco grande *(oon 'poh-koh 'grahn-deh)*	a little big
muy grande *('moo-ee 'grahn-deh)*	very big
demasiado grande *(deh-mah-see-'ah-doh 'grahn-deh)*	too big
tan grande *(tahn 'grahn-deh)*	so big

PRIVATE PRACTICE Práctica privada

(8) Match these opposites:

1. **viejo**	**fácil**
2. **limpio**	**chico**
3. **malo**	**sucio**
4. **gordo**	**joven**
5. **difícil**	**pobre**
6. **rico**	**delgado**
7. **grande**	**bueno**

TO BE
Estar y Ser
(ehs-'tahr ee sehr)

There are two ways to say *to be* in Spanish: **estar** *(ehs-'tahr)* and **ser** *(sehr)*. **Estar** is used to indicate the location or condition of someone or something, while **ser** is used for everything else. Here are the eight forms:

TO BE	ESTAR	SER
I am	**estoy** *(ehs-'toh-ee)*	**soy** *('soh-ee)*
You are (sing); He, She, It is	**está** *(ehs-'tah)*	**es** *(ehs)*
You are (pl); They are	**están** *(ehs-'tahn)*	**son** *(sohn)*
We are	**estamos** *(ehs-'tah-mohs)*	**somos** *('soh-mohs)*

Notice how both **está** and **es** mean *is* in Spanish, but are used differently. The word **está** expresses a temporary state, condition, or location, while **es** expresses an inherent characteristic or quality, including origin and ownership:

The man is fine.	**El hombre está bien.** *(ehl 'ohm-breh ehs-'tah bee-'ehn)*
The man is in the room.	**El hombre está en el cuarto.**
	(ehl 'ohm-breh ehs-'tah ehn ehl 'kwahr-toh)
The man is big.	**El hombre es grande.** *(ehl 'ohm-breh ehs 'grahn-deh)*
The man is American.	**El hombre es americano.**
	(ehl 'ohm-breh ehs ah-meh-ree-'kah-noh)

Now, to talk about more than one person, place, or thing, replace **está** with **están**, and **es** with **son** (see the table above). Don't forget that all words must agree when you change to plurals:

The paper is on the table.	**El papel está en la mesa.**
	(ehl pah-'pehl ehs-'tah ehn lah 'meh-sah)
The papers are on the table.	**Los papeles están en la mesa.**
	(lohs pah-'peh-lehs ehs-'tahn ehn lah 'meh-sah)
It's a neighbor.	**Es un vecino.** *(ehs oon veh-'see-noh)*
They are neighbors.	**Son vecinos.** *(sohn veh-'see-nohs)*

Check out these other examples and read them aloud as you focus on their structure and meaning:

Are the papers yellow?	**¿Son amarillos los papeles?**
	(sohn ah-mah-'ree-yohs lohs pah-'peh-lehs)
The clients are in the office.	**Los clientes están en la oficina.**
	(lohs klee-'ehn-tehs ehs-'tahn ehn lah oh-fee-'see-nah)
They are not important.	**No son importantes.** *(noh sohn eem-pohr-'tahn-tehs)*
Are they clean?	**¿Están limpios?** *(ehs-'tahn 'leem-pee-ohs)*

To say *I am* and *we are* in Spanish, you must also learn the different forms. As with **está** and **están**, the words **estoy** and **estamos** refer to the location or condition of a person, place, or thing. And, just like **es** and **son**, the words **soy** and **somos** are used with everything else:

I am fine.	**Estoy bien.** *(ehs-'toh-ee bee-'ehn)*
We are in the car.	**Estamos en el carro.** *(ehs-'tah-mohs ehn ehl 'kahr-roh)*
I am Lupe.	**Soy Lupe.** *('soh-ee 'loo-peh)*
We are Cuban.	**Somos cubanos.** *('soh-mohs koo-'bah-nohs)*

There are two other words, **estás** and **eres** (from the informal **tú** form), which may be used among friends, family and small children:

How are you, Mary? You are very pretty.
¿Cómo estás, María? Tú eres muy bonita.
('koh-moh ehs-'tahs mah-'ree-ah too 'eh-rehs 'moo-ee boh-'nee-tah)

NOTICE! ¡Fíjese!

As you've probably learned, sometimes it's OK to drop the subject pronoun since it's usually understood who is involved:

I am fine.	**(Yo) Estoy bien.** *(yoh ehs-'toh-ee bee-'ehn)*
They are not at home.	**(Ellos) No están en casa.**
	('eh-yohs noh ehs-'tahn ehn 'kah-sah)

PRIVATE PRACTICE Práctica privada

9 A. Fill in the blanks with the correct form of **estar**:

1. Yo _____ bien.

2. Ella no _____ en su casa.

3. Ellas _____ en la mesa.

B. Fill in the blanks with the correct form of **ser**:

1. Nosotros _____ americanos.

2. Yo _____ hombre.

3. Juan _____ doctor.

TO HAVE
Tener
(teh-'nehr)

Tener (*to have*) is another basic verb that must be learned.

TO HAVE	**Tener** *(teh-'nehr)*
I have	**tengo** *('tehn-goh)*
You have (sing); He has, She has, It has	**tiene** *(tee-'eh-neh)*
You have (pl); They have	**tienen** *(tee-'eh-nehn)*
We have	**tenemos** *(teh-'neh-mohs)*

Read these sample sentences aloud:

I have a problem.	**Tengo un problema.** *('tehn-goh oon proh-'bleh-mah)*
He has a white car.	**Tiene un carro blanco.**
	(tee-'eh-neh oon 'kahr-roh 'blahn-koh)
They have four children.	**Tienen cuatro niños.** *(tee-'eh-nehn 'kwah-troh 'neen-yohs)*
We have a big house.	**Tenemos una casa grande.**
	(teh-'neh-mohs 'oo-nah 'kah-sah 'grahn-deh)

Even though **tener** literally means *to have*, sometimes it's used instead to mean *to be* in order to express the following:

(I am) afraid	**(tengo) miedo** (*'tehn-goh mee-'eh-doh*)
(we are) at fault	**(tenemos) la culpa** (*teh-'neh-mohs lah 'kool-pah*)
(they are) cold	**(tienen) frío** (*tee-'eh-nehn 'free-oh*)
(she is) 15 years old	**(tiene) quince años** (*tee-'eh-neh 'keen-seh 'ahn-yohs*)
(I am) hot	**(tengo) calor** (*'tehn-goh kah-'lohr*)
(they are) hungry	**(tienen) hambre** (*tee-'eh-nehn 'ahm-breh*)
(he is) sleepy	**(tiene) sueño** (*tee-'eh-neh 'swehn-yoh*)
(we are) thirsty	**(tenemos) sed** (*teh-'neh-mohs sehd*)
(you are) right	**(tienes) razón** (*tee-'eh-nehs rah-'sohn*)
(I am) lucky	**(tengo) suerte** (*'tehn-goh 'swehr-teh*)

PRIVATE PRACTICE **Práctica privada**

(10) Use **tengo** (*I have*) to answer these personal questions:

¿Tiene usted un carro blanco? _____

¿Cuántos amigos tiene usted? _____

¿Tienes mucha hambre? _____

THERE IS AND THERE ARE
Hay
('ah-ee)

For both *there is* and *there are* you use the little word **hay** (*'ah-ee*):

There's one case.	**Hay un caso.** (*'ah-ee oon 'kah-soh*)
There are two cases.	**Hay dos casos.** (*'ah-ee dohs 'kah-sohs*)

NO!
¡No!
(noh)

To express the negative in Spanish, put the word **no** (*noh*) in front of the verb.

There are no more.	**No hay más.** (*noh 'ah-ee mahs*)
José is not my friend.	**José no es mi amigo.** (*hoh-'seh noh ehs mee ah-'mee-goh*)
I do not have the job.	**No tengo el trabajo.** (*noh 'tehn-goh ehl trah-'bah-hoh*)

Spanish also uses the double negative, so when you respond, say **no** twice in your sentences. To ask a question, simply raise your voice at the end:

¿Hay problemas?   **No, no hay problemas.**

PRIVATE PRACTICE   **Práctica privada**

11 Translate these:

1. Hay dos hombres en la casa. _____

2. No hay agua. _____

3. ¿Hay un problema? _____

VERBS IN ACTION!   **¡Verbos activos!**

Although the verb forms of **estar**, **ser**, and **tener** are critical in the legal profession, they do not express everyday action. Learning how to use key Spanish verbs allows us to talk about what's going on. Take as much time as you need with this brief list of verb infinitives. Notice how they end in the letters **ar**, **er**, or **ir**:

to come	**venir** (veh-'neer)
to drink	**beber** (beh-'behr)
to drive	**manejar** (mah-neh-'hahr)
to eat	**comer** (koh-'mehr)
to go	**ir** (eer)
to leave	**salir** (sah-'leer)
to listen	**escuchar** (ehs-koo-'chahr)
to look	**mirar** (mee-'rahr)
to lose	**perder** (pehr-'dehr)
to read	**leer** (leh-'ehr)
to sleep	**dormir** (dohr-'meer)
to speak	**hablar** (ah-'blahr)
to wait	**esperar** (ehs-peh-'rahr)
to walk	**caminar** (kah-mee-'nahr)
to win	**ganar** (gah-'nahr)
to work	**trabajar** (trah-bah-'hahr)
to write	**escribir** (ehs-kree-'beer)

NOTICE!   **¡Fíjese!**

Many Spanish verb infinitives related to law are similar to English. Look at these examples.

defender (deh-fehn-'dehr)	to defend
reportar (reh-pohr-'tahr)	to report
investigar (een-vehs-tee-'gahr)	to investigate
disputar (dees-poo-'tahr)	to dispute
examinar (ex-ah-mee-'nahr)	to examine
confrontar (kohn-frohn-'tahr)	to confront

THE SENTENCE! ¡La frase!

The Sentence sections will introduce a variety of conjugated verb forms. By practicing the patterns, you'll soon be able to discuss past, present, and future events.

One of the most effective ways to put your verbs into action is to combine them with simple phrases that create complete sentences. For example, look what happens when you add these verb infinitives to **Favor de...** *(fah-'vohr deh)*, which means, *Would you please...*:

Please ...	**Favor de . . .** *(fah-'vohr deh)*
write everything	**escribir todo** *(ehs-kree-'beer 'toh-doh)*
come tomorrow	**venir mañana** *(veh-'neer mahn-'yah-nah)*
speak slowly	**hablar despacio** *(ah-'blahr dehs-'pah-see-oh)*

By adding the word **no** in front of the verb, you say *don't*:

Please don't come tomorrow. **Favor de no venir mañana.**
(fah-'vohr deh noh veh-'neer mahn-'yah-nah)

Here's a more extensive list of phrases that are used before infinitives. Study the examples, and then add a few infinitives of your own:

I have to... **Tengo que ... salir** *(tehn-goh keh sah-'leer)*
Tengo que salir mañana. *('tehn-goh keh sah-'leer mahn-'yah-nah)*

I should... **Debo ... leer** *('deh-boh leh-'ehr)*
Debo leer el documento. *('deh-boh leh-'ehr ehl doh-koo-'mehn-toh)*

I need (to)...	**Necesito ...** *(neh-seh-'see-toh)*	_____
I want (to)...	**Quiero ...** *(kee-'eh-roh)*	_____
I'd like to...	**Quisiera ...** *(kee-see-'eh-rah)*	_____
I can...	**Puedo ...** *('pweh-doh)*	_____
I like (to)...	**Me gusta ...** *(meh 'goos-tah)*	_____
I'm going to...	**Voy a ...** *('voh-ee ah)*	_____
I prefer (to) ...	**Prefiero ...** *(preh-fee-'eh-roh)*	_____

PRIVATE PRACTICE   **Práctica privada**

(12) A. These verbs are so similar to their English counterparts that you can translate them on your own:

1. aceptar _____

2. acusar _____

3. admitir _____

4. autorizar _____

5. causar _____

6. compensar _____

7. comunicar _____

8. confirmar _____

9. confiscar _____

10. consultar _____

11. cooperar _____

12. determinar _____

B. Translate:

1. I'm going to eat. _____

2. Please don't come tomorrow. _____

3. I'd like to investigate. _____

CULTURAL COMMENT   **Comentario cultural**

If you get stuck in the middle of a phrase or sentence, don't be afraid to send messages using hand gestures or facial expressions. Body signals are frequently used in conversations throughout the Spanish-speaking world. And remember, there's nothing wrong with repeating your message several times until you're understood!

Chapter Two

Capítulo Dos
(kah-'pee-too-loh dohs)

The Law Office
La oficina de abogados

(lah oh-fee-'see-nah deh ah-boh-'gah-dohs)

WELCOME TO OUR OFFICE
Bienvenidos a nuestra oficina

(bee-ehn-veh-'nee-dohs ah 'nwehs-trah oh-fee-'see-nah)

This chapter focuses on life around the law office. As you meet and greet someone in Spanish, be sure to shake hands, smile, and make eye contact briefly. Use short phrases, including those that were presented earlier:

Good afternoon.
Buenas tardes. *('bweh-nahs 'tahr-dehs)*

How may I help you?
¿En qué puedo servirle? *(ehn keh 'pweh-doh sehr-'veer-leh)*

I'm sorry, but I don't speak Spanish very well.
Lo siento, pero no hablo español muy bien.
(loh see-'ehn-toh 'peh-roh noh 'ah-bloh ehs-pahn-'yohl 'moo-ee bee-'ehn)

Do you need an interpreter?
¿Necesita un/una intérprete? *(neh-seh-'see-tah oon/'oo-nah een-'tehr-preh-teh)*

Please take a seat.
Tome asiento, por favor. *('toh-meh ah-see-'ehn-toh pohr fah-'vohr)*

Someone will be with you in a moment.
Alguien le atenderá en un momento.
('ahl-ghee-ehn leh ah-tehn-deh-'rah ehn oon moh-'mehn-toh)

Is he/she expecting you?
¿Lo/la está esperando? *(loh/leh ehs-'tah ehs-peh-'rahn-doh)*

I'll tell him/her that you're here.
Le diré que usted está aquí. *(leh dee-'reh keh oos-'tehd ehs-'tah ah-'kee)*

Thank you for your patience.
Gracias por su paciencia. *('grah-see-ahs pohr soo pah-see-'ehn-see-ah)*

What time was your appointment?
¿A qué hora tenía cita? *(ah keh 'oh-rah teh-'nee-ah 'see-tah)*

Please sign the waiting list.
Favor de firmar la lista de espera. *(fah-'vohr deh feer-'mahr lah 'lees-tah deh ehs-'peh-rah)*

Are you a new client?
¿Es usted un cliente nuevo/una clienta nueva?
(ehs oos-'tehd oon klee-'ehn-teh noo-'eh-voh/'oo-nah klee-'ehn-tah noo-'eh-vah)

My name is Mr./Mrs./Ms. ...
Me llamo el Señor/la Señora/la Señorita...
(meh 'yah-moh ehl sehn-'yohr/lah sehn-'yoh-rah/ lah sehn-yoh-'ree-tah)

I'd like to introduce...
Quisiera presentarle a... *(kee-see-'eh-rah preh-sehn-'tahr-leh ah)*

Nice to meet you.
Mucho gusto. *('moo-choh 'goos-toh)*

Now find out what the person is looking for:

Do you need...?	**¿Necesita...?** *(neh-seh-'see-tah)*
legal assistance	**ayuda jurídica/legal** *(ah-'yoo-dah hoo-'ree-dee-kah/leh-'gahl)*
legal counsel	**consejos jurídicos/legales** *(kohn-'seh-hohs hoo-'ree-dee-kohs leh-'gah-lehs)*
legal defense	**defensa jurídica/legal** *(deh-'fehn-sah hoo-'ree-dee-kah/leh-'gahl)*
legal protection	**protección jurídica/legal** *(proh-tehk-see-'ohn hoo-'ree-dee-kah/leh-'gahl)*
legal resources	**recursos jurídicos/legales** *(reh-'koor-sohs hoo-'ree-dee-kohs leh-'gah-lehs)*
legal services	**servicios jurídicos/legales** *(sehr-'vee-see-ohs hoo-'ree-dee-kohs/leh-'gah-lehs)*
legal support	**apoyo jurídico/legal** *(ah-'poh-yoh hoo-'ree-dee-koh leh-'gahl)*

Does it concern (the)...?	**¿Tiene que ver con...?** *(tee-'eh-neh keh vehr kohn)*
contracts	**los contratos** *(lohs kohn-'trah-tohs)*
discrimination	**la discriminación** *(lah dees-kree-mee-nah-see-'ohn)*
divorce	**el divorcio** *(ehl dee-'vohr-see-oh)*
insurance	**el seguro** *(ehl seh-'goo-roh)*
malpractice	**la negligencia professional** *(lah neh-glee-'ghen-see-ah proh-feh-see-oh-'nahl)*
small claims	**los reclamos menores** *(lohs reh-'klah-mohs meh-'noh-rehs)*

taxes	**los impuestos** *(lohs eem-'pwehs-tohs)*
traffic	**el tráfico** *(ehl 'trah-fee-koh)*
will	**el testamento** *(ehl tehs-tah-'mehn-toh)*

Is it a..?	**¿Es un...?** *(ehs oon)*
civil trial	**juicio civil** *(hoo-'ee-see-oh see-'veel)*
jury trial	**juicio con jurado** *(hoo-'ee-see-oh kohn hoo-'rah-doh)*
criminal trial	**juicio penal** *(hoo-'ee-see-oh peh-'nahl)*

Do you understand (the)...?	**¿Entiende...?** *(ehn-tee-'ehn-deh)*
continuance	**el aplazamiento** *(el ah-plah-sah-mee-'ehn-toh)*
countersuit	**la contrademanda** *(lah kohn-trah-deh-'mahn-dah)*
judgment by default	**el juicio en rebeldía** *(ehl hoo-'ee-see-oh ehn reh-behl-'dee-ah)*
lawsuit	**el pleito** *(ehl 'pleh-ee-toh)*
restraining order	**el interdicto** *(ehl een-tehr-'deek-toh)*
ruling	**la resolución** *(lah reh-soh-loo-see-'ohn)*
settlement	**el convenio** *(ehl kohn-'veh-nee-oh)*
warrant	**la orden** *(lah 'ohr-dehn)*

Is it your...?	**¿Es su...?** *(ehs soo)*
business	**negocio** *(neh-'goh-see-oh)*
car	**carro** *('kahr-roh)*
child	**hijo/hija** *('ee-hoh/'ee-hah)*
family	**familia** *(fah-'mee-lee-ah)*
health	**salud** *(sah-'lood)*
home	**casa** *('kah-sah)*
job	**trabajo** *(trah-'bah-hoh)*
money	**dinero** *(dee-'neh-roh)*
property	**propiedad** *(proh-pee-eh-'dahd)*
spouse	**cónyugue** *('kohn-yoo-gheh)*

Are you (the)...?	**¿Es usted...?** *(ehs oos-'tehd)*
client	**el cliente/la clienta** *(ehl klee-'ehn-teh/lah klee-'ehn-tah)*
defendant (civil)	**el demandado/la demandada** *(ehl deh-mahn-'dah-doh/lah deh-mahn-'dah-dah)*
defendant (criminal)	**el acusado/la acusada** *(ehl ah-koo-'sah-doh/lah ah-koo-'sah-dah)*
family member	**el/la pariente** *(ehl/lah pah-ree-'ehn-teh)*
friend	**el amigo/la amiga** *(ehl ah-'mee-goh/lah ah-'mee-gah)*
plaintiff	**el/la demandante** *(ehl/lah deh-mahn-'dahn-teh)*
roommate	**el compañero/la compañera de cuarto** *(ehl kohm-pahn-'yeh-roh/lah kohm-pahn-'yeh-rah deh 'kwahr-toh)*
suspect	**el sospechoso/la sospechosa** *(ehl sohs-peh-'choh-soh/lah sohs-peh-'choh-sah)*

victim	**la víctima** *(lah 'veek-tee-mah)*
witness	**el/la testigo** *(ehl/lah tehs-'tee-goh)*

Be sure to mention your title as well:

I'm (the)...	**Soy...** *('soh-ee)*
administrator	**el administrador/la administradora** *(ehl ahd-mee-nees-trah-'dohr/lah ahd-mee-nees-trah-'doh-rah)*
agent	**el/la agente** *(ehl/lah ah-'hehn-teh)*
assistant	**el/la asistente** *(ehl/lah ah-sees-'tehn-teh)*
associate	**el asociado/la asociada** *(ehl ah-soh-see-'ah-doh/lah ah-soh-see-'ah-dah)*
law clerk	**el oficinista jurídico/la oficinista jurídica** *(ehl oh-fee-see-'nees-tah hoo-'ree-dee-koh/lah oh-fee-see-'nees-tah hoo-'ree-dee-kah)*
records clerk	**el/la oficinista de archivos** *(ehl/lah oh-fee-see-'nees-tah deh ahr-'chee-vohs)*
director	**el director/la directora** *(ehl dee-rehk-'tohr/lah dee-rehk-'toh-rah)*
employee	**el empleado/la empleada** *(ehl ehm-pleh-'ah-doh/lah ehm-pleh-'ah-dah)*
interpreter	**el/la intérprete** *(ehl/lah een-'tehr-preh-teh)*
investigator	**el investigador/ la investigadora** *(ehl een-vehs-tee-gah-'dohr/lah een-vehs-tee-gah-'doh-rah)*
lawyer	**el abogado/la abogada** *(ehl ah-boh-'gah-doh/lah ah-boh-'gah-dah)*
legal representative	**el/la representante legal** *(ehl/lah reh-preh-sehn-'tahn-teh leh-'gahl)*
manager	**el/la gerente** *(eh/lah heh-'rehn-teh)*
notary public	**el notario público/la notaria pública** *(ehl noh-'tah-ree-oh 'poob-lee-koh/lah noh-'tah-ree-ah 'poob-lee-kah)*
officer	**el funcionario/la funcionaria** *(ehl foon-see-oh-'nah-ree-oh/lah foon-see-oh-'nah-ree-ah)*
owner	**el dueño/la dueña** *(ehl 'dwehn-yoh/lah 'dwehn-yah)*
paralegal	**el/la ayudante de abogado** *(ehl/lah ah-yoo-'dahn-teh/lah ah-yoo-'dahn-tah deh ah-boh-'gah-doh)*
partner	**el socio/la socia** *(ehl 'soh-see-oh/lah 'soh-see-ah)*
president	**el presidente/la presidenta** *(ehl preh-see-'dehn-teh/lah preh-see-'dehn-tah)*
receptionist	**el/la recepcionista** *(ehl/lah reh-sehp-see-oh-'nees-tah)*
legal secretary	**el secretario/la secretaria legal** *(ehl seh-kreh-'tah-ree-oh/lah seh-kreh-'tah-ree-ah leh-'gahl)*
librarian	**el bibliotecario/la bibliotecaria** *(ehl beeb-lee-oh-teh-'kah-ree-oh/lah beeb-lee-oh-teh-'kah-ree-ah)*

supervisor	**el supervisor/la supervisora**
	(ehl soo-pehr-vee-sohr/lah soo-pehr-vee-'soh-rah)
vice-president	**el vicepresidente/la vicepresidenta**
	(ehl vee-seh-preh-see-'dehn-teh/lah vee-seh-preh-see-'dehn-tah)

We are _____ lawyers.	**Somos abogados de _____.**
	('soh-mohs ah-boh-'gah-dohs deh)
appeal	**la apelación** *(lah ah-peh-lah-see-'ohn)*
bankruptcy	**la bancarrota** *(lah bahn-kahr-'roh-tah)*
civil rights	**los derechos civiles** *(lohs deh-'reh-chohs see-'vee-lehs)*
drunk driving	**los conductores ebrios**
	(lohs kohn-dook-'toh-rehs 'ehb-ree-ohs)
defense	**la defensa** *(lah deh-'fehn-sah)*
environmental	**el medio ambiente** *(ehl 'meh-dee-oh ahm-bee-'ehn-teh)*
immigration	**la inmigración** *(lah een-mee-grah-see-'ohn)*
legal aid	**la ayuda legal** *(lah ah-'yoo-dah leh-'gahl)*
litigation	**la litigación** *(lah lee-tee-gah-see-'ohn)*
patent	**las patentes** *(lahs pah-'tehn-tehs)*
personal injury	**las lesiones personales**
	(lahs leh-see-'oh-nehs pehr-soh-'nah-lehs)
probate	**la validación de testamentos**
	(lah vah-lee-dah-see-'ohn deh tehs-tah-'mehn-tohs)
small business	**las pequeñas empresas**
	(lahs peh-'kehn-yahs ehm-'preh-sahs)
tax	**la ley tributaria, los impuestos**
	(lah 'leh-ee tree-boo-'tah-ree-ah, lohs eem-'pwehs-tohs)
trial	**el juicio** *(ehl hoo-'ee-see-oh)*
union	**el sindicato** *(ehl seen-dee-'kah-toh)*
Workers'	**la compensación laboral**
Compensation	*(lah kohm-pehn-sah-see-'ohn lah-boh-'rahl)*

It's _____ law	**Es la ley _____.** *(ehs lah 'leh-ee)*
maritime	**marítima** *(mah-'ree-tee-mah)*
property	**de propiedad** *(deh proh-pee-eh-'dahd)*
corporate	**de empresas** *(deh ehm-'preh-sahs)*

NOTICE!   **¡Fíjese!**

Continue to list those words that are simple to remember:

Is it a _____ case?	**¿Es un caso _____?** *(ehs oon 'kah-soh)*
civil	**civil** *(see-'veel)*
criminal	**penal** *(peh-'nahl)*
federal	**federal** *(feh-deh-'rahl)*
international	**internacional** *(een-tehr-nah-see-oh-'nahl)*
labor	**laboral** *(lah-boh-'rahl)*

local	**local** *(loh-'kahl)*
regional	**regional** *(reh-ee-oh-'nahl)*
state	**estatal** *(ehs-tah-'tahl)*

PRIVATE PRACTICE   **Práctica privada**

 Read this dialogue aloud. You should also be able to translate everything:

—**¿En qué puedo servirle?**
—**Necesito ayuda jurídica.**
—**¿Es usted un cliente nuevo?**
—**Sí. ¿Ustedes son abogados de inmigración, ¿verdad?**
—**Sí, pero yo no soy abogada. Soy la recepcionista. Tome un asiento,
   por favor. Alguien le atenderá en un momento.**

THE CLIENT INTERVIEW
La entrevista con el cliente
(lah ehn-treh-'vees-tah kohn ehl klee-'ehn-teh)

One of the first things you do is gather information. Use the following one-liners
to get the client interview started:

I need some information.
Necesito alguna información. *(neh-seh-'see-toh ahl-'goo-nah een-fohr-mah-see-'ohn)*

I have a few questions for you.
Tengo algunas preguntas para usted.
('tehn-goh ahl-'goo-nahs preh-'goon-tahs 'pah-rah oos-'tehd)

This will only take us a few minutes.
Esto nos tomará solo unos minutos.
('ehs-toh nohs toh-mah-'rah 'soh-loh 'oo-nohs mee-'noo-tohs)

Please answer the questions the best you can.
Favor de contestar las preguntas lo mejor que pueda.
(fah-'vohr deh kohn-tehs-'tahr loh meh-'hohr keh 'pweh-dah)

Is all this information correct?
¿Es correcta toda la información? *(ehs kohr-'rehk-tah 'toh-dah lah een-fohr-mah-see-'ohn)*

Now confirm any personal data. Notice the pattern:

What is your...	**¿Cuál es su...?** *(kwahl ehs soo)*
address	**dirección** *(dee-rehk-see-'ohn)*
area code	**código telefónico** *('koh-dee-goh teh-leh-'foh-nee-koh)*

cell phone	**teléfono celular** *(teh-'leh-foh-noh seh-loo-'lahr)*
date of birth	**fecha de nacimiento** *('feh-chah deh nah-see-mee-'ehn-toh)*
e-mail	**correo electrónico** *(kohr-'reh-oh eh-lehk-'troh-nee-koh)*
first name	**primer nombre** *(pree-'mehr 'nohm-breh)*
full name	**nombre completo** *('nohm-breh kohm-'pleh-toh)*
last name	**apellido** *(ah-peh-'yee-doh)*
place of employment	**lugar de empleo** *(loo-'gahr deh ehm-'pleh-oh)*
license number	**número de licencia** *('noo-meh-roh deh lee-'sehn-see-ah)*
maiden name	**nombre de soltera** *('nohm-breh deh sohl-'teh-rah)*
marital status	**estado civil** *(eh-'stah-doh see-'veel)*
name	**nombre** *('nohm-breh)*
nationality	**nacionalidad** *(nah-see-oh-nah-lee-'dahd)*
place of birth	**lugar de nacimiento** *(loo-'gahr deh nah-see-mee-'ehn-toh)*
relationship	**relación** *(reh-lah-see-'ohn)*
social security number	**número de seguro social** *('noo-meh-roh deh seh-'goo-roh soh-see-'ahl)*
telephone number	**número de teléfono** *('noo-meh-roh deh teh-'leh-foh-noh)*
zip code	**zona postal** *('soh-nah pohs-'tahl)*

Are you...?	**¿Es...?** *(ehs)*
married	**casado/casada** *(kah-'sah-doh/kah-'sah-dah)*
single	**soltero/soltera** *(sohl-'teh-roh/sohl-'teh-rah)*

And don't forget to ask about citizenship:

Are you a U.S. citizen?
¿Es usted ciudadano/ciudadana de Estados Unidos?
(ehs oos-'tehd see-oo-dah-'dah-noh/see-oo-dah-'dah-nah deh ehs-'tah-dohs oo-'nee-dohs)

What's your resident number?
¿Cuál es su número de residente? *(kwahl ehs soo 'noo-meh-roh deh reh-see-'dehn-teh)*

Do you have a green card?
¿Tiene usted una tarjeta de residente?
(tee-'eh-neh oos-'tehd 'oo-nah tahr-'heh-tah deh reh-see-'dehn-teh)

 NOTICE!   **¡Fíjese!**

All these words will be useful in an interview:

Tell me (the)...	**Dígame...** *('dee-gah-meh)*
city	**la ciudad** *(lah see-oo-'dahd)*
county	**el condado** *(ehl kohn-'dah-doh)*
district	**el distrito** *(ehl dees-'tree-toh)*
country	**el país** *(ehl pah-'ees)*
state	**el estado** *(ehl ehs-'tah-doh)*
town	**el pueblo** *(ehl 'pweh-bloh)*

PRIVATE PRACTICE **Práctica privada**

(14) Answer these questions about yourself:

¿Cuál es su fecha de nacimiento? _____

¿Cuál es su lugar de empleo? _____

¿Cuál es su número de seguro social? _____

¿Cuál es su correo electrónico? _____

¿Es usted casado/casada? _____

¿Es usted ciudadano de Estados Unidos? _____

MORE KEY QUESTIONS
Más preguntas claves
(mahs preh-'goon-tahs 'klah-vehs)

As you chat, listen for the answers, **sí** or **no**:

Do you have (the)...?	**¿Tiene usted...?** *(tee-'eh-neh oos-'tehd)*
application	**la solicitud** *(lah soh-lee-see-'tood)*
appointment	**la cita** *(lah 'see-tah)*
business card	**la tarjeta comercial** *(lah tahr-'heh-tah koh-mehr-see-'ahl)*
calendar	**el calendario** *(ehl kah-lehn-'dah-ree-oh)*
case number	**el número del caso** *(ehl 'noo-meh-roh dehl 'kah-soh)*
contract	**el contrato** *(ehl kohn-'trah-toh)*
driver's license	**la licencia de manejar** *(lah lee-'sehn-see-ah deh mah-neh-'hahr)*
form	**el formulario** *(ehl fohr-moo-'lah-ree-oh)*
identification	**la identificación** *(lah ee-dehn-tee-fee-kah-see-'ohn)*
information	**la información** *(lah een-fohr-mah-see-'ohn)*
insurance	**el seguro** *(ehl seh-'goo-roh)*
meeting	**la reunión** *(lah reh-oo-nee-'ohn)*
records	**los archivos** *(lohs ahr-'chee-vohs)*
schedule	**el horario** *(ehl oh-'rah-ree-oh)*
transportation	**el transporte** *(ehl trahns-'pohr-teh)*
Can you...?	**¿Puede usted...?** *('pweh-deh oos-'tehd)*
answer	**contestar** *(kohn-tehs-'tahr)*
come back	**regresar** *(reh-greh-'sahr)*
drive	**manejar** *(mah-neh-'hahr)*
pay	**pagar** *(pah-'gahr)*

read and write	**leer y escribir** *(leh-'ehr ee ehs-kree-'beer)*
speak some English	**hablar algo de inglés** *(ah-'blahr 'ahl-goh deh een-'glehs)*
travel	**viajar** *(vee-ah-'hahr)*
understand everything	**entender todo** *(ehn-tehn-'dehr 'toh-doh)*
work	**trabajar** *(trah-bah-'hahr)*

Are you...?	**¿Está usted...?** *(ehs-'tah oos-'tehd)*
available	**disponible** *(dees-poh-'nee-bleh)*
busy	**ocupado/ocupada** *(oh-koo-'pah-doh/oh-koo-'pah-dah)*
employed	**empleado/empleada** *(ehm-pleh-'ah-doh/ehm-pleh-'ah-dah)*
interested	**interesado/interesada** *(een-teh-reh-'sah-doh/een-teh-reh-'sah-dah)*
ready	**listo/lista** *('lees-toh/'lees-tah)*

Be careful with your pronunciation as you try out this new question pattern:

Have you ever ____?	**¿Ha____alguna vez?** *(ah ____ ahl-'goo-nah vehs)*
been arrested	**sido arrestado** *('see-doh ahr-rehs-'tah-doh)*
been charged	**sido acusado** *('see-doh ah-koo-'sah-doh)*
been sued	**sido demandado** *('see-doh deh-mahn-'dah-doh)*
hired a lawyer	**contratado un abogado** *(kohn-trah-'tah-doh oon ah-boh-'gah-doh)*
sued anyone	**demandado a alguien** *(deh-mahn-'dah-doh ah ahl-ghee-'ehn)*

These may look easy, but you'll have to listen carefully if you want to understand their responses:

Who is your ___?	**¿Quién es su ___?** *(kee-'ehn ehs soo)*
closest relative	**pariente mas cercano** *(pah-ree-'ehn-teh mahs sehr-'kah-noh)*
co-worker	**compañero de trabajo** *(kohm-pahn-'yeh-roh deh trah-'bah-hoh)*
employer	**empresario** *(ehm-preh-'sah-ree-oh)*
family physician	**médico familiar** *('meh-dee-koh fah-mee-lee-'ahr)*
landlord	**arrendador** *(ahr-rehn-dah-'dohr)*
legal advisor	**asesor jurídico** *(ah-seh-'sohr hoo-'ree-dee-koh)*
neighbor	**vecino** *(veh-'see-noh)*

When did you ___?	**¿Cuándo ___ usted?** *('kwahn-doh ___ oos-'tehd)*
send it	**lo mandó** *(loh mahn-'doh)*
arrive	**llegó** *(yeh-'goh)*
call	**llamó** *(yah-'moh)*

Where ___?	¿Dónde ___? *('dohn-deh)*
were you born	**nació** *(nah-see-'oh)*
do you live	**vive** *('vee-veh)*
did it happen	**pasó** *(pah-'soh)*

NOTICE!   ¡Fíjese!

There are two contractions in Spanish:

a *(to)* + **el** *(the)* = **al**
Vamos al carro *('vah-mohs ahl 'kahr-roh)*   Let's go to the car.

de *(from)* + **el** *(the)* = **del**
Es del abogado *(ehs dehl ah-boh-'gah-doh)*   It's from the lawyer.

WHAT'S YOUR OCCUPATION?
¿Cuál es su ocupación?
(kwahl ehs soo oh-koo-pah-see-'ohn)

The following occupations refer to males. Remember that for females you should use the article **la** and change the **o** ending to **a**, or add an **a** to words ending in **r**:

Are you (the)...?	¿Es usted...? *(ehs oos-'tehd)*
artist	**el artista** *(ehl ahr-'tees-tah)*
bartender	**el cantinero** *(ehl kahn-tee-'neh-roh)*
busboy	**el ayudante de camarero** *(ehl ah-yoo-'dahn-teh deh kah-mah-'reh-roh)*
carpenter	**el carpintero** *(ehl kahr-peen-'teh-roh)*
cashier	**el cajero** *(ehl kah-'heh-roh)*
clerk	**el oficinista** *(ehl oh-fee-see-'nees-tah)*
cook	**el cocinero** *(ehl koh-see-'neh-roh)*
dishwasher	**el lavaplatos** *(ehl lah-vah-'plah-tohs)*
employee	**el empleado** *(ehl ehm-pleh-'ah-doh)*
gardener	**el jardinero** *(ehl hahr-dee-'neh-roh)*
guide	**el guía** *(ehl 'ghee-ah)*
janitor	**el conserje** *(ehl kohn-'sehr-heh)*
laborer	**el obrero** *(ehl oh-'breh-roh)*
mechanic	**el mecánico** *(ehl meh-'kah-nee-koh)*
painter	**el pintor** *(ehl peen-'tohr)*
plumber	**el plomero** *(ehl ploh-'meh-roh)*
receptionist	**el receptionista** *(ehl reh-sehp-see-oh-'nees-tah)*
sales rep	**el vendedor** *(ehl vehn-deh-'dohr)*
secretary	**el secretario** *(ehl seh-kreh-'tah-ree-oh)*

machinist	**el operario de máquina**
	(ehl oh-peh-'rah-ree-oh deh 'mah-kee-nah)
truck driver	**el camionero** *(ehl kah-mee-oh-'neh-roh)*
waiter	**el mesero** *(ehl meh-'seh-roh)*
worker	**el trabajador** *(ehl trah-bah-hah-'dohr)*
technician	**el técnico** *(ehl 'tehk-nee-koh)*
student	**el estudiante** *(ehl ehs-too-dee-'ahn-teh)*

Here are some more professions. Notice how both males and females are listed:

He/She is (the)...	**Él/Ella es...** *(ehl/'eh-yah ehs)*
accountant	**el contador/la contadora**
	(ehl kohn-tah-'dohr/lah kohn-tah-'doh-rah)
architect	**el arquitecto/la arquitecta**
	(ehl ahr-kee-'tehk-toh/lah ahr-kee-'tehk-tah)
dentist	**el/la dentista** *(ehl/lah dehn-'tees-tah)*
doctor	**el médico/la médica**
	(ehl 'meh-dee-koh/lah 'meh-dee-kah)
engineer	**el ingeniero/la ingeniera**
	(ehl een-heh-nee-'eh-roh/lah een-heh-nee-'eh-rah)
farmer	**el granjero/la granjera**
	(ehl grahn-'heh-roh/lah grahn-'heh-rah)
firefighter	**el/la bombero** *(ehl/lah bohm-'beh-roh)*
librarian	**el bibliotecario/la bibliotecaria**
	(ehl bee-blee-oh-teh-'kah-ree-oh/lah bee-blee-oh-teh-'kah-ree-ah)
mail carrier	**el cartero/la cartera**
	(ehl kahr-'teh-roh/lah kahr-'teh-rah)
musician	**el músico/la música** *(ehl 'moo-see-koh/lah 'moo-see-kah)*
nurse	**el enfermero/la enfermera**
	(ehl ehn-fehr-'meh-roh/lah ehn-fehr-'meh-rah)
pilot	**el/la piloto** *(ehl/lah pee-'loh-toh)*
police officer	**el/la policía** *(ehl/lah poh-lee-'see-ah)*
tailor	**el/la sastre** *(ehl/lah 'sahs-treh)*
teacher	**el maestro/la maestro**
	(ehl mah-'ehs-troh/lah mah-'ehs-trah)

NOTICE! ¡Fíjese!

Here are more words that might surface during the initial conversation:

first language	**el primer idioma** *(ehl pre-'mehr ee-dee-'oh-mah)*
race	**la raza** *(lah 'rah-sah)*
religion	**la religión** *(lah reh-lee-hee-'ohn)*
school	**la escuela** *(lah ehs-'kweh-lah)*
sex	**el sexo** *(ehl 'sehks-oh)*
signature	**la firma** *(lah 'feer-mah)*

AT YOUR SERVICE
A su servicio
(ah soo sehr-'vee-see-oh)

Now that you have information about the client, it's time to talk about yourself. The following questions and statements allow you to converse with others about your legal services.

We offer you...	**Le ofrecemos...** *(leh oh-freh-'seh-mohs)*
advice	**el consejo** *(ehl kohn-'seh-hoh)*
opportunity	**la oportunidad** *(lah oh-pohr-too-nee-'dahd)*
protection	**la protección** *(lah proh-tehk-see-'ohn)*
representation	**la representación** *(lah reh-preh-sehn-tah-see-'ohn)*
support	**el apoyo** *(ehl ah-'poh-yoh)*
We have (the)...	**Tenemos...** *(teh-'neh-mohs)*
confidence	**la confianza** *(lah kohn-fee-'ahn-sah)*
experience	**la experiencia** *(lah ex-peh-ree-'ehn-see-ah)*
expertise	**la competencia** *(lah kohm-peh-'tehn-see-ah)*
references	**las referencias** *(lahs reh-feh-'rehn-see-ahs)*
resources	**los recursos** *(lohs reh-'koor-sohs)*
results	**los resultados** *(lohs reh-sool-'tah-dohs)*
success	**el éxito** *(ehl 'ex-ee-toh)*
title	**el título** *(ehl 'tee-too-loh)*
training	**el entrenamiento** *(ehl ehn-treh-nah-mee-'ehn-toh)*
We're...	**Somos...** *('soh-mohs)*
advisors	**asesores** *(ah-seh-'soh-rehs)*
experts	**expertos** *(ex-'pehr-tohs)*
members	**miembros** *(mee-'ehm-brohs)*
professionals	**profesionales** *(proh-feh-see-oh-'nah-lehs)*
specialists	**especialistas** *(ehs-peh-see-ah-'lees-tahs)*
You can...	**Puede usted...** *('pweh-deh oos-'tehd)*
trust	**confiar** *(kohn-fee-'ahr)*
relax	**relajarse** *(reh-lah-'hahr-seh)*
rest	**descansar** *(dehs-kahn-'sahr)*
It's our _____	**Es nuestro _____** *(ehs 'nwehs-troh)*
job	**trabajo** *(trah-'bah-hoh)*
business	**negocio** *(neh-'goh-see-oh)*
field	**campo de trabajo** *('kahm-poh deh trah-'bah-hoh)*

NOTICE!   ¡Fíjese!

Keep describing your place of employment:

We are...	**Somos...** ('soh-mohs)
aggressive	**agresivos** (ah-greh-'see-vohs)
capable	**capaces** (kah-'pah-sehs)
certified	**certificados** (sehr-tee-fee-'kah-dohs)
funded	**financiados** (fee-nahn-see-'ah-dohs)
honest	**honestos** (oh-'nehs-tohs)
licensed	**licenciados** (lee-sehn-see-'ah-dohs)
qualified	**calificados** (kah-lee-fee-'kah-dohs)

PRIVATE PRACTICE   Práctica privada

(15) A. Name five common occupations in Spanish:

_____ _____ _____

_____ _____

B. Connect the words that belong together:

1. empresario	**experiencia**
2. disponible	**empleado**
3. bombero	**horario**
4. competencia	**policía**
5. calendario	**listo**

TO WORK WITH THE CLIENT
Trabajar con el cliente
(trah-bah-'hahr kohn ehl klee-'ehn-teh)

Once you set up a working relationship, let the client know what needs to be done next:

You need (the)...	**Necesita...** (neh-seh-'see-tah)
consultation	**la consulta** (lah kohn-'sool-tah)
meeting	**la reunión** (lah reh-oo-nee-'ohn)
conference	**la conferencia** (lah kohn-feh-'rehn-see-ah)

Let's discuss (the)...	**Conversemos de...** (kohn-vehr-'seh-mohs deh)
case	**el caso** (ehl 'kah-soh)
matter	**el asunto** (ehl ah-'soon-toh)
order	**el orden** (ehl 'ohr-dehn)
plan	**el plan** (ehl plahn)

problem	**el problema** (*ehl proh-'bleh-mah*)
procedure	**el procedimiento** (*ehl proh-seh-dee-mee-'ehn-toh*)
stages	**las etapas** (*lahs eh-'tah-pahs*)
steps	**los pasos** (*lohs 'pah-sohs*)
Here's info about (the)..	**Aquí tiene información sobre...**
	(*ah-'kee tee-'eh-neh een-fohr-mah-see-'ohn 'soh-breh*)
crime	**el crimen** (*ehl 'kree-mehn*)
defense	**la defensa** (*lah deh-'fehn-sah*)
jurisdiction	**la jurisdicción** (*lah hoo-rees-deek-see-'ohn*)
law	**la ley** (*lah 'leh-ee*)
lawsuit	**el pleito** (*ehl 'pleh-ee-toh*)
legal team	**el equipo legal** (*ehl eh-'kee-poh leh-gahl*)
prosecution	**el enjuiciamiento** (*ehl ehn-hoo-ee-see-ah-mee-'ehn-toh*)
trial	**el juicio** (*ehl hoo-'ee-see-oh*)
media coverage	**la cobertura informativa**
	(*lah koh-behr-'too-rah een-fohr-mah-'tee-vah*)

Now memorize a few of these. They can make clients feel more at ease:

Don't worry.
No se preocupe. (*nos seh preh-oh-'koo-peh*)

You have rights.
Usted tiene derechos. (*oos-'tehd tee-'eh-neh deh-'reh-chohs*)

We can help you.
Le podemos ayudar. (*leh poh-'deh-mohs ah-yoo-'dahr*)

We fight for you.
Luchamos por usted. (*loo-'chah-mohs pohr oos-'tehd*)

We look after your interests.
Defendemos sus intereses. (*deh-fehn-'deh-mohs soos een-teh-'reh-sehs*)

We want to keep you informed.
Queremos mantenerlo informado. (*keh-'reh-mohs mahn-teh-'nehr-loh een-fohr-'mah-doh*)

All of your questions will be answered.
Todas sus preguntas serán contestadas.
(*'toh-dahs soos preh-'goon-tahs seh-'rahn kohn-tehs-'tah-dahs*)

We decide what needs to be done.
Nosotros decidimos lo que hay que hacer.
(*noh-'soh-trohs deh-see-'dee-mohs loh keh 'ah-ee keh ah-'sehr*)

We'll determine the best way.
Determinaremos la mejor manera.
(*deh-tehr-mee-nah-'reh-mohs lah meh-'hohr mah-'neh-rah*)

Here's your case number.
Aquí tiene el número de su caso. (*ah-'kee tee-'eh-neh ehl 'noo-meh-roh deh soo 'kah-soh*)

Call this number.
Llame este número. (*'yah-meh 'ehs-teh 'noo-meh-roh*)

Where else can we reach you?
¿Dónde más podemos contactarlo? (*'dohn-deh mahs poh-'deh-mohs kohn-tahk-'tahr-loh*)

We will call you if we have more information.
Lo llamaremos si tenemos más información.
(*loh yah-mah-'reh-mohs see teh-'neh-mohs mahs een-fohr-mah-see-'ohn*)

We'll do everything possible.
Haremos todo lo que sea posible. (*ah-'reh-mohs 'toh-doh loh keh 'seh-ah poh-'see-bleh*)

I can't promise you anything.
No puedo prometerle nada. (*noh 'pweh-doh proh-meh-'tehr-leh 'nah-dah*)

THE SENTENCE!   ¡La frase!

The legal profession is packed with important words and phrases, so create your own list:

We follow the judicial process.
Seguimos el proceso judicial. (*seh-'ghee-mohs ehl proh-'seh-soh hoo-dee-see-'ahl*)

You have the Constitutional right.
Tiene el derecho constitucional. (*tee-'eh-neh ehl deh-'reh-choh kohns-tee-too-see-oh-'nahl*)

She passed the bar exam.
Pasó el examen de abogacía. (*pah-'soh ehl ex-'ah-mehn deh ah-boh-gah-'see-ah*)

THE CONTRACT
El contrato
(*ehl kohn-'trah-toh*)

In most cases, you'll want to discuss some form of contractual agreement that includes all payments, fees, or charges involved:

Here's (the)...	**Aquí tiene...** (*ah-'kee tee-'eh-neh*)
agreement	**el acuerdo** (*ehl ah-'kwehr-doh*)
amendment	**la enmienda** (*lah ehn-mee-'ehn-dah*)
arrangement	**el arreglo** (*ehl ahr-'reh-gloh*)

contract	**el contrato** *(ehl kohn-'trah-toh)*
disclosure	**la revelación** *(lah reh-veh-lah-see-'ohn)*
transaction	**la transacción** *(lah trahns-ahk-see-'ohn)*
understanding	**el entendimiento** *(ehl ehn-tehn-dee-mee-'ehn-toh)*

Let's check (the)...	**Revisemos...** *(reh-vee-'seh-mohs)*
terms	**los términos** *(lohs 'tehr-mee-nohs)*
conditions	**las condiciones** *(lahs kohn-dee-see-'oh-nehs)*
details	**los detalles** *(lohs deh-'tah-yehs)*

It's...	**Es...** *(ehs)*
concise	**conciso** *(kohn-'see-soh)*
expensive	**caro** *('kah-roh)*
free	**gratuito** *(grah-'twee-toh)*
inexpensive	**barato** *(bah-'rah-toh)*
itemized	**detallado** *(deh-tah-'yah-doh)*
low-cost	**de bajo costo** *(deh 'bah-hoh 'kohs-toh)*
monthly	**mensual** *(mehn-soo-'ahl)*
personalized	**personalizado** *(pehr-soh-nah-lee-'sah-doh)*
private	**privado** *(pree-'vah-doh)*
public	**público** *('poo-blee-koh)*

You need to pay (the)...	**Necesita pagar...** *(neh-seh-'see-tah pah-'gahr)*
balance	**el saldo** *(ehl 'sahl-doh)*
bill	**la cuenta** *(lah 'kwehn-tah)*
charge	**el cargo** *(ehl 'kahr-goh)*
cost	**el costo** *(ehl 'kohs-toh)*
down payment	**el pago inicial** *(ehl 'pah-goh ee-nee-see-'ahl)*
expense	**el gasto** *(ehl 'gahs-toh)*
fee	**el honorario** *(ehl oh-noh-'rah-ree-oh)*
installment	**la cuota** *(lah koo-'oh-tah)*
invoice	**la factura** *(lah fahk-'too-rah)*
payment	**el pago** *(ehl 'pah-goh)*
rate	**el precio fijado** *(ehl 'preh-see-oh fee-'hah-doh)*
tax	**el impuesto** *(ehl eem-'pwehs-toh)*
total	**el total** *(ehl toh-'tahl)*

We accept (the)...	**Aceptamos...** *(ah-sehp-'tah-mohs)*
cash	**el efectivo** *(ehl eh-fehk-'tee-voh)*
cashier's check	**el cheque de banco** *(ehl 'che-keh deh 'bahn-koh)*
check	**el cheque** *(ehl 'cheh-keh)*
credit card	**la tarjeta de crédito** *(lah tahr-'heh-tah deh 'kreh-dee-toh)*
money order	**el giro postal** *(ehl 'hee-roh pohs-'tahl)*

Do you understand (the)...?	**¿Entiende...?** *(ehn-tee-'ehn-deh)*
discount	**el descuento** *(ehl dehs-'kwehn-toh)*
document	**el documento** *(ehl doh-koo-'mehn-toh)*
guarantee	**la garantía** *(lah gah-rahn-'tee-ah)*
program	**el programa** *(ehl proh-'grah-mah)*
reduction	**la rebaja** *(lah reh-'bah-hah)*
refund	**el reembolso** *(ehl reh-ehm-'bohl-soh)*

VERBS IN ACTION!   ¡Verbos activos!

Interject commands whenever you can:

Call me at this number.	**Llámeme a este número.** *('yah-meh-meh ah 'ehs-teh 'noo-meh-roh)*
Check out our website.	**Revise nuestra página web.** *(reh-'vee-seh 'nwehs-trah 'pah-hee-nah web)*
Sign here.	**Firme aquí.** *('feer-meh ah-'kee)*

ENDING THE CONVERSATION
Al terminar la conversación
(ahl tehr-mee-'nahr lah kohn-vehr-sah-see-'ohn)

Close out the meeting or consultation with a few traditional one-liners:

Thank you for your time.
Gracias por su tiempo. *('grah-see-ahs pohr soo tee-'ehm-poh)*

Do you have any questions?
¿Tiene alguna pregunta? *(tee-'eh-neh ahl-'goo-nah pre-'goon-tah)*

It was a pleasure meeting you.
Fue un gusto conocerle. *(foo-'eh oon 'goos-toh koh-noh-'sehr-leh)*

Let me explain the next step.
Déjeme explicar el siguiente paso.
('deh-heh-meh ex-plee-'kahr ehl see-ghee-'ehn-teh 'pah-soh)

I would like...	**Quisiera...** *(kee-see-'eh-rah)*
to help you	**ayudarle** *(ah-yoo-'dahr-leh)*
to explain why	**explicar por qué** *(ex-plee-'kahr pohr keh)*
to study your case	**estudiar su caso** *(ehs-too-dee-'ahr soo 'kah-soh)*
to give you something	**darle algo** *('dahr-leh 'ahl-goh)*
to meet him/her	**reunirme con él/ella** *(reh-oo-'neer-meh kohn ehl/'eh-yah)*
to know more about it	**saber más sobre eso** *(sah-'behr mahs 'soh-breh 'eh-soh)*

to talk to the others	**hablar con los demás** *(ah-'blahr kohn lohs deh-'mahs)*
to call you later	**llamarle más tarde** *(yah-'mahr-leh mahs 'tahr-deh)*
to send you an e-mail	**mandarle un correo electrónico**
	(mahn-'dahr-leh oon kohr-'reh-oh eh-lehk-'troh-nee-koh)
to recommend someone	**recomendarle a alguien**
	(reh-koh-mehn-'dahr-leh ah 'ahl-ghee-ehn)
to confirm everything	**confirmar todo** *(kohn-feer-'mahr 'toh-doh)*
to have another meeting	**tener otra reunión** *(teh-'nehr 'oh-trah reh-oo-nee-'ohn)*
to think about it	**pensarlo** *(pehn-'sahr-loh)*

You can't help everyone, so learn how to share the bad news, too:

I'm sorry, but...	**Lo siento, pero...** *(loh see-'ehn-toh 'peh-roh)*

We are not taking more cases.
No aceptamos más casos. *(noh ah-sehp-'tah-mohs mahs 'kah-sohs)*

We don't handle those cases.
No trabajamos con tales casos. *(noh trah-bah-'hah-mohs kohn 'tah-lehs 'kah-sohs)*

That isn't much of a case   .
No parece ser un caso fuerte. *(noh pah-'reh-seh sehr oon 'kah-soh 'fwehr-teh)*

You don't need a lawyer for that.
No necesita abogado para hacer eso.
(noh neh-seh-'see-tah ah-boh-'gah-doh 'pah-rah ah-'sehr 'eh-soh)

We are tied up with another case.
Estamos ocupados con otro caso. *(esh-'tah-mohs oh-koo-'pah-dohs kohn 'oh-troh 'kah-soh)*

You could try another law office.
Podría encontrar otro bufete. *(poh-'dree-ah ehn-kohn-'trahr 'oh-troh boo-'feh-teh)*

         NOTICE!   **¡Fíjese!**

Use these sentences as marketing tools:

Every client is important to us.
Cada cliente es importante para nosotros.
('kah-dah klee-'ehn-teh ehs eem-pohr-'tahn-teh 'pah-rah noh-'soh-trohs)

It doesn't matter how large or small the case is.
No importa cuan grande o pequeño el caso.
(noh eem-'pohr-tah kwahn 'grahn-deh oh peh-'kehn-yoh ehl 'kah-soh)

If we don't win, we don't charge.
Si no ganamos, no cobramos. *(see noh gah-'nah-mohs noh koh-'brah-mohs)*

PRIVATE PRACTICE   **Práctica privada**

(16) A. Translate:

1. Usted necesita la consulta. _____

2. Conversemos del caso. _____

3. Determinaremos la mejor manera. _____

B. Underline the word in each group that does not belong with the others:

1. contrato, archivo, arreglo, acuerdo
2. costo, condado, cargo, cuenta
3. resultado, rebaja, descuento, reembolso

CULTURAL COMMENT   **Comentario cultural**

Take an interest in your Hispanic clients, but be careful to control your tone of voice and nonverbal actions when you speak: cultural differences may rub the wrong way. The more comfortable they feel, the more information they will share. One way to connect is to mention something positive about their native country or point out pictures of your home and family members.

THE OFFICE BUILDING
El edificio de oficinas
(ehl eh-dee-'fee-see-oh deh oh-fee-'see-nahs)

Assist Spanish-speakers as they move around the office building:

Do you know where the ___ is?	**¿Sabe dónde está ___?** *('sah-beh 'dohn-deh ehs-'tah)*

entrance	**la entrada** *(lah ehn-'trah-dah)*
exit	**la salida** *(lah sah-'lee-dah)*
hallway	**el corredor** *(ehl kohr-reh-'dohr)*
parking area	**el estacionamiento** *(ehl ehs-tah-see-oh-nah-mee-'ehn-toh)*
reception desk	**la recepción** *(lah reh-sehp-see-'ohn)*
restroom	**el servicio** *(ehl sehr-'vee-see-oh)*
vending machine	**la máquina vendedora** *(lah 'mah-kee-nah vehn-deh-'doh-rah)*
water fountain	**el surtidor de agua** *(ehl soor-tee-'dohr deh 'ah-gwah)*

Let's go to (the) _____ . **Vamos a _____.** *('vah-mohs ah)*

conference room **la sala de conferencias**
(lah 'sah-lah deh kohn-feh-'rehn-see-ahs)

first floor **el primer piso** *(ehl pre-'mehr 'pee-soh)*
library **la biblioteca** *(lah bee-blee-oh-'teh-kah)*
lobby **el vestíbulo** *(ehl vehs-'tee-boo-loh)*
main office **la oficina principal** *(lah oh-fee-'see-nah preen-see-'pahl)*
waiting room **la sala de espera** *(lah 'sah-lah deh ehs-'peh-rah)*

Please use (the)... **Favor de usar...** *(fah-'vohr deh oo-'sahr)*

double doors **la puerta doble** *(lah 'pwehr-tah 'doh-bleh)*
elevator **el ascensor** *(ehl ah-sehn-'sohr)*
escalator **la escalera mecánica**
(lah ehs-kah-'leh-rah meh-'kah-nee-kah)

stairway **la escalera** *(lah ehs-kah-'leh-rah)*
steps **los escalones** *(lohs ehs-kah-'loh-nehs)*

Be sure to send your clients to the appropriate department:

Call (the) _____ **Llame el departamento de _____.**
department. *('yah-meh ahl deh-pahr-tah-'mehn-toh deh)*

accounting **contabilidad** *(kohn-tah-bee-lee-'dahd)*
advertising **publicidad** *(poo-blee-see-'dahd)*
credit **crédito** *('kreh-dee-toh)*
customer service **servicio para clientes**
(sehr-'vee-see-oh 'pah-rah klee-'ehn-tehs)

maintenance **mantenimiento** *(mahn-teh-nee-mee-'ehn-toh)*
research **investigación** *(een-vehs-tee-gah-see-'ohn)*
security **seguridad** *(seh-goo-ree-'dahd)*

You may also need to speak Spanish around the office cafeteria or dining area:

This is the cafeteria and dining area.
Esta es la cafetería y el comedor.
('ehs-tah ehs lah kah-feh-teh-'ree-ah ee ehl koh-meh-'dohr)

You may sit where you want.
Puede sentarse dónde quiera.
('pweh-deh sehn-'tahr-seh 'dohn-deh kee-'eh-rah)

These are the hours of service.
Estas son las horas de servicio.
('ehs-tahs sohn lahs 'oh-rahs deh sehr-'vee-see-oh)

They sell ...	**Venden ...** (*'vehn-dehn*)
breakfast	**el desayuno** (*ehl deh-sah-'yoo-noh*)
lunch	**el almuerzo** (*ehl ahl-'mwehr-soh*)
dinner	**la cena** (*lah 'seh-nah*)
snacks	**la comida ligera** (*lah koh-'mee-dah lee-'heh-rah*)
drinks	**las bebidas** (*lahs beh-'bee-dahs*)

THE FURNITURE AND EQUIPMENT
Los muebles y los equipos
(lohs 'mweh-blehs ee lohs eh-'kee-pohs)

Conversations around the office also include the names for office equipment, furniture, and décor. One practice technique is to apply removable stickers to everything, so that you can read the Spanish as you walk by:

Let's use (the) _____.	**Usemos _____.** (*oo-'seh-mohs*)
armchair	**el sillón** (*ehl see-'yohn*)
bench	**la banca** (*lah 'bahn-kah*)
bookshelf	**el librero** (*ehl lee-'breh-roh*)
chair	**la silla** (*lah 'see-yah*)
counter	**el mostrador** (*ehl mohs-trah-'dohr*)
desk	**el escritorio** (*ehl ehs-kree-'toh-ree-oh*)
seat	**el asiento** (*ehl ah-see-'ehn-toh*)
sofa	**el sofá** (*ehl soh-'fah*)
table	**la mesa** (*lah 'meh-sah*)

I'll put it in (the)...	**Lo pondré en...** (*loh pohn-'dreh ehn*)
cabinet	**el gabinete** (*ehl gah-bee-'neh-teh*)
drawer	**el cajón** (*ehl kah-'hohn*)
file cabinet	**el archivo** (*ehl ahr-'chee-voh*)
safe	**la caja fuerte** (*lah 'kah-hah 'fwehr-teh*)
shredder	**la trituradora** (*lah tree-too-rah-'doh-rah*)
storeroom	**el almacén** (*ehl ahl-mah-'sehn*)
trash basket	**el cesto de basura** (*ehl 'sehs-toh deh bah-'soo-rah*)

Now ask your client some more yes-no questions:

Have you seen (the)...?	**¿Ha visto...?** (*ah 'vees-toh*)
calendar	**el calendario** (*ehl kah-lehn-'dah-ree-oh*)
chart	**la gráfica** (*lah 'grah-fee-kah*)
map	**el mapa** (*ehl 'mah-pah*)
planner	**el planificador** (*ehl pla-nee-fee-kah-'dohr*)
schedule	**el horario** (*ehl oh-'rah-ree-oh*)

Can I turn on (the)...?	¿Puedo prender...? *('pweh-doh prehn-'dehr)*
air conditioner	el acondicionador de aire *(ehl ah-kohn-dee-see-oh-nah-'dohr deh 'ah-ee-reh)*
camcorder	la filmadora *(lah feel-mah-'doh-rah)*
fan	el ventilador *(ehl vehn-tee-lah-'dohr)*
heater	el calentador *(ehl kah-lehn-tah-'dohr)*
lamp	la lámpara *(lah 'lahm-pah-rah)*
microphone	el micrófono *(ehl mee-'kroh-foh-noh)*
monitor	el monitor *(ehl moh-nee-'tohr)*
projector	el proyector *(ehl proh-yehk-'tohr)*
recorder	la grabadora *(lah grah-bah-'doh-rah)*
television	el televisor *(ehl teh-leh-vee-'sohr)*

Do you need (the)...?	¿Necesita...? *(neh-seh-'see-tah)*
calculator	la calculadora *(lah kahl-koo-lah-'doh-rah)*
cell phone	el celular *(ehl seh-loo-'lahr)*
computer	la computadora *(lah kohm-poo-tah-'doh-rah)*
copier	la copiadora *(lah koh-pee-ah-'doh-rah)*
fax machine	la máquina de fax *(lah 'mah-kee-nah deh fax)*
laptop	la computadora portátil *(lah kohm-poo-tah-'doh-rah pohr-'tah-teel)*
PDA	la computadora de bolsillo *(lah kohm-poo-tah-'doh-rah deh bohl-'see-yoh)*
phone	el teléfono *(ehl teh-'leh-foh-noh)*
printer	la impresora *(lah eem-preh-'soh-rah)*
remote control	el control remoto *(ehl kohn-'trohl reh-'moh-toh)*
scanner	el escáner *(ehl ehs-'kah-nehr)*

☞ NOTICE! ¡Fíjese!

Keep learning new vocabulary by interacting with it:

Point to (the)...	Señale... *(sehn-'yah-leh)*
answering machine	el contestador telefónico *(ehl kohn-tehs-tah-'dohr teh-leh-'foh-nee-koh)*
carpet	la alfombra *(lah ahl-'fohm-brah)*
clock	el reloj *(ehl reh-'loh)*
dictaphone	el dictáfono *(ehl deek-'tah-foh-noh)*
digital camera	la cámara digital *(lah 'kah-mah-rah dee-hee-'tahl)*
screen	la pantalla *(lah pahn-'tah-yah)*
speaker	el altavoz *(ehl ahl-tah-'vohs)*

Take (the)...	Tome... *('toh-meh)*
envelope	el sobre *(ehl 'soh-breh)*
folder	la carpeta *(lah kahr-'peh-tah)*
paper clips	los sujetapapeles *(lohs soo-heh-tah-pah-'peh-lehs)*

paper	**el papel** *(ehl pah-'pehl)*
pen	**el lapicero** *(ehl lah-pee-'seh-roh)*
pencil	**el lápiz** *(ehl 'lah-pees)*
rubber bands	**las ligas** *(lahs 'lee-gahs)*
scissors	**las tijeras** *(lahs tee-'heh-rahs)*
scotch tape	**la cinta adhesiva** *(lah 'seen-tah ah-deh-'see-vah)*
stamps	**las estampillas** *(lahs ehs-tahm-'pee-yahs)*
stapler	**la engrapadora** *(lah ehn-grah-pah-'doh-rah)*

PRIVATE PRACTICE **Práctica privada**

17 A. Fill in the word that completes each series:

asiento, ascensor, gabinete, lápiz, planificador, impresora

1. **escalones, escaleras, _____**

2. **horario, calendario, _____**

3. **archivo, cajón, _____**

4. **copiadora, computadora, _____**

5. **sofá, silla, _____**

6. **papel, lapicero, _____**

B. Fill in these lines with words you have just learned:

¿Dónde está _____?

¡_____ es muy grande!

No trabajo con _____.

USING THE TELEPHONE
Uso del teléfono
('oo-soh dehl teh-'leh-foh-noh)

Despite the rapid changes in technology, most legal professionals still rely on the telephone to communicate. Practice each group of words:

Did you check (the)...?	**¿Revisó...?** *(reh-vee-'soh)*
connection	**la conexión** *(lah kohn-ex-see-'ohn)*
message	**el recado, el mensaje** *(ehl reh-'kah-doh, ehl mehn-'sah-heh)*
line	**la línea** *(lah 'lee-neh-ah)*
reception	**la recepción** *(lah reh-sehp-see-'ohn)*
service	**el servicio** *(ehl sehr-'vee-see-oh)*

Do you have (the)...?	**¿Tiene...?** *(tee-'eh-neh)*
caller ID	**el identificador de llamada** *(ehl ee-dehn-tee-fee-kah-'dohr deh yah-'mah-dah)*
call-waiting	**la llamada en espera** *(lah yah-'mah-dah ehn ehs-'peh-rah)*
webcam	**la cámara de web** *(lah 'kah-mah-rah deh web)*
conference call	**la llamada-conferencia** *(lah yah-'mah-dah-kohn-feh-'rehn-see-ah)*
voice mail	**el telemensajes** *(ehl teh-leh-mehn-'sah-hehs)*

Do you know (the)...?	**¿Sabe...?** *('sah-beh)*
phone number	**el número de teléfono** *(ehl 'noo-meh-roh deh teh-'leh-foh-noh)*
area code	**el código de area** *(ehl 'koh-dee-goh deh 'ah-reh-ah)*
extension	**la extensión** *(lah ex-tehn-see-'ohn)*

Place the following phrases near your office phone, and wait for the chance to practice:

Hello, is _____ there?	**¿Aló, está _____?** *(ah-'loh ehs-'tah)*
May I speak to _____?	**Puedo hablar con _____.** *('pweh-doh ah-'blahr kohn)*
I'm calling about _____.	**Estoy llamando sobre _____.** *(ehs-'toh-ee yah-'mahn-doh 'soh-breh)*
I'd like to leave a message.	**Quisiera dejar un recado.** *(kee-see-'eh-rah deh-'hahr oon reh-'kah-doh)*
Tell him/her that _____.	**Dígale que _____.** *('dee-gah-leh keh)*
I'll call back later.	**Llamaré más tarde.** *(yah-mah-'reh mahs 'tahr-deh)*

THE SENTENCE! ¡La frase!

Who are you calling, please?
¿A quién está llamando, por favor? *(ah kee-'ehn ehs-'tah yah-'mahn-doh pohr fah-'vohr)*

I'm going to transfer you.
Lo/la voy a transferir. *(loh/lah 'voh-ee ah trahns-feh-'reer)*

Sorry, but he/she doesn't answer.
Lo siento, pero no contesta. *(loh see-'ehn-toh 'peh-roh noh kohn-'tehs-tah)*

Do you want to leave a message?
¿Quiere dejarle un recado? *(kee-'eh-reh deh-hahr-leh oon reh-'kah-doh)*

I will give him/her your message.
Le voy a dejar su mensaje. *(leh 'voh-ee ah deh-'hahr soo mehn-'sah-heh)*

Can you call back later?
¿Puede llamar más tarde? *('pweh-deh yah-'mahr mahs 'tahr-deh)*

He/She will call you later.
Él/ella lo llamará más tarde. *(ehl/'eh-yah loh yah-mah-'rah mahs 'tahr-deh)*

Continue to practice aloud, and remember to say, **por favor**:

More slowly, please.
Más despacio, por favor. *(mahs dehs-'pah-see-oh pohr fah-'vohr)*

Wait a moment, please.
Espere un momento, por favor. *(ehs-'peh-reh oon moh-'mehn-toh pohr fah-'vohr)*

Could you please repeat that?
¿Puede repetirlo, por favor? *('pweh-deh reh-peh-'teer-loh pohr fah-'vohr)*

Please...	**...por favor.** *(pohr fah-'vohr)*
answer the telephone.	**Conteste el teléfono.** *(kohn-'tehs-teh ehl teh-'leh-foh-noh)*
dial this number.	**Marque este número.** *('mahr-keh 'ehs-teh 'noo-meh-roh)*
hang up the phone.	**Cuelgue el teléfono.** *('kwehl-gheh ehl teh-'leh-foh-noh)*
press this number.	**Oprima este número.** *(oh-'pree-mah 'ehs-teh 'noo-meh-roh)*
wait for the tone.	**Espere por el tono.** *(ehs-'peh-reh pohr ehl 'toh-noh)*

Now break your comments and questions into topic-specific sets:

He/She isn't here right now.
No está aquí en este momento. *(noh ehs-'tah ah-'kee ehn 'ehs-teh moh-'mehn-toh)*
He/She can't come to the phone.
No puede contestar la llamada. *(noh 'pweh-deh kohn-tehs-'tahr lah yah-'mah-dah)*

He/She is in a meeting.
Está en conferencia. *(ehs-'tah ehn kohn-feh-'rehn-see-ah)*
He/She is on the other line.
Está en la otra línea. *(ehs-'tah ehn lah 'oh-trah 'lee-neh-ah)*

Is it long distance?
¿Es de larga distancia? *(ehs deh 'lahr-gah dees-'tahn-see-ah)*
Is it a local call?
¿Es una llamada local? *(ehs 'oo-nah yah-'mah-dah loh-'kahl)*

You have the wrong number.
Tiene el número equivocado. *(tee-'eh-neh ehl 'noo-meh-roh eh-kee-voh-'kah-doh)*
The number has been changed.
Ha cambiado el número. *(ah kahm-bee-'ah-doh ehl 'noo-meh-roh)*

THE INTERNET
El internet
(ehl een-tehr-'neht)

Now give instructions to clients who'll be using the Internet:

Go to our website.
Visite nuestro sitio web. *(vee-'see-teh 'nwehs-troh 'see-tee-oh web)*

Enter your password.
Teclee su contraseña. *(teh-'klee-eh soo kohn-trah-'sehn-yah)*

Download the information.
Descargue la información. *(dehs-'kahr-gheh soo een-fohr-mah-see-'ohn)*

Did you see (the)...?	¿Vió...? *(vee-'oh)*
attachment	**el adjunto** *(ehl ahd-'hoon-toh)*
file	**el fichero** *(ehl fee-'cheh-roh)*
database	**la base de datos** *(lah 'bah-seh deh 'dah-tohs)*
disc	**el disco** *(ehl 'dees-koh)*
e-mail	**el correo electrónico** *(ehl kohr-'reh-oh eh-lehk-'troh-nee-koh)*
folder	**el directorio** *(ehl dee-rehk-'toh-ree-oh)*
home page	**la página inicial** *(lah 'pah-ee-nah ee-nee-see-'ahl)*
icon	**el ícono** *(ehl 'ee-koh-noh)*
log-in box	**el registro** *(ehl reh-'ees-troh)*
mailbox	**el buzón** *(ehl boo-'sohn)*
menu	**el menú** *(ehl meh-'noo)*
message	**el mensaje** *(ehl mehn-'sah-heh)*
program	**el programa** *(ehl proh-'grah-mah)*

You'll need ...	Necesitará... *(neh-seh-see-tah-'rah)*
to click	**hacer clic** *(ah-'sehr kleek)*
to connect	**conectar** *(koh-nehk-'tahr)*
to copy	**copiar** *(koh-pee-'ahr)*
to delete	**eliminar** *(eh-lee-mee-'nahr)*
to download	**descargar** *(dehs-'kahr-gahr)*
to drag	**mover** *(moh-'vehr)*
to find	**encontrar** *(ehn-kohn-'trahr)*
to forward	**reenviar** *(reh-ehn-vee-'ahr)*
to log in	**conectar** *(kohn-ehk-'tahr)*
to press	**oprimir** *(oh-pree-'meer)*
to print	**imprimir** *(eem-pree-'meer)*
to reply	**responder** *(rehs-pohn-'dehr)*
to save	**guardar** *('gwahr-dahr)*

to scroll down	**desplazar hacia abajo**
	(dehs-plah-'sahr 'ah-see-ah ah-'bah-hoh)
to scroll up	**desplazar hacia arriba**
	(dehs-plah-'sahr 'ah-see-ah ahr-'ree-bah)
to search	**buscar** *(boos-'kahr)*
to select	**escoger** *(ehs-koh-'hehr)*
to send	**enviar** *(ehn-vee-'ahr)*
to upgrade	**actualizar** *(ahk-too-ah-lee-'sahr)*

And these are the basic parts of an e-mail in Spanish:

Silvia	@	alegre	.	provider	.	es
nombre del usario[1]	**arroba**[2]	**nombre de dominio**[3]	**punto**[4]	**proveedor de acceso al internet**[5]	**punto**	**país**[6]
(user name)	(at)	(domain name)	(dot)	(provider)	(dot)	(country)

[1] *('nohm-breh dehl oo-'swah-ree-oh)*
[2] *(ahr-'roh-bah)*
[3] *('nohm-breh deh doh-'mee-nee-oh)*
[4] *('poon-toh)*
[5] *(proh-veh-eh-'dohr deh ahk-'seh-soh ahl een-tehr-'neht)*
[6] *(pah-'ees)*

And, as you can guess, a lot of technical terminology is the same in both Spanish and English:

CD	DVD	PC
DSL	Wifi	podcast
iPod	MP3	webcam
url	LED	plasma
USB	Blackberry	LCD
Blu-ray	Bluetooth	flash drive
HD	software	hardware

PRIVATE PRACTICE   **Práctica privada**

(18) A. Translate this simple telephone conversation into Spanish:

> Hello, is Raul there?

_____

< No, I'm sorry. Do you want to leave a message?

_____

> Yes, thank you. My name is Smith, and I'm calling from his lawyer's office.

_____

B. Put each group of words in correct order:

¿datos de la vió base?   **¿Vió la base de datos?**

1. sitio visite nuestro web   _____

2. el está buzón el no mensaje en   _____

3. ¿necesito directorio cuándo el abrir? _____

VERBS IN ACTION!   **¡Verbos activos!**

These verbs are basic for conversation. Feel free to create a sentence or two:

to answer	**contestar** *(kohn-tehs-'tahr)*	**Necesita contestar la pregunta.**
to bring	**traer** *(trah-'ehr)*	**Tiene que traer el documento.**
to call	**llamar** *(yah-'mahr)*	**Voy a llamar a la oficina.**
to check	**revisar** *(reh-vee-'sahr)*	_____
to deal with	**atender** *(ah-tehn-'dehr)*	_____
to defend	**defender** *(deh-fehn-'dehr)*	_____
to describe	**describir** *(dehs-kree-'beer)*	_____
to explain	**explicar** *(ex-plee-'kahr)*	_____
to give	**dar** *(dahr)*	_____
to hire	**contratar** *(kohn-trah-'tahr)*	_____
to learn	**aprender** *(ah-prehn-'dehr)*	_____
to live	**vivir** *(vee-'veer)*	_____
to protect	**proteger** *(proh-teh-'hehr)*	_____

to provide	**proveer** (*proh-veh-'ehr*)	_____
to receive	**recibir** (*reh-see-'beer*)	_____
to recommend	**recomendar** (*reh-koh-mehn-'dahr*)	_____
to return	**regresar** (*reh-greh-'sahr*)	_____
to study	**estudiar** (*ehs-too-dee-'ahr*)	_____
to take	**tomar** (*toh-'mahr*)	_____
to tell	**decir** (*deh-'seer*)	_____

THE SENTENCE! ¡La frase!

One of the easiest verb forms to use is the Present Progressive Tense, which refers to actions that are taking place at this moment. It is similar to our -ing form in English. Simply change the base verb ending slightly, and then combine the new form with the four forms of the verb **estar** (*to be*). The **-ar**-ending verbs become **-ando**, while the **-er**-ending and **-ir**-ending verbs become **-iendo**. Study these examples:

to talk, to speak   **hablar** (*ah-'blahr*)
speaking   **hablando** (*ah-'blahn-doh*)
We are speaking Spanish.
Estamos hablando español. (*ehs-'tah-mohs ah-'blahn-doh ehs-pahn-'yohl*)

to eat   **comer** (*koh-'mehr*)
eating   **comiendo** (*koh-mee-'ehn-doh*)
The man is eating.
El hombre está comiendo. (*ehl 'ohm-breh ehs-'tah koh-mee-'ehn-doh*)

to write   **escribir** (*ehs-kree-'beer*)
writing   **escribiendo** (*ehs-kree-bee-'ehn-doh*)
I'm writing the report.
Estoy escribiendo el informe. (*ehs-'toh-ee ehs-kree-bee-'ehn-doh ehl een-'fohr-meh*)

VERBS IN ACTION! ¡Verbos activos!

A few Spanish verbs change in spelling when you add the **-ndo** ending. Study these two examples:

to follow   **seguir** (*seh-'gheer*)
following   **siguiendo** (*see-ghee-'ehn-doh*)

to sleep   **dormir** (*dohr-'meer*)
sleeping   **durmiendo** (*door-mee-'ehn-doh*)

PRIVATE PRACTICE **Práctica privada**

(19) Follow the examples and change each verb to the Present Progressive Tense:

trabajar	**Estamos trabajando**
defender	**Estamos defendiendo**
1. estudiar	_____
2. aprender	_____
3. observar	_____
4. verificar	_____
5. salir	_____

CULTURAL COMMENT **Comentario cultural**

Are your Spanish-speaking clients confused about our language and culture? When you find the time, share a few insights on U.S. customs toward tipping, making appointments, holidays, and even dating or other social practices. You can also teach them a new word or two! Make new immigrants feel welcome by respecting their perspective, and watch your relationship grow!

Chapter Three

The Courthouse
El tribunal

(ehl tree-boo-'nahl)

THE COURTS
Los tribunales
(lohs tree-boo-'nah-lehs)

Now that everyone has been introduced and the legal matters have been discussed, let's head directly to the courthouse. **La corte** *(lah 'kohr-teh)* is often used in everyday conversation to mean court. However, a more appropriate word to use is **el tribunal**:

It's called (the)...   **Se llama...** *(seh 'yah-mah)*

- supreme court   **el tribunal supremo** *(ehl tree-boo-'nahl soo-'preh-moh)*
- superior court   **el tribunal superior** *(ehl tree-boo-'nahl soo-peh-ree-'ohr)*
- court of appeals   **el tribunal de apelaciones**
  (ehl tree-boo-'nahl deh ah-peh-lah-see-'oh-nehs)
- civil court   **el tribunal civil** *(ehl tree-boo-nahl see-'veel)*
- criminal court   **el tribunal penal** *(ehl tree-boo-'nahl peh-'nahl)*
- juvenile court   **el tribunal de menores**
  (elh tree-boo-'nahl deh meh-'noh-rehs)

It's a case for (the)...   **Es un caso para...** *(ehs oon 'kah-soh 'pah-rah)*

- circuit court   **el tribunal de circuito**
  (ehl tree-boo-'nahl deh seer-'kwee-toh)
- county court   **el tribunal de condado**
  (ehl tree-boo-'nahl deh kohn-'dah-doh)
- district court   **el tribunal de distrito**
  (ehl tree-boo-nahl deh dees-'tree-toh)
- federal court   **el tribunal federal** *(ehl tree-boo-'nahl feh-deh-'rahl)*
- municipal court   **el tribunal municipal**
  (ehl tree-boo-'nahl moo-nee-see-'pahl)
- state court   **el tribunal estatal** *(ehl tree-boo-'nahl ehs-tah-'tahl)*

You need (the)...   **Necesita...** *(neh-seh-'see-tah)*

- small claims court   **el tribunal de reclamos menores**
  (ehl tree-boo-'nahl deh reh-'klah-mohs meh-'noh-rehs)
- family law court   **el tribunal de derecho familiar**
  (ehl tree-boo-'nahl deh deh-'reh-choh fah-mee-lee-'ahr)

probate court	**el tribunal testamentario**
	(ehl tree-boo-'nahl tehs-tah-mehn-'tah-ree-oh)
drug court	**el tribunal de drogas ilegales**
	(ehl tree-boo-'nahl deh 'droh-gahs ee-leh-'gah-lehs)

NOTICE!　¡Fíjese!

Another word for *court* in Spanish is **el juzgado**. Remember to change the contraction **a el** to **al**:

Let's go to...	**Vamos...** *('vah-mohs)*
lower court	**al juzgado menor** *(ahl hoos-'gah-doh meh-'nohr)*
higher court	**al juzgado de primera instancia**
	(ahl hoos-'gah-doh deh pree-'meh-rah eens-'tahn-see-ah)
traffic court	**el juzgado de tráfico**
	(ehl hoos-'gah-doh deh 'trah-fee-koh)
trial court	**al juzgado de enjuiciamiento**
	(ah hoos-'gah-doh deh ehn-hoo-ee-see-ah-mee-'ehn-toh)

TRAFFIC COURT
El juzgado de tráfico
(ehl hoos-'gah-doh deh 'trah-fee-koh)

Each court has its own vocabulary. For example, the following words and phrases relate to everyday conversations at the traffic court. Why not begin by asking a few yes-no questions:

Are you looking for (the)...?	**¿Busca...?** *('boos-kah)*
amount	**el total** *(ehl toh-'tahl)*
application	**la solicitud** *(lah soh-lee-see-'tood)*
court date	**la fecha de la audiencia**
	(lah 'feh-chah deh lah aw-dee-'ehn-see-ah)
extension	**la extensión** *(lah ex-tehn-see-'ohn)*
refund	**el reembolso** *(ehl reh-ehm-'bohl-soh)*
traffic school	**la escuela de tráfico** *(lah ehs-'kweh-lah deh 'trah-fee-koh)*
trial by declaration	**el juicio por declaración**
	(ehl hoo-'ee-see-oh pohr deh-klah-rah-see-'ohn)

Do you have (the)...?	**¿Tiene usted...?** *(tee-'eh-neh oos-'tehd)*
driver's license	**la licencia de conducir**
	(lah lee-'sehn-see-ah deh kohn-doo-'seer)
I.D.	**la identificación** *(lah ee-dehn-tee-fee-kah-see-'ohn)*
plate number	**el número de la placa**
	(ehl 'noo-meh-roh deh lah 'plah-kah)
proof of correction	**la prueba de corrección**
	(lah proo-'eh-bah deh kohr-rehk-see-'ohn)

proof of insurance	**la prueba de seguro** *(lah proo-'eh-bah deh seh-'goo-roh)*
registration	**el registro** *(ehl reh-'hees-troh)*
ticket	**la boleta** *(lah boh-'leh-tah)*
warrant	**la orden** *(lah 'ohr-dehn)*

Was it (the)...?	**¿Fue...?** *(foo-'eh)*
fix-it ticket	**la boleta para reparar el vehículo** *(lah boh-'leh-tah 'pah-rah reh-pah-'rahr ehl veh-'ee-koo-loh)*
insurance violation	**la violación del seguro** *(lah vee-oh-lah-see-'ohn dehl seh-'goo-roh)*
parking ticket	**la boleta de estacionamiento** *(lah boh-'leh-tah deh ehs-tah-see-oh-nah-mee-'ehn-toh)*
photo citation	**la boleta de fotografía** *(lah boh-'leh-tah deh foh-toh-grah-'fee-ah)*
ownership violation	**la violación de la propiedad** *(lah vee-oh-lah-see-'ohn deh lah proh-pee-eh-'dahd)*

Now discuss the payment procedure in detail:

Go there to pay (the)...	**Vaya allí para pagar...** *('vah-yah ah-'yee 'pah-rah pah-'gahr)*
bail	**la fianza** *(lah fee-'ahn-sah)*
fine	**la multa** *(lah 'mool-tah)*
payment	**el pago** *(ehl 'pah-goh)*
tax	**el impuesto** *(ehl eem-'pwehs-toh)*

The court accepts (the)...	**El tribunal acepta...** *(ehl tree-boo-'nahl ah-'sehp-tah)*
cash	**el efectivo** *(ehl eh-fehk-'tee-voh)*
cashier check	**el cheque de caja** *(ehl 'cheh-keh deh 'kah-hah)*
credit card	**la tarjeta de crédito** *(lah tahr-'heh-tah deh 'kreh-dee-toh)*
money order	**el giro postal** *(ehl 'hee-roh pohs-'tahl)*
personal check	**el cheque personal** *(ehl 'cheh-keh pehr-soh-'nahl)*

Do it...	**Hágalo...** *('ah-gah-loh)*
on-line	**por correo electrónico** *(pohr kohr-'reh-oh eh-lehk-'troh-nee-koh)*
by mail	**por correo** *(pohr kohr-'reh-oh)*
in person	**en persona** *(ehn pehr-'soh-nah)*

NOTICE!   ¡Fíjese!

If you do a lot of work in traffic court, these words should be acquired right away:

accident	**el accidente** *(ehl ahk-see-'dehn-teh)*
driver	**el chofer** *(ehl choh-'fehr)*
fault	**la culpa** *(lah 'kool-pah)*
hazard	**el peligro** *(ehl peh-'lee-groh)*
pedestrian	**el peatón** *(ehl peh-ah-'tohn)*

seat belt	**el cinturón de seguridad**
	(ehl seen-too-'rohn deh seh-goo-ree-'dahd)
stop sign	**la señal de pare** *(lah sehn-'yahl deh 'pah-reh)*
tow truck	**la grúa** *(lah 'groo-ah)*
warning sign	**el aviso de advertencia**
	(ehl ah-'vee-soh deh ahd-vehr-'tehn-see-ah)

PRIVATE PRACTICE   **Práctica privada**

(20) A. Answer in Spanish:

1. In what court would a 10-year-old be tried for a felony?

   En _____

2. Use two words to translate the word *court*.

   _____

3. Where would a settlement usually be reached in a divorce case?

   En _____

B. Translate into English:

1. El tribunal penal   _____

2. El juzgado de tráfico   _____

3. El tribunal de reclamos menores   _____

C. Connect the words that belong together best:

1. la licencia	**el efectivo**
2. la multa	**el registro**
3. el cheque	**la boleta**

LOCAL OFFICES AND AGENCIES
Oficinas y agencias locales
(oh-fee-'see-nahs ee ah-'hehn-see-ahs loh-'kah-lehs)

There are usually several important offices, businesses, or agencies near the courthouse, so it will be a good idea to mention a few:

The _____ will help you.   _____ **le ayudará.** *(leh ah-yoo-dah-'rah)*

agency	**la agencia** *(lah ah-'hehn-see-ah)*
branch office	**la sucursal** *(lah soo-koor-'sahl)*
bureau	**el departamento** *(ehl deh-pahr-tah-'mehn-toh)*
business	**el negocio** *(ehl neh-'goh-see-oh)*
company	**la compañía** *(lah kohm-pahn-'ee-ah)*
division	**la división** *(lah dee-vee-see-'ohn)*

group	**el grupo** *(ehl 'groo-poh)*
office	**la oficina** *(lah oh-fee-'see-nah)*
organization	**la organización** *(lah ohr-gah-nee-sah-see-'ohn)*
unit	**la unidad** *(lah oo-nee-'dahd)*

It's an agency for...	**Es una agencia para...**
	(ehs 'oo-nah ah-'hehn-see-ah 'pah-rah)
education	**la educación** *(lah eh-doo-kah-see-'ohn)*
health care	**el cuidado médico** *(ehl kwee-'dah-doh 'meh-dee-koh)*
housing	**las viviendas** *(lahs vee-vee-'ehn-dahs)*
small business development	**el desarrollo de pequeños negocios**
	(ehl deh-sahr-'roh-yoh deh peh-'kehn-yohs neh-'goh-see-ohs)
veterans	**los veteranos** *(lohs veh-teh-'rah-nohs)*

They have (the)...	**Tienen...** *(tee-'eh-nehn)*
administrative support	**apoyo administrativo**
	(ah-'poh-yoh ahd-mee-nees-trah-'tee-voh)
bailment	**fianza** *(fee-'ahn-sah)*
Latino assistance	**ayuda para latinos** *(ah-'yoo-dah 'pah-rah lah-'tee-nohs)*
legal aid	**ayuda para asuntos legales**
	(ah-'yoo-dah 'pah-rah ah-'soon-tohs leh-'gah-lehs)
public records	**archivos públicos** *(ahr-'chee-vohs 'poo-blee-kohs)*
referral services	**servicios de referencia**
	(sehr-'vee-see-ohs deh reh-feh-'rehn-see-ah)

Now focus on the local government facilities:

The courthouse is near (the)...	**El tribunal está cerca de...**
	(ehl tree-boo-'nahl ehs-'tah 'sehr-kah deh)
chamber of commerce	**la cámera de comercio**
	(lah 'kah-mah-rah deh koh-'mehr-see-oh)
city hall	**el municipio** *(ehl moo-nee-'see-pee-oh)*
fire department	**el departamento de bomberos**
	(ehl deh-pahr-tah-'mehn-toh deh bohm-'beh-rohs)
jail	**la cárcel** *(lah 'kahr-sehl)*
library	**la biblioteca** *(lah bee-blee-oh-'teh-kah)*
police station	**la estación de policía**
	(lah ehs-tah-see-'ohn deh poh-lee-'see-ah)
post office	**el correo** *(ehl kohr-'reh-oh)*

It's (the) _____ department.	**Es el departamento de _____.**
	(ehs ehl deh-pahr-tah-'mehn-toh deh)
code enforcement	**cumplimiento de códigos**
	(koom-plee-mee-'ehn-toh deh 'koh-dee-gohs)
community services	**servicios comunitarios**
	(sehr-'vee-see-ohs koh-moo-nee-'tah-ree-ohs)

economic development	**desarrollo económico**
	(deh-sahr-'roh-yoh eh-koh-'noh-mee-koh)
finance	**finanzas** *(fee-'nahn-sahs)*
homeland security	**protección de la patria**
	(proh-tehk-see-'ohn deh lah 'pah-tree-ah)
human resources	**recursos humanos** *(reh-'koor-sohs oo-'mah-nos)*
parks and recreation	**parques y recreo** *('pahr-kehs ee reh-'kreh-oh)*
permits and licenses	**permisos y licencias** *(pehr-'mee-sohs ee lee-'sehn-see-ahs)*
planning	**planificación** *(plah-nee-fee-kah-see-'ohn)*
public works	**obras públicas** *('oh-brahs 'poo-blee-kahs)*
utilities	**servicios públicos** *(sehr-'vee-see-ohs 'poo-blee-kohs)*

It's next to (the) _____	**Está al lado del centro de _____.**
center.	*(ehs-'tah ahl 'lah-doh dehl 'sehn-troh deh)*
community	**comunidad** *(koh-moo-nee-'dahd)*
convention	**convenciones** *(kohn-vehn-see-'oh-nehs)*
health	**salud** *(sah-'lood)*
recreation	**recreo** *(reh-'kreh-oh)*
shopping	**comercio** *(koh-'mehr-see-oh)*
visitor	**visitantes** *(vee-see-'tahn-tehs)*

Continue to name buildings and sites around the courthouse:

Turn at (the)...	**Dé vuelta en...** *(deh voo-'ehl-tah ehn)*
airport	**el aeropuerto** *(ehl ah-eh-roh-'pwehr-toh)*
bank	**el banco** *(ehl 'bahn-koh)*
car lot	**el lote de carros** *(ehl 'loh-teh deh 'kahr-rohs)*
church	**la iglesia** *(lah eeg-'leh-see-ah)*
clinic	**la clínica** *(lah 'klee-nee-kah)*
factory	**la fábrica** *(lah 'fah-bree-kah)*
gas station	**la gasolinera** *(lah gah-soh-lee-'neh-rah)*
hospital	**el hospital** *(ehl ohs-pee-'tahl)*
movie theater	**el cine** *(ehl 'see-neh)*
museum	**el museo** *(ehl moo-'seh-oh)*
park	**el parque** *(ehl 'pahr-keh)*
restaurant	**el restaurante** *(ehl rehs-tah-oo-'rahn-teh)*
school	**la escuela** *(lah ehs-'kweh-lah)*
store	**la tienda** *(lah tee-'ehn-dah)*
supermarket	**el supermercado** *(ehl soo-pehr-mehr-'kah-doh)*
university	**la universidad** *(lah oo-nee-vehr-see-'dahd)*

The _____ station	**la estación de _____** *(lah ehs-tah-see-'ohn deh)*
bus	**autobús** *(aw-toh-'boos)*
subway	**metro** *('meh-troh)*
train	**tren** *(trehn)*

Do you know (the)...	¿Conoce usted...? *(koh-'noh-seh oos-'tehd)*
avenue	**la avenida** *(lah ah-veh-'nee-dah)*
bridge	**el puente** *(ehl 'pwehn-teh)*
building	**el edificio** *(ehl eh-dee-'fee-see-oh)*
hotel	**el hotel** *(ehl oh-'tehl)*
apartments	**los apartamentos** *(lohs ah-pahr-tah-'mehn-tohs)*
corner	**la esquina** *(lah ehs-'kee-nah)*
courtyard	**el patio** *(ehl 'pah-tee-oh)*
downtown	**el centro** *(ehl 'sehn-troh)*
fountain	**la fuente** *(lah 'fwehn-teh)*
highway	**la carretera** *(lah kahr-reh-'teh-rah)*
neighborhood	**el barrio** *(ehl 'bahr-ree-oh)*
road	**el camino** *(ehl kah-'mee-noh)*
skyscaper	**el rascacielos** *(ehl rahs-kah-see-'eh-lohs)*
statue	**la estatua** *(lah ehs-'tah-twah)*
sign	**la señal** *(lah sehn-'yahl)*
street	**la calle** *(lah 'kah-yeh)*
traffic signal	**el semáforo** *(ehl seh-'mah-foh-roh)*
tunnel	**el túnel** *(ehl 'too-nehl)*

Use (the)...	Use ... *('oo-seh)*
bus stop	**la parada de autobús** *(lah pah-'rah-dah deh aw-toh-'boos)*
crosswalk	**el cruce de peatones** *(ehl 'kroo-seh deh peh-ah-'toh-nehs)*
elevator	**el ascensor** *(ehl ah-sehn-'sohr)*
parking meter	**el parquímetro** *(ehl pahr-'kee-meh-troh)*
parking lot	**el estacionamiento** *(ehl ehs-tah-see-oh-nah-mee-'ehn-toh)*
restroom	**el baño** *(ehl 'bahn-yoh)*
sidewalk	**la acera** *(lah ah-'seh-rah)*
stairs	**las escaleras** *(lahs ehs-kah-'leh-rahs)*
steps	**los escalones** *(lohs ehs-kah-'loh-nehs)*
toll booth	**la caseta de peaje** *(lah kah-'seh-tah deh peh-'ah-heh)*

PRIVATE PRACTICE Práctica privada

(21) Circle the one word in each group that doesn't belong with the others:
1. **comercio, camino, calle, carretera**
2. **agencia, semáforo, compañía, negocio**
3. **escalones, cruce de peatones, acera, desarrollo**

CULTURAL COMMENT **Comentario cultural**

Many lawyers work with clients who know little or nothing about local, state, or federal laws and regulations. By contacting a variety of service agencies, one can pick up literature and website information in Spanish concerning citizenship, taxes, health care, education, transportation, and residence, as well as personal rights and privileges.

GIVING DIRECTIONS
Dar las direcciones
(dahr lahs dee-rehk-see-'oh-nehs)

Guide your Spanish-speaking clients to your exact location using words you know:

Where is it?	**¿Dónde está?** *('dohn-deh ehs-'tah)*
It's...	**Está...** *(ehs-'tah)*

behind   **detrás** *(deh-'trahs)*
Está detrás del estacionamiento. *(ehs-'tah deh-'trahs dehl ehs-tah-see-oh-nah-mee-'ehn-toh)*

far   **lejos** *('leh-hohs)*
Está lejos de aquí. *(ehs-'tah 'leh-hohs deh ah-'kee)*

in front   **enfrente** *(ehn-'frehn-teh)*
Está enfrente de la oficina. *(ehs-'tah ehn-'frehn-teh deh lah oh-fee-'see-nah)*

near   **cerca** *('sehr-kah)*
Está cerca del edificio. *(ehs-'tah 'sehr-kah dehl eh-dee-'fee-see-oh)*

beside   **al lado** *(ahl 'lah-doh)*
Está al lado del tribunal. *(ehs-'tah ahl 'lah-doh dehl tree-boo-'nahl)*

Also use these new phrases to direct folks to the courthouse:

Head...	**Vaya hacia el...** *('vah-yah 'ah-see-ah ehl)*
north	**norte** *('nohr-teh)*
south	**sur** *(soor)*
east	**este** *('ehs-teh)*
west	**oeste** *(oh-'ehs-teh)*

On what floor?	**¿En qué piso?** *(ehn keh 'pee-soh)*
The room is...	**El cuarto está...** *(ehl 'kwahr-toh ehs-'tah)*
on the first floor	**en el primer piso** *(ehn ehl pree-'mehr 'pee-soh)*
on the second floor	**en el segundo piso** *(ehn ehl seh-'goon-doh 'pee-soh)*
on this floor	**en este piso** *(ehn 'ehs-teh 'pee-soh)*

Many of these comments are used with numbers:

We'll meet there at _____ o'clock.
Nos encontramos allí a las _____. *(nohs ehn-kohn-'trah-mohs ah-'ee ah lahs)*

It's _____ blocks from here.
Está a _____ cuadras de aquí. *(ehs-'tah ah ___ 'kwah-drahs deh ah-'kee)*

It should take you _____ minutes.
Debe tomarle _____ minutos. *('deh-beh toh-'mahr-leh ___ mee-'noo-tohs)*

Now get them seated in the courtroom:

Where do I sit?	**¿Dónde me siento?** *('dohn-deh meh see-'ehn-toh)*
Sit...	**Siéntese...** *(see-'ehn-teh-seh)*
on the right side	**en el lado derecho** *(ehn ehl 'lah-doh deh-'reh-choh)*
on the left side	**en el lado izquierdo** *(ehn ehl 'lah-doh ees-kee-'ehr-doh)*
on the other side	**en el otro lado** *(ehn ehl 'oh-troh 'lah-doh)*
Move ...	**Muévase...** *(moo-'eh-vah-seh)*
to the center	**hacia el medio** *('ah-see-ah ehl 'meh-dee-oh)*
back	**hacia atrás** *('ah-see-ah ah-'trahs)*
forward	**hacia adelante** *('ah-see-ah ah-deh-'lahn-teh)*

VERBS IN ACTION!   ¡Verbos activos!

When giving formal affirmative and negative commands in Spanish, try to combine them with the pronouns **me**, **le**, **les**, and **nos**. Notice how they are positioned:

Answer (me)	**Contésteme** *(kohn-'tehs-teh-meh)*
Answer (him or her)	**Contéstele** *(kohn-'tehs-teh-leh)*
Answer (them)	**Contésteles** *(kohn-'tehs-teh-lehs)*
Answer (us)	**Contéstenos** *(kohn-'tehs-teh-nohs)*

Add some negative phrases. Continue to read aloud:

Listen to me.	**Escúcheme.** *(ehs-'koo-cheh-meh)*
Don't listen to Lupe.	**No le escuche a Lupe.** *(noh leh ehs-'koo-cheh ah 'loo-peh)*
Tell us.	**Díganos.** *('dee-gah-nohs)*
Don't tell them.	**No les diga.** *(noh lehs 'dee-gah)*

PRIVATE PRACTICE **Práctica privada**

22 Translate into English:

1. **Muévase hacia atrás.** _____

2. **Llámeme mañana.** _____

3. **No le dé el número.** _____

4. **Vaya al oeste.** _____

5. **Tráiganos los documentos** _____

6. **No les mande el dinero** _____

INSIDE THE COURTROOM
Dentro del tribunal
('dehn-troh dehl tree-boo-'nahl)

Now take a moment to identify a few parts of the courthouse and rooms around you:

Look at (the)...   **Mire...** *('mee-reh)*

bench	**la banca** *(lah 'bahn-kah)*
ceiling	**el techo** *(ehl 'teh-choh)*
chair	**la silla** *(lah 'see-yah)*
clock	**el reloj** *(ehl reh-'loh)*
elevator	**el ascensor** *(ehl ah-sehn-'sohr)*
entrance	**la entrada** *(lah ehn-'trah-dah)*
escalator	**la escalera mecánica** *(lah ehs-kah-'leh-rah meh-'kah-nee-kah)*
exit	**la salida** *(lah sah-'lee-dah)*
flag	**la bandera** *(lah bahn-'deh-rah)*
floor	**el piso** *(ehl 'pee-soh)*
front desk	**el escritorio principal** *(ehl ehs-kree-'toh-ree-oh preen-see-'pahl)*
gallery	**la galería** *(lah gah-leh-'ree-ah)*
guardrail	**la baranda** *(lah bah-'rahn-dah)*
hallway	**el pasillo** *(ehl pah-'see-yoh)*
lobby	**el vestíbulo** *(ehl vehs-'tee-boo-loh)*
seat	**el asiento** *(ehl ah-see-'ehn-toh)*
security area	**la zona de seguridad** *(lah 'soh-nah deh seh-goo-ree-'dahd)*
side door	**la puerta lateral** *(lah 'pwehr-tah lah-teh-'rahl)*
stand	**el estrado de testigos** *(ehl ehs-'trah-doh deh tehs-'tee-gohs)*
stool	**el taburete** *(ehl tah-boo-'reh-teh)*
table	**la mesa** *(lah 'meh-sah)*

viewing window	**la ventana de observación**
	(lah vehn-'tah-nah deh ohb-sehr-vah-see-'ohn)
wall	**la pared** *(lah pah-'rehd)*
whiteboard	**la pizarra** *(lah pee-'sahr-rah)*

They use (the)...	**Usan...** *('oo-sahn)*
earphones	**los audífonos** *(lohs aw-'dee-foh-nohs)*
computers	**las computadoras** *(lahs kohm-poo-tah-'doh-rahs)*
monitors	**los monitores** *(lohs moh-nee-'toh-rehs)*
screens	**las pantallas** *(lahs pahn-'tah-yahs)*
microphones	**los micrófonos** *(lohs mee-'kroh-foh-nohs)*
videocameras	**las videocámaras** *(lahs vee-deh-oh-'kah-mah-rahs)*

Did you see (the)...	**¿Vío usted...?** *(vee-'oh oos-'tehd)*
aisles	**los pasillos** *(los pah-'see-yohs)*
partitions	**los tabiques** *(lohs tah-'bee-kehs)*
rows	**las filas** *(lahs 'fee-lahs)*
sections	**las secciones** *(lahs sehk-see-'oh-nehs)*

That's called...	**Eso se llama...** *('eh-soh seh 'yah-mah)*
clerk's desk	**el escritorio del escribano**
	(ehl ehs-kree-'toh-ree-oh dehl ehs-kree-'bah-noh)
defendant's table	**el banquillo del acusado**
	(ehl bahn-'kee-yoh dehl ah-koo-'sah-doh)
exhibit area	**el área de pruebas instrumentales**
	(ehl 'ah-reh-ah deh proo-'eh-bahs eens-troo-mehn-'tah-lehs)
judge's bench	**la banca del juez** *(lah 'bahn-kah dehl hwehs)*
jury box	**la tribuna del jurado**
	(lah tree-'boo-nah dehl hoo-'rah-doh)

THE PEOPLE IN COURT
La gente en el tribunal
(lah 'hehn-teh ehn ehl tree-boo-'nahl)

Not everyone is included on the following list, but these are the major players in a courtroom setting. Try them out with both opening phrases:

He's/She's (the) ...	**Él/Ella es ...** *(ehl/'eh-yah ehs)*
I just spoke with...	**Acabo de hablar con...** *(ah-'kah-boh deh ah-'blahr kohn)*
assistant	**el/la asistente** *(ehl/lah ah-sees-'tehn-teh)*
bailiff	**el/la alguacil** *(ehl/lah ahl-gwah-'seel)*
court clerk	**el actuario/la actuaria**
	(ehl ahk-too-'ah-ree-oh/lah ahk-too-'ah-ree-ah)
court recorder	**el estenógrafo/ la estenógrafa**
	(ehl ehs-teh-'noh-grah-foh/lah ehs-teh-'noh-grah-fah)

court referee	**el/la árbitro del tribunal**
	(ehl/lah 'ahr-bee-troh dehl tree-boo-'nahl)
defendant (criminal)	**el acusado/la acusada**
	(ehl ah-koo-'sah-doh/lah ah-koo-'sah-dah)
defendant (civil)	**el demandado/la demandada**
	(ehl deh-mahn-'dah-doh/lah deh-mahn-'dah-dah)
defense attorney	**el abogado defensor/la abogada defensora**
	(ehl ah-boh-'gah-doh deh-fehn-'sohr/lah ah-boh-'gah-dah deh-fehn-'soh-rah)
detective	**el/la detective** *(ehl/lah deh-tehk-'tee-veh)*
filing clerk	**el secretario/la secretaria de actas**
	(ehl seh-kreh-'tah-ree-oh/lah seh-kreh-'tah-ree-ah deh 'ahk-tahs)
guard	**el/la guardia** *(ehl/lah 'gwahr-dee-ah)*
helper	**el ayudante/la ayudanta**
	(ehl ah-yoo-'dahn-teh/lah ah-yoo-'dahn-tah)
interpreter	**el/la intérprete** *(ehl/lah een-'tehr-preh-teh)*
investigator	**el investigador/la investigadora**
	(ehl een-vehs-tee-gah-'dohr/lah een-vehs-tee-gah-'doh-rah)
judge	**el juez/ la jueza** *(ehl hwehs/lah 'hweh-sah)*
jury member	**el/la miembro del jurado**
	(ehl/lah mee-'ehm-broh dehl hoo-'rah-doh)
law clerk	**el oficinista jurídico/la oficinista jurídica**
	(ehl oh-fee-see-'nees-tah hoo-'ree-dee-koh/lah oh-fee-see-'nees-tah hoo-'ree-dee-kah)
records clerk	**el/la oficinista de archivos**
	(ehl/lah oh-fee-see-'nees-tah deh ahr-'chee-vohs)
legal advisor	**el asesor/la asesora legal**
	(ehl ah-seh-'sohr/lah ah-seh-'soh-rah leh-'gahl)
paralegal	**el/la asistente legal** *(ehl/lah ah-sees-'tehn-teh leh-'gahl)*
plaintiff	**el/la demandante** *(ehl/lah deh-mahn-'dahn-teh)*
police officer	**el/la policía** *(ehl/lah poh-lee-'see-ah)*
prosecuting attorney	**el/la fiscal** *(ehl/lah fees-'kahl)*
public defender	**el defensor público/la defensora pública**
	(ehl deh-fehn-'sohr 'poo-blee-koh/lah deh-fehn-'soh-rah 'poo-blee-kah)
relative	**el/la pariente** *(ehl/lah pah-ree-'ehn-teh)*
reporter	**el reportero/ la reportera**
	(ehl reh-pohr-'teh-roh/lah reh-pohr-'teh-rah)
secretary	**el secretario/la secretaria**
	(ehl seh-kreh-'tah-ree-oh/lah seh-kreh-'tah-ree-ah)
suspect	**el sospechoso/ la sospechosa**
	(ehl sohs-peh-'choh-soh/lah sohs-peh-'choh-sah)
other party	**la otra parte** *(lah 'oh-trah 'pahr-teh)*
translator	**el traductor/la traductora**
	(ehl trah-dook-'tohr/lah trah-dook-'toh-rah)

victim	**la víctima** *(lah 'veek-tee-mah)*
viewer	**el espectador/ la espectadora**
	(ehl ehs-pehk-tah-'dohr/lah ehs-pehk-tah-'doh-rah)
witness	**el/la testigo** *(ehl/lah tehs-'tee-goh)*

Be sure to identify those government officials who might be involved in the case:

Here comes (the)...	**Aquí viene...** *(ah-'kee vee-'eh-neh)*
city manager	**el gerente/la gerenta municipal**
	(ehl heh-'rehn-teh/lah heh-'rehn-tah moo-nee-see-'pahl)
coroner	**el/la médico legista**
	(ehl/lah 'meh-dee-koh leh-'hees-tah)
counsel member	**el consejal/la consejala**
	(ehl kohn-seh-'hahl/lah kohn-seh-'hah-lah)
district attorney	**el/la fiscal del distrito**
	(ehl/lah fees-'kahl dehl dees-'tree-toh)
governor	**el gobernador/la gobernadora**
	(ehl goh-behr-nah-'dohr/lah goh-behr-nah-'doh-rah)
mayor	**el alcalde/la alcaldesa**
	(ehl ahl-'kahl-deh/lah ahl-kahl-'deh-sah)
police chief	**el jefe/la jefa de policía**
	(ehl 'heh-feh/lah 'heh-fah deh poh-lee-'see-ah)
supervisor	**el supervisor/la supervisora**
	(ehl soo-pehr-vee-'sohr/lah soo-pehr-vee-'soh-rah)

They're...	**Son...** *(sohn)*
government officials	**funcionarios gubernamentales**
	(foon-see-oh-'nah-ree-ohs goo-behr-nah-mehn-'tah-lehs)
administrators	**administradores** *(ahd-mee-nees-trah-'doh-rehs)*
coordinators	**coordinadores** *(koh-ohr-dee-nah-'doh-rehs)*
directors	**directores** *(dee-rehk-'toh-rehs)*
managers	**gerentes** *(heh-'rehn-tehs)*

NOTICE! ¡Fíjese!

How about the little details in the courtroom?

There's a...	**Hay...** *('ah-ee)*
gavel	**un mazo** *(oon 'mah-soh)*
nameplate	**una placa** *('oo-nah 'plah-kah)*
seal	**un sello** *(oon 'seh-yoh)*

PRIVATE PRACTICE   **Práctica privada**

(23) A. Answer in Spanish:

1. **¿Cuántas personas hay en el jurado – doce o quince?**

   _____

2. **¿Dónde está la banca del juez – enfrente o detrás?**

   _____

3. **¿Cuáles son más grandes – los asientos o los audífonos?**

   _____

B. Match the opposites:

1. **arriba**	**detrás**
2. **enfrente**	**afuera**
3. **lejos**	**izquierda**
4. **adentro**	**abajo**
5. **derecha**	**cerca**

C. Write in the correct job title following each descriptive sentence.
   The first one is done for you:

Esta persona escucha lo que las dos partes del desacuerdo dicen y luego decide quién ganó: el miembro del jurado

1. **Esta persona lleva uniforme y mantiene orden en el tribunal:**

   _____

2. **Esta persona viene al tribunal para decir la verdad y contar lo que ha oído o visto:**

   _____

3. **Esta persona usa una máquina para escribir todo lo que se dice en el tribunal:**

   _____

THE PROCEDURE
El procedimiento
(ehl proh-seh-dee-mee-'ehn-toh)

Let's check the court procedures. Many of these words should look familiar to you:

Do you understand (the)...?   **¿Entiende usted ...?** *(ehn-tee-'ehn-deh oos-'tehd)*

plan	**el plan** *(ehl plahn)*
process	**el proceso** *(ehl proh-'seh-soh)*
strategy	**la estrategia** *(lah ehs-trah-'teh-ee-ah)*
procedure	**el procedimiento** *(ehl proh-seh-dee-mee-'ehn-toh)*
proceedings	**el acto procesal** *(ehl 'ahk-toh proh-seh-'sahl)*
requirements	**los requisitos** *(lohs reh-kee-'see-tohs)*
rules	**las reglas** *(lahs 'reh-glahs)*
steps	**los pasos** *(lohs 'pah-sohs)*
system	**el sistema** *(ehl sees-'teh-mah)*

Would you like to talk   **¿Quisiera hablar de...?**
about (the)...?   *(kee-see-'eh-rah ah-'blahr deh)*

affidavit	**el afidávit** *(ehl ah-fee-'dah-veet)*
appeal	**la apelación** *(lah ah-peh-lah-see-'ohn)*
arraignment	**la lectura de cargos** *(lah lehk-'too-rah deh 'kahr-gohs)*
arrest	**el arresto** *(ehl ahr-'rehs-toh)*
brief	**el sumario** *(ehl soo-'mah-ree-oh)*
calendar	**el calendario** *(ehl kah-lehn-'dah-ree-oh)*
case	**el caso** *(ehl 'kah-soh)*
change	**el cambio** *(ehl 'kahm-bee-oh)*
charges	**los cargos** *(lohs 'kahr-gohs)*
claim	**la demanda** *(lah deh-'mahn-dah)*
conduct	**la conducta** *(lah kohn-'dook-tah)*
decision	**la decision** *(lah deh-see-see-'ohn)*
defense	**la defensa** *(lah deh-'fehn-sah)*
deposition	**la declaración** *(lah deh-klah-rah-see-'ohn)*
docket	**el horario de juicios** *(ehl oh-'rah-ree-oh deh hoo-'ee-see-ohs)*
evidence	**las pruebas** *(lahs proo-'eh-bahs)*
exhibit	**la prueba instrumental** *(lah proo-'eh-bah eens-troo-mehn-'tahl)*
fines	**las multas** *(lahs 'mool-tahs)*
hearing	**la audiencia** *(lah aw-dee-'ehn-see-ah)*
indictment	**la acusación** *(lah ah-koo-sah-see-'ohn)*
information	**la información** *(lah een-fohr-mah-see-'ohn)*
judgment	**el fallo** *(ehl 'fah-yoh)*
jury selection	**la selección del jurado** *(lah seh-lehk-see-'ohn dehl hoo-'rah-doh)*
lawsuit	**el pleito** *(ehl 'pleh-ee-toh)*
list	**la lista** *(lah 'lees-tah)*

motion	**la petición** *(lah peh-tee-see-'ohn)*
plea	**el alegato** *(ehl ah-leh-'gah-toh)*
ruling	**la resolución** *(lah reh-soh-loo-see-'ohn)*
sentence	**la sentencia** *(lah sehn-'tehn-see-ah)*
settlement	**el acuerdo** *(ehl ah-'kwehr-doh)*
subpoena	**la citación** *(lah see-tah-see-'ohn)*
testimony	**el testimonio** *(ehl tehs-tee-'moh-nee-oh)*
trial	**el juicio** *(ehl hoo-'ee-see-oh)*
warrant	**la orden** *(lah 'ohr-dehn)*

Notice the value of this familiar verb pattern when it comes to discussing legal procedures:

I'm going to...	**Voy a...** *('voh-ee ah)*
We're going to...	**Vamos a...** *('vah-mohs ah)*

announce	**anunciar** *(ah-noon-see-'ahr)*
answer	**contestar** *(kohn-tehs-'tahr)*
ask for	**pedir** *(peh-'deer)*
ask	**preguntar** *(preh-goon-'tahr)*
attend	**asistir** *(ah-sees-'teer)*
call	**llamar** *(yah-'mahr)*
check	**revisar** *(reh-vee-sahr)*
enter	**entrar** *(ehn-'trahr)*
exchange	**cambiar** *(kahm-bee-'ahr)*
file	**archivar** *(ahr-chee-'vahr)*
give	**dar** *(dahr)*
go	**ir** *(eer)*
leave	**salir** *(sah-'leer)*
listen	**escuchar** *(ehs-koo-'chahr)*
meet	**juntarse** *(hoon-'tahr-seh)*
present	**presentar** *(preh-sehn-'tahr)*
prove	**demostrar** *(deh-mohs-'trahr)*
receive	**recibir** *(reh-see-'beer)*
say	**decir** *(deh-'seer)*
show	**mostrar** *(mohs-'trahr)*
sit	**sentarse** *(sehn-'tahr-seh)*
speak	**hablar** *(ah-'blahr)*
stand	**pararse** *(pah-'rahr-seh)*
suggest	**sugerir** *(soo-heh-'reer)*
try	**probar** *(proh-'bahr)*

He/She is going to say...
Él/Ella va a decir... *(ehl/'eh-yah vah ah deh-'seer)*

All rise.
Favor de pararse todos. *(fah-'vohr deh pah-'rahr-seh 'toh-dohs)*

The honorable judge ____ is in the courtroom.
El honorable juez ____ está en el tribunal.
(ehl oh-noh-'rah-bleh hwehs ehs-'tah ehn ehl tree-boo-'nahl)

You may be seated.
Pueden sentarse. *('pweh-dehn sehn-'tahr-seh)*

Continue to work on those words that are a lot like English:

It's...   **Es...** *(ehs)*

ethical	**ético** *('eh-tee-koh)*
formal	**formal** *(fohr-'mahl)*
illegal	**ilegal** *(ee-leh-'gahl)*
important	**importante** *(eem-pohr-'tahn-teh)*
informal	**informal** *(een-fohr-'mahl)*
legal	**legal** *(leh-'gahl)*
necessary	**necesario** *(neh-seh-'sah-ree-oh)*
official	**oficial** *(oh-fee-see-'ahl)*
provisional	**provisional** *(proh-vee-see-oh-'nahl)*
respectful	**respetuoso** *(rehs-peh-too-'oh-soh)*
serious	**serio** *('seh-ree-oh)*
traditional	**tradicional** *(trah-dee-see-oh-'nahl)*
typical	**típico** *('tee-pee-koh)*

NOTICE!   ¡Fíjese!

Note how effective the ordinal numbers can be in court:

First, we file a case and schedule a hearing.
Primero, registramos el caso y programamos una audiencia.

Second, we present the strategy and the procedure to the client.
Segundo, presentamos la estrategia y el procedimiento al cliente.

Third, we go to the hearing and talk to the judge.
Tercero, vamos a la audiencia y conversamos con el juez.

MORE INSTRUCTIONS
Más instrucciones
(mahs eens-trook-see-'oh-nehs)

Keep using brief phrases to guide clients through the process. If necessary, rehearse the actions as much as possible:

Watch and listen.	**Mire y escuche.** *('mee-reh ee ehs-'koo-cheh)*
Pay attention.	**Preste atención.** *('prehs-teh ah-tehn-see-'ohn)*
This way.	**De esta manera.** *(deh 'ehs-tah mah-'neh-rah)*
This way.	**Así.** *(ah-'see)*

Remember this.	**Recuerde esto.** *(reh-'kwehr-deh 'ehs-toh)*
It's very important.	**Es muy importante.** *(ehs 'moo-ee eem-pohr-'tahn-teh)*

Envision how, when, or where each of these can be used:

Again.	**Otra vez.** *('oh-trah vehs)*
The same thing.	**La misma cosa.** *(lah 'mees-mah 'koh-sah)*
This one, too.	**Este también.** *('ehs-teh tahm-bee-'ehn)*
Not that one.	**Ese no.** *('eh-seh noh)*
The other one.	**El otro.** *(ehl 'oh-troh)*
Not like that.	**Así no.** *(ah-'see noh)*
That's better.	**Está mejor.** *(ehs-'tah meh-'hohr)*
Keep going.	**Siga.** *('see-gah)*

THE SENTENCE! ¡La frase!

These phrases communicate caution or warning:

Don't do it.	**No lo haga.** *(noh loh 'ah-gah)*
Stay calm.	**Manténgase tranquilo.** *(mahn-'tehn-gah-seh trahn-'kee-loh)*
Be very careful.	**Tenga mucho cuidado.**
	('tehn-gah 'moo-choh koo-ee-'dah-doh)

PRIVATE PRACTICE Práctica privada

(24) A. Translate:

1. Pay attention! _____

2. You may be seated. _____

3. Here is the procedure. _____

B. Unscramble the letters to form common legal words:

¿Quisiera hablar del/de la...?

1. toelag _____

2. addmaen _____

3. icijou _____

C. Write in the opposite:

1. preguntar _____

2. escuchar _____

3. recibir _____

FRIENDLY REMINDERS
Recordatorios amistosos
(reh-kohr-dah-'toh-ree-ohs ah-mees-'toh-sohs)

Instruction to clients is an ongoing process, so it's best to learn sentence patterns that can be used effectively time and again:

Make sure that (you) ...
Asegúrese de ... *(ah-seh-'goo-reh-seh deh)*

Remember to ...
Recuerde ... *(reh-'kwehr-deh)*

It's important to...
Es importante ... *(ehs eem-pohr-'tahn-teh)*

ask me if you don't understand	**preguntarme si no entiende** *(preh-goon-'tahr-meh see noh ehn-tee-'ehn-deh)*
call me at this number	**llamarme a este número** *(yah-'mahr-meh ah 'ehs-teh 'noo-meh-roh)*
arrive early	**llegar temprano** *(yeh-'gahr tehm-'prah-noh)*
bring the paperwork	**traer los papeles** *(trah-'ehr lohs pah-'peh-lehs)*
read the documents	**leer los documentos** *(leh-'ehr lohs doh-koo-'mehn-tohs)*

Here are more examples:

When you finish ...
Cuando termine ... *('kwahn-doh tehr-'mee-neh)*

When you finish, call me at this number.
Cuando termine, llámeme a este número.
('kwah-doh tehr-'mee-neh 'yah-meh-meh ah 'ehs-teh 'noo-meh-roh)

If it's possible...
Si es posible ... *(see ehs poh-'see-bleh)*

If it's possible, come at eight o'clock.
Si es posible, venga a las ocho. *(see ehs poh-'see-bleh 'vehn-gah ah lahs 'oh-choh)*

Before you go ...
Antes de irse ... *('ahn-tehs deh 'eer-seh)*

Before you go, talk to the secretary.
Antes de irse, hable con la secretaria.
('ahn-tehs deh 'eer-seh 'ah-bleh kohn lah seh-kreh-'tah-ree-ah)

THE SCHEDULE
El horario
(ehl oh-'rah-ree-oh)

After you firm up a plan or schedule, use the following to tell your client when events related to their case take place.

This is the calendar.	**Este es el calendario.** *('ehs-teh ehs ehl kah-lehn-'dah-ree-oh)*
Check the schedule.	**Revise el horario.** *(reh-'vee-seh ehl oh-'rah-ree-oh)*
These are the dates and times.	**Estas son las fechas y horas.** *('ehs-tahs sohn lahs 'feh-chahs ee 'oh-rahs)*
I'll send you (the) ...	**Le voy a mandar...** *(leh 'voh-ee ah mahn-'dahr)*
plan	**el plan** *(ehl plahn)*
agenda	**la orden del día** *(lah 'ohr-dehn dehl 'dee-ah)*
change	**el cambio** *(ehl 'kahm-bee-oh)*

Remember the expression *at* in reference to time is **a la(s)** *(ah lah/s)* (at 2:00, **a las dos**). To refer to days, dates, or months, simply include the article **el** or **los**:

We start ___	**Empezamos ___** *(ehm-peh-'sah-mohs)*
We start at nine.	**Empezamos a las nueve.** *(em-peh-'sah-mohs ah lahs 'nweh-veh)*
We finish ___	**Terminamos ___** *(tehr-mee-'nah-mohs)*
We finish on Friday.	**Terminamos el viernes.** *(tehr-mee-'nah-mohs ehl vee-'ehr-nehs)*

VERBS IN ACTION! ¡Verbos activos!

Again, be firm about the need for punctuality in the courthouse:

Be here for sure!
¡Venga aquí sin falta! *('vehn-gah ah-'kee seen 'fahl-tah)*

Please arrive early!
¡Favor de llegar temprano! *(fah-'vohr deh yeh-'gahr tehm-'prah-noh)*

Do not miss the appointment!
¡No falte a la cita! *(noh 'fahl-teh ah lah 'see-tah)*

Call if you have a problem!
¡Llame si tiene un problema! *('yah-meh see tee-'eh-neh oon proh-'bleh-mah)*

You will need a medical excuse!
¡Necesitará una excusa médica! *(neh-seh-see-tah-'rah 'oo-nah ex-'koo-sah 'meh-dee-kah)*

CULTURAL COMMENT   Comentario cultural

Many cultures put less emphasis on beating the clock than others, so you may have to be more patient with some of your clients. However, if punctuality is a concern, be sincere and direct as you discuss your cultural differences. Like it or not, many immigrants need to learn the value and benefits of trying to arrive on time.

COURTROOM CONDUCT
El comportamiento en el tribunal
(ehl kohm-pohr-tah-mee-'ehn-toh ehn ehl tree-'boo-nahl)

Most people are unaware of the rules for courtroom behavior. The following guidelines will cover most of your concerns:

Use the expression *honorable judge.*
Use la expresión *el honorable señor juez (la honorable señora jueza).*
('oo-seh lah ex-preh-see-'ohn ehl oh-noh-'rah-bleh sehn-'yohr hwehs lah oh-noh-'rah-bleh sehn-'yoh-rah hweh-sah)

Let us know when you don't understand something.
Avísenos cuando no entiende algo.
(ah-'vee-seh-nohs 'kwahn-doh noh ehn-tee-'ehn-deh 'ahl-goh)

Please remain quiet.
Favor de guardar silencio. *(fah-'vohr deh gwahr-'dahr see-'lehn-see-'oh)*

If possible, have your instructions translated into Spanish. Use words that are easy for Spanish speakers to understand:

You may not...	**No puede...** *(noh 'pweh-deh)*
drink	**beber** *(beh-'behr)*
eat	**comer** *(koh-'mehr)*
leave	**salir** *(sah-'leer)*
shout	**gritar** *(gree-'tahr)*
smoke	**fumar** *(foo-'mahr)*
talk	**hablar** *(ah-'blahr)*

You have to...	**Tiene que...** *(tee-'eh-neh keh)*
leave the children at home	**dejar los niños en casa** *(deh-'hahr lohs 'neen-yohs ehn 'kah-sah)*
arrive early	**llegar temprano** *(yeh-'gahr tehm-'prah-noh)*
bring the documents	**traer los documentos** *(trah-'ehr lohs doh-koo-'mehn-tohs)*
pass through security	**pasar por seguridad** *(pah-'sahr pohr seh-goo-ree-'dahd)*

empty your pockets	**vaciar los bolsillos** (*vah-see-'ahr lohs bohl-'see-yohs*)
use the interpreter	**usar el intérprete** (*oo-'sahr ehl een-'tehr-preh-teh*)
turn off the cell phone	**apagar el celular** (*ah-pah-'gahr ehl seh-loo-'lahr*)
put away the iPod	**guardar el iPod** (*gwahr-'dahr ehl 'ah-ee-pohd*)
complete the forms	**llenar los formularios**
	(*yeh-'nahr lohs fohr-moo-'lah-ree-ohs*)

It's important to...	**Es importante...** (*eh seem-pohr-'tahn-teh*)
be well groomed	**arreglarse bien** (*ahr-reh-'glahr-seh bee-'ehn*)
dress appropriately	**vestirse apropiadamente**
	(*vehs-'teer-seh ah-proh-pee-ah-dah-'mehn-teh*)
stay healthy	**estar con buena salud**
	(*ehs-'tahr kohn 'bweh-nah sah-'lood*)
look confident	**verse seguro/a de sí mismo/a**
	(*'vehr-seh seh-'goo-roh/ah deh see 'mees-moh/ah*)
remember everything	**acordarse de todo** (*ah-kohr-'dahr-seh deh 'toh-doh*)
speak clearly	**hablar claramente** (*ah-'blahr klah-rah-'mehn-teh*)

Please do not...	**Favor de no...** (*fah-'vohr deh noh*)
change your story	**alterar su historia** (*ahl-teh-'rahr soo ees-'toh-ree-ah*)
chew gum	**masticar chicle** (*mahs-tee-'kahr 'chee-kleh*)
commit perjury	**perjurar** (*pehr-hoo-'rahr*)
curse	**decir groserías** (*deh-'seer groh-seh-'ree-ahs*)
lie	**mentir** (*mehn-'teer*)
point	**señalar** (*sehn-yah-'lahr*)

PROPER ATTIRE
La ropa apropiada
(lah 'roh-pah ah-proh-pee-'ah-dah)

Another important part of courtroom demeanor involves one's physical appearance before the judge. Here are a few words and phrases that relate to clothing and accessories:

Take off (the)...	**Quítese...** (*'kee-teh-seh*)
cap	**la gorra** (*lah 'gohr-rah*)
hat	**el sombrero** (*ehl sohm-'breh-roh*)
gloves	**los guantes** (*lohs 'gwahn-tehs*)
handkerchief	**el pañuelo** (*ehl pahn-yoo-'eh-loh*)
jacket	**la chaqueta** (*lah chah-'keh-tah*)
jewelry	**las joyas** (*lahs 'hoh-yahs*)
overcoat	**el abrigo** (*ehl ah-'bree-goh*)
raincoat	**el impermeable** (*ehl eem-pehr-meh-'ah-bleh*)
scarf	**la bufunda** (*lah boo-'fahn-dah*)

Your clothes must be clean.
Su ropa debe estar limpia. (*soo 'roh-pah 'deh-beh ehs-'tahr 'leem-pee-ah*)

| Wear (the)... | **Póngase...**(*'pohn-gah-seh*) |
| Don't wear (the)... | **No se ponga...** (*noh seh 'pohn-gah*) |

dress	**el vestido** (*ehl vehs-'tee-doh*)
jacket	**el saco** (*ehl 'sah-koh*)
jeans	**los bluyines** (*lohs bloo-'yee-nehs*)
pants	**los pantalones** (*lohs pahn-tah-'loh-nehs*)
sandals	**las sandalias** (*lahs sahn-'dah-lee-ahs*)
shirt	**la camisa** (*lah kah-'mee-sah*)
shoes	**las zapatos** (*lohs sah-'pah-tohs*)
skirt	**la falda** (*lah 'fahl-dah*)
sneakers	**las zapatillas** (*lahs sah-pah-'tee-yahs*)
socks	**los calcetines** (*lohs kahl-seh-'tee-nehs*)
suit	**el traje** (*ehl 'trah-heh*)
sweatsuit	**las sudaderas** (*lahs soo-dah-'deh-rahs*)
T-shirt	**la camiseta** (*lah kah-mee-'seh-tah*)
tie	**la corbata** (*lah kohr-'bah-tah*)
uniform	**el uniforme** (*ehl oo-nee-'fohr-meh*)

NOTICE!　¡Fíjese!

Remember that indirect pronouns can be placed at the end of an infinitive. Try some of these one-liners around the courthouse:

I want to...	**Quiero...** (*kee-'eh-roh*)
ask you something	**preguntarle algo** (*preh-goon-'tahr-leh 'ahl-goh*)
assure you	**asegurarle** (*ah-seh-goo-'rahr-leh*)
call you	**llamarle** (*yah-'mahr-leh*)
explain to you	**explicarle** (*ex-plee-'kahr-leh*)
inform you	**informarle** (*een-fohr-'mahr-leh*)
show you something	**mostrarle algo** (*mohs-'trahr-leh*)

PRIVATE PRACTICE　Práctica privada

(25) A. Name three activities that are not allowed in the courtroom:

Favor de no... _____ _____ _____

B. Circle the one word in each group that doesn't belong with the others:

1. **serio, importante, abrigo, necesario**

2. **plan, pizarra, proceso, procedimiento**

3. **gorra, algo, corbata, sombrero**

VERBS IN ACTION!   ¡Verbos activos!

So many verbs related to activities at the courthouse! Memorize the most important ones first:

to adjust	**ajustar** *(ah-hoos-'tahr)*
to admonish	**amonestar** *(ah-moh-nehs-'tahr)*
to affirm	**afirmar** *(ah-feer-'mahr)*
to allege	**alegar** *(ah-leh-'gahr)*
to amend	**enmendar** *(ehn-mehn-'dahr)*
to appeal	**apelar** *(ah-peh-'lahr)*
to bind	**compeler, obligar** *(kohm-peh-'lehr, oh-blee-'gahr)*
to challenge	**recusar** *(reh-koo-'sahr)*
to commit	**cometer** *(koh-meh-'tehr)*
to confiscate	**confiscar** *(kohn-fees-'kahr)*
to continue	**continuar** *(kohn-tee-'nwahr)*
to convey	**transmitir** *(trahns-mee-'teer)*
to deem	**estimar** *(ehs-tee-'mahr)*
to delete	**borrar** *(bohr-'rahr)*
to deliberate	**deliberar** *(deh-lee-beh-'rahr)*
to dismiss	**despedir** *(dehs-peh-'deer)*
to divide	**dividir** *(dee-vee-'deer)*
to endorse	**endosar** *(ehn-doh-'sahr)*
to enforce	**hacer cumplir** *(ah-'sehr koom-'pleer)*
to enjoin	**prohibir** *(proh-ee-'beer)*
to establish	**establecer** *(ehs-tah-bleh-'sehr)*
to execute	**ejecutar** *(eh-heh-koo-'tahr)*
to exonerate	**exonerar** *(ex-oh-neh-'rahr)*
to expunge	**erradicar** *(ehr-rah-dee-'kahr)*
to include	**incluir** *(een-kloo-'eer)*
to incriminate	**incriminar** *(een-kree-mee-'nahr)*
to issue	**emitir** *(eh-mee-'teer)*
to litigate	**litigar** *(lee-tee-'gahr)*
to plea	**declararse** *(deh-klah-'rahr-seh)*
to possess	**poseer** *(poh-seh-'ehr)*
to post	**dar aviso** *(dahr ah-'vee-soh)*
to postpone	**posponer** *(pohs-poh-'nehr)*
to process	**procesar** *(proh-seh-'sahr)*
to promise	**prometer** *(proh-meh-'tehr)*
to prosecute	**procesar** *(proh-seh-'sahr)*
to punish	**castigar** *(kahs-tee-'gahr)*
to release	**liberar** *(lee-beh-'rahr)*
to reverse	**anular el fallo** *(ah-noo-'lahr ehl 'fah-yoh)*
to seal	**sellar** *(seh-'yahr)*
to serve	**servir** *(sehr-'veer)*
to strike	**eliminar** *(eh-lee-mee-'nahr)*
to submit	**entregarse** *(ehn-treh-'gahr-seh)*

to subrogate	**subrogar** *(soob-roh-'gahr)*
to suppress	**suprimir** *(soo-pree-'meer)*
to suspend	**suspender** *(soos-pehn-'dehr)*
to testify	**testificar** *(tehs-tee-fee-'kahr)*
to uphold	**confirmar** *(kohn-feer-'mahr)*
to visit	**visitar** *(vee-see-'tahr)*
to warn	**conminar** *(kohn-mee-'nahr)*

NOTICE!   ¡Fíjese!

Add the suffix -**mente** to some descriptive words in Spanish, and you can create an adverb. An adverb tells *how* something is done:

slow	**lento(a)** *(lehn-toh/ah)*
slowly	**lentamente** *(lehn-tah-'mehn-teh)*

He walks slowly.
Él camina lentamente. *(ehl kah-'mee-nah lehn-tah-'mehn-teh)*

dangerous	**peligroso(a)** *(peh-lee-'groh-soh/ah)*
dangerously	**peligrosamente** *(peh-lee-groh-sah-'mehn-teh)*

She's driving dangerously.
Ella está manejando peligrosamente.
(eh-yah ehs-'tah mah-neh-'hahn-doh peh-lee-groh-sah-'mehn-teh)

THE SENTENCE!   ¡La frase!

Like the commands, verb infinitives also must be changed when we refer to everyday activities. In the examples below, notice how the Present Tense forms change based on *who* completes the action. These final letter patterns are the same for most verbs:

TO SPEAK	**Hablar** *(ah-'blahr)*
I speak	**hablo** *('ah-bloh)*
You speak (sing.); He, She speaks	**habla** *('ah-blah)*
You speak (pl.); They speak	**hablan** *('ah-blahn)*
We speak	**hablamos** *(ah-'blah-mohs)*

Hablo español y mi amiga habla inglés.
('ah-bloh ehs-pahn-'yohl ee mee ah-'mee-gah 'ah-blah een-'glehs)

TO EAT	Comer *(koh-'mehr)*
I eat	**como** *('koh-moh)*
You eat (sing.); He, She eats	**come** *('koh-meh)*
You eat (pl.); They eat	**comen** *('koh-mehn)*
We eat	**comemos** *(koh-'meh-mohs)*

Usted <u>come</u> hamburguesas y ellos <u>comen</u> tacos.
(oos-'tehd 'koh-meh ahm-boor-'gheh-sahs ee 'eh-yohs 'koh-mehn 'tah-kohs)

TO WRITE	Escribir *(ehs-kree-'beer)*
I write	**escribo** *(ehs-'kree-boh)*
You write (sing.); He, She writes	**escribe** *(ehs-'kree-beh)*
You write (pl.); They write	**escriben** *(ehs-'kree-behn)*
We write	**escribimos** *(ehs-kree-'bee-mohs)*

Ustedes <u>escriben</u> en el papel y nosotros <u>escribimos</u> en el libro.
(oos-'teh-dehs ehs-'kree-behn ehn ehl pah-'pehl ee noh-'soh-trohs ehs-kree-'bee-mohs ehn ehl 'lee-broh)

Notice how the **-ar** verb, **hablar**, doesn't change the same as the **-er** and **-ir** verbs! This will be explained as you pick up more verbs later on. Also note that some verbs are irregular because they don't follow the pattern above:

to begin	**empezar** *(ehm-peh-'sahr)*
I begin.	**Empiezo.** *(ehm-pee-'eh-soh)*
to bring	**traer** *(trah-'ehr)*
I bring.	**Traigo.** *('trah-ee-goh)*
to do	**hacer** *(ah-'sehr)*
I do.	**Hago.** *('ah-goh)*
to find	**encontrar** *(ehn-kohn-'trahr)*
I find.	**Encuentro.** *(ehn-'kwehn-troh)*
to give	**dar** *(dahr)*
I give.	**Doy.** *('doh-ee)*
to leave	**salir** *(sah-'leer)*
I leave.	**Salgo.** *('sahl-goh)*
to offer	**ofrecer** *(oh-freh-'sehr)*
I offer.	**Ofrezco.** *(oh-'frehs-koh)*

| to see | **ver** *(vehr)* |
| I see. | **Veo.** *('veh-oh)* |

| to tell | **decir** *(deh-'seer)* |
| I tell. | **Digo.** *('dee-goh)* |

| to think | **pensar** *(pehn-'sahr)* |
| I think. | **Pienso.** *(pee-'ehn-soh)* |

| to understand | **entender** *(ehn-tehn-'dehr)* |
| I understand. | **Entiendo.** *(ehn-tee-'ehn-doh)* |

And this is how you ask a question and express the negative in the Present Indicative:

| Do they work here? | **¿Trabajan aquí?** *(trah-'bah-hahn ah-'kee)* |
| No, they don't work here. | **No, no trabajan aquí.** *(noh noh trah-'bah-hahn ah-'kee)* |

NOTICE!   ¡Fíjese!

Be on the lookout for verbs ending with **-se**. They refer to *-self* actions:

to stand up	**pararse** *(pah-'rahr-seh)*
to retire	**retirarse** *(reh-tee-'rahr-seh)*
to meet	**reunirse** *(reh-oo-'neer-seh)*

And, here are two more irregular verbs that you'll be using every day:

TO BE ABLE TO	**Poder** *(poh-'dehr)*
I can	**puedo** *('pweh-doh)*
You can (sing.); He, She, It can	**puede** *('pweh-deh)*
You can (pl.); They can	**pueden** *('pweh-dehn)*
We can	**podemos** *(poh-'deh-mohs)*

Puedo leer y él puede escribir.
('pweh-doh leh-'ehr ee ehl 'pweh-deh ehs-kree-'beer)

TO WANT	**Querer** *(keh-'rehr)*
I want	**quiero** *(kee-'eh-roh)*
You want (sing.); He, She wants	**quiere** *(kee-'eh-reh)*
You want (pl.); They want	**quieren** *(kee-'eh-rehn)*
We want	**queremos** *(keh-'reh-mohs)*

Quiero trabajar hoy y ella quiere trabajar mañana.
(kee-'eh-roh trah-bah-'hahr 'oh-ee ee 'eh-yah kee-'eh-reh trah-bah-'hahr mahn-'yah-nah)

PRIVATE PRACTICE   **Práctica privada**

(26) Using what you learned about the Present Indicative tense in Spanish, make changes to these verbs and then translate the sentences into English.

COMER (to eat)   **Yo como temprano.**
(I eat early.)

1. **TRABAJAR** (to work)   **Ella _____ mucho.**

(_____)

2. **MANDAR** (to send)   **Nosotros _____ el dinero.**

(_____)

3. **REGRESAR** (to return)   **Ellos _____ tarde.**

(_____)

4. **ESCRIBIR** (to write)   **Yo _____ la información.**

(_____)

5. **USAR** (to use)   **Él _____ el lápiz.**

(_____)

Chapter Four

Capítulo Cuatro
(kah-'pee-too-loh 'kwah-troh)

Immigration, Personal Injury, and Family Law
La inmigración, la lesión corporal y la ley familiar

(lah een-mee-grah-see-'ohn, lah leh-see-'ohn kohr-poh-'rahl ee lah 'leh-ee fah-mee-lee-'ahr)

IMMIGRATION LAW
La ley de inmigración
(lah 'leh-ee deh een-mee-grah-see-'ohn)

One of the most common areas of discussion today is immigration law, so spend plenty of time studying the following vocabulary lists. Although some of these words were presented earlier, this first group refers to race, countries, and nationalities:

African-American	**afroamericano** *(ah-froh-ah-meh-ree-'kah-noh)*
Anglo-Saxon	**anglosajón** *(ahn-gloh-sah-'hohn)*
Asian-American	**asiático-americano** *(ah-see-ah-tee-koh-ah-meh-ree-'kah-noh)*
Are you a/an ...?	**¿Es usted...?** *(ehs oos-'tehd)*
American	**norteamericano/norteamericana** *(nohr-teh-ah-meh-ree-'kah-noh/nohr-teh-ah-meh-ree-'kah-nah)*
European	**europeo/europea** *(eh-oo-roh-'peh-oh/eh-oo-roh-'peh-ah)*
Latin American	**latinoamericano/latinoamericana** *(lah-tee-noh-ah-meh-ree-'kah-noh/lah-tee-noh-ah-meh-ree-'kah-nah)*
South American	**sudamericano/sudamericana** *(soo-dah-meh-ree-'kah-noh/soo-dah-meh-ree-'kah-nah)*
U.S. citizen	**ciudadano/ciudadana estadounidense** *(see-oo-dah-'dah-noh/see-oo-dah-'dah-nah ehs-tah-doh-oo-nee-'dehn-seh)*

Now target the native countries of the Spanish-speakers you serve:

Is she from...? — Is he ....?   **¿Es ella de...? — ¿Es él...?** *(ehs 'eh-yah deh...ehs ehl deh)*

Argentina — argentino *(ahr-hehn-'tee-nah/ahr-hehn-'tee-noh)*
Brasil — brasileño *(brah-'seel/brah-see-'lehn-yoh)*
Bolivia — boliviano *(boh-'lee-vee-ah/boh-lee-vee-'ah-noh)*
Chile — chileno *('chee-leh/chee-'leh-noh)*
Colombia — colombiano *(koh-'lohm-bee-ah/koh-lohm-bee-'ah-noh)*
Costa Rica —costarricense *('kohs-tah 'ree-kah/kohs-tahr-ree-'sehn-seh)*
Cuba — cubano *('koo-bah/koo-'bah-noh)*
Ecuador — ecuatoriano *(eh-kwah-'dohr/eh-kwah-toh-ree-'ah-noh)*
El Salvador — salvadoreño *(ehl sahl-vah-'dohr/sahl-vah-doh-'rehn-yoh)*
España — español *(ehs-'pahn-yah/ehs-pahn-'yohl)*
Guatemala — guatemalteco *(goo-ah-teh-'mah-lah/goo-ah-teh-mahl-'teh-koh)*
Honduras — hondureño *(ohn-'doo-rahs/ohn-doo-'rehn-yoh)*
México — mejicano *('meh-ee-koh/meh-ee-'kah-noh)*
Nicaragua — nicaragüense *(nee-kah-'rah-gwah/nee-kah-rah-'gwehn-seh)*
Panamá — panameño *(pah-nah-'mah/pah-nah-'mehn-yoh)*
Paraguay — paraguayo *(pah-rah-'gwah-ee/pah-rah-'gwah-yoh)*
Perú — peruano *(peh-'roo/peh-roo-'ah-noh)*
Puerto Rico — puertorriqueño *(poo-ehr-tohr-'ree-koh/poo-'ehr-tohr-ree-'kehn-yoh)*
República Dominicana — dominicano
(reh-'poo-blee-kah doh-mee-nee-'kah-nah/doh-mee-nee-'kah-noh)
Uruguay — uruguayo *(oo-roo-'gwah-ee/oo-roo-'gwah-yoh)*
Venezuela — venezolano *(veh-neh-'sweh-lah/veh-neh-soh-'lah-noh)*

It's also wise to check on everyone's paperwork:

Do you have (the)...?   **¿Tiene...?** *(tee-'eh-neh)*

affidavit   **la declaración jurada**
(lah deh-klah-rah-see-'ohn hoo-'rah-dah)
application   **la solicitud** *(lah soh-lee-see-'tood)*
card   **la tarjeta** *(lah tahr-'heh-tah)*
certificate   **el certificado** *(ehl sehr-tee-fee-'kah-doh)*
document   **el documento** *(ehl doh-koo-'mehn-toh)*
form   **el formulario** *(ehl fohr-moo-'lah-ree-oh)*

letter   **la carta** *(lah 'kahr-tah)*
license   **la licencia** *(lah lee-'sehn-see-ah)*
packet   **el paquete** *(ehl pah-'keh-teh)*
pamphlet   **el folleto** *(ehl foh-'yeh-toh)*
permit   **el permiso** *(ehl pehr-'mee-soh)*
petition   **la petición** *(lah peh-tee-see-'ohn)*
visa   **la visa** *(lah 'vee-sah)*

Can I see (the)...?	**¿Puedo ver...?** *(poo-'eh-doh vehr)*
birth certificate	**el certificado de nacimiento** *(ehl sehr-tee-fee-'kah-doh deh nah-see-mee-'ehn-toh)*
driver's license	**la licencia de conducir** *(lah lee-'sehn-see-ah deh kohn-doo-'seer)*
green card	**la tarjeta verde** *(lah tahr-'heh-tah 'vehr-deh)*
passport	**el pasaporte** *(ehl pah-sah-'pohr-teh)*
picture ID	**la identificación con foto** *(lah ee-dehn-tee-fee-kah-see-'ohn kohn 'foh-toh)*
social security card	**la tarjeta de seguro social** *(lah tahr-'heh-tah deh seh-'goo-roh soh-see-'ahl)*

NOTICE!   ¡Fíjese!

In immigration affairs, what is more basic than visas?

Let's check (the)...	**Revisemos...** *(reh-vee-'seh-mohs)*
education visa	**la visa educativa** *(lah 'vee-sah eh-doo-kah-'tee-vah)*
permanent visa	**la visa permanente** *(lah 'vee-sah pehr-mah-'nehn-teh)*
reentry permit	**el permiso de reingreso** *(ehl pehr-'mee-soh deh reh-een-'greh-soh)*
residence card	**la tarjeta de residencia** *(lah tahr-'heh-tah deh reh-see-'dehn-see-ah)*
temporary visa	**la visa temporal** *(lah 'vee-sah tehm-poh-'rahl)*
treaty trader visa	**la visa de comerciante por tratado** *(lah 'vee-sah deh koh-mehr-see-'ahn-teh pohr trah-'tah-doh)*
work visa	**la visa de trabajo** *(lah 'vee-sah deh trah-'bah-hoh)*

MORE IMMIGRATION QUESTIONS
Más preguntas inmigratorias
(mahs preh-'goon-tahs een-mee-grah-'toh-ree-ahs)

Would you like information about (the)...?	**¿Quisiera información sobre...?** *(kee-see-'eh-rah een-fohr-mah-see-'ohn 'soh-breh)*
asylum	**el asilo** *(ehl ah-'see-loh)*
border control	**el control de la frontera** *(ehl kohn-'trohl deh lah frohn-'teh-rah)*
citizenship	**la ciudadanía** *(lah see-oo-dah-dah-'nee-ah)*
deportation	**la deportación** *(lah deh-pohr-tah-see-'ohn)*
dual citizenship	**la doble ciudadanía** *(lah 'doh-bleh see-oo-dah-dah-'nee-ah)*
exclusion	**la exclusión** *(lah ex-kloo-see-'ohn)*
immigration laws	**las leyes inmigratorias** *(lahs 'leh-yehs een-mee-grah-'toh-ree-ahs)*
immigration status	**el estado inmigratorio** *(ehl ehs-'tah-doh een-mee-grah-'toh-ree-oh)*

immunity	**la inmunidad** *(lah een-moo-nee-'dahd)*
learning English	**el aprendizaje del inglés**
	(ehl ah-prehn-dee-'sah-heh dehl een-'glehs)
lottery	**la lotería** *(lah loh-teh-'ree-ah)*
NAFTA	**la NAFTA** *(lah 'nahf-tah)*
naturalization	**la naturalización** *(lah nah-too-rah-lee-sah-see-'ohn)*
quotas	**las cuotas** *(lahs 'kwoh-tahs)*
refugees	**los refugiados** *(lohs reh-foo-hee-'ah-dohs)*
sponsorship	**el patrocinio** *(ehl pah-troh-'see-nee-oh)*
USA	**Estados Unidos** *(ehs-'tah-dohs oo-'nee-dohs)*
Does it have to do with...?	**¿Tiene que ver con...?** *(tee-'eh-neh keh vehr kohn)*
business	**el negocio** *(ehl neh-'goh-see-oh)*
education	**la educación** *(lah eh-doo-kah-see-'ohn)*
exceptional ability	**la habilidad excepcional**
	(lah ah-bee-lee-'dahd ex-sehp-see-oh-'nahl)
health	**la salud** *(lah sah-'lood)*
marriage	**el matrimonio** *(ehl mah-tree-'moh-nee-oh)*
religion	**la religión** *(lah reh-lee-hee-'ohn)*
visitation	**la visita** *(lah vee-'see-tah)*
Do you need (the)...?	**¿Necesita...?** *(neh-seh-'see-tah)*
classes	**las clases** *(lahs 'klah-sehs)*
clearance	**la aprobación** *(lah ah-proh-bah-see-'ohn)*
consultation	**la consulta** *(lah kohn-'sool-tah)*
counsel	**el asesoramiento** *(ehl ah-seh-soh-rah-mee-'ehn-toh)*
declaration	**la declaración** *(lah deh-klah-rah-see-'ohn)*
exam	**el examen** *(ehl ex-'ah-mehn)*
extension	**la extensión** *(lah ex-tehn-see-'ohn)*
information	**la información** *(lah een-fohr-mah-see-'ohn)*
interview	**la entrevista** *(lah ehn-treh-'vees-tah)*
registration	**el registro** *(ehl reh-'hees-troh)*
renewal	**la renovación** *(lah reh-noh-vah-see-'ohn)*
replacement	**el reemplazo** *(ehl reh-ehm-'plah-soh)*
Is it for a (an)...?	**¿Es para...?** *(ehs 'pah-rah)*
artist	**un/una artista** *(oon/'oo-nah ahr-'tees-tah)*
athlete	**un/una atleta** *(oon/'oo-nah aht-'leh-tah)*
emigrant	**un/una emigrante** *(oon/'oo-nah eh-mee-'grahn-teh)*
employee	**un empleado/una empleada**
	(oon ehm-pleh-'ah-doh/'oo-nah ehm-pleh-'ah-dah)
family member	**un/una pariente** *(oon/'oo-nah pah-ree-'ehn-teh)*
foreign national	**un extranjero/una extranjera**
	(oon ex-trahn-'heh-roh/'oo-nah ex-trahn-'heh-rah)
fugitive	**un fugitivo/una fugitiva**
	(oon foo-hee-'tee-voh/'oo-nah foo-hee-'tee-vah)
immigrant	**un/una inmigrante** *(oon/'oo-nah een-mee-'grahn-teh)*

investor	**un/una inversionista**
	(oon/'oo-nah een-vehr-see-oh-'nees-tah)
sponsor	**un patrocinador/una patrocinadora**
	(oon pah-troh-see-nah-'dohr/'oo-nah pah-troh-see-nah-'doh-rah)
student	**un/una estudiante** *(oon/'oo-nah ehs-too-dee-'ahn-teh)*
tourist	**un/una turista** *(oon/'oo-nah too-'rees-tah)*
visitor	**un/una visitante** *(oon/'oo-nah vee-see-'tahn-teh)*
worker	**un obrero/una obrera**
	(oon oh-'breh-roh/'oo-nah oh-'breh-rah)
undocumented	**un indocumentado/una indocumentada**
	(oon een-doh-koo-mehn-'tah-doh/'oo-nah een-doh-koo-mehn-'tah-dah)

Do you understand (the)...?	**¿Entiende...?** *(ehn-tee-'ehn-deh)*
certification	**la certificación** *(lah sehr-tee-fee-kah-see-'ohn)*
changes	**los cambios** *(lohs 'kahm-bee-ohs)*
complications	**las complicaciones** *(lahs kohm-plee-kah-see-'oh-nehs)*
conditions	**las condiciones** *(lahs kohn-dee-see-'oh-nehs)*
delays	**los retrasos** *(lohs reh-'trah-sohs)*
guidelines	**las pautas** *(lahs 'pah-oo-tahs)*
preferences	**las preferencias** *(lahs preh-feh-'rehn-see-ahs)*
proceedings	**los trámites** *(lohs 'trah-mee-tehs)*
process	**el proceso** *(ehl proh-'seh-soh)*
steps	**los pasos** *(lohs 'pah-sohs)*

NOTICE!   ¡Fíjese!

You will need to know your numbers and letters in Spanish when discussing visas (**visas**—*'vee-sahs*):

Visa – B1, B2 *(beh 'oo-noh, beh dohs)*
Visa – K-1 *(kah 'oo-noh)*
Visa – H-1B *('ah-cheh 'oo-noh beh)*
Visa – E1, E2 *(eh 'oo-noh, eh dohs)*
Visa – F *('eh-feh)*
Visa – J1 *('hoh-tah 'oo-noh)*

IMMIGRATION CONCERNS
Problemas inmigratorios
(proh-'bleh-mahs een-mee-grah-'toh-ree-ohs)

Make sure that your client included all of the information:

Did you write (the)...?	**¿Escribió...?** *(ehs-kree-bee-'oh)*
native language	**la lengua materna** *(lah 'lehn-gwah mah-'tehr-nah)*
birth date	**la fecha de nacimiento**
	(lah 'feh-chah deh nah-see-mee-'ehn-toh)

country of birth	**el país natal** *(ehl pah-'ees nah-'tahl)*
I-94 number	**el número de residente** *(ehl 'noo-meh-roh deh reh-see-'dehn-teh)*
expiration date	**la fecha de vencimiento** *(lah 'feh-chah deh vehn-see-mee-'ehn-toh)*
last entry date	**la última fecha de entrada** *(lah 'ool-tee-mah 'feh-chah deh ehn-'trah-dah)*
visa type	**el tipo de visa** *(ehl 'tee-poh deh 'vee-sah)*

Does it include (the)...?	**¿Incluye...?** *(een-'kloo-yeh)*
fingerprints	**las huellas digitales** *(lahs hoo-'eh-yahs dee-hee-'tah-lehs)*
blood type	**el tipo de sangre** *(ehl 'tee-poh deh 'sahn-greh)*
DNA testing	**la prueba de ADN** *(lah proo-'eh-bah deh ah-deh-'eh-neh)*

Can I see (the)...?	**¿Puedo ver...?** *(poo-'eh-doh vehr)*
proof	**la prueba** *(lah proo-'eh-bah)*
evidence	**la evidencia** *(lah eh-vee-'dehn-see-ah)*
testimony	**el testimonio** *(ehl tehs-tee-'moh-nee-oh)*

Have you talked to (the)...?	**¿Ha hablado con...?** *(ah ah-'blah-doh kohn)*
immigration authorities	**las autoridades de inmigración** *(lahs aw-toh-ree-'dah-dehs deh een-mee-grah-see-'ohn)*
police department	**el departamento de policía** *(ehl deh-pahr-tah-'mehn-toh deh poh-lee-'see-ah)*
ICE	**el Servicio de Inmigración y Control de Aduanas** *(ehl sehr-'vee-see-oh deh een-mee-grah-see-'ohn ee kohn-'trohl deh ah-'dwah-nahs)*
Homeland Security	**el Departamento de Seguridad Nacional** *(ehl deh-pahr-tah-'mehn-toh deh seh-goo-ree-'dahd nah-see-oh-'nahl)*
consulate	**el consulado** *(ehl kohn-soo-'lah-doh)*
customs	**la aduana** *(lah ah-doo-'ah-nah)*

Now discuss the issue in more detail:

The pamphlet explains (the)...	**El folleto explica...** *(ehl foh-'yeh-toh ex-'plee-kah)*
detention	**la detención** *(lah deh-tehn-see-'ohn)*
fines	**las multas** *(lahs 'mool-tahs)*
incarceration	**el encarcelamiento** *(ehl ehn-kahr-seh-lah-mee-'ehn-toh)*
inspection	**la inspección** *(lah eens-pehk-see-'ohn)*
laws	**las leyes** *(lahs 'leh-yehs)*
requirements	**los requisitos** *(lohs reh-kee-'see-tohs)*
rules	**los reglamentos** *(lohs reh-glah-'mehn-tohs)*

It's about (the)...	**Tiene que ver con...** *(tee-'eh-neh keh vehr kohn)*
criminal activity	**la actividad criminal** *(lah ahk-tee-vee-'dahd kree-mee-'nahl)*
length of stay	**la duración de la estadía** *(lah doo-rah-see-'ohn deh lah ehs-tah-'dee-ah)*
waiting period	**el período de espera** *(ehl peh-'ree-oh-doh deh ehs-'peh-rah)*

Let's discuss (the)...	**Conversemos de...** *(kohn-vehr-'seh-mohs deh)*
domestic violence	**la violencia doméstica** *(lah vee-oh-'lehn-see-ah doh-'mehs-tee-kah)*
drugs	**las drogas** *(lahs 'droh-gahs)*
drunk driving	**conducir embriagado** *(kohn-doo-'seer ehm-bree-ah-'gah-doh)*
firearms	**las armas de fuego** *(lahs 'ahr-mahs deh 'fweh-goh)*
homicide	**el homicidio** *(ehl oh-mee-'see-dee-oh)*
illegal entry	**la entrada ilegal** *(lah ehn-'trah-dah ee-leh-'gahl)*
sex crimes	**los delitos sexuales** *(lohs deh-'lee-tohs sehk-soo-'ah-lehs)*
violent crimes	**los delitos violentos** *(lohs deh-'lee-tohs vee-oh-'lehn-tohs)*

It's...	**Es...** *(ehs)*
illegal	**ilegal** *(ee-leh-'gahl)*
complicated	**complejo** *(kohm-'pleh-hoh)*
difficult	**difícil** *(dee-'fee-seel)*
expensive	**caro** *('kah-roh)*
inconvenient	**inconveniente** *(een-kohn-veh-nee-'ehn-teh)*
very serious	**grave** *('grah-veh)*
tragic	**trágico** *('trah-hee-koh)*

These are questions when there's trouble with the immigration papers:

Is it...?	**¿Está...?** *(ehs-'tah)*
destroyed	**destruido** *(dehs-troo-'ee-doh)*
expired	**vencido** *(vehn-'see-doh)*
fake	**falsificado** *(fahl-see-fee-'kah-doh)*
invalid	**inválido** *(een-'vah-lee-doh)*
lost	**perdido** *(pehr-'dee-doh)*
overdue	**atrasado** *(ah-trah-'sah-doh)*
postponed	**aplazado** *(ah-plah-'sah-doh)*
rejected	**rechazado** *(reh-chah-'sah-doh)*
stolen	**robado** *(roh-'bah-doh)*
unsigned	**sin firma** *(seen 'feer-mah)*

PRIVATE PRACTICE   **Práctica privada**

(27) A. Name three nationalities in Spanish where Spanish is spoken:

_____   _____   _____

B. Name three types of visas in Spanish:

_____   _____   _____

C. Connect the words that belong together best:

1. requisito	**proceso**
2. asilo	**inmunidad**
3. trámite	**ley**
4. difícil	**aplazado**
5. atrasado	**grave**

PERSONAL INJURY LAW
La ley de lesiones corporales
(lah 'leh-ee deh leh-see-'oh-nehs kohr-poh-'rah-lehs)

Personal injury lawyers, these are for you.

What happened?
¿Qué pasó? *(keh pah-'soh)*

How long ago?
¿Desde cuándo? *('dehs-deh 'kwahn-doh)*

Are you injured?
¿Está herido/herida? *(ehs-'tah eh-'ree-doh/eh-'ree-dah)*

Are you ill?
¿Está enfermo/enferma? *(ehs-'tah ehn-'fehr-moh/ehn-'fehr-mah)*

Do you need a personal injury lawyer?
¿Necesita un abogado de lesiones corporales?
(neh-seh-'see-tah oon ah-boh-'gah-doh deh leh-see-'oh-nehs kohr-poh-'rah-lehs)

Do you have a lot of pain?
¿Tiene mucho dolor? *(tee-'eh-neh 'moo-choh doh-'lohr)*

Where does it hurt?
¿Dónde le duele? *('dohn-deh leh 'dweh-leh)*

Are you under a doctor's care?
¿Está bajo el cuidado de un doctor?
(ehs-'tah 'bah-hoh ehl koo-ee-'dah-doh deh oon dohk-'tohr)

What's the diagnosis?
¿Cuál es el diagnóstico? *(kwahl ehs ehl dee-ahg-'nohs-tee-koh)*

Are you taking medications?
¿Toma medicamentos? *('toh-mah meh-dee-kah-'mehn-tohs)*

Whose fault was it?
¿Quién tenía la culpa? *(kee-'ehn teh-'nee-ah lah 'kool-pah)*

Were there witnesses?
¿Había testigos? *(ah-'bee-ah tehs-'tee-gohs)*

Did you document everything?
¿Ha archivado todo? *(ah ahr-chee-'vah-doh 'toh-doh)*

Did you take pictures?
¿Ha tomado fotos? *(ah toh-'mah-doh 'foh-tohs)*

Did you record it?
¿Lo grabó? *(loh grah-'boh)*

Have you called your insurance company?
¿Ha llamado a su compañía de seguros?
(ah yah-'mah-doh ah soo kohm-pah-'nee-ah deh seh-'goo-rohs)

Did you call the police?
¿Llamó a la policía? *(yah-'moh ah lah poh-lee-'see-ah)*

Would you like to sue for damages?
¿Quisiera demandar por daños? *(kee-see-'eh-rah deh-mahn-'dahr pohr 'dahn-yohs)*

Now calm the victim's fears:

You will be OK.	**Estará bien.** *(ehs-tah-'rah bee-'ehn)*
You have legal rights.	**Tiene derechos jurídicos.**
	(tee-'eh-neh deh-'reh-chos hoo-'ree-dee-kohs)
I will help you.	**Le ayudaré.** *(leh ah-yoo-dah-'reh)*
We handle ____ cases.	**Trabajamos con casos de ____.**
	(trah-bah-'hah-mos kohn 'kah-sohs deh)

all kinds of	**todo tipo** *('toh-doh 'tee-poh)*
asbestos injury	**asbestosis** *(ahs-behs-'toh-sees)*
assault	**agresión** *(ah-greh-see-'ohn)*
car accident	**accidente de carro** *(ahk-see-'dehn-teh deh kahr-roh)*

defective product	**productos defectuosos** *(proh-'dook-tohs deh-fehk-too-'oh-sohs)*
disability	**subsidios por incapacidad laboral** *(soob-'see-dee-ohs pohr een-kah-pah-see-'dahd lah-boh-'rahl)*
dog bite	**mordidas de perro** *(mohr-'dee-dahs deh 'pehr-roh)*
drunk driving	**manejo con embriaguez** *(mah-'neh-hoh kohn ehm-bree-ah-'ghes)*
elder abuse	**abuso de ancianos** *(ah-'boo-soh deh ahn-see-'ah-nohs)*
environmental	**medio ambiente** *('meh-dee-oh ahm-bee-'ehn-teh)*
handicapped person	**gente incapacitada** *('hehn-teh een-kah-pah-see-'tah-dah)*
insurance litigation	**litigios con compañías de seguros** *(lee-'tee-hee-ohs kohn kohm-pah-'nee-ahs deh seh-'goo-rohs)*
lead poisoning	**intoxicación de plomo** *(een-tohk-see-kah-see-'ohn deh 'ploh-moh)*
libel	**difamación** *(dee-fah-mah-see-'ohn)*
medical negligence	**negligencia médica** *(neh-glee-'hehn-see-ah 'meh-dee-kah)*
mold	**moho** *('moh-hoh)*
negligent security	**negligencias de seguridad** *(neh-glee-'hehn-see-ahs deh seh-goo-ree-'dahd)*
pharmaceutical negligence	**negligencia farmacéutica** *(neh-glee-'hehn-see-ah fahr-mah-'seh-oo-tee-kah)*
premises liability	**responsabilidad legal del local** *(rehs-pohn-sah-bee-lee-'dahd leh-'gahl dehl loh-'kahl)*
prescription error	**error de receta médica** *(ehr-'rohr deh reh-'seh-tah 'meh-dee-kah)*
slip and fall	**rebalón y caída** *(rehs-bah-'lohn ee kah-'ee-dah)*
sport	**deporte** *(deh-'pohr-teh)*
toxic substances	**sustancias tóxicas** *(soos-'tahn-see-ahs 'tohk-see-kahs)*
workers' compensation	**compensación laboral** *(kohm-pehn-sah-see-'ohn lah-boh-'rahl)*
wrongful death	**muerte por negligencia** *('mwehr-teh pohr neh-glee-'hehn-see-ah)*

ACCIDENTS
Accidentes
(akh-see-'dehn-tehs)

Many personal injury cases involve accidents. Continue to ask yes-no questions:

Was it a/an ____ accident?	**¿Fue un accidente de ____?** *(foo-'eh oon ahk-see-'dehn-teh deh)*
airline	**aerolíneas** *(ah-eh-roh-'lee-neh-ahs)*
auto	**carro** *('kahr-roh)*
bicycle	**bicicleta** *(bee-see-'kleh-tah)*
boat	**bote** *('boh-teh)*
bus	**autobús** *(aw-toh-'boos)*
construction	**construcción** *(kohns-trook-see-'ohn)*

crane	**grúa** *('groo-ah)*
cruise ship	**crucero** *(kroo-'seh-roh)*
elevator	**ascensor** *(ah-sehn-'sohr)*
fire	**incendio** *(een-'sehn-dee-oh)*
motorcycle	**moto** *('moh-toh)*
pedestrian	**peatón** *(peh-ah-'tohn)*
rental car	**carro alquilado** *('kahr-roh ahl-'kee-lah-doh)*
subway	**metro** *('meh-troh)*
swimming pool	**piscina** *(pees-'see-nah)*
train	**tren** *(trehn)*
truck	**camión** *(kah-mee-'ohn)*
work-related	**trabajo** *(trah-'bah-hoh)*

Have you suffered...?	**¿Ha sufrido...?** *(ah soo-'free-doh)*
emotional problems	**problemas emocionales** *(proh-'bleh-mahs eh-moh-see-oh-'nah-lehs)*
great damages	**grandes perjuicios** *('grahn-dehs per-hoo-'ee-see-ohs)*
loss of income	**pérdida de ingresos** *('pehr-dee-dah deh een-'greh-sohs)*
lost time at work	**tiempo perdido de trabajo** *(tee-'ehm-poh pehr-'dee-doh deh trah-'bah-hoh)*
medical charges	**cuentas médicas** *('kwehn-tahs 'meh-dee-kahs)*
pain and suffering	**dolor y sufrimiento** *(doh-'lohr ee soo-free-mee-'ehn-toh)*
physical injury	**heridas físicas** *(eh-'ree-dahs 'fee-see-kahs)*
post-traumatic stress	**estrés postraumático** *(ehs-'trehs pohs-trah-oo-'mah-tee-koh)*

Is it a ____ injury?	**¿Es un trauma de ____?** *(ehs oon 'trah-oo-mah deh)*
back	**la espalda** *(lah ehs-'pahl-dah)*
brain	**el cerebro** *(ehl seh-'reh-broh)*
head	**la cabeza** *(lah kah-'beh-sah)*
neck	**el cuello** *(ehl koo-'eh-yoh)*
spinal cord	**la médula espinal** *(lah 'meh-doo-lah ehs-pee-'nahl)*

Are you feeling...?	**¿Se siente...?** *(seh see-'ehn-teh)*
exhausted	**agotado/agotada** *(ah-goh-'tah-doh/ah-goh-'tah-dah)*
faint	**desfallecido/desfallecida** *(dehs-fah-yeh-'see-doh/dehs-fah-yeh-'see-dah)*
poorly	**mal** *(mahl)*
sore	**adolorido/adolorida** *(ah-doh-loh-'ree-doh/ah-doh-loh-'ree-dah)*
weak	**débil** *('deh-beel)*

Injuries can take place just about anywhere:

Did it happen at/in/on (the)...? **¿Ocurrió en...?** *(oh-koor-ree-'oh ehn)*

amusement park **el parque de diversión** *(ehl 'pahr-keh deh dee-vehr-see-'ohn)*
street **la calle** *(lah 'kah-yeh)*
highway **la carretera** *(lah kahr-reh-'teh-rah)*
hospital **el hospital** *(ehl ohs-pee-'tahl)*
playground **el campo de recreo** *(ehl 'kahm-poh deh reh-'kreh-oh)*
private property **la propiedad privada** *(lah proh-pee-eh-'dahd pre-'vah-dah)*
public place **el lugar público** *(ehl loo-'gahr 'poo-blee-koh)*
rest home **la casa de reposo** *(lah 'kah-sah deh reh-'poh-soh)*
shopping center **el centro comercial** *(ehl 'sehn-troh koh-mehr-see-'ahl)*
worksite **el lugar de empleo** *(ehl loo-'gahr deh ehm-'pleh-oh)*

After evaluating the situation you may give some advice:

Let's talk about (the)... **Conversemos de...** *(kohn-vehr-'seh-mohs deh)*

cause **la causa** *(lah 'kah-oo-sah)*
consequence **la consecuencia** *(lah kohn-seh-'kwehn-see-ah)*
damage **el daño** *(ehl 'dahn-yoh)*
danger **el peligro** *(ehl peh-'lee-groh)*
harm **el perjuicio** *(ehl pehr-hoo-'ee-see-oh)*
hazard **el riesgo** *(ehl ree-'ehs-goh)*
pain **el dolor** *(ehl doh-'lohr)*
reason **la razón** *(lah rah-'sohn)*
recall **el retiro** *(ehl reh-'tee-roh)*
responsibility **la responsabilidad** *(lah rehs-pohs-sah-bee-lee-'dahd)*
suffering **el sufrimiento** *(ehl soo-free-mee-'ehn-toh)*
warning **la advertencia** *(lah ahd-vehr-'tehn-see-ah)*

Was it...? **¿Fue...?** *(foo-'eh)*

carelessness **descuido** *(dehs-'koo-ee-doh)*
dangerous **peligroso** *(peh-lee-'groh-soh)*
illegal **ilegal** *(ee-leh-'gahl)*
irresponsible **irresponsable** *(eer-rehs-pohn-'sah-bleh)*
low quality **baja calidad** *('bah-hah kah-lee-'dahd)*
unfair **injusto** *(een-'hoos-toh)*
unprofessional **poco profesional** *('poh-koh proh-feh-see-oh-'nahl)*
unsafe **arriesgado** *(ahr-ree-ehs-'gah-doh)*
wrong **equivocado** *(eh-kee-voh-'kah-doh)*

You should...	**Debe ...** *('deh-beh)*
be compensated	**ser recompensado/recompensada** *(sehr reh-kohm-pehn-'sah-doh/reh-kohm-pehn-'sah-dah)*
defend yourself	**defenderse** *(deh-fehn-'dehr-seh)*
fight it	**lucharlo** *(loo-'chahr-loh)*
get another opinion	**conseguir otra opinión** *(kohn-seh-'gheer 'oh-trah oh-pee-nee-'ohn)*
heal	**sanar** *(sah-'nahr)*
receive something	**recibir algo** *(reh-see-'beer 'ahl-goh)*
recover	**recuperarse** *(reh-koo-peh-'rahr-seh)*
see a doctor	**ver un medico** *(vehr oon 'meh-see-koh)*
take care of yourself	**cuidarse** *(koo-ee-'dahr-seh)*

You deserve (a) (an)...	**Merece...** *(meh-'reh-seh)*
apology	**una disculpa** *('oo-nah dees-'kool-pah)*
explanation	**una explicación** *('oo-nah ex-plee-kah-see-'ohn)*
indemnization	**una indemnización** *('oo-nah een-dehm-nee-sah-see-'ohn)*
payment	**una recompensa** *('oo-nah reh-kohm-'pehn-sah)*
protection	**protección** *(proh-tehk-see-'ohn)*
reimbursement	**un reembolso** *(oon reh-ehm-'bohl-soh)*
repair	**una reparación** *('oo-nah reh-pah-rah-see-'ohn)*
treatment	**un tratamiento** *(oon trah-tah-mee-'ehn-toh)*

We're going to...	**Vamos a...** *('vah-mohs ah)*
interpret the information	**interpretar la información** *(een-tehr-preh-'tahr lah een-fohr-mah-see-'ohn)*
look for resources	**buscar recursos** *(boos-'kahr reh-'koor-sohs)*
manage your affairs	**manejar sus asuntos** *(mah-neh-'hahr soos ah-'soon-tohs)*
solve the problem	**resolver el problema** *(reh-sohl-'vehr ehl proh-'bleh-mah)*
take care of the paperwork	**cuidar del papeleo** *(koo-ee-'dahr dehl pah-peh-'leh-oh)*

Before you go any further, gather some insurance information:

What is (the)...?	**¿Cuál es . . .?** *(kwahl ehs)*
due date	**la fecha de vencimiento** *(lah 'feh-chah deh vehn-see-mee-'ehn-toh)*
group number	**el número del grupo** *(ehl 'noo-meh-roh dehl 'groo-poh)*
insurance company	**la compañía de seguros** *(lah kohm-pah-'nee-ah deh seh-'goo-rohs)*
monthly premium	**la prima mensual** *(lah 'pree-mah mehn-soo-'ahl)*
policy number	**el número de póliza** *(ehl 'noo-meh-roh deh 'poh-lee-sah)*

Who is (the)...?	**¿Quién es...?** *(kee-'ehn ehs)*
agent	**el/la agente** *(ehl/lah ah-'hehn-teh)*
doctor	**el médico/la médica** *(ehl 'meh-dee-koh/lah 'meh-dee-kah)*
guilty party	**el/la culpable** *(ehl/lah kool-'pah-bleh)*

manufacturer	**el/la fabricante** *(ehl/lah fah-bree-'kahn-teh)*
member	**el/la miembro** *(ehl/lah mee-'ehm-broh)*
merchant	**el/la comerciante** *(ehl/lah koh-mehr-see-'ahn-teh)*
nurse	**el enfermero/la enfermera**
	(ehl ehn-fehr-'meh-roh/lah ehn-fehr-'meh-rah)
owner	**el dueño/la dueña** *(ehl 'dwehn-yoh/lah 'dwehn-yah)*

Have you seen (the)...?	**¿Ha visto al...?** *(ah 'vees-toh ahl)*
anesthetist	**anestesista** *(ah-nehs-teh-'sees-tah)*
bacteriologist	**bacteriólogo** *(bahk-teh-ree-'oh-loh-goh)*
cardiologist	**cardiólogo** *(kahr-dee-'oh-loh-goh)*
chiropractor	**quiropráctico** *(kee-roh-'prahk-tee-koh)*
dermatologist	**dermatólogo** *(dehr-mah-'toh-loh-goh)*
gynecologist	**ginecólogo** *(hee-neh-'koh-loh-goh)*
neurologist	**neurólogo** *(neh-oo-'roh-loh-goh)*
obstetrician	**obstetra** *(ohbs-'teh-trah)*
ophthalmologist	**oftalmólogo** *(ohf-tahl-'moh-loh-goh)*
orthodontist	**ortodoncista** *(ohr-toh-dohn-'sees-tah)*
orthopedist	**ortopeda** *(ohr-toh-'peh-dah)*
pediatrician	**pediatra** *(peh-dee-'ah-trah)*
pharmacist	**farmacéutico** *(fahr-mah-'seh-oo-tee-koh)*
psychiatrist	**psiquiatra** *(see-kee-'ah-trah)*
psychologist	**psicólogo** *(see-'koh-loh-goh)*
radiologist	**radiólogo** *(rah-dee-'oh-loh-goh)*
specialist	**especialista** *(ehs-peh-see-ah-'lees-tah)*
surgeon	**cirujano** *(see-roo-'hah-noh)*
therapist	**terapeuta** *(the-rah-'peh-oo-tah)*
urologist	**urólogo** *(oo-'roh-loh-goh)*

NOTICE!   ¡Fíjese!

You know that there are several kinds of insurance:

It's ___ insurance.	**Es seguro ___.** *(ehs seh-'goo-roh)*
auto	**de carro** *(deh 'kahr-roh)*
collision	**contra choques** *('kohn-trah 'choh-kehs)*
dental	**dental** *(dehn-'tahl)*
disability	**de subsidio por incapacidad laboral**
	(deh soob-'see-dee-oh pohr een-kah-pah-see-'dahd lah-boh-'rahl)
home	**de casa** *(deh 'kah-sah)*
life	**de vida** *(deh 'vee-dah)*
medical	**médico** *('meh-dee-koh)*
mental health	**de salud mental** *(deh sah-'lood mehn-'tahl)*
unemployment	**de desempleo** *(deh deh-sehm-'pleh-oh)*
vision	**para la vista** *('pah-rah lah 'vees-tah)*
workers' compensation	**de compensación laboral**
	(deh kohm-pehn-sah-see-'ohn lah-boh-'rahl)

PRIVATE PRACTICE   **Práctica privada**

(28) A. Translate:

1. Do you need a personal injury lawyer? _____

2. Would you like to sue for damages? _____

3. We handle medical negligence cases. _____

B. Choose the appropriate word to complete each list:

cuello   terapeuta   advertencia   autobús   póliza

1. **cirujano, pediatra,** _____

2. **seguros, grupo,** _____

3. **espalda, cabeza,** _____

4. **riesgo, peligro,** _____

5. **camion, tren,** _____

WHAT IS THE TROUBLE?
¿Cuál es el problema?
(kwahl ehs ehl proh-'bleh-mah)

Find out more medical information as you target the victim's physical condition:

Have you had...?	**¿Ha tenido...?** *(ah teh-'nee-doh)*
allergies	**alergias** *(ah-'lehr-hee-ahs)*
convulsions	**convulsiones** *(kohn-vool-see-'oh-nehs)*
dizziness	**mareos** *(mah-'reh-ohs)*
a fever	**fiebre** *(fee-'eh-breh)*
headaches	**dolores de cabeza** *(doh-'loh-rehs deh kah-'beh-sah)*
seizures	**ataques** *(ah-'tah-kehs)*
spasms	**espasmos** *(ehs-'pahs-mohs)*

Is it...?	**¿Está...?** *(ehs-'tah)*
broken	**roto** *('roh-toh)*
cut	**cortado** *(kohr-'tah-doh)*
infected	**infectado** *(een-fehk-'tah-doh)*
sprained	**dislocado** *(dees-loh-'kah-doh)*
swollen	**hinchado** *(een-'chah-doh)*

Do you have...?	**¿Tiene ...?** *(tee-'eh-neh)*
bruises	**contusiones** *(kohn-too-see-'oh-nehs)*
burns	**quemaduras** *(keh-mah-'doo-rahs)*
cuts	**cortaduras** *(kohr-tah-'doo-rahs)*
rashes	**erupciones** *(eh-roop-see-'oh-nehs)*
scratches	**rasguños** *(rahs-'goon-yohs)*

Keep asking questions:

How do you feel?
¿Cómo se siente? *('koh-moh she see-'ehn-teh)*

Did you lose consciousness?
¿Perdió el conocimiento? *(pehr-dee-'oh ehl koh-noh-see-mee-'ehn-toh)*

Do you have heart trouble?
¿Tiene problemas cardíacos? *(tee-'eh-neh proh-'bleh-mahs kahr-'dee-ah-kohs)*

Are you allergic?
¿Es alérgico/alérgica? *(ehs ah-'lehr-hee-koh/ah-'lehr-hee-kah)*

Are you pregnant?
¿Está embarazada? *(ehs-'tah ehm-bah-rah-'sah-dah)*

Were you in the hospital?
¿Estuvo en el hospital? *(ehs-'too-voh ehn ehl ohs-pee-'tahl)*

☞ NOTICE! **¡Fíjese!**

When death is the topic, here's what you need to know:

autopsy	**la autopsia** *(lah aw-'tohp-see-ah)*
cadaver	**el cadaver** *(ehl kah-'dah-vehr)*
cemetery	**el cementerio** *(ehl seh-mehn-'teh-ree-oh)*
coffin	**el ataúd** *(ehl ah-tah-'ood)*
coroner	**el médico legista** *(ehl 'meh-dee-koh leh-'hees-tah)*
funeral	**el funeral** *(ehl foo-neh-'rahl)*
morgue	**la morgue** *(lah 'mohr-gheh)*
mortician	**el director/la directora de pompas fúnebres** *(ehl dee-rehk-'tohr/lah dee-rehk-'toh-rah deh 'pohm-pahs 'foo-neh-brehs)*

He/she's dead.	**Está muerto/muerta.** *(ehs-'tah 'mwehr-toh/'mwehr-tah)*
He/she's dying.	**Se está muriendo.** *(seh ehs-'tah moo-ree-'ehn-doh)*
He/she died.	**Se murió.** *(she moo-ree-'oh)*
I'm very sorry.	**Lo siento mucho.** *(loh see-'ehn-toh 'moo-choh)*
My deepest sympathies.	**Mi más sentido pésame.** *(mee mahs sehn-'tee-doh 'peh-sah-meh)*

THE HUMAN BODY
El cuerpo humano
(ehl 'kwehr-poh oo-'mah-noh)

In order to discuss any aspect of a personal injury case, you must learn the parts of the body. The best practice technique is to touch, point, or move as you say each one aloud:

Move...	**Mueva . . .** *(moo-'eh-vah)*
Point to...	**Señale . . .** *(sehn-'yah-leh)*
Touch...	**Toque . . .** *('toh-keh)*

arm	**el brazo** *(ehl 'brah-soh)*
back	**la espalda** *(lah ehs-'pahl-dah)*
chest	**el pecho** *(ehl 'peh-choh)*
ear	**la oreja** *(lah oh-'reh-hah)*
elbow	**el codo** *(ehl 'koh-doh)*
eye	**el ojo** *(ehl 'oh-hoh)*
face	**la cara** *(lah 'kah-rah)*
finger	**el dedo** *(ehl 'deh-doh)*
foot	**el pie** *(ehl pee-'eh)*
hand	**la mano** *(lah 'mah-noh)*
head	**la cabeza** *(lah kah-'beh-sah)*
knee	**la rodilla** *(lah roh-'dee-yah)*
leg	**la pierna** *(lah pee-'ehr-nah)*
mouth	**la boca** *(lah 'boh-kah)*
neck	**el cuello** *(ehl 'kweh-yoh)*
nose	**la nariz** *(lah nah-'rees)*
shoulder	**el hombro** *(ehl 'ohm-broh)*
stomach	**el estómago** *(ehl ehs-'toh-mah-goh)*
toe	**el dedo del pie** *(ehl 'deh-doh dehl pee-'eh)*

PRIVATE PRACTICE   Práctica privada

(29) A. Answer these questions about yourself:

¿Cómo se siente hoy? _____

¿Ha tenido dolores de cabeza? _____

¿Necesita Ud. cirugía? _____

B. Name ten body parts in Spanish:

_____ _____

_____ _____

_____ _____

_____ _____

_____ _____

FURTHER INVESTIGATION
Más investigación
(mahs een-vehs-tee-gah-see-'ohn)

Was there a/an...?	**¿Hubo...?** *('hoo-boh)*
beating	**paliza** *(pah-'lee-sah)*
birth defect	**defecto natal** *(deh-'fehk-toh nah-'tahl)*
coma	**coma** *('koh-mah)*
concussion	**conmoción** *(kohn-moh-see-'ohn)*
drowning	**ahogamiento** *(ah-oh-gah-mee-'ehn-toh)*
gunshot wound	**herida de bala** *(eh-'ree-dah deh 'bah-lah)*
illness	**enfermedad** *(ehn-fehr-meh-'dahd)*
overdose	**sobredosis** *(soh-breh-'doh-sees)*
poisoning	**intoxicación** *(een-tohk-see-kah-see-'ohn)*
stabbing	**puñalada** *(poon-yah-'lah-dah)*
stroke	**derrame celebral** *(dehr-'rah-meh seh-reh-'brahl)*
Was it...?	**¿Fue...?** *(foo-'eh)*
dehydration	**deshidratación** *(dehs-ee-drah-tah-see-'ohn)*
frostbite	**congelamiento** *(kohn-heh-lah-mee-'ehn-toh)*
heatstroke	**insolación** *(een-soh-lah-see-'ohn)*
Did you need (the)...?	**¿Necesita...?** *(neh-seh-'see-tah)*
counseling	**terapia psicológica** *(teh-'rah-pee-ah see-koh-'loh-hee-kah)*
medicine	**medicina** *(meh-dee-'see-nah)*
oxygen	**oxígeno** *(ox-'ee-heh-noh)*
physical therapy	**terapia física** *(teh-'rah-pee-ah 'fee-see-kah)*
shots	**inyecciones** *(een-yehk-see-'oh-nehs)*
stitches	**puntadas** *(poon-'tah-dahs)*
surgery	**cirugía** *(see-roo-'hee-ah)*
treatment	**tratamiento** *(trah-tah-mee-'ehn-toh)*
Was it (the)...?	**¿Fue...?** *(foo-'eh)*
application	**la aplicación** *(lah ah-plee-kah-see-'ohn)*
care	**el cuidado** *(ehl koo-ee-'dah-doh)*
construction	**la construcción** *(lah kohns-trook-see-'ohn)*
design	**el diseño** *(ehl dee-'sehn-yoh)*
use	**el uso** *(ehl 'oo-soh)*

NOTICE!   ¡Fíjese!

Find out if safety precautions were in place before the injury occurred:

Were you wearing (the)...   **¿Tenía(n) puesto...?** *(teh-'nee-ah(n) poo-'ehs-toh)*

back support	**la faja** *(lah 'fah-hah)*
boots	**las botas** *(lahs 'boh-tahs)*
earplugs	**los tapones de oído** *(lohs tah-'poh-nehs deh oh-'ee-doh)*
fall equipment	**el equipo contra caídas** *(ehl eh-'kee-poh 'kohn-trah kah-'ee-dahs)*
gloves	**los guantes** *(lohs 'gwahn-tehs)*
goggles	**las gafas** *(lahs 'gah-fahs)*
hard hat	**el casco duro** *(ehl 'kahs-koh 'doo-roh)*
mask	**la máscara** *(lah 'mahs-kah-rah)*
reflectors	**los reflectores** *(lohs reh-flehk-'toh-rehs)*
respirator	**el respirador** *(ehl rehs-pee-rah-'dohr)*
safety glasses	**los lentes de protección** *(lohs 'lehn-tehs deh proh-tehk-see-'ohn)*
safety line	**la cuerda de seguridad** *(lah 'kwehr-dah deh seh-goo-ree-'dahd)*
seat belt	**el cinturón de seguridad** *(ehl seen-too-'rohn deh seh-goo-ree-'dahd)*
strap	**la correa** *(lah kohr-'reh-ah)*
vest	**el chaleco** *(ehl chah-'leh-koh)*

Do you have...?   **¿Tiene...?** *(tee-'eh-neh)*

proof	**prueba** *(proo-'eh-bah)*
evidence	**evidencia** *(eh-vee-'dehn-see-ah)*
verification	**confirmación** *(kohn-feer-mah-see-'ohn)*

Most medical words in Spanish are similar to English in their spellings. Guess at the meanings of these:

paralysis	**diabetes**	**epilepsia**	**tifoidea**
difteria	**hepatitis**	**fiebre reumática**	**leucemia**
meningitis	**polio**	**pulmonía**	**tétano**
tuberculosis			

AUTO ACCIDENTS
Accidentes del carro
(ahk-see-'dehn-tehs dehl 'kahr-roh)

If the personal injury case is based on a car accident, you may want to learn the names for items on the street or even a few auto parts:

ABS	**el sistema de frenos antibloqueo** *(ehl sees-'teh-mah deh 'freh-nohs ahn-tee-bloh-'keh-oh)*
air bag	**la bolsa de aire** *(lah 'bohl-sah deh 'ah-ee-reh)*
brakes	**los frenos** *(lohs 'freh-nohs)*
bumper	**el parachoques** *(ehl pah-rah-'choh-kehs)*
crash	**el choque** *(ehl 'choh-keh)*
engine	**el motor** *(ehl moh-'tohr)*
highway	**la carretera** *(lah kahr-reh-'teh-rah)*
road	**el camino** *(ehl kah-'mee-noh)*
seat belt	**el cinturón de seguridad** *(ehl seen-too-'rohn deh seh-goo-ree-'dahd)*
stop sign	**el señal de pare** *(lah sehn-'yahl deh 'pah-reh)*
street	**la calle** *(lah 'kah-yeh)*
tires	**los neumáticos** *(lohs neh-oo-'mah-tee-kohs)*
traffic	**el tráfico** *(ehl 'trah-fee-koh)*
traffic light	**el semáforo** *(ehl seh-'mah-foh-roh)*
wheel	**el volante** *(ehl voh-'lahn-teh)*

Note how the following questions simply require a **sí** or **no** response:

Did someone crash into you?
¿Alguién lo chocó? *('ahl-ghee-ehn loh choh-'koh)*

Were you driving?
¿Estaba manejando usted? *(ehs-'tah-bah mah-neh-'hahn-doh oos-'tehd)*

Was anyone else hurt?
¿Había más heridos? *(ah-'bee-ah mahs eh-'ree-dohs)*

Do you have the police report?
¿Tiene el reporte policial? *(tee-'eh-neh ehl reh-'pohr-teh poh-lee-see-'ahl)*

Does your car need repairs?
¿Necesita reparar su carro? *(neh-seh-'see-tah reh-pah-'rahr soo 'kahr-roh)*

Are you (the)...?	**¿Es usted...?** *(ehs oos-'tehd)*
registered owner	**el dueño registrado/la dueña registrada** *(ehl 'dwehn-yoh reh-hees-'trah-doh/lah 'dwehn-yah reh-hees-'trah-dah)*
driver	**el/la chofer** *(ehl/lah choh-'fehr)*
passenger	**el pasajero/la pasajera** *(ehl pah-sah-'heh-roh/lah pah-sah-'heh-rah)*

pedestrian	**el peatón/la peatona**
	(ehl peh-ah-'tohn/lah peh-ah-'toh-nah)
witness	**el/la testigo** *(ehl/lah tehs-'tee-goh)*

Did you call (the)...?	**¿Llamó a...?** *(yah-'moh ah)*
ambulance	**la ambulancia** *(lah ahm-boo-'lahn-see-ah)*
garage	**el garaje** *(ehl gah-'rah-heh)*
gas station	**la gasolinera** *(lah gah-soh-lee-'neh-rah)*
mechanic	**el mecánico** *(ehl meh-'kah-nee-koh)*
towing company	**la compañía de remolque**
	(lah kohm-pah-'nee-ah deh reh-'mohl-keh)

Was it...?	**¿Estaba...?** *(ehs-'tah-bah)*
blocked off	**obstruída** *(ohbs-troo-'ee-dah)*
flooded	**inundada** *(ee-noon-'dah-dah)*
slippery	**resbaladiza** *(rehs-bah-lah-'dee-sah)*

PRIVATE PRACTICE   **Práctica privada**

(30) A. Fill in the blanks with words or expressions of your choice as you discuss an auto accident case:

¿Es usted....? _____

¿Llamó usted a...? _____

¿Vió usted...? _____

B. Delete the word in each group that does not belong with the others:

1. paliza, oreja, puñalada, herida de bala
2. llamada, puntadas, cirugía, terapia
3. fuego, ácido, volante, químico

FAMILY LAW
La ley familiar
(lah 'leh-ee fah-mee-lee-'ahr)

Before you initiate any conversation on family law, take a few minutes to memorize the names in Spanish for all the family members:

Are you (the)...?	**¿Es usted...?** *(ehs oos-'tehd)*
aunt	**la tía** *(lah 'tee-ah)*
brother	**el hermano** *(ehl ehr-'mah-noh)*
brother-in-law	**el cuñado** *(ehl koon-'yah-doh)*

cousin	**la prima/el primo** *(lah 'pree-mah/ehl 'pree-moh)*
daughter	**la hija** *(lah 'ee-hah)*
daughter-in-law	**la nuera** *(lah 'nweh-rah)*
father	**el padre** *(ehl 'pah-dreh)*
father-in-law	**el suegro** *(ehl 'sweh-groh)*
granddaughter	**la nieta** *(lah nee-'eh-tah)*
grandfather	**el abuelo** *(ehl ah-'bweh-loh)*
grandmother	**la abuela** *(lah ah-'bweh-lah)*
grandson	**el nieto** *(ehl nee-'eh-toh)*
husband	**el esposo** *(ehl ehs-'poh-soh)*
mother	**la madre** *(lah 'mah-dreh)*
mother-in-law	**la suegra** *(lah 'sweh-grah)*
nephew	**el sobrino** *(ehl soh-'bree-noh)*
niece	**la sobrina** *(lah soh-'bree-nah)*
sister	**la hermana** *(lah ehr-'mah-nah)*
sister-in-law	**la cuñada** *(lah koon-'yah-dah)*
son	**el hijo** *(ehl 'ee-hoh)*
son-in-law	**el yerno** *(ehl 'yehr-noh)*
stepdaughter	**la hijastra** *(lah ee-'hahs-trah)*
stepfather	**el padrastro** *(ehl pah-'drahs-troh)*
stepmother	**la madrastra** *(lah mah-'drahs-trah)*
stepson	**el hijastro** *(ehl ee-'hahs-troh)*
uncle	**el tío** *(ehl 'tee-oh)*
wife	**la esposa** *(lah ehs-'poh-sah)*

 CULTURAL COMMENT **Comentario cultural**

Because the traditional Hispanic family includes more than just its immediate members, you may want to consider learning the names for those other "relations."

boyfriend	**el novio** *(ehl 'noh-vee-oh)*
close friends	**los amigos íntimos** *(lohs ah-'mee-gohs 'een-tee-mohs)*
girlfriend	**la novia** *(lah 'noh-vee-ah)*
godfather	**el compadre** *(ehl kohm-'pah-dreh)*
godmother	**la comadre** *(lah koh-'mah-dreh)*
godparents	**los padrinos** *(lohs pah-'dree-nohs)*
neighbors	**los vecinos** *(lohs veh-'see-nohs)*
parents	**los padres** *(lohs 'pah-drehs)*
relatives	**los parientes** *(lohs pah-ree-'ehn-tehs)*
roommates	**los compañeros de cuarto**
	(lohs kohm-pahn-'yeh-rohs deh 'kwahr-toh)

FAMILY PROBLEMS
Los problemas familiares
(lohs proh-'bleh-mahs fah-mee-lee-'ah-rehs)

These are typical family law concerns:

Is it (the)...?	**¿Es...?** *(ehs)*
adoption	**la adopción** *(lah ah-dohp-see-'ohn)*
annulment	**la anulación** *(lah ah-noo-lah-see-'ohn)*
dissolution	**la disolución** *(lah dee-soh-loo-see-'ohn)*
divorce	**el divorcio** *(ehl dee-'vohr-see-oh)*
domestic violence	**la violencia doméstica**
	(lah vee-oh-'lehn-see-ah doh-'mehs-tee-kah)
foster care	**la crianza de niños ajenos**
	(lah kree-'ahn-sah deh 'neen-yohs ah-'heh-nohs)
guardianship	**la tutela** *(lah too-'teh-lah)*
joint custody	**la custodia en común**
	(lah koos-'toh-dee-ah ehn koh-'moon)
legal custody	**la custodia legal** *(lah koos-'toh-dee-ah leh-'gahl)*
legal separation	**la separación legal** *(lah seh-pah-rah-see-'ohn leh-gahl)*
marriage	**el matrimonio** *(ehl mah-tree-'moh-nee-oh)*
paternity	**la paternidad** *(lah pah-tehr-nee-'dahd)*
physical custody	**la custodia física** *(lah koos-'toh-dee-ah 'fee-see-kah)*
probate	**la validación testamentaria**
	(lah vah-lee-dah-see-'ohn tehs-tah-mehn-'tah-ree-ah)
visitation rights	**el derecho de visita** *(ehl deh-'reh-choh deh vee-'see-tah)*
Is there _____ abuse?	**¿Hay abuso _____?** *('ah-ee ah-'boo-soh)*
economic	**económico** *(eh-koh-'noh-mee-koh)*
physical	**físico** *('fee-see-koh)*
psychological	**sicológico** *(see-koh-'loh-hee-koh)*
sexual	**sexual** *(sehk-soo-'ahl)*
spousal	**conyugal** *(kohn-yoo-'gahl)*
verbal	**verbal** *(vehr-'bahl)*
Ask him/her about (the)...	**Pregúntele de...** *(preh-'goon-teh-leh deh)*
communication	**la comunicación** *(lah koh-moo-nee-kah-see-'ohn)*
cooperation	**la cooperación** *(lah koh-oh-peh-rah-see-'ohn)*
friendship	**el compañerismo** *(ehl kohm-pahn-yeh-'rees-moh)*
upbringing	**la crianza** *(lah kree-'ahn-sah)*
well-being	**el bienestar** *(ehl bee-eh-nehs-'tahr)*
Do you understand (the)...?	**¿Entiende...?** *(ehn-tee-'ehn-deh)*
agreement	**el acuerdo** *(ehl ah-'kwehr-doh)*
alimony	**la manutención conyugal**
	(lah mah-noo-tehn-see-'ohn kohn-yoo-'gahl)

allocation of assets	**el reparto de bienes** *(ehl reh-ˈpahr-toh deh bee-ˈeh-nehs)*
arrest warrant	**la orden de detención** *(lah ˈohr-dehn deh deh-tehn-see-ˈohn)*
child support	**la manutención infantil** *(lah mah-noo-tehn-see-ˈohn een-fahn-ˈteel)*
civil suit	**la demanda civil** *(lah deh-ˈmahn-dah see-ˈveel)*
countersuit	**la contrademanda** *(lah kohn-trah-deh-ˈmahn-dah)*
joint agreement	**el acuerdo mutuo** *(ehl ah-ˈkwehr-doh ˈmoo-too-oh)*
juvenile law	**la ley de menores** *(lah ˈleh-ee deh meh-ˈnoh-rehs)*
law	**la ley** *(lah ˈleh-ee)*
legal action	**la demanda judicial** *(lah deh-ˈmahn-dah hoo-dee-see-ˈahl)*
petition	**la petición** *(lah peh-tee-see-ˈohn)*
prenuptial agreement	**el contrato prematrimonial** *(ehl kohn-ˈtrah-toh preh-mah-tree-moh-nee-ˈahl)*
proposition	**la proposición** *(lah proh-poh-see-see-ˈohn)*
protection order	**la orden de protección** *(lah ˈohr-dehn deh proh-tehk-see-ˈohn)*
restraining order	**la orden de restricción** *(lah ˈohr-dehn deh rehs-treek-see-ˈohn)*
rights	**los derechos** *(lohs deh-ˈreh-chohs)*
search warrant	**la orden de registro** *(lah ˈohr-dehn deh reh-ˈhees-troh)*
settlement	**el convenio** *(ehl kohn-ˈveh-nee-oh)*
Who is (the)...?	**¿Quién es...?** *(kee-ˈehn ehs)*
suspect	**el sospechoso/la sospechosa** *(ehl sohs-peh-ˈchoh-soh/lah sohs-peh-ˈchoh-sah)*
victim	**el/la víctima** *(ehl/lah ˈveek-tee-mah)*
witness	**el/la testigo** *(ehl/lah tehs-ˈtee-goh)*
We help (the)...	**Ayudamos ...** *(ah-yoo-ˈdah-mohs)*
adolescents	**a los adolescentes** *(ah lohs ah-doh-lehs-ˈsehn-tehs)*
both parties	**a ambas partes** *(ah ˈahm-bahs ˈpahr-tehs)*
defendant	**al/demandado/a la demandada** *(ahl deh-mahn-ˈdah-doh/ah lah deh-mahn-ˈdah-dah)*
dependent	**al/a la dependiente** *(ahl/ah lah deh-pehn-dee-ˈehn-teh)*
elderly	**a los ancianos** *(ah lohs ahn-see-ˈah-nohs)*
ex-spouse	**al ex-esposo/a la ex-esposa** *(ahl ex-ehs-ˈpoh-soh/ah lah ex-ehs-ˈpoh-sah)*
family	**a la familia** *(ah lah fah-ˈmee-lee-ah)*
guardian	**al guardian/a la guardiana** *(ahl gwahr-dee-ˈahn/ah lah gwahr-dee-ˈah-nah)*
husband	**al esposo** *(ahl ehs-ˈpoh-soh)*
married couple	**a los cónyuges** *(ah lohs ˈkohn-yoo-ghehs)*
minors	**a los/a las menores de edad** *(ah lohs/ah lahs meh-ˈnoh-rehs deh eh-ˈdahd)*

petitioners	**a los peticionarios/a las peticionarias** *(ah lohs peh-tee-see-oh-'nah-ree-ohs/ah lahs peh-tee-see-oh-'nah-ree-ahs)*
plaintiff	**al/a la demandante** *(ahl/ah lah deh-mahn-'dahn-teh)*
wife	**a la esposa** *(ah lah ehs-'poh-sah)*

Do you agree with (the)...?	**¿Entiende...?** *(ehn-tee-'ehn-deh)*

allegations	**los alegatos** *(lohs ah-leh-'gah-tohs)*
charge	**la acusación** *(lah ah-koo-sah-see-'ohn)*
differences	**las diferencias** *(lahs dee-fee-'rehn-see-ahs)*
duration	**la duración** *(lah doo-rah-see-'ohn)*
explanation	**la explicación** *(lah ex-plee-kah-see-'ohn)*
final decision	**la decisión final** *(lah deh-see-see-'ohn fee-'nahl)*
justification	**la justificación** *(lah hoos-tee-fee-kah-see-'ohn)*
plea	**la alegación** *(lah ah-leh-gah-see-'ohn)*
requirement	**el requisito** *(ehl reh-kee-'see-toh)*
response	**la respuesta** *(lah rehs-'pwehs-tah)*
rules	**las reglas** *(lahs 'reh-glahs)*
ruling	**la resolución** *(lah reh-soh-loo-see-'ohn)*

AVAILABLE HELP
La ayuda disponible
(lah ah-'yoo-dah dees-poh-'nee-bleh)

Your client may not even be aware of these benefits:

Do you need...?	**¿Necesita...?** *(neh-seh-'see-tah)*

child welfare	**el bienestar infantil** *(ehl bee-eh-nehs-'tahr een-fahn-'teel)*
counseling	**el asesoramiento** *(ehl ah-seh-soh-rah-mee-'ehn-toh)*
family court	**el tribunal de asuntos familiares** *(ehl tree-boo-'nahl deh ah-'soon-tohs fah-mee-lee-'ah-rehs)*
food stamps	**los cupones de alimentos** *(lohs koo-'poh-nehs deh ah-lee-'mehn-tohs)*
government assistance	**la asistencia del gobierno** *(lah ah-sees-'tehn-see-ah dehl goh-bee-'ehr-noh)*
housing	**la vivienda** *(lah vee-vee-'ehn-dah)*
mediation	**la mediación** *(lah meh-dee-ah-see-'ohn)*
medical care	**el cuidado médico** *(ehl koo-ee-'dah-doh 'meh-dee-koh)*
orientation	**la orientación** *(lah oh-ree-ehn-tah-see-'ohn)*
prevention	**la prevención** *(lah preh-vehn-see-'ohn)*
protection	**la protección** *(lah proh-tehk-see-'ohn)*
resources	**los recursos** *(lohs reh-'koor-sohs)*
services	**los servicios** *(lohs sehr-'vee-see-ohs)*
social services	**los servicios sociales** *(lohs sehr-'vee-see-ohs soh-see-'ah-lehs)*
tutorage	**la tutoría** *(lah too-toh-'ree-ah)*

Have you seen (the)...?	**¿Ha visto...?** *(ah 'vees-toh)*
agent	**el/la agente** *(ehl/lah ah-'hehn-teh)*
doctor	**el médico/la médica** *(ehl 'meh-dee-koh/lah 'meh-dee-kah)*
investigator	**el investigador/la investigadora** *(ehl een-vehs-tee-gah-'dohr/lah een-vehs-tee-gah-'doh-rah)*
judge	**el juez/la jueza** *(ehl hwehs/lah 'hweh-sah)*
mediator	**el mediador/la mediadora** *(ehl meh-dee-ah-'dohr/lah meh-dee-ah-'doh-rah)*
official	**el funcionario/la funcionaria** *(ehl foon-see-oh-'nah-ree-oh/lah foon-see-oh-'nah-ree-ah)*
therapist	**el/la terapeuta** *(ehl/lah teh-rah-'peh-oo-tah)*

It's...	**Está.../Es...** *(ehs-'tah/ehs)*
approved	**aprobado** *(ah-proh-'bah-doh)*
available	**disponible** *(dees-poh-'nee-bleh)*
disputed	**disputado** *(dees-poo-'tah-doh)*
equal	**igual** *(ee-'gwahl)*
fair	**justo** *('hoos-toh)*
included	**incluído** *(een-kloo-'ee-doh)*
introduced	**presentado** *(preh-sehn-'tah-doh)*
irrevocable	**irrevocable** *(eer-reh-voh-'kah-bleh)*
obligatory	**obligatorio** *(oh-blee-gah-'toh-ree-oh)*
personal	**personal** *(pehr-soh-'nahl)*
published	**publicado** *(poo-blee-'kah-doh)*
rejected	**rechazado** *(reh-chah-'sah-doh)*
resolved	**resuelto** *(reh-'swehl-toh)*
shared	**compartido** *(kohm-pahr-'tee-doh)*
signed	**firmado** *(feer-'mah-doh)*
supervised	**supervisado** *(soo-pehr-vee-'sah-doh)*

There's an allocation of...	**Hay un reparto de...** *('ah-ee oon reh-'pahr-toh deh)*
assets	**los bienes** *(lohs bee-'eh-nehs)*
debts	**las deudas** *(lahs 'deh-oo-dahs)*
expenses	**los gastos** *(lohs 'gahs-tohs)*
money	**el dinero** *(ehl dee-'neh-roh)*
responsibilities	**las responsabilidades** *(lahs rehs-pohn-sah-bee-lee-'dah-dehs)*
rights	**los derechos** *(lohs deh-'reh-chohs)*
time	**el tiempo** *(ehl tee-'ehm-poh)*

Are you fighting for (the)...?	**¿Lucha por...?** *('loo-chah pohr)*
active assets	**los bienes activos** *(lohs bee-'eh-nehs ahk-'tee-vohs)*
assets acquired beforehand	**los bienes obtenidos de antemano** *(lohs bee-'eh-nehs ohb-teh-'nee-dohs deh ahn-teh-'mah-noh)*

intangible assets	**los bienes intangibles** *(lohs bee-'eh-nehs een-tahn-'hee-blehs)*
personal property	**los bienes muebles** *(lohs bee-'eh-nehs 'mweh-blehs)*
real estate	**los bienes raíces** *(lohs bee-'eh-nehs rah-'ee-sehs)*
shared assets	**los bienes gananciales** *(lohs bee-'eh-nehs gah-nahn-see-'ah-lehs)*
Does it include (the)...?	**¿Incluye...?** *(een-'kloo-yeh)*
bank accounts	**las cuentas bancarias** *(lahs 'kwehn-tahs bahn-'kah-ree-ahs)*
credit cards	**las tarjetas de crédito** *(lahs tahr-'heh-tahs deh 'kreh-dee-toh)*
earnings	**los ingresos** *(lohs een-'greh-sohs)*
funds	**los fondos** *(lohs 'fohn-dohs)*
gifts	**los regalos** *(lohs reh-'gah-lohs)*
increase in value	**el aumento de su valor** *(ehl aw-'mehn-toh deh soo vah-'lohr)*
inheritance	**la herencia** *(lah eh-'rehn-see-ah)*
insurance	**el seguro** *(ehl seh-'goo-roh)*
loan	**el préstamo** *(ehl 'prehs-tah-moh)*
mortgage	**la hipoteca** *(lah ee-poh-'teh-kah)*
property	**la propiedad** *(lah proh-pee-eh-'dahd)*
rent	**el alquiler** *(ehl ahl-kee-'lehr)*
retirement plan	**el plan de jubilación** *(ehl plahn deh hoo-bee-lah-see-'ohn)*
salary	**el salario** *(ehl sah-'lah-ree-oh)*
stocks and bonds	**las acciones y los bonos** *(lahs ahk-see-'oh-nehs ee lohs 'boh-nohs)*
taxes	**los impuestos** *(lohs eem-'pwehs-tohs)*
trust	**el fideicomiso** *(ehl fee-deh-ee-koh-'mee-soh)*
will	**el testamento** *(ehl tehs-tah-'mehn-toh)*
Do you have the... ?	**¿Tiene... ?** *(tee-'eh-neh)*
appointment	**la cita** *(lah 'see-tah)*
copy	**la copia** *(lah 'koh-pee-ah)*
documents	**los documentos** *(lohs doh-koo-'mehn-tohs)*
e-mail	**el correo electrónico** *(ehl kohr-'reh-oh eh-lehk-'troh-nee-koh)*
Do you know when the ___ is?	**¿Sabe cuándo es ... ?** *('sah-beh 'kwahn-doh ehs)*
hearing	**la audiencia** *(lah ah-oo-dee-'ehn-see-ah)*
meeting	**la reunión** *(lah reh-oo-nee-'ohn)*
session	**la sesión** *(lah seh-see-'ohn)*
visit	**la visita** *(lah vee-'see-tah)*

Think about the child's...	**Piense en ____ del niño.**
	(pee-'ehn-seh ehn ____ dehl 'neen-yoh)
behavior	**el comportamento** *(kohm-pohr-tah-mee-'ehn-toh)*
desires	**los deseos** *(lohs deh-'seh-ohs)*
education	**la educación** *(lah eh-doo-kah-see-'ohn)*
feelings	**los sentimientos** *(lohs sehn-tee-mee-'ehn-tohs)*
handicap	**la incapacidad** *(lah een-kah-pah-see-'dahd)*
mental development	**el desarrollo mental** *(ehl deh-sahr-'roh-yoh mehn-'tahl)*
needs	**las necesidades** *(lahs neh-seh-see-'dah-dehs)*
opinion	**la opinión** *(lah oh-pee-nee-'ohn)*
psychological health	**la salud psicológica** *(lah sah-'lood see-koh-'loh-hee-kah)*
quality of life	**la calidad de vida** *(lah kah-lee-'dahd deh 'vee-dah)*
relationships	**las relaciones** *(lahs reh-lah-see-'oh-nehs)*
Has he/she...?	**¿Ha...?** *(ah)*
committed	**comprometido** *(kohm-proh-meh-'tee-doh)*
contributed	**contribuido** *(kohn-tree-boo-'ee-doh)*
helped	**ayudado** *(ah-yoo-'dah-doh)*
paid	**pagado** *(pah-'gah-doh)*
visited	**visitado** *(vee-see-'tah-doh)*
Talk to me about ...	**Hábleme de...** *('ah-bleh-meh deh)*
abuse	**el abuso** *(ehl ah-'boo-soh)*
conflict	**el conflicto** *(ehl kohn-'fleek-toh)*
crisis	**la crisis** *(lah 'kree-sees)*
damage	**el daño** *(ehl 'dahn-yoh)*
danger	**el peligro** *(ehl peh-'lee-groh)*
dispute	**la disputa** *(lah dees-'poo-tah)*
emergency	**la emergencia** *(lah eh-mehr-'hehn-see-ah)*
loss	**la pérdida** *(lah 'pehr-dee-dah)*
mistreatment	**el maltrato** *(ehl mahl-'trah-toh)*
neglect	**la negligencia** *(lah neh-glee-'hehn-see-ah)*
trauma	**el trauma** *(ehl 'trah-oo-mah)*
violence	**la violencia** *(lah vee-oh-'lehn-see-ah)*
Would you like to talk about (the)...?	**¿Quisiera hablar de...?**
	(kee-see-'eh-rah ah-'blahr deh)
alcohol	**el alcohol** *(ehl ahl-koh-'ohl)*
assault	**la agresión** *(lah ah-greh-see-'ohn)*
death	**la muerte** *(lah 'mwehr-teh)*
depression	**la depresión** *(lah deh-preh-see-'ohn)*
drugs	**las drogas** *(lahs 'droh-gahs)*
emotional problems	**los problemas emocionales**
	(lohs proh-'bleh-mahs eh-moh-see-oh-'nah-lehs)
felony	**el delito mayor** *(ehl deh-'lee-toh mah-'yohr)*
fighting	**la pelea** *(lah peh-'leh-ah)*

financial trouble	**el problema financiero** (ehl proh-'bleh-mah fee-nahn-see-'eh-roh)
harassment	**el acosamiento** (ehl ah-koh-sah-mee-'ehn-toh)
illegal status	**el estado ilegal** (ehl ehs-'tah-doh ee-leh-'gahl)
incest	**el incesto** (ehl een-'sehs-toh)
kidnapping	**el secuestro** (ehl seh-'kwehs-troh)
lost child	**el niño desaparecido** (ehl 'neen-yoh deh-sah-pah-reh-'see-doh)
misdemeanor	**el delito menor** (ehl deh-'lee-toh meh-'nohr)
rape	**la violación** (lah vee-oh-lah-see-'ohn)
runaway child	**el niño fugitivo** (ehl 'neen-yoh foo-hee-'tee-voh)
threats	**las amenazas** (lahs ah-meh-'nah-sahs)
Do you want...?	**¿Quiere...?** (kee-'eh-reh)
to approve	**aprobar** (ah-proh-'bahr)
to avoid	**evitar** (eh-vee-'tahr)
to divide	**dividir** (dee-vee-'deer)
to file for custody	**reclamar la custodia** (reh-klah-'mahr lah koos-'toh-dee-ah)
to file for divorce	**entablar pleito de divorcio** (ehn-tah-'blahr 'pleh-ee-toh deh dee-'vohr-see-oh)
to finalize	**finalizar** (fee-nah-lee-'sahr)
to keep	**mantener** (mahn-teh-'nehr)
to negociate	**negociar** (neh-goh-see-'ahr)
to pay	**pagar** (peh-'gahr)
to process	**tramitar** (trah-mee-'tahr)
to receive	**recibir** (reh-see-'beer)
to report	**reportar** (reh-pohr-'tahr)
to request	**solicitar** (soh-lee-see-'tahr)
to separate	**separar** (seh-pah-'rahr)
to share	**compartir** (kohm-pahr-'teer)
to start	**iniciar** (ee-nee-see-'ahr)
to sue	**demandar** (deh-mahn-'dahr)

NOTICE! ¡Fíjese!

You may need more vocabulary that refers to people and relationships:

childhood	**la niñez** (lah neen-'yehs)
civil union	**la unión civil** (lah oo-nee-'ohn see-'veel)
old age	**la vejez** (lah veh-'hehs)
older child	**el hijo mayor** (ehl 'ee-hoh mah-'yohr)
orphan	**el huérfano/la huérfana** (ehl oo-'ehr-fah-noh/lah oo-'ehr-fah-nah)
parenthood	**la paternidad** (lah pah-tehr-nee-'dahd)

twin	el gemelo/la gemela *(ehl heh-'meh-loh/lah heh-'meh-lah)*
young person	el joven/la joven *(ehl 'hoh-vehn/lah 'hoh-vehn)*
younger child	el hijo menor *(ehl 'ee-hoh meh-'nohr)*

 CULTURAL COMMENT **Comentario cultural**

The extended family may include in-laws, friends, or neighbors who have lent their support to family members in the past, so they may be asked to assist in decision-making. Hispanic families also respect the elderly. Older children, too, are given more responsibilities and are treated differently. When dealing with a large family, it is usually a good idea to find out who is in charge.

 PRIVATE PRACTICE **Práctica privada**

(31) A. Connect the words that go together best:

1. la orden	los ingresos
2. el salario	la necesidad
3. el cónyuge	el cargo
4. el alegato	la demanda
5. el deseo	el esposo

B. Translate:

1. el hijo menor _____

2. secuestro _____

3. delito mayor _____

4. relaciones _____

5. maltrato _____

6. reunión _____

C. In Spanish, list three family members, three legal issues related to children, and three action words related to family law.

_____ _____ _____

_____ _____ _____

_____ _____ _____

MORE PERSONAL INFORMATION
Más información personal
(mahs een-fohr-mah-see-'ohn pehr-soh-'nahl)

To build a relationship with your client, several topics usually are discussed:

Do you drink?	**¿Toma licor?** *('toh-mah lee-'kohr)*
Do you smoke?	**¿Fuma?** *('foo-mah)*
Do you take drugs?	**¿Toma drogas?** *('toh-mah 'droh-gahs)*

Are you...?   **¿Es usted...?** *(ehs oos-'tehd)*

   divorced   **divorciado/divorciada**
                                (dee-vohr-see-'ah-doh/dee-vohr-see-'ah-dah)
   gay   **homosexual** *(oh-moh-sehk-soo-'ahl)*
   married   **casado/casada** *(kah-'sah-doh/kah-'sah-dah)*
   separated   **separado/separada** *(seh-pah-'rah-doh/seh-pah-'rah-dah)*
   single   **soltero/soltera** *(sohl-'teh-roh/sohl-'teh-rah)*
   straight   **heterosexual** *(eh-teh-roh-sehk-soo-'ahl)*
   widowed   **viudo/viuda** *(vee-'oo-doh/vee-'oo-dah)*

Do you live together?
¿Viven ustedes juntos? *('vee-vehn oos-'teh-dehs 'hoon-tohs)*

How many children do you have?
¿Cuántos hijos tienen? *('kwahn-tohs 'ee-hohs tee-'eh-nehn)*

Have you been married before?
¿Ha estado casado/casada antes?
(ah ehs-'tah-doh kah-'sah-doh/kah-'sah-dah 'ahn-tehs)

Are you currently employed?
¿Está con trabajo ahora? *(ehs-'tah kohn trah-'bah-hoh ah-'oh-rah)*

Are you over 18 years of age?
¿Tiene más de dieciocho años? *(tee-'eh-neh mahs deh dee-eh-see-'oh-choh 'ahn-yohs)*

Who lives with you?
¿Quién vive con usted? *(kee-'ehn 'vee-veh kohn oos-'tehd)*

Who do the children live with?
¿Con quién viven los niños? *(kohn kee-'ehn 'vee-vehn lohs 'neen-yohs)*

Who is his/her lawyer?
¿Quién es su abogado? *(kee-'ehn ehs soo ah-boh-'gah-doh)*

Who is legally responsible?
¿Quién es legalmante responsable? *(kee-'ehn ehs leh-gahl-'mehn-teh rehs-pohn-'sah-bleh)*

Who filed the lawsuit?
¿Quién presentó la demanda? *(kee-'ehn preh-sehn-'toh lah deh-'mahn-dah)*

How long have you...?	**¿Por cuánto tiempo ha...?**
	(pohr 'kwahn-toh tee-'ehm-poh ah)
been divorced	**estado divorciado/divorciada**
	(ehs-'tah-doh dee-vohr-see-'ah-doh/dee-vohr-see-'ah-dah)
been married	**estado casado/casada**
	(ehs-'tah-doh kah-'sah-doh/kah-'sah-dah)
been separated	**estado separado/separada**
	(ehs-'tah-doh seh-pah-'rah-doh/seh-pah-'rah-dah)
had marital problems	**tenido problemas matrimoniales**
	(teh-'nee-doh proh-'bleh-mahs mah-tree-moh-nee-'ah-lehs)
lived there	**vivido allí** *(vee-'vee-doh ah-'yee)*
Write (the)...	**Escriba...** *(ehs-'kree-bah)*
case number	**el número del caso** *(ehl 'noo-meh-roh dehl 'kah-soh)*
court date	**la fecha de corte** *(lah 'feh-chah deh 'kohr-teh)*
minor's name	**el nombre del menor** *(ehl 'nohm-breh dehl meh-'nohr)*
relationship to minor	**la relación con el menor de edad**
	(lah reh-lah-see-'ohn kohn ehl meh-'nohr deh eh-'dahd)

NOTICE!   ¡Fíjese!

Check out the new pattern below:

Did he/she...?	**¿Le...?** *(leh)*
abuse you	**abusó** *(ah-boo-'soh)*
hit you	**pegó** *(peh-'goh)*
kick you	**pateó** *(pah-teh-'oh)*
knock you down	**tumbó** *(toom-'boh)*
push you	**empujó** *(ehm-poo-'hoh)*
rape you	**violó** *(vee-oh-'loh)*
threaten you	**amenazó** *(ah-meh-nah-'soh)*
touch you	**tocó** *(toh-'koh)*
yell at you	**gritó** *(gree-'toh)*

WHAT KIND OF PERSON?
¿Qué tipo de persona?
(keh 'tee-poh deh pehr-'soh-nah)

These are words to describe your client and others involved in the case.

You're...   **Usted es...** *(oos-'tehd ehs)*

brave	**valiente** *(vah-lee-'ehn-teh)*
fair	**justo/justa** *('hoos-toh/'hoos-tah)*
friendly	**amistoso/amistosa** *(ah-mees-'toh-soh/ah-mees-'toh-sah)*
healthy	**saludable** *(sah-loo-'dah-bleh)*
honest	**honesto/honesta** *(oh-'nehs-toh/oh-'nehs-tah)*
industrious	**trabajador/trabajadora** *(trah-bah-hah-'dohr/trah-bah-hah-'doh-rah)*
intelligent	**inteligente** *(een-teh-lee-'hehn-teh)*
kind	**amable** *(ah-'mah-bleh)*
likable	**simpatico/simpática** *(seem-'pah-tee-koh/seem-'pah-tee-kah)*
patient	**paciente** *(pah-see-'ehn-teh)*
polite	**cortés** *(kohr-'tehs)*
punctual	**puntual** *(poon-too-'ahl)*
quiet	**quieto/quieta** *(kee-'eh-toh/kee-'eh-tah)*
sensitive	**sensible** *(sehn-'see-bleh)*
strong	**fuerte** *('fwehr-teh)*

Is he/she...?   **¿Es él/ella...?** *(ehs ehl/'eh-yah)*

dangerous	**peligroso/peligrosa** *(peh-lee-'groh-soh/peh-lee-'groh-sah)*
deceitful	**engañoso/engañosa** *(ehn-gahn-'yoh-soh/ehn-gahn-'yoh-sah)*
hurtful	**ofensivo/ofensiva** *(oh-fehn-'see-voh/oh-fehn-'see-vah)*
mean	**cruel** *(kroo-'ehl)*
rude	**grosero/grosera** *(groh-'seh-roh/groh-'seh-rah)*

The more you discuss family concerns, the greater the chances of an emotional response. These next words delve into the heart of the matter:

Do you feel...?   **¿Se siente...?** *(seh see-'ehn-teh)*

afraid	**asustado/asustada** *(ah-soos-'tah-doh/ah-soos-'tah-dah)*
angry	**enojado/enojada** *(eh-noh-'hah-doh/eh-noh-'hah-dah)*
bitter	**amargado/amargada** *(ah-mahr-'gah-doh/ah-mahr-'gah-dah)*
distracted	**distraído/distraída** *(dees-trah-'ee-doh/dees-trah-'ee-dah)*
frustrated	**frustrado/frustrada** *(froos-'trah-doh/froos-'trah-dah)*
guilty	**culpable** *(kool-'pah-bleh)*
hostile	**hostil** *(ohs-'teel)*
impatient	**impaciente** *(eem-pah-see-'ehn-teh)*
nervous	**nervioso/nerviosa** *(nehr-vee-'oh-soh/nehr-vee-'oh-sah)*
sad	**triste** *('trees-teh)*

Don't stop talking about how the person feels. One method is to hold up a list of feelings, in Spanish, and then ask the client to point to the word that best describes his or her emotions.

I feel...	**Me siento...** *(meh see-'ehn-toh)*
abused	**abusado/abusada** *(ah-boo-'sah-doh/ah-boo-'sah-dah)*
anxious	**ansioso/ansiosa** *(ahn-see-'oh-soh/ahn-see-'oh-sah)*
bothered	**molesto/molesta** *(moh-'lehs-toh/moh-'lehs-tah)*
confused	**confundido/confundida** *(kohn-foon-'dee-doh/kohn-foon-'dee-doh)*
desperate	**desesperado/deseperada** *(deh-sehs-peh-'rah-doh/deh-sehs-peh-'rah-dah)*
embarrassed	**turbado/turbada** *(toor-'bah-doh/toor-'bah-dah)*
exhausted	**agotado/agotada** *(ah-goh-'tah-doh/ah-goh-'tah-dah)*
fed up	**harto/harta** *('ahr-toh/'ahr-tah)*
furious	**furioso/furiosa** *(foo-ree-'oh-soh/foo-ree-'oh-sah)*
hated	**odiado/odiada** *(oh-dee-'ah-doh/oh-dee-'ah-dah)*
jealous	**celoso/celosa** *(seh-'loh-soh/seh-'loh-sah)*
resentful	**resentido/resentida** *(reh-sehn-'tee-doh/reh-sehn-'tee-dah)*
restless	**inquieto/inquieta** *(een-kee-'eh-toh/een-kee'eh-tah)*
suspicious	**suspicaz** *(soos-pee-'kahs)*
trapped	**atrapado/atrapada** *(ah-trah-'pah-doh/ah-trah-'pah-dah)*
uncomfortable	**incómodo/incómoda** *(een-'koh-moh-doh/een-'koh-moh-dah)*
unhappy	**descontento/descontenta** *(dehs-kohn-'tehn-toh/dehs-kohn-'tehn-tah)*
worried	**preocupado/preocupada** *(preh-oh-koo-'pah-doh/preh-oh-koo-'pah-dah)*

DOMESTIC VIOLENCE
La violencia doméstica
(lah vee-oh-'lehn-see-ah doh-'mehs-tee-kah)

With the help of an interpreter, inquire about domestic violence using some of the lines below:

What happened?
¿Qué pasó? *(keh pah-'soh)*

Is anyone hurt?
¿Hay alguién lastimado? *('ah-ee 'ahl-ghee-ehn lahs-tee-'mah-doh)*

What did he/she do to you?
¿Qué le hizo a usted? *(keh leh 'ee-soh ah oos-'tehd)*

Is he/she a violent person?
¿Es una persona violenta? *(ehs ʿoo-nah pehr-ʿsoh-nah vee-oh-ʿlehn-tah)*

Does he/she do drugs?
¿Toma drogas? *(ʿtoh-mah ʿdroh-gahs)*

Does he/she have a firearm?
¿Tiene un arma de fuego? *(tee-ʿeh-neh oon ʿahr-mah deh ʿfweh-goh)*

Was this the first time?
¿Ha pasado antes? *(ah pah-ʿsah-doh ʿahn-tehs)*

How many times?
¿Cuántas veces? *(ʿkwahn-tahs ʿveh-sehs)*

How long ago?
¿Cuánto tiempo atrás? *(ʿkwahn-toh tee-ʿehm-poh ah-ʿtrahs)*

How often?
¿Cuán a menudo? *(kwahn ah meh-ʿnoo-doh)*

Do you want...?	**¿Quiere...?** *(kee-ʿeh-reh)*
a court order	**una orden de la corte** *(ʿoo-nah ʿohr-dehn deh lah ʿkohr-teh)*
to press charges	**acusarle legalmente** *(ah-koo-ʿsahr-leh leh-gahl-ʿmehn-teh)*
him/her arrested	**que se le arreste** *(keh seh leh ahr-ʿrehs-teh)*

Do you have a place to go?
¿Tiene un lugar adónde ir? *(tee-ʿeh-neh oon loo-ʿgahr ah-ʿdohn-deh eer)*

Will you be safe?
¿Estará protegido/protegida? *(ehs-tah-ʿrah proh-teh-ʿhee-doh/proh-teh-ʿhee-dah)*

Who's going to accompany you?
¿Quién le va a acompañar? *(kee-ʿehn leh vah ah ah-kohm-pahn-ʿyahr)*

Could you...?	**¿Podría...?** *(pohd-ʿree-ah)*
call this agency	**llamar a esta agencia** *(yah-ʿmahr ah ʿehs-tah ah-ʿhehn-see-ah)*
move out	**mudarse** *(moo-ʿdahr-seh)*
separate for awhile	**separarse por un tiempo** *(seh-pah-ʿrahr-seh pohr oon tee-ʿehm-poh)*

PRIVATE PRACTICE   **Práctica privada**

(32) A. Join the words that have related meanings:

1. **ofensivo**	**relajarse**
2. **furioso**	**grosero**
3. **burlarse**	**menor**
4. **nervioso**	**ansioso**
5. **joven**	**molestar**
6. **calmarse**	**enojado**

B. Talk about yourself:

¿Fuma usted?

¿Es usted paciente?

¿Es usted una persona valiente?

VERBS IN ACTION!   **¡Verbos activos!**

This list includes verbs in the areas of immigration, personal injury, and family law:

to antagonize	**antagonizar** *(ahn-tah-goh-nee-'sahr)*
to argue	**argüir** *(ahr-goo-'eer)*
to beat	**golpear** *(gohl-peh-'ahr)*
to bother	**molestar** *(moh-lehs-'tahr)*
to counsel	**aconsejar** *(ah-kohn-seh-'hahr)*
to crash	**chocar** *(choh-'kahr)*
to curse	**maldecir** *(mahl-deh-'seer)*
to gossip	**chismear** *(chees-meh-'ahr)*
to hit	**pegar** *(peh-'gahr)*
to humiliate	**humillar** *(oo-mee-'yahr)*
to immigrate	**inmigrar** *(een-mee-'grahr)*
to injure	**herir** *(eh-'reer)*
to joke	**bromear** *(broh-meh-'ahr)*
to protect	**proteger** *(proh-teh-'hehr)*
to recover	**recuperar** *(reh-koo-peh-'rahr)*
to suffer	**sufrir** *(soo-'freer)*
to tease	**burlarse** *(boor-'lahr-seh)*
to threaten	**amenazar** *(ah-meh-nah-'sahr)*
to yell	**gritar** *(gree-'tahr)*

Notice how reflexive verbs are used in a sentence:

to divorce   **divorciarse** *(dee-vohr-see-'ahr-seh)*
They are divorcing.
Se están divorciando. *(seh ehs-'tahn dee-vohr-see-'ahn-doh)*

to get sick   **enfermarse** *(ehn-fehr-'mahr-seh)*
I am getting sick.
Me estoy enfermando. *(meh ehs-'toh-ee ehn-fehr-'mahn-doh)*

to get married   **casarse** *(kah-'sahr-seh)*
We are getting married.
Nos estamos casando. *(nohs ehs-'tah-mohs kah-'sahn-doh)*

I'll bet you can figure out the meanings of these verbs. Cover the English column and guess at the translation:

calmar *(kahl-'mahr)*	to calm
causar *(kah-oo-'sahr)*	to cause
comunicar *(koh-moo-nee-'kahr)*	to communicate
confirmar *(kohn-feer-'mahr)*	to confirm
consultar *(kohn-sool-'tahr)*	to consult
conversar *(kohn-vehr-'sahr)*	to converse
cooperar *(koh-oh-peh-'rahr)*	to cooperate
defender *(deh-fehn-'dehr)*	to defend
determinar *(deh-tehr-mee-'nahr)*	to determine
eliminar *(eh-lee-mee-'nahr)*	to eliminate
explorar *(ex-ploh-'rahr)*	to explore
identificar *(ee-dehn-tee-fee-'kahr)*	to identify
informar *(een-fohr-'mahr)*	to inform
justificar *(hoos-tee-fee-'kahr)*	to justify
modificar *(moh-dee-fee-'kahr)*	to modify
notar *(noh-'tahr)*	to note
observer *(ohb-sehr-'vahr)*	to observe
obtener *(ohb-teh-'nehr)*	to obtain
participar *(pahr-tee-see-'pahr)*	to participate
permitir *(pehr-mee-'teer)*	to permit
planear *(plah-neh-ahr)*	to plan
practicar *(prahk-tee-'kahr)*	to practice
recomendar *(reh-koh-mehn-'dahr)*	to recommend
referir *(reh-feh-'reer)*	to refer
representar *(reh-preh-sehn-'tahr)*	to represent
restaurar *(rehs-tah-oo-'rahr)*	to restore
separar *(seh-pah-'rahr)*	to separate
transferir *(trahns-feh-'reer)*	to transfer
verificar *(veh-ree-fee-'kahr)*	to verify
visitar *(vee-see-'tahr)*	to visit

Be careful—some verb infinitives are *not* what they seem to be:

embarazar *(ehm-bah-rah-'sahr)*	to impregnate
molestar *(moh-lehs-'tahr)*	to bother
violar *(vee-oh-'lahr)*	to rape

 ## NOTICE!   ¡Fíjese!

In Spanish, there are two common ways to express *to know*. "To know something" requires the verb **saber**, whereas "to know someone" requires the verb **conocer**. Carefully read through these examples:

I don't know.	**No sé.** *(noh seh)*
I don't know him.	**No lo conozco.** *(noh loh koh-'nohs-koh)*
Do you know the time?	**¿Sabe la hora?** *('sah-beh lah 'oh-rah)*
Do you know her?	**¿La conoce?** *(lah koh-'noh-seh)*
I didn't know it.	**No lo sabía.** *(noh loh sah-'bee-ah)*
I didn't know him.	**No lo conocía.** *(noh loh koh-noh-'see-ah)*

THE FUTURE
El futuro
(ehl foo-'too-roh)

To discuss the future—what's going to happen—in Spanish, all you need are the basic forms of the verb *to go* (**ir**) before a verb infinitive:

I'm going to...	...read.
Voy a... *('voh-ee ah)*	**...leer.** *(leh-'ehr)*
You're (sing.); He's, She's going to...	...drive.
Va a... *('vah ah)*	**...manejar.** *(mah-neh-'hahr)*
You're (pl.); They're going to...	...check.
Van a... *('vahn ah)*	**...revisar.** *(reh-vee-'sahr)*
We're going to...	...investigate.
Vamos a... *('vah-mohs ah)*	**...investigar.** *(een-vehs-tee-'gahr)*

Notice how these other statements refer to future actions:

I'm going to the office.	**Voy a la oficina.** *('voh-ee ah lah oh-fee-'see-nah)*
I'm going <u>to call</u>.	**Voy a <u>llamar</u>.** *('voh-ee ah yah-'mahr)*
We're going to the courtroom.	**Vamos al tribunal.** *('vah-mohs ahl tree-boo-'nahl)*
We're going <u>to listen</u> to the judge.	**Vamos a <u>escuchar</u> al juez.**
	('vah-mohs ah ehs-koo-'chahr ahl hwehs)
She's going to the post office.	**Va al correo.** *(vah ahl kohr-'reh-oh)*
She's going to <u>pick up</u> the envelope.	**Va a <u>recoger</u> el sobre.**
	(vah ah reh-koh-'hehr ehl 'soh-breh)

TO CALL	**Llamar** *(yah-'mahr)*
I will call	**Yo llamaré** *(yoh yah-mah-'reh)*
You (sing.); He, She will call	**Usted, Él, Ella llamará**
	(oos-'tehd, ehl, 'eh-yah yah-mah-'rah)
You (pl.); They will call	**Ustedes, Ellos llamarán**
	(oos-'teh-dehs, 'eh-yohs yah-mah-'rahn)
We will call	**Nosotros llamaremos**
	(noh-'soh-trohs yah-mah-'reh-mohs)

I'll work on Monday.   **Trabajaré el lunes.** *(trah-bah-hah-'reh ehl 'loo-nehs)*

He'll eat at six.   **Comerá a las seis.** *(koh-meh-'rah ah lahs 'seh-ees)*

They'll go in August.   **Irán en agosto.** *(ee-'rahn ehn ah-'gohs-toh)*

We'll finish tomorrow.   **Terminaremos mañana.**
     (tehr-mee-nah-'reh-mohs mahn-'yah-nah)

PRIVATE PRACTICE   Práctica privada

(33) A. Translate the verb into English and then say what you're going to do in the future in Spanish. Follow the example:

recuperar	recuperate	**Voy a recuperar.**
1. llamar	_____	_____
2. descansar	_____	_____
3. hacer ejercicio	_____	_____
4. tomar medicina	_____	_____
5. gritar	_____	_____

B. Conjugate the same verbs. Follow the example:

recuperar	**recuperaré, recuperará, recuperarán, recuperaremos**
1. llamar	_____
2. descansar	_____
3. hacer	_____
4. tomar	_____
5. gritar	_____

Chapter Five	**Capítulo Cinco** *(kah-'pee-too-loh 'seen-koh)*

Business, Finances, and Real Estate Law
Leyes comerciales, financieras y de bienes raíces

('leh-yehs koh-mehr-see-'ah-lehs, fee-nahn-see-'eh-rahs
ee deh bee-'eh-nes rah-'ee-sehs)

Prior to working through any legal concerns related to finances, check the basic vocabulary needed to discuss **el dinero** *(ehl dee-'neh-roh)* in Spanish:

What happened to (the)...?	**¿Qué pasó con...?** *(keh pah-'soh kohn)*
ATM card	**la tarjeta para el cajero automático** *(lah tahr-'heh-tah 'pah-rah ehl kah-'heh-roh aw-toh-'mah-tee-koh)*
bills	**los billetes** *(lohs bee-'yeh-tehs)*
cash	**el efectivo** *(ehl eh-fehk-'tee-voh)*
cashier's check	**el cheque de banco** *(ehl 'cheh-keh deh 'bahn-koh)*
cents	**los centavos** *(lohs sehn-'tah-vohs)*
change	**el cambio** *(ehl 'kahm-bee-oh)*
check	**el cheque** *(ehl 'cheh-keh)*
coins	**las monedas** *(lahs moh-'neh-dahs)*
credit card	**la tarjeta de crédito** *(lah tahr-'heh-tah deh 'kreh-dee-toh)*
dollars	**los dólares** *(lohs 'doh-lah-rehs)*
money order	**el giro postal** *(ehl 'hee-roh pohs-'tahl)*

Do you have (the)...?	**¿Tiene...?** *(tee-'eh-neh)*
application	**la solicitud** *(lah soh-lee-see-'tood)*
bill	**la cuenta** *(lah 'kwehn-tah)*
claim	**la reclamación** *(lah reh-klah-mah-see-'ohn)*
document	**el documento** *(ehl doh-koo-'mehn-toh)*
form	**el formulario** *(ehl fohr-moo-'lah-ree-oh)*
invoice	**la factura** *(lah fahk-'too-rah)*
order	**el pedido** *(ehl peh-'dee-doh)*
paperwork	**el papeleo** *(ehl pah-peh-'leh-oh)*
receipt	**el recibo** *(ehl reh-'see-boh)*

What do you know about (the)...?	¿Qué sabe Ud. de...? *(keh 'sah-beh oos-'tehd deh)*
annuity	**la anualidad** *(lah ah-nwah-lee-'dahd)*
assets	**los bienes** *(lohs bee-'eh-nehs)*
bond	**el bono** *(ehl 'boh-noh)*
budget	**el presupuesto** *(ehl preh-soo-'pwehs-toh)*
certificate	**el certificado** *(ehl sehr-tee-fee-'kah-doh)*
checking account	**la cuenta de cheques** *(lah 'kwehn-tah deh 'cheh-kehs)*
collection agency	**la agencia de cobros** *(lah ah-'hehn-see-ah deh 'koh-brohs)*
commodity	**la mercancía** *(lah mehr-kahn-'see-ah)*
credit rating	**las clasificación de crédito** *(lah klah-see-fee-kah-see-'ohn deh 'kreh-dee-toh)*
dividend	**el dividendo** *(ehl dee-vee-'dehn-doh)*
donation	**la donación** *(lah doh-nah-see-'ohn)*
down payment	**la entrega inicial** *(lah ehn-'treh-gah ee-nee-see-'ahl)*
equity	**el valor líquido** *(ehl vah-'lohr 'lee-kee-doh)*
fundraising	**la recaudación de fondos** *(lah reh-kah-oo-dah-see-'ohn deh 'fohn-dohs)*
inheritance	**la herencia** *(lah eh-'rehn-see-ah)*
insurance company	**la compañía de seguros** *(lah kohm-pah-'nee-ah deh seh-'goo-rohs)*
interest rate	**la tasa de interés** *(lah 'tah-sah deh een-teh-'rehs)*
investment	**la inversión** *(lah een-vehr-see-'ohn)*
lease	**el alquiler** *(ehl ahl-kee-'lehr)*
liability	**el pasivo** *(ehl pah-'see-voh)*
loan	**el préstamo** *(ehl 'prehs-tah-moh)*
money market	**el mercado de valores** *(ehl mehr-'kah-doh deh vah-'loh-rehs)*
mortgage	**la hipoteca** *(lah ee-poh-'teh-kah)*
mutual fund	**el fondo mutualista** *(ehl 'fohn-doh moo-too-ah-'lees-tah)*
patent	**la patente** *(lah pah-'tehn-teh)*
payment plan	**el plan de pago a plazos** *(ehl plahn deh 'pah-goh ah 'plah-sohs)*
pension plans	**el plan de pensión** *(ehl plahn deh pehn-see-'ohn)*
probate	**la validación testamentaria** *(lah vah-lee-dah-see-'ohn tehs-tah-mehn-'tah-ree-ah)*
real estate	**los bienes raíces** *(lohs bee-'eh-nehs rah-'ee-sehs)*
rebate	**el reembolso** *(ehl reh-ehm-'bohl-soh)*
savings account	**la cuenta de ahorros** *(lah 'kwehn-tah deh ah-'ohr-rohs)*
scholarship	**la beca** *(lah 'beh-kah)*
securities portfolio	**la cartera de valores** *(lah kahr-'teh-rah deh vah-'loh-rehs)*
social security	**el seguro social** *(ehl seh-'goo-roh soh-see-'ahl)*
stocks	**las acciones** *(lahs ahk-see-'oh-nehs)*
student loan	**el préstamo estudiantil** *(ehl 'prehs-tah-moh ehs-too-dee-ahn-'teel)*
tax	**el impuesto** *(ehl eem-'pwehs-toh)*
trust fund	**el fondo fiduciario** *(ehl 'fohn-doh fee-doo-see-'ah-ree-oh)*

VA benefit	**el beneficio de veterano** *(ehl beh-neh-'fee-see-oh deh veh-teh-'rah-noh)*
W-2 form	**el formulario W-2** *(ehl fohr-moo-'lah-ree-oh 'doh-bleh veh dohs)*
will	**el testamento** *(ehl tehs-tah-'mehn-toh)*

Did you speak with (the)...?	**¿Habló con...?** *(ah-'bloh kohn)*
accountant	**el contador/la contadora** *(ehl kohn-tah-'dohr/lah kohn-tah-'doh-rah)*
administrator	**el administrador/la administradora** *(ehl ahd-mee-nees-trah-'dohr/lah ahd-mee-nees-trah-'doh-rah)*
agent	**el/la agente** *(ehl/lah ah-'hehn-teh)*
analyst	**el/la analista** *(ehl/lah ah-nah-'lees-tah)*
applicant	**el/la solicitante** *(ehl/lah soh-lee-see-'tahn-teh)*
attorney	**el abogado/la abogada** *(ehl ah-boh-'gah-doh/lah ah-boh-'gah-dah)*
auditor	**el auditor/la auditora** *(ehl aw-dee-'tohr/lah aw-dee-'toh-rah)*
beneficiary	**el beneficiario/la beneficiaria** *(ehl beh-neh-fee-see-'ah-ree-oh/lah beh-neh-fee-see-'ah-ree-ah)*
bookkeeper	**el/la contable** *(ehl/lah kohn-'tah-bleh)*
borrower	**el prestatario/la prestataria** *(ehl prehs-tah-'tah-ree-oh/lah prehs-tah-'tah-ree-ah)*
broker	**el corredor/la corredora** *(ehl kohr-reh-'dohr/lah kohr-reh-'doh-rah)*
buyer	**el jefe/la jefa de compras** *(ehl 'heh-feh/lah 'heh-fah deh 'kohm-prahs)*
cashier	**el cajero/la cajera** *(ehl kah-'heh-roh/lah kah-'heh-rah)*
claimant	**el/la reclamante** *(ehl/lah reh-klah-'mahn-teh)*
clerk	**el dependiente/la dependienta** *(ehl deh-pehn-dee-'ehn-teh/lah deh-pehn-dee-'ehn-tah)*
client	**el cliente/la clienta** *(ehl klee-'ehn-teh/lah klee-'ehn-tah)*
competitor	**el competidor/la competidora** *(ehl kohm-peh-tee-'dohr/lah kohm-peh-tee-'doh-rah)*
consultant	**el consultor/la consultora** *(ehl kohn-sool-'tohr/lah kohn-sool-'toh-rah)*
consumer	**el consumidor/la consumidora** *(ehl kohn-soo-mee-'dohr/lah kohn-soo-mee-'doh-rah)*
courier	**el mensajero/la mensajera** *(ehl mehn-sah-'heh-roh/lah mehn-sah-'heh-rah)*
CPA	**el contador público/la contadora pública** *(ehl kohn-tah-'dohr 'poo-blee-koh/lah kohn-tah-'doh-rah 'poo-blee-kah)*
creditor	**el acreedor/la acreedora** *(ehl ah-kreh-eh-'dohr/lah ah-kreh-eh-'doh-rah)*
customer	**el cliente/la clienta** *(ehl klee-'ehn-teh/lah klee-'ehn-tah)*
dealer	**el concesionario/la concesionaria** *(ehl kohn-seh-see-oh-'nah-ree-oh/lah kohn-seh-see-oh-'nah-ree-ah)*

expert	**el experto/la experta** *(ehl ex-'pehr-toh/lah ex-'pehr-tah)*
heir	**el heredero/la heredera** *(ehl eh-reh-'deh-roh/lah eh-reh-'deh-rah)*
investigator	**el investigador/la investigadora** *(ehl een-vehs-tee-gah-'dohr/lah een-vehs-tee-gah-'doh-rah)*
investor	**el/la inversionista** *(ehl/lah een-vehr-see-oh-'nees-tah)*
manager	**el gerente/la gerenta** *(ehl heh-'rehn-teh/lah heh-'rehn-tah)*
manufacturer	**el/la fabricante** *(ehl/lah fah-bree-'kahn-teh)*
member	**el/la miembro** *(ehl/lah mee-'ehm-broh)*
notary public	**el notario público/la notaria pública** *(ehl noh-'tah-ree-oh 'poo-blee-koh/lah noh-'tah-ree-ah 'poo-blee-kah)*
office clerk	**el/la oficinista** *(ehl/lah oh-fee-see-'nees-tah)*
owner	**el dueño/la dueña** *(ehl 'dwehn-yoh/lah 'dwehn-yah)*
partner	**el socio/la socia** *(ehl 'soh-see-oh/lah 'soh-see-ah)*
salesperson	**el vendedor/la vendedora** *(ehl vehn-deh-'dohr/lah vehn-deh-'doh-rah)*
shipper	**el fletador/la fletadora** *(ehl fleh-tah-'dohr/lah fleh-tah-'doh-rah)*
supplier	**el abastecedor/la abastecedora** *(ehl ah-bahs-teh-seh-'dohr/lah ah-bahs-teh-seh-'doh-rah)*
tax collector	**el recaudador/la recaudadora de impuestos** *(ehl reh-kah-oo-dah-'dohr/lah reh-kah-oo-dah-'doh-rah deh eem-'pwehs-tohs)*
third party	**la tercera persona** *(lah tehr-'seh-rah pehr-'soh-nah)*
trustee	**el fideicomisario/la fideicomisaria** *(ehl fee-deh-ee-koh-mee-'sah-ree-oh/lah fee-deh-ee-koh-mee-'sah-ree-ah)*

 NOTICE!   **¡Fíjese!**

Here are descriptive words to discuss about financial concerns:

Was it...?	**¿Fue...?** *(fweh)*
better	**mejor** *(meh-'hohr)*
enough	**suficiente** *(soo-fee-see-'ehn-teh)*
expensive	**caro** *('kah-roh)*
free	**gratuito** *(grah-too-'ee-toh)*
inexpensive	**barato** *(bah-'rah-toh)*
less	**menos** *('meh-nohs)*
more	**más** *(mahs)*
overdue	**atrasado** *(ah-trah-'sah-doh)*
worse	**peor** *(peh-'ohr)*

THE BANK
El banco
(ehl 'bahn-koh)

The following words focus on banking procedures. However, many also relate to *insurance*, *tax*, and *property* law. Some you should already know:

Does it have to do with (the)...?	**¿Tiene que ver con...?** *(tee-'eh-neh keh vehr kohn)*
agreement	**el acuerdo** *(ehl ah-'kwehr-doh)*
auto loan	**el préstamo de carro** *(ehl 'prehs-tah-moh deh 'kahr-roh)*
bank	**el banco** *(ehl 'bahn-koh)*
certificate of deposit	**el certificado de depósito** *(ehl sehr-tee-fee-'kah-doh deh deh-'poh-see-toh)*
checking account	**la cuenta de cheques** *(lah 'kwehn-tah deh 'cheh-kehs)*
credit union	**el banco cooperativo** *(ehl 'bahn-koh koh-oh-peh-rah-'tee-voh)*
equity loan	**el préstamo de valor líquido** *(ehl 'prehs-tah-moh deh vah-'lohr 'lee-kee-doh)*
grace period	**el período de gracia** *(ehl peh-'ree-oh-doh deh 'grah-see-ah)*
home loan	**el préstamo para comprar casa** *(ehl 'prehs-tah-moh 'pah-rah kohm-'prahr 'kah-sah)*
insurance	**el seguro** *(ehl seh-'goo-roh)*
interest	**el interés** *(ehl een-teh-'rehs)*
IRA	**la cuenta de jubilación individual** *(lah 'kwehn-tah deh hoo-bee-lah-see-'ohn een-dee-vee-doo-'ahl)*
joint account	**la cuenta conjunta** *(lah 'kwehn-tah kohn-'hoon-tah)*
lease	**el arrendamiento** *(ehl ahr-rehn-dah-mee-'ehn-toh)*
loan	**el préstamo** *(ehl 'prehs-tah-moh)*
loan officer	**el/la agente de préstamos** *(ehl/lah ah-'hehn-teh deh 'prehs-tah-mohs)*
loan servicer	**el administrador/la administradora de préstamos** *(ehl ahd-mee-nees-trah-'dohr/lah ahd-mee-nees-trah-'doh-rah deh 'prehs-tah-mohs)*
maturity date	**la fecha de vencimento** *(lah 'feh-chah deh vehn-see-mee-'ehn-toh)*
money order	**el giro postal** *(ehl 'hee-roh pohs-'tahl)*
mortgage	**la hipoteca** *(lah ee-poh-'teh-kah)*
notary	**el notario** *(ehl noh-'tah-ree-oh)*
online banking	**la banca en línea** *(lah 'bahn-kah ehn 'lee-neh-ah)*
overdraw	**el sobregiro** *(ehl soh-breh-'hee-roh)*
payroll deduction	**la deducción de nómina** *(lah deh-dook-see-'ohn deh 'noh-mee-nah)*
pin number	**número de identificación personal (NIP)** *(ehl 'noo-meh-roh deh ee-dehn-tee-fee-kah-see-'ohn pehr-so-'nahl)*

points	**los puntos hipotecarios** *(lohs 'poon-tohs ee-poh-teh-'kah-ree-ohs)*
power of attorney	**el poder notarial** *(ehl poh-'dehr noh-tah-ree-'ahl)*
rate	**la tasa** *(lah 'tah-sah)*
real estate	**los bienes raíces** *(lohs bee-'eh-nehs rah-'ee-sehs)*
real estate agent	**el/la agente de bienes raíces** *(ehl/lah ah-'hehn-teh deh bee-'eh-nehs rah-'ee-sehs)*
refinance	**el refinanciamiento** *(ehl reh-fee-nahn-see-ah-mee-'ehn-toh)*
registration	**el registro** *(ehl reh-'hees-troh)*
reward	**la recompensa** *(lah reh-kohm-'pehn-sah)*
savings	**los ahorros** *(lohs ah-'ohr-rohs)*
savings account	**la cuenta de ahorros** *(lah 'kwehn-tah deh ah-'ohr-rohs)*
statement	**el estado de cuenta** *(ehl ehs-'tah-doh deh 'kwehn-tah)*
tax	**el impuesto** *(ehl eem-'pwehs-toh)*
teller	**el cajero/la cajera** *(ehl kah-'heh-roh/lah kah-'heh-rah)*
terms	**los términos** *(lohs 'tehr-mee-nohs)*
transfer	**la transferencia** *(lah trahns-feh-'rehn-see-ah)*
wire transfer	**la transferencia electrónica** *(lah trahns-feh-'rehn-see-ah eh-lehk-'troh-nee-kah)*
withdrawal	**el retiro** *(ehl reh-'tee-roh)*

Did they help you with...?	**¿Le ayudaron con...?** *(leh ah-yoo-'dah-rohn kohn)*
financial planning	**la planificación financiera** *(lah plah-nee-fee-kah-see-'ohn fee-nahn-see-'eh-rah)*
money management	**el manejo de las finanzas** *(ehl mah-'neh-hoh deh lahs fee-'nahn-sahs)*
financial services	**los servicios financieros** *(lohs sehr-'vee-see-ohs fee-nahn-see-'eh-rohs)*

Is it...?	**¿Es...?** *(ehs)*
a fiscal year	**un año financiero** *(oon 'ahn-yoh fee-nahn-see-'eh-roh)*
bimonthly	**cada dos meses** *('kah-dah dohs 'meh-sehs)*
quarterly	**cada tres meses** *('kah-dah trehs 'meh-sehs)*
long-term	**a largo plazo** *(ah 'lahr-goh 'plah-soh)*
semi-annual	**semianual** *(she-mee-ah-'nwahl)*
short-term	**a corto plazo** *(a 'kohr-toh 'plah-soh)*

Is it...?	**¿Está... ? Es...?** *(ehs-'tah...ehs)*
accrued	**acumulado** *(ah-koo-moo-'lah-doh)*
active	**activo** *(ahk-'tee-voh)*
conventional	**convencional** *(kohn-vehn-see-oh-'nahl)*
eligible	**elegible** *(eh-leh-'hee-bleh)*
fixed	**fijo** *('fee-hoh)*
prepaid	**prepagado** *(preh-pah-'gah-doh)*
variable	**variable** *(vah-ree-'ah-bleh)*

What's the...?	¿Cuál es...? *(kwahl ehs)*
adjustment	**el ajuste** *(ehl ah-'hoos-teh)*
appreciation	**la revalorización** *(lah reh-vah-loh-ree-sah-see-'ohn)*
APR	**la tasa de interés annual** *(lah 'tah-sah deh een-teh-'rehs ahn-'wahl)*
cycle	**el ciclo** *(ehl 'see-kloh)*
estimate	**el estimado** *(ehl ehs-tee-'mah-doh)*
expiration date	**la fecha de vencimiento** *(lah 'feh-chah deh vehn-see-mee-'ehn-toh)*
figure	**la cifra** *(lah 'see-frah)*
growth	**el crecimiento** *(ehl kreh-see-mee-'ehn-toh)*
index	**el índice** *(ehl 'een-dee-seh)*
limit	**el límite** *(ehl 'lee-mee-teh)*
market value	**el valor de mercado** *(ehl vah-'lohr deh mehr-'kah-doh)*
penalty	**la multa** *(lah 'mool-tah)*
percentage	**el porcentaje** *(ehl pohr-sehn-'tah-heh)*
regulation	**el reglamento** *(ehl reh-glah-'mehn-toh)*
requirement	**el requisito** *(ehl reh-kee-'see-toh)*
term	**el término** *(ehl 'tehr-mee-noh)*
yield	**el rendimiento** *(ehl rehn-dee-mee-'ehn-toh)*

Do you have (the)...?	¿Tiene usted...? *(tee-'eh-neh oos-'tehd)*
appraisal	**el avalúo** *(ehl ah-vah-'loo-oh)*
appreciation	**la apreciación** *(lah ah-preh-see-ah-see-'ohn)*
capital	**el capital** *(ehl kah-pee-'tahl)*
cash flow	**el flujo de efectivo** *(ehl 'floo-hoh deh eh-fehk-'tee-voh)*
collateral	**el colateral** *(ehl koh-lah-teh-'rahl)*
grant	**la beca** *(lah 'beh-kah)*
lien	**el embargo** *(ehl ehm-'bahr-goh)*
liquidity	**la liquidez** *(lah lee-kee-'dehs)*
portfolio	**los valores en cartera** *(lohs vah-'loh-rehs ehn kahr-'teh-rah)*
securities	**los valores** *(lohs vah-'loh-rehs)*

NOTICE!   ¡Fíjese!

The topic of **los impuestos** *(lohs eem-'pwehs-tohs)* is unavoidable when it comes to finances and the law:

We'll help you with...	Le ayudamos con... *(leh ah-yoo-'dah-mohs kohn)*
deferred taxes	**los impuestos diferidos** *(lohs eem-'pwehs-tohs dee-feh-'ree-dohs)*
federal income tax	**el impuesto de ingresos federal** *(ehl eem-'pwehs-toh deh een-'greh-sohs feh-deh-'rahl)*
gross income	**los ingresos brutos** *(lohs een-'greh-sohs 'broo-tohs)*
net income	**los ingresos netos** *(lohs een-'greh-sohs 'neh-tohs)*

state income tax	**el impuesto de ingresos estatal**
	(ehl eem-'pwehs-toh deh een-'greh-sohs ehs-tah-'tahl)
tax return (check)	**la devolución de los impuestos**
	(lah deh-voh-loo-see-'ohn deh lohs eem-'pwehs-tohs)
tax return (forms)	**la declaración de ingresos**
	(lah deh-klah-rah-see-'ohn deh een-'greh-sohs)
tax shelter	**la protección contra los impuestos**
	(lah proh-tehk-see-'ohn 'kohn-trah los eem-'pwehs-tohs)
withholding tax	**la retención de impuestos**
	(lah reh-tehn-see-'ohn deh eem-'pwehs-tohs)

Do you understand (the)...?	**¿Entiende...?** *(ehn-tee-'ehn-deh)*
tax allowance	**el descuento impositivo**
	(ehl dehs-'kwehn-toh eem-poh-see-'tee-voh)
tax bracket	**el grupo impositivo** *(ehl 'groo-poh eem-poh-see-'tee-voh)*
tax code	**el código impositivo**
	(ehl 'koh-dee-goh eem-poh-see-'tee-voh)
tax collection	**la recaudación de impuestos**
	(lah reh-kah-oo-dah-see-'ohn deh eem-'pwehs-tohs)
tax cuts	**las reducciones en los impuestos**
	(lahs reh-dook-see-'oh-nehs ehn lohs eem-'pwehs-tohs)
tax evasion	**la evasión fiscal** *(lah eh-vah-see-'ohn fees-'kahl)*
tax exemption	**la exención de impuestos**
	(lah ex-ehn-see-'ohn deh eem-'pwehs-tohs)

PRIVATE PRACTICE **Práctica privada**

(34) A. Name five professionals who work in the world of finance:

_____

B. Connect the words that belong together:

1. el cambio	**el formulario**
2. el pedido	**las monedas**
3. la solicitud	**la factura**

C. Fill in the blanks as you translate each phrase into Spanish:

1. interest rates	**la _____ de interés**
2. saving account	**la cuenta de _____**
3. down payment	**el _____ adelantado**
4. credit card	**la _____ de crédito**
5. real estate	**los bienes _____**

D. What is the opposite?

el retiro　　　　　<u>el depósito</u>

1. a largo plazo　　　_____

2. fijo　　　　　　　_____

3. caro　　　　　　　_____

 CULTURAL COMMENT　**Comentario cultural**

You don't need to translate all the names of businesses, brands, streets, or professional titles. Nor do you have to change your name to Spanish in order to communicate. All over the world, most formal titles in English remain the same.

FINANCIAL AND LEGAL ASSISTANCE
El auxilio financiero y la ayuda jurídica
*(ehl ah-oo-'xee-lee-oh fee-nahn-see-'eh-roh
ee lah ah-'yoo-dah hoo-'ree-dee-kah)*

Once you identify the financial issue of concern, tell the client what you intend to do:

We work with cases of...	**Trabajamos con casos de...**
	(trah-bah-'hah-mohs kohn 'kah-sohs deh)
extortion	**extorsión** *(ex-tohr-see-'ohn)*
forgery	**falsificación** *(fahl-see-fee-kah-see-'ohn)*
fraud	**fraude** *('frah-oo-deh)*
harassment	**acosamiento** *(ah-koh-sah-mee-'ehn-toh)*
identity theft	**robo de identidad** *('roh-boh deh ee-dehn-tee-'dahd)*
laundering	**blanqueo de dinero** *(blahn-'keh-oh deh dee-'neh-roh)*

We help you with (the)...	**Le ayudamos con...** *(leh ah-yoo-'dah-mohs kohn)*
bad checks	**los cheques fraudulentos** *(lohs 'cheh-kehs frah-oo-doo-'lehn-tohs)*
balance due	**el saldo deudor** *(ehl 'sahl-doh deh-oo-'dohr)*
debt consolidation	**la consolidación de deudas** *(lah kohn-soh-lee-dah-see-'ohn deh 'deh-oo-dahs)*
eviction	**el desalojo** *(ehl deh-sah-'loh-hoh)*
foreclosure	**el juicio hipotecario** *(ehl hoo-'ee-see-oh ee-poh-teh-'kah-ree-oh)*
insufficient funds	**los fondos insuficientes** *(lohs 'fohn-dohs een-soo-fee-see-'ehn-tehs)*

loan modification	**la modificación del préstamo** *(lah moh-dee-fee-kah-see-'ohn dehl 'prehs-tah-moh)*
refinancing	**refinanciación** *(reh-fee-nahn-see-ah-see-'ohn)*
undeclared taxes	**los impuestos no declarados** *(lohs eem-'pwehs-tohs noh deh-klah-'rah-dohs)*
unpaid bills	**las cuentas no pagadas** *(lahs 'kwehn-tahs noh pah-'gah-dahs)*
wage garnishment	**el embargo de salario** *(ehl ehm-'bahr-goh deh sah-'lah-ree-oh)*

We examine (the)...	**Examinamos...** *(ex-ah-mee-'nanh-mohs)*
audit	**la auditoría** *(lah aw-dee-toh-'ree-ah)*
cause	**la causa** *(lah 'kah-oo-sah)*
debt	**la deuda** *(lah 'deh-oo-dah)*
delay	**la tardanza** *(lah tahr-'dahn-sah)*
error	**el error** *(ehl ehr-'rohr)*
fee	**la comisión** *(lah koh-mee-see-'ohn)*
liability	**la obligación** *(lah oh-blee-gah-see-'ohn)*
loss	**la pérdida** *(lah 'pehr-dee-dah)*
penalty	**la penalidad** *(lah peh-nah-lee-'dahd)*
reduction	**la reducción** *(lah reh-dook-see-'ohn)*

We check (the)...	**Revisamos...** *(reh-vee-'sah-mohs)*
agreement	**el acuerdo** *(ehl ah-'kwehr-doh)*
court orders	**los mandatos judiciales** *(lohs mahn-'dah-tohs hoo-dee-see-'ah-lehs)*
contracts	**los contratos** *(lohs kohnm-'trah-tohs)*
copies	**las copias** *(lahs 'koh-pee-ahs)*
instructions	**las instrucciones** *(lahs eens-trook-see-'oh-nehs)*
options	**las opciones** *(lahs ohp-see-'oh-nehs)*
original	**el original** *(ehl oh-ree-hee-'nahl)*
petitions	**las peticiones** *(lahs peh-tee-see-'oh-nehs)*
regulations	**los reglamentos** *(lohs reh-glah-'mehn-tohs)*
recommendations	**las recomendaciones** *(lahs reh-koh-mehn-dah-see-'oh-nehs)*
requirements	**los requisitos** *(lohs reh-kee-'see-tohs)*
responses	**las respuestas** *(lahs rehs-'pwehs-tahs)*
threatening letters	**las cartas de amenaza** *(lahs 'kahr-tahs kohn ah-meh-'nah-sah)*

We are familiar with...	**Estamos familiarizados con...** *(ehs-'tah-mohs fah-mee-lee-ah-ree-'sah-dohs kohn)*
disability income insurance	**el seguro de ingresos por incapacidad** *(ehl seh-'goo-roh deh een-'greh-sohs pohr een-kah-pah-see-'dahd)*

unemployment benefits	**los beneficios del seguro de desempleo** *(lohs beh-neh-'fee-see-ohs dehl seh-'goo-roh deh deh-sehm-'pleh-oh)*
workers' compensation	**la compensación laboral** *(lah kohm-pehn-sah-see-'ohn lah-boh-'rahl)*

Return to the pattern of asking related sets of questions. Again, practice by reading aloud:

How much is (the)...	**¿Cuánto es...?** *('kwahn-toh ehs)*
amount	**el monto** *(ehl 'mohn-toh)*
total	**el total** *(ehl toh-'tahl)*
sum	**la suma** *(lah 'soo-mah)*
Are they...?	**¿Están...?** *(ehs-'tahn)*
invested	**invertidos** *(een-vehr-'tee-dohs)*
purchased	**comprados** *(kohm-'prah-dohs)*
sold	**vendidos** *(vehn-'dee-dohs)*
Were they...?	**¿Estaban...?** *(ehs-'tah-bahn)*
rented	**alquilados** *(ahl-kee-'lah-dohs)*
leased	**arrendados** *(ahr-rehn-'dah-dohs)*
loaned	**prestados** *(prehs-'tah-dohs)*
Is it...?	**¿Es...?** *(ehs)*
mandated	**ordenado** *(ohr-deh-'nah-doh)*
recommended	**recomendado** *(reh-koh-mehn-'dah-doh)*
required	**obligatorio** *(oh-blee-gah-'toh-ree-oh)*
Will it be...?	**¿Será...?** *(seh-'rah)*
cancelled	**cancelado** *(kahn-seh-'lah-doh)*
null and void	**nulo y sin efecto** *('noo-loh ee seen eh-'fehk-toh)*
worthless	**sin valor** *(seen vah-lohr)*
Has it been...?	**¿Ha sido...?** *(ah 'see-doh)*
accepted	**aceptado** *(ah-sehp-'tah-doh)*
anticipated	**anticipado** *(ahn-tee-see-'pah-doh)*
proposed	**propuesto** *(proh-'pwehs-toh)*
Would it be...?	**¿Sería...?** *(seh-'ree-ah)*
payable	**pagadero** *(pah-gah-'deh-roh)*
accrued	**acumulado** *(ah-koo-moo-'lah-doh)*
matured	**pagadero** *(pah-gah-'deh-roh)*

NOTICE! ¡Fíjese!

Note the similarities here:

cancellation	**la cancelación** *(lah kahn-seh-lah-see-'ohn)*
compensation	**la compensación** *(lah kohm-pehn-sah-see-'ohn)*
deduction	**la deducción** *(lah deh-dook-see-'ohn)*
extension	**la extensión** *(lah ex-tehn-see-'ohn)*
legalization	**la legalización** *(lah leh-gah-lee-sah-see-'ohn)*
motion	**la moción** *(lah moh-see-'ohn)*
negociation	**la negociación** *(lah neh-goh-see-ah-see-'ohn)*
participation	**la participación** *(lah pahr-tee-see-pah-see-'ohn)*
possession	**la posesión** *(lah poh-seh-see-'ohn)*
regulation	**la regulación** *(lah reh-goo-lah-see'ohn)*

PROBATE
La validación testamentaria
(lah vah-lee-dah-see-'ohn tehs-tah-mehn-'tah-ree-ah)

Picture a scenario where the following phrases would be used in a probate case. You picked up some of these terms before:

Would you like to discuss (the)...?	**¿Quisiera hablar de...?** *(kee-see-'eh-rah ah-'blahr deh)*
allocation	**la asignación** *(lah ah-seeg-nah-see-'ohn)*
assets	**los bienes** *(lohs bee-'eh-nehs)*
back taxes	**los impuestos atrasados** *(lohs eem-'pwehs-tohs ah-trah-'sah-dohs)*
burial	**el entierro** *(ehl ehn-tee-'ehr-roh)*
charity	**la caridad** *(lah kah-ree-'dahd)*
death certificate	**el certificado de defunción** *(ehl sehr-tee-fee-'kah-doh deh deh-foon-see-'ohn)*
debt amount	**el monto de deuda** *(ehl 'mohn-toh deh 'deh-oo-dah)*
distribution	**la distribución** *(lah dees-tree-boo-see-'ohn)*
donation	**la donación** *(lah doh-nah-see-'ohn)*
estate planning	**la planificación de bienes** *(lah plah-nee-fee-kah-see-'ohn deh bee-'eh-nehs)*
expenses	**los gastos de sucesión** *(lohs 'gahs-tohs deh soo-seh-see-'ohn)*
forms and instructions	**los formularios y las instrucciones** *(lohs fohr-moo-'lah-ree-ohs ee lahs soo-seh-see-'oh-nehs)*
funeral arrangements	**los arreglos funerarios** *(lohs ahr-'reh-glohs foo-neh-'rah-ree-ohs)*
inheritance	**la herencia** *(lah eh-'rehn-see-ah)*
inventory	**el inventario** *(ehl een-vehn-'tah-ree-oh)*

joint property	**la propiedad conjunta**
	(lah proh-pee-eh-'dahd kohn-'hoon-tah)
living trust	**el fideicomiso activo**
	(ehl fee-deh-ee-koh-'mee-soh ahk-'tee-voh)
living will	**el testamento en vida**
	(ehl tehs-tah-'mehn-toh ehn 'vee-dah)
probate court	**el tribunal testamentario**
	(ehl tree-boo-'nahl tehs-tah-mehn-'tah-ree-oh)
procedures	**los trámites** *(lohs 'trah-mee-tehs)*
property	**la propiedad** *(lah proh-pee-eh-'dahd)*
sale	**la venta** *(lah 'vehn-tah)*
state law	**la ley estatal** *(lah 'leh-ee ehs-tah-'tahl)*
transfer	**el traspaso** *(ehl trahs-'pah-soh)*
trust	**el fideicomiso** *(ehl fee-deh-ee-koh-'mee-soh)*
will	**el testamento** *(ehl tehs-tah-'mehn-toh)*
Who is the...?	**¿Quién es...?** *(kee-'ehn ehs)*
administrator	**el administrador/la administradora**
	(ehl ahd-mee-nees-trah-'dohr/lah ahd-mee-nees-trah-'doh-rah)
author	**el autor/la autora** *(ehl aw-'tohr/lah aw-'toh-rah)*
beneficiary	**el beneficiario/la beneficiaria**
	(ehl beh-neh-fee-see-'ah-ree-oh/lah beh-neh-fee-see-'ah-ree-ah)
biological child	**el hijo biológico** *(ehl 'ee-hoh bee-oh-'loh-hee-koh)*
blood relative	**el familiar consanguíneo**
	(fah-mee-lee-'ahr kohn-sahn-'ghee-neh-oh)
clergyman	**el clérigo/la clériga** *(ehl 'kleh-ree-goh/lah 'kleh-ree-gah)*
custodian	**el/la custodio** *(ehl/lah koos-'toh-dee-oh)*
deceased	**el difunto/la difunta** *(ehl dee-'foon-toh/lah dee-foon-tah)*
descendent	**el/la descendiente** *(ehl/lah dehs-sehn-dee-'ehn-teh)*
executor	**el/la albacea** *(ehl/lah ahl-bah-'seh-ah)*
expert witness	**el testigo pericial** *(ehl tehs-'tee-goh peh-ree-see-'ahl)*
family member	**el miembro de la familia**
	(ehl mee-'ehm-broh deh lah fah-'mee-lee-ah)
guardian	**el tutor/la tutora** *(ehl too-'tohr/lah too-'toh-rah)*
inheritor	**el heredero/la heredera**
	(ehl eh-reh-'deh-roh/lah eh-reh-'deh-rah)
minor	**el/la menor de edad** *(ehl/lah meh-'nohr deh eh-'dahd)*
next of kin	**el pariente más cercano**
	(ehl pah-ree-'ehn-teh mahs sehr-'kah-noh)
notary	**el notario/la notaria**
	(ehl noh-'tah-ree-oh/lah noh-'tah-ree-ah)
owner	**el propietario/la propietaria**
	(ehl proh-pee-eh-'tah-ree-oh/lah proh-pee-eh-'tah-ree-ah)
parent	**el padre/la madre** *(ehl 'pah-dreh/lah 'mah-dreh)*
partner	**el socio/la socia** *(ehl 'soh-see-oh/lah 'soh-see-ah)*

personal representative	**el/la representante personal** *(ehl/lah reh-preh-sehn-ˈtahn-teh pehr-soh-ˈnahl)*
sibling	**el hermano/la hermana** *(ehl ehr-ˈmah-noh/lah ehr-ˈmah-nah)*
testator	**el testador/la testadora** *(ehl tehs-tah-ˈdohr/lah tehs-tah-ˈdoh-rah)*
third party	**la tercera parte** *(lah tehr-ˈseh-rah ˈpahr-teh)*

In any legal argument, there are at least two parties who don't see eye to eye. Use these words to describe the issue at hand:

What do you know about (the)...?	**¿Qué sabe usted de...?** *(keh ˈsah-beh oos-ˈtehd deh)*
conflict	**el conflicto** *(ehl kohn-ˈfleek-toh)*
debate	**el debate** *(ehl deh-ˈbah-teh)*
deliberation	**la deliberación** *(lah deh-lee-beh-rah-see-ˈohn)*
differences	**las diferencias** *(lahs dee-fee-ˈrehn-see-ahs)*
disagreement	**el desacuerdo** *(ehl deh-sah-ˈkwehr-doh)*
discrepancy	**la discrepancía** *(lah dees-kreh-ˈpahn-see-ah)*
disparity	**la disparidad** *(lah dees-pah-ree-ˈdahd)*
dispute	**la disputa** *(lah dees-ˈpoo-tah)*
fight	**la pelea** *(lah peh-ˈleh-ah)*
legal battle	**el pleito jurídico** *(ehl ˈpleh-ee-toh hoo-ˈree-dee-koh)*
quarrel	**la discusión** *(lah dees-koo-see-ˈohn)*
Is it...?	**¿Es/Está...?** *(ehs/ehs-ˈtah)*
annulled	**anulado** *(ah-noo-ˈlah-doh)*
bequeathed	**legado** *(leh-ˈgah-doh)*
cancelled	**cancelado** *(kahn-seh-ˈlah-doh)*
declared	**declarado** *(deh-klah-ˈrah-doh)*
detailed	**detallado** *(deh-tah-ˈyah-doh)*
doubtful	**dudoso** *(doo-ˈdoh-soh)*
forged	**falsificado** *(fahl-see-fee-ˈkah-doh)*
legal	**legal** *(leh-ˈgahl)*
legitimate	**legítimo** *(leh-ˈhee-tee-moh)*
modified	**modificado** *(moh-dee-fee-ˈkah-doh)*
notarized	**notarizado** *(noh-tah-ree-ˈsah-doh)*
sealed	**sellado** *(seh-ˈyah-doh)*
signed	**firmado** *(feer-ˈmah-doh)*
stipulated	**estipulado** *(ehs-tee-poo-ˈlah-doh)*
written	**escrito** *(ehs-ˈkree-toh)*

OPPOSITE MEANINGS
Significados opuestos
(seeg-nee-fee-'kah-dohs oh-'pwehs-tohs)

Learning two words with opposite meanings will make memorizing a lot easier.

simple	**sencillo** *(sehn-'see-yoh)*
complicated	**complicado** *(kohm-plee-'kah-doh)*
included	**incluido** *(een-kloo-'ee-doh)*
excluded	**excluido** *(ex-kloo-'ee-doh)*
valid	**válido** *('vah-le-doh)*
invalid	**inválido** *(een-'vah-lee-doh)*
surviving	**sobreviviente** *(soh-breh-vee-vee-'ehn-teh)*
deceased	**fallecido** *(fah-yeh-'see-doh)*
clear	**claro** *('klah-roh)*
confusing	**confuso** *(kohn-'foo-soh)*

PRIVATE PRACTICE   Práctica privada

(35) A. Underline the one word in each group that doesn't belong with the others:

1. la carta, la extorsión, el fraude, el robo
2. el total, la suma, el monto, el socio
3. alquilados, jurados, arrendados, prestados

B. Fill in the missing letters as you translate:

1. assets   **los b _____ s**

2. trust   **el f _____ o**

3. will   **el t _____ o**

BUSINESS-RELATED VOCABULARY
Vocabulario relacionado con comercio
(voh-kah-boo-'lah-ree-oh reh-lah-see-oh-'nah-doh kohn koh-'mehr-see-oh)

Since our focus is finance, spend some time working on terminology linked to business and corporate law.

Is it a...?	¿Es un/una...? *(eh soon/'oo-nah)*
business	**negocio** *(neh-'goh-see-oh)*
corporation	**sociedad mercantil** *(soh-see-eh-'dahd mehr-kahn-'teel)*
family business	**empresa familiar** *(ehm-'preh-sah fah-mee-lee-'ahr)*
limited liability corporation	**sociedad de responsabilidad limitada** *(soh-see-eh-'dahd deh rehs-pohn-sah-bee-lee-'dahd lee-mee-'tah-dah)*
major company	**gran empresa** *(grahn ehm-'preh-sah)*
nonprofit organization	**oganización sin fines lucrativos** *(ohr-gah-nee-sah-see-'ohn seen 'fee-nehs loo-krah-'tee-vohs)*
small business	**pequeña empresa** *(peh-'kehn-yah ehm-'preh-sah)*
sole proprietorship	**empresa de propiedad individual** *(ehm-'preh-sah deh proh-pee-eh-'dahd een-dee-vee-doo-'ahl)*

Is it ...?	¿Es ...? *(ehs)*
domestic	**nacional** *(nah-see-oh-'nahl)*
foreign	**extranjero** *(ex-trahn-'heh-roh)*
global	**mundial** *(moon-dee-'ahl)*
interim	**provisional** *(proh-vee-see-oh-'nahl)*
international	**internacional** *(een-tehr-nah-see-oh-'nahl)*
interstate	**interestatal** *(een-tehr-ehs-tah-'tahl)*
local	**local** *(loh-kahl)*
national	**nacional** *(nah-see-oh-'nahl)*
private	**privado** *(pre-'vah-doh)*
public	**público** *('poob-lee-koh)*
seasonal	**estacional** *(ehs-tah-see-oh-'nahl)*

Do you (pl.) work with...?	¿Trabajan con...? *(trah-'bah-hahn kohn)*
commerce	**el comercio** *(ehl koh-'mehr-see-oh)*
deliveries	**las entregas** *(lahs ehn-'treh-gahs)*
goods	**los bienes** *(lohs bee-'eh-nehs)*
inventory	**las existencias** *(lahs ex-ees-'tehn-see-ahs)*
merchandise	**las mercancías** *(lahs mehr-kahn-'see-ahs)*
products	**los productos** *(lohs proh-'dook-tohs)*
raw materials	**las materias primas** *(lahs mah-'teh-ree-ahs 'pree-mahs)*
services	**los servicios** *(lohs sehr-'vee-see-ohs)*
shipments	**los envíos** *(lohs ehn-'vee-ohs)*
stock	**las reservas** *(lahs reh-'sehr-vahs)*
supplies	**los suministros** *(lohs soo-mee-'nees-trohs)*
surplus	**el exceso** *(ehl ex-'seh-soh)*

Are you going...?	**¿Va a ...?** *(vah ah)*
to arrange	**arreglar** *(ahr-reh-'glahr)*
to build	**construir** *(kohns-troo-'eer)*
to buy	**comprar** *(kohm-'prahr)*
to develop	**desarrollar** *(deh-sahr-roh-'yahr)*
to install	**instalar** *(eens-tah-'lahr)*
to invest	**invertir** *(een-vehr-'teer)*
to lease	**arrendar** *(ahr-rehn-'dahr)*
to make	**hacer** *(ah-sehr)*
to manage	**manejar** *(mah-neh-'hahr)*
to offer	**ofrecer** *(oh-freh-'sehr)*
to prepare	**preparar** *(preh-pah-'rahr)*
to produce	**producir** *(proh-doo-'seer)*
to provide	**proveer** *(proh-veh-'ehr)*
to repair	**reparar** *(reh-pah-'rahr)*
to sell	**vender** *(vehn-'dehr)*
to send	**enviar** *(ehn-vee-'ahr)*

Many legal matters are based on the sales of products or services. Study these questions:

What was (the)...?	**¿Cuál fue...?** *(kwahl foo-'eh)*
balance	**el saldo** *(ehl 'sahl-doh)*
charge	**el cargo** *(ehl 'kahr-goh)*
cost	**el costo** *(ehl 'kohs-toh)*
deposit	**el depósito** *(ehl deh-'poh-see-toh)*
down payment	**el pago inicial** *(ehl 'pah-goh ee-nee-see-'ahl)*
payment	**el pago** *(ehl 'pah-goh)*
price	**el precio** *(ehl 'preh-see-oh)*
tax	**el impuesto** *(ehl eem-'pwehs-toh)*

Do you understand (the)...?	**¿Entiende...?** *(ehn-tee-'ehn-deh)*
bargain	**la ganga** *(lah 'gahn-gah)*
discount	**el descuento** *(ehl dehs-'kwehn-toh)*
guarantee	**la garantía** *(lah gah-rahn-'tee-ah)*
installment	**el plazo** *(ehl 'plah-soh)*
offer	**la oferta** *(lah oh-'fehr-tah)*
purchase	**la compra** *(lah 'kohm-prah)*
rebate	**la rebaja** *(lah reh-'bah-hah)*
refund	**el reembolso** *(ehl reh-ehm-'bohl-soh)*
sale	**la venta** *(lah 'vehn-tah)*

Do you know (the) ...?	**¿Sabe...?** *('sah-beh)*
average	**el promedio** *(ehl proh-'meh-dee-oh)*
comparison	**la comparación** *(lah kohm-pah-rah-see-'ohn)*
index	**el índice** *(ehl 'een-dee-seh)*

level	**el nivel** *(ehl nee-'vehl)*
loss	**la pérdida** *(lah 'pehr-dee-dah)*
margin	**el margen** *(ehl 'mahr-hehn)*
maximum	**el máximo** *(ehl 'mahk-see-moh)*
minimum	**el mínimo** *(ehl 'mee-nee-moh)*
percentage	**el porcentaje** *(ehl pohr-sehn-'tah-heh)*
profit	**la ganancia** *(lah gah-'nahn-see-ah)*
quota	**la cuota** *(lah koo-'oh-tah)*
rate	**la tasa** *(lah 'tah-sah)*
ratio	**la proporción** *(lah proh-pohr-see-'ohn)*
reduction	**la reducción** *(lah reh-dook-see-'ohn)*
return	**la devolución** *(lah deh-voh-loo-see-'ohn)*
value	**el valor** *(ehl vah-'lohr)*
variance	**la variación** *(lah vah-ree-ah-see-'ohn)*
yield	**el rédito** *(ehl 'reh-dee-toh)*
Was it ...?	**¿Fue...?** *(foo-'eh)*
delayed	**retrasado** *(reh-trah-'sah-doh)*
duty free	**libre de derechos** *('lee-breh deh deh-'reh-chohs)*
exported	**exportado** *(ex-pohr-'tah-doh)*
free	**gratuito** *(grah-too-'ee-toh)*
imported	**importado** *(eem-pohr-'tah-doh)*
included	**incluido** *(een-kloo-'ee-doh)*
overdue	**vencido** *(vehn-'see-doh)*
paid	**pagado** *(pah-'gah-doh)*
repossessed	**recobrado** *(reh-koh-'brah-doh)*
used	**usado** *(oo-'sah-doh)*
voided	**cancelado** *(kahn-seh-'lah-doh)*
Did it include (the)...?	**¿Incluyó...?** *(een-kloo-'yoh)*
delivery	**la entrega** *(lah ehn-'treh-gah)*
express mail	**el correo expreso** *(ehl kohr-'reh-oh ex-'preh-soh)*
handling	**los gastos de tramitación**
	(lohs 'gahs-tohs deh trah-mee-tah-see-'ohn)
packaging	**el empaque** *(ehl ehm-'pah-keh)*
service	**el servicio** *(ehl sehr-'vee-see-oh)*
shipping	**el envío** *(ehl ehn-'vee-oh)*

Use verbs in both the present and the past tenses:

How much...?	**¿Cuánto ...?** *('kwahn-toh)*
does it cost	**cuesta** *('kwehs-tah)*
did you pay	**pagó** *(pah-'goh)*
is it worth	**vale** *('vah-leh)*

PRIVATE PRACTICE   **Práctica privada**

(36) A. Translate and read aloud:

Tengo una empresa familiar. Es un negocio local y trabajamos con varios productos y servicios.

B. Follow the example and answer the questions with the correct verb form:

¿Producen Uds.?	**Sí, producimos.**
1. **¿Venden Uds.?**	_____
2. **¿Instalan Uds.?**	_____
3. **¿Compran Uds.?**	_____
4. **¿Construyen Uds.?**	_____
5. **¿Invierten Uds.?**	_____

C. Link the words that belong together:

1. **compra**	**costo**
2. **precio**	**envío**
3. **ganga**	**descuento**
4. **proporción**	**venta**
5. **correo**	**porcentaje**

REAL ESTATE
Los bienes raíces
(lohs bee-'eh-nehs rah-'ee-sehs)

Take on this next selection when the legal case deals with real estate law:

Do you own (the)...?   **¿Es usted propietario/propietaria de...?**
(ehs oos-'tehd proh-pee-eh-'tah-ree-oh/proh-pee-eh-'tah-ree-ah deh)

apartment	**el apartamento** *(ehl ah-pahr-tah-'mehn-toh)*
building	**el edificio** *(ehl eh-dee-'fee-see-oh)*
business	**la empresa** *(lah ehm-'preh-sah)*
condominium	**el condominio** *(ehl kohn-doh-'mee-nee-oh)*
duplex	**el dúplex** *(ehl 'doo-plex)*
estate	**la finca** *(lah 'feen-kah)*
farm	**la granja** *(lah 'grahn-hah)*
hotel	**el hotel** *(ehl oh-'tehl)*
house	**la casa** *(lah 'kah-sah)*
land	**el terreno** *(ehl tehr-'reh-noh)*
mobile home	**la casa rodante** *(lah 'kah-sah roh-'dahn-teh)*

property	**la propiedad** *(lah proh-pee-eh-'dahd)*
ranch	**el rancho** *(ehl 'rahn-choh)*
residence	**el domicilio** *(ehl doh-mee-'see-lee-oh)*
shopping center	**el centro comercial** *(ehl 'sehn-troh koh-mehr-see-'ahl)*

Are you (the)...?	**¿Es usted ...?** *(ehs oos-'tehd)*
agent	**el/la agente** *(ehl/lah ah-'hehn-teh)*
appraiser	**el tasador/la tasadora** *(ehl tah-sah-'dohr/lah tah-sah-'doh-rah)*
banker	**el banquero/la banquera** *(ehl bahn-'keh-roh/lah bahn-'keh-rah)*
borrower	**el prestatario/la prestataria** *(ehl prehs-tah-'tah-ree-oh/lah prehs-tah-'tah-ree-ah)*
broker	**el corredor/la corredora** *(ehl kohr-reh-'dohr/lah kohr-reh-'doh-rah)*
buyer	**el comprador/la compradora** *(ehl kohm-prah-'dohr/lah kohm-prah-'doh-rah)*
contractor	**el/la contratista** *(ehl/lah kohn-trah-'tees-tah)*
developer	**el urbanizador/la urbanizadora** *(ehl oor-bah-nee-sah-'dohr/lah oor-bah-nee-sah-'doh-rah)*
inspector	**el inspector/la inspectora** *(ehl eens-pehk-'tohr/lah eens-pehk-'toh-rah)*
lender	**el/la prestamista** *(ehl/lah prehs-tah-'mees-tah)*
lessee	**el arrendatario/la arrendataria** *(ehl ahr-rehn-dah-'tah-ree-oh/lah ahr-rehn-dah-'tah-ree-ah)*
lessor	**el arrendador/la arrendadora** *(ehl ahr-rehn-dah-'dohr/lah ahr-rehn-dah-'doh-rah)*
manager	**el/la gerente** *(ehl/lah heh-'rehn-teh)*
owner	**el propietario/la propietaria** *(ehl proh-pee-eh-'tah-ree-oh/lah proh-pee-eh-'tah-ree-ah)*
resident	**el/la residente** *(ehl/lah reh-see-'dehn-teh)*
salesperson	**el vendedor/la vendedora** *(ehl vehn-deh-'dohr/lah vehn-deh-'doh-rah)*
tenant	**el inquilino/la inquilina** *(ehl een-kee-'lee-noh/lah een-kee-'lee-nah)*
trustee	**el fiduciario/la fiduciaria** *(ehl fee-doo-see-'ah-ree-oh/lah fee-doo-see-'ah-ree-ah)*

Are there problems with (the)...?	**¿Hay problemas con...?** *('ah-ee proh-'bleh-mahs kohn)*
appraisal	**el avalúo** *(ehl ah-vah-'loo-oh)*
building code	**las normas de construcción** *(lahs 'nohr-mahs deh kohns-trook-see-'ohn)*
certificate	**el certificado** *(ehl sehr-tee-fee-'kah-doh)*
closing	**el cierre** *(ehl see-'ehr-reh)*
credit company	**la entidad crediticia** *(lah ehn-tee-'dahd kreh-dee-'tee-see-ah)*

credit report	**el informe de crédito** *(ehl een-'fohr-meh deh 'kreh-dee-toh)*
credit score	**el puntaje de crédito** *(ehl poon-'tah-heh deh 'kreh-dee-toh)*
deed	**la escritura** *(lah ehs-kree-'too-rah)*
equity	**la equidad** *(lah eh-kee-'dahd)*
escrow	**la plica** *(lah 'plee-kah)*
estimate	**el cálculo** *(ehl 'kahl-koo-loh)*
financing	**la financiación** *(lah fee-nahn-see-ah-see-'ohn)*
improvement	**la mejora** *(lah meh-'hoh-rah)*
insurance	**el seguro** *(ehl seh-'goo-roh)*
interest	**el interés** *(ehl een-teh-'rehs)*
lease	**el arrendamiento** *(ehl ahr-rehn-dah-mee-'ehn-toh)*
loan	**el préstamo** *(ehl 'prehs-tah-moh)*
monthly payments	**los pagos mensuales** *(lohs 'pah-gohs mehn-soo-'ah-lehs)*
payment	**el pago** *(ehl 'pah-goh)*
permit	**el permiso** *(ehl pehr-'mee-soh)*
points	**los puntos** *(lohs 'poon-tohs)*
policy	**la póliza** *(lah 'poh-see-sah)*
price	**el precio** *(ehl 'preh-see-oh)*
promissory note	**el pagaré** *(ehl pah-gah-'reh)*
proposal	**la propuesta** *(lah proh-'pwehs-tah)*
recording	**el registro** *(ehl reh-'hees-troh)*
rent	**el alquiler** *(ehl ahl-kee-'lehr)*
security deposit	**el depósito de garantía** *(ehl deh-'poh-see-toh deh gah-rahn-'tee-ah)*
taxes	**los impuestos** *(lohs eem-'pwehs-tohs)*
title	**el título** *(ehl 'tee-too-loh)*
W-2 forms	**los formularios W-2** *(lohs fohr-moo-'lah-ree-ohs 'doh-bleh veh dohs)*

Do you understand (the)...?	**¿Entiende ...?** *(ehn-tee-'ehn-deh)*
approval	**la aprobación** *(lah ah-proh-bah-see-'ohn)*
assessment	**la tasación** *(lah tah-sah-see-'ohn)*
balloon payment	**el pago mayor** *(ehl 'pah-goh mah-'yohr)*
capital gains	**la ganancia de capital** *(lah gah-'nahn-see-ah deh kah-pee-'tahl)*
charges	**los cargos** *(lohs 'kahr-gohs)*
claim	**el reclamo** *(ehl reh-'klah-moh)*
clause	**la cláusula** *(lah 'klah-oo-soo-lah)*
commission	**la comisión** *(lah koh-mee-see-'ohn)*
compound interest	**el interés compuesto** *(ehl een-teh-'rehs kohm-'pwehs-toh)*
counteroffer	**la contraoferta** *(lah kohn-trah-oh-'fehr-tah)*
default	**el incumplimiento** *(ehl een-koom-plee-mee-'ehn-toh)*
fee	**el honorario** *(ehl oh-noh-'rah-ree-oh)*
government program	**el programa gubernamental** *(ehl proh-'grah-mah goo-behr-nah-mehn-'tahl)*

guarantee	**la garantía** *(lah gah-rahn-'tee-ah)*
investment	**la inversión** *(lah een-vehr-see-'ohn)*
jumbo loan	**el préstamo jumbo** *(ehl 'prehs-tah-moh 'hoom-boh)*
lien	**el gravamen** *(ehl grah-'vah-mehn)*
market price	**el precio de mercado**
	(ehl 'preh-see-oh deh mehr-'kah-doh)
offer	**la oferta** *(lah oh-'fehr-tah)*
options	**las opciones** *(lahs ohp-see-'oh-nehs)*
prime rate	**la tasa de interés preferencial**
	(lah 'tah-sah deh een-teh-'rehs preh-feh-rehn-see-'ahl)
rating	**la clasificación** *(lah klah-see-fee-kah-see-'ohn)*
restrictions	**las restricciones** *(lahs rehs-treek-see-'oh-nehs)*
ruling	**la resolución** *(lah reh-soh-loo-see-'ohn)*
statement	**la declaración** *(lah deh-klah-rah-see-'ohn)*
terms	**los términos** *(lohs 'tehr-mee-nohs)*
transfer	**el traspaso** *(ehl trahs-'pah-soh)*
Have you heard of...?	**¿Ha escuchado de...?** *(ah ehs-koo-'chah-doh deh)*
easement	**el derecho de vía** *(ehl deh-'reh-choh deh 'vee-ah)*
eminent domain	**el dominio eminente**
	(ehl doh-'mee-nee-oh eh-mee-'nehn-teh)
misrepresentation	**la representación fraudulenta**
	(lah reh-preh-sehn-tah-see-'ohn frah-oo-doo-'lehn-tah)
price fixing	**la fijación de precios**
	(lah fee-hah-see-'ohn deh 'preh-see-ohs)
variance	**la variación** *(lah vah-ree-ah-see-'ohn)*
It's called...	**Se llama...** *(seh 'yah-mah)*
amoritization	**la amortización** *(lah ah-mohr-tee-sah-see-'ohn)*
appreciation	**la apreciación** *(lah ah-preh-see-ah-see-'ohn)*
depreciation	**la depreciación** *(lah deh-preh-see-ah-see-'ohn)*

NOTICE! ¡Fíjese!

Often, more Spanish words are required to translate its English equivalent:

home equity loan
el préstamo sobre la equidad de una vivienda
(ehl 'prehs-tah-moh 'soh-breh lah eh-kee-'dahd deh 'oo-nah vee-vee-'ehn-dah)

homeowners insurance policy
la póliza de seguro para propietarios de vivienda
(lah 'poh-lee-sah deh seh-'goo-roh 'pah-rah proh-pee-eh-'tah-ree-ohs deh vee-vee-'ehn-dah)

title insurance
el seguro contra defectos en títulos de propiedad
(ehl seh-'goo-roh 'kohn-trah deh-'fehk-tohs ehn 'tee-too-lohs deh proh-pee-eh-'dahd)

LANDLORD AND TENANT PROBLEMS
Problemas entre propietario e inquilino
(proh-'bleh-mahs 'ehn-treh proh-pee-eh-'tah-ree-oh eh een-kee-'lee-noh)

For owners as well as tenants, there are several basic words that relate to areas of legal concern. Use each one in a complete sentence:

Do you live at (the)...?	**¿Vive usted en...?** *('vee-veh oos-'tehd ehn)*
apartment building	**el edificio de apartamentos** *(ehl eh-dee-'fee-see-oh deh ah-pahr-tah-'mehn-tohs)*
hotel	**el hotel** *(ehl oh-'tehl)*
house	**la casa** *(lah 'kah-sah)*
motel	**el motel** *(ehl moh-'tehl)*
rest home	**el hogar de ancianos** *(ehl oh-'gahr deh ahn-see-'ah-nohs)*
student housing	**la vivienda universitaria** *(lah vee-vee-'ehn-dah oo-nee-vehr-see-'tah-ree-ah)*
Which is (the)...?	**¿Cuál es...?** *(kwahl ehs)*
floor	**el piso** *(ehl 'pee-soh)*
apartment	**el apartamento** *(ehl ah-pahr-tah-'mehn-toh)*
room	**el cuarto** *(ehl 'kwahr-toh)*
Are there problems with (the)...?	**¿Hay problemas con...?** *('ah-ee proh-'bleh-mahs kohn)*
contract	**el contrato** *(ehl kohn-'trah-toh)*
deposit	**el depósito** *(ehl deh-'poh-see-toh)*
landlord	**el propietario** *(ehl proh-pee-eh-'tah-ree-oh)*
lease	**el arrendamiento** *(ehl ahr-rehn-dah-mee-'ehn-toh)*
rent	**el alquiler** *(ehl ahl-kee-lehr)*
tenants	**los inquilinos** *(lohs een-kee-'lee-nohs)*
Does it have to do with (the)...?	**¿Tiene que ver con...?** *(tee-'eh-neh keh vehr kohn)*
deterioration	**el deterioro** *(ehl deh-teh-ree-'oh-roh)*
discrimination	**la discriminación** *(lah dees-kree-mee-nah-see-'ohn)*
eviction notice	**el aviso de desalojo** *(ehl ah-'vee-soh deh deh-sah-'loh-hoh)*
location	**la ubicación** *(lah oo-bee-kah-see-'ohn)*
mold	**el moho** *(ehl 'moh-hoh)*
noise	**el ruido** *(ehl roo-'ee-doh)*
parking	**el estacionamiento** *(ehl ehs-tah-see-oh-nah-mee-'ehn-toh)*
pests	**las plagas** *(lahs 'plah-gahs)*
pets	**los animals domésticos** *(lohs ah-nee-'mah-lehs doh-'mehs-tee-kohs)*
sewage	**el desagüe** *(ehl dehs-'ah-gweh)*
smell	**el olor** *(ehl oh-'lohr)*
trash	**la basura** *(lah bah-'soo-rah)*

utilities	**los servicios públicos** *(lohs sehr-'vee-see-ohs 'poo-blee-kohs)*
view	**la vista** *(lah 'vees-tah)*

Is there a lack of...?	**¿Hay falta de...?** *('ah-ee 'fahl-tah deh)*
care	**cuidado** *(koo-ee-'dah-doh)*
cleaning	**limpieza** *(leem-pee-'eh-sah)*
light	**luz** *(loos)*
privacy	**privacidad** *(pree-vah-see-'dahd)*
reparation	**reparación** *(reh-pah-rah-see-'ohn)*
security	**seguridad** *(seh-goo-ree-'dahd)*
service	**servicio** *(sehr-'vee-see-oh)*
trash containers	**basureros** *(bah-soo-'reh-rohs)*

What happened to (the)...?	**¿Qué pasó con...?** *(keh pah-'soh kohn)*
air conditioning	**el aire acondicionado** *(ehl 'ah-ee-reh ah-kohn-dee-see-oh-'nah-doh)*
carpet	**la alfombra** *(lah ahl-'fohm-brah)*
electricity	**la electricidad** *(lah eh-lehk-tree-see-'dahd)*
elevator	**el ascensor** *(ehl ah-sehn-'sohr)*
foundation	**los cimientos** *(lohs see-mee-'ehn-tohs)*
furniture	**los muebles** *(lohs 'mweh-blehs)*
gate	**el portón** *(ehl pohr-'tohn)*
gym	**el gimnasio** *(ehl heem-'nah-see-oh)*
heating	**la calefacción** *(lah kah-leh-fahk-see-'ohn)*
paint	**la pintura** *(lah peen-'too-rah)*
plumbing	**las tuberías** *(lahs too-beh-'ree-ahs)*
pool	**la piscina** *(lah pees-'see-nah)*
roof	**el techo** *(ehl 'teh-choh)*
ventilation	**la ventilación** *(lah vehn-tee-lah-see-'ohn)*
windows	**las ventanas** *(lahs vehn-'tah-nahs)*

Do you know (the)...?	**¿Sabe...?** *('sah-beh)*
rules	**las reglas** *(lahs 'reh-glahs)*
codes	**los códigos** *(lohs 'koh-dee-gohs)*
law	**la ley** *(lah 'leh-ee)*

Is it...?	**¿Es...?** *(ehs)*
exclusive	**exclusivo** *(ex-kloo-'see-voh)*
guaranteed	**garantizado** *(gah-rahn-tee-'sah-doh)*
habitable	**habitable** *(ah-bee-'tah-bleh)*
legitimate	**legítimo** *(leh-'hee-tee-moh)*
private	**privado** *(pree-'vah-doh)*
residential	**residencial** *(reh-see-dehn-see-'ahl)*
sanitary	**sanitario** *(sah-nee-'tah-ree-oh)*

Is it...?	**¿Está...?** *(ehs-'tah)*
broken	**roto** *('roh-toh)*
dangerous	**peligroso** *(peh-lee-'groh-soh)*
dirty	**sucio** *('soo-see-oh)*
lost	**perdido** *(pehr-'dee-doh)*
old	**viejo** *(vee-'eh-hoh)*
overdue	**vencido** *(vehn-'see-doh)*
replaced	**cambiado** *(kahm-bee-'ah-doh)*

You/He/She cannot...	**No puede...** *(noh 'pweh-deh)*
abuse	**abusar** *(ah-boo-'sahr)*
allow	**permitir** *(pehr-mee-'teer)*
avoid	**evitar** *(eh-vee-'tahr)*
bother	**molestar** *(moh-lehs-'tahr)*
cut	**cortar** *(kohr-'tahr)*
discriminate	**discriminar** *(dees-kree-mee-'nahr)*
enter	**entrar** *(ehn-'trahr)*
evict	**desahuciar** *(dehs-ah-oo-see-'ahr)*
forget about	**olvidarse de** *(ohl-vee-'dahr-seh deh)*
harass	**acosar** *(ah-koh-'sahr)*
impound	**embargar** *(ehm-bahr-'gahr)*
increase	**aumentar** *(ah-oo-mehn-'tahr)*
keep	**guardar** *(gwahr-'dahr)*
leave	**salir** *(sah-'leer)*
limit	**limitar** *(lee-mee-'tahr)*
lose	**perder** *(pehr-'dehr)*
move	**mover** *(moh-'vehr)*
punish	**castigar** *(kahs-tee-'gahr)*
reduce	**reducir** *(reh-doo-'seer)*
refuse	**rechazar** *(reh-chah-'sahr)*
remove	**quitar** *(kee-'tahr)*
surrender	**entregar** *(ehn-treh-'gahr)*
withhold	**retirar** *(reh-tee-'rahr)*

You/He/She needs to...	**Necesita...** *(neh-seh-'see-tah)*
advise	**avisar** *(ah-vee-'sahr)*
call	**llamar** *(yah-'mahr)*
complain	**quejarse** *(keh-'hahr-seh)*
comply with	**cumplir con** *(koom-'pleer kohn)*
demand	**exigir** *(ex-ee-'heer)*
demonstrate	**demostrar** *(deh-mohs-'trahr)*
document	**documentar** *(doh-koo-mehn-'tahr)*
fight	**luchar** *(loo-'chahr)*
fix	**reparar** *(reh-pah-'rahr)*
improve	**mejorar** *(meh-oh-'rahr)*
join	**unirse** *(oo-'neer-seh)*

maintain	**mantener** *(mahn-teh-'nehr)*
move away	**mudarse** *(moo-'dahr-seh)*
pressure	**presionar** *(preh-see-oh-'nahr)*
protect	**proteger** *(proh-teh-'hehr)*
renovate	**renovar** *(reh-noh-'vahr)*
request	**pedir** *(peh-'deer)*
respect	**respetar** *(rehs-peh-'tahr)*
take pictures	**tomar fotos** *(toh-'mahr 'foh-tohs)*
turn in	**entregar** *(ehn-treh-'gahr)*

NOTICE! ¡Fíjese!

Name a few domestic animals that may cause concerns on the rental property:

bird	**el pájaro** *(ehl 'pah-hah-roh)*
cat	**el gato** *(ehl 'gah-toh)*
dog	**el perro** *(ehl 'pehr-roh)*
lizard	**la lagartija** *(lah lah-gahr-'tee-hah)*
mouse	**el ratón** *(ehl rah-'tohn)*
rat	**la rata** *(lah 'rah-tah)*
snake	**la culebra** *(lah koo-'leh-brah)*

PRIVATE PRACTICE Práctica privada

(37) A. Answer these questions:

¿Cuál es la diferencia entre el avalúo y el precio?
¿Cuál es la diferencia entre el arrendamiento y el alquiler?
¿Cuál es la diferencia entre los puntos y los pagos de hipoteca?

B. Connect the vocabulary words that are closely related:

1. propietario	privado
2. ruido	piso
3. tuberías	inquilino
4. techo	olor
5. exclusivo	electricidad

C. Fill in the missing word as you translate each of the following:

1. eviction notice	**el aviso de** _____
2. security deposit	**el depósito de** _____
3. home equity	**la** _____ **de una vivienda**

MORE INSURANCE INFORMATION
Más información sobre seguros
(mahs een-fohr-mah-see-'ohn 'soh-breh seh-'goo-rohs)

Is it _____ insurance?	**¿Es seguro _____?** *(ehs seh-'goo-roh)*
accident	**de accidentes** *(deh ahk-see-'dehn-tehs)*
accidental death	**de muerte accidental** *(deh 'mwehr-teh ahk-see-dehn-'tahl)*
auto	**de carro** *(deh 'kahr-roh)*
bodily injury	**de lesiones corporales** *(deh leh-see-'oh-nehs kohr-poh-'rah-lehs)*
business	**para el negocio** *('pah-rah ehl neh-'goh-see-oh)*
collision	**de choques** *(deh 'choh-kehs)*
dental	**dental** *(dehn-'tahl)*
disability	**de incapacidad** *(deh een-kah-pah-see-'dahd)*
endowment	**de póliza dotal** *(deh 'poh-lee-sah doh-'tahl)*
fire	**de incendio** *(deh een-'sehn-dee-oh)*
group	**de grupo** *(deh 'groo-poh)*
health	**de salud** *(deh sah-'lood)*
individual	**individual** *(een-dee-vee-doo-'ahl)*
liability	**de responsabilidad civil** *(deh rehs-pohn-sah-bee-lee-'dahd see-'veel)*
life	**de vida** *(deh 'vee-dah)*
long-term care	**de cuidado a largo plazo** *(deh koo-ee-'dah-doh ah 'lahr-goh 'plah-soh)*
medical	**médico** *('meh-dee-koh)*
mortgage	**hipotecario** *(ee-poh-teh-'kah-ree-oh)*
unemployment	**de desempleo** *(deh deh-sehm-'pleh-oh)*
vision	**de la vista** *(deh lah 'vees-tah)*

Are there problems with (the)...?	**¿Hay problemas con...?** *('ah-ee proh-'bleh-mahs kohn)*
adjustment	**el ajuste** *(ehl ah-'hoos-teh)*
annuity	**la anualidad** *(lah ah-noo-ah-lee-'dahd)*
benefits	**los beneficios** *(lohs beh-neh-'fee-see-ohs)*
binder	**la cobertura provisional** *(lah koh-behr-'too-rah proh-vee-see-oh-'nahl)*
claim	**el reclamo** *(ehl reh-'klah-moh)*
clause	**la cláusula** *(lah 'klah-oo-soo-lah)*
cost	**el costo** *(ehl 'kohs-toh)*
coverage	**la cobertura** *(lah koh-behr-'too-rah)*
disclosure	**la revelación** *(lah reh-veh-lah-see-'ohn)*
medical exam	**el examen médico** *(ehl ex-'ah-mehn 'meh-dee-koh)*
notice	**el aviso** *(ehl ah-'vee-soh)*
plan	**el plan** *(ehl plahn)*
policy	**la póliza** *(lah 'poh-lee-sah)*

premium	**la prima** *(lah 'pree-mah)*
public records	**los archivos públicos**
	(lohs ahr-'chee-vohs 'poo-blee-kohs)
rates	**las tarifas** *(lahs tah-'ree-fahs)*
report	**el informe** *(ehl een-'fohr-meh)*
rider	**la cláusula adicional**
	(lah 'klah-oo-soo-lah ah-dee-see-oh-'nahl)
service	**el servicio** *(ehl sehr-'vee-see-oh)*
standards	**las normas** *(lahs 'nohr-mahs)*
waiver	**la renuncia** *(lah reh-'noon-see-ah)*

Do you understand (the)...?	**¿Entiende...?** *(ehn-tee-'ehn-deh)*
compensation	**la indemnización** *(lah een-dehm-nee-sah-see-'ohn)*
conditions	**las condiciones** *(lahs kohn-dee-see-'oh-nehs)*
duration	**la duración** *(lah doo-rah-see-'ohn)*
exclusions	**las exclusiones** *(lahs ex-kloo-see-'oh-nehs)*
expiration	**el vencimiento** *(ehl vehn-see-mee-'ehn-toh)*
loss	**la pérdida** *(lah 'pehr-dee-dah)*
maximum	**el máximo** *(ehl 'mahk-see-moh)*
minimum	**el mínimo** *(ehl 'mee-nee-moh)*
provision	**la estipulación** *(lah ehs-tee-poo-lah-see-'ohn)*
rating	**la clasificación** *(lah klah-see-fee-kah-see-'ohn)*
reduction	**la dismunición** *(lah dees-mee-noo-see-'ohn)*
requirements	**los requisitos** *(lohs reh-kee-'see-tohs)*
risk	**el riesgo** *(ehl ree-'ehs-goh)*
terms	**los términos** *(lohs 'tehr-mee-nohs)*
value	**el valor** *(ehl vah-'lohr)*
waiting period	**el período de espera**
	(ehl peh-'ree-oh-doh deh ehs-'peh-rah)

Did you talk to (the)...?	**¿Habló con...?** *(ah-'bloh kohn)*
administrator	**el administrador/la administradora**
	(ehl ahd-mee-nees-trah-dohr/lah ahd-mee-nees-trah-'doh-rah)
agent	**el/la agente** *(ehl/lah ah-'hehn-teh)*
assignor	**el/la cedente** *(ehl/lah seh-'dehn-teh)*
beneficiary	**el beneficiario/la beneficiaria**
	(ehl beh-neh-fee-see-'ah-ree-oh/lah beh-neh-fee-see-'ah-ree-ah)
broker	**el corredor/la corredora**
	(ehl kohr-reh-'dohr/lah kohr-reh-'doh-rah)
claimant	**el/la reclamante** *(ehl/lah reh-klah-'mahn-teh)*
dependent	**el dependiente/la dependienta**
	(ehl deh-pehn-dee-'ehn-teh/lah deh-pehn-dee-'ehn-tah)
doctor	**el médico/la médica**
	(ehl 'meh-dee-koh/lah 'meh-dee-kah)

employee	**el empleado/la empleada** *(ehl ehm-pleh-'ah-doh/lah ehm-pleh-'ah-dah)*
examiner	**el examinador/la examinadora** *(ehl ex-ah-mee-nah- 'dohr/lah ex-ah-mee-nah-'doh-rah)*
fiduciary	**el fiduciario/la fiduciaria** *(ehl fee-doo-see-'ah-ree-oh/lah fee-doo-see-'ah-ree-ah)*
insurance company	**la compañía de seguros** *(lah kohm-pahn-'ee-ah deh seh-'goo-rohs)*
insured	**la persona asegurada** *(lah pehr-'soh-nah ah-seh-goo-'rah-dah)*
insurer	**el asegurador/la aseguradora** *(ehl ah-seh-goo-rah-'dohr/lah ah-seh-goo-rah-'doh-rah)*
owner	**el propietario/la propietaria** *(ehl proh-pee-eh-'tah-ree-oh/lah proh-pee-eh-'tah-ree-ah)*
payor	**el pagador/la pagadora** *(ehl pah-gah-'dohr/lah pah-gah-'doh-rah)*
provider	**el proveedor/la proveedora** *(ehl proh-veh-eh-'dohr/lah proh-veh-eh-'doh-rah)*
representative	**el/la representante** *(ehl/lah reh-preh-sehn-'tahn-teh)*
victim	**la víctima** *(lah 'veek-tee-mah)*

Short one-liners can be effective when you need to make a comment. Say them aloud:

The policy is...	**La póliza es/está...** *(lah 'poh-lee-sah ehs/ehs-'tah)*
comprehensive	**amplia** *('ahm-plee-ah)*
conditional	**condicional** *(kohn-dee-see-oh-'nahl)*
current	**actual** *(ahk-too-'ahl)*
deductible	**deducible** *(deh-doo-'see-bleh)*
deferred	**diferida** *(dee-feh-'ree-dah)*
fixed	**fija** *('fee-hah)*
immediate	**inmediata** *(een-meh-dee-'ah-tah)*
in force	**en fuerza** *(ehn foo-'ehr-sah)*
joint	**mancomunada** *(mahn-koh-moo-'nah-dah)*
modified	**modificada** *(moh-dee-fee-'kah-dah)*
mutual	**mutua** *('moo-too-ah)*
partial	**parcial** *(pahr-see-'ahl)*
renewable	**renovable** *(reh-noh-'vah-bleh)*
term life	**de vida a término** *(deh 'vee-dah ah 'tehr-mee-noh)*
variable	**variable** *(vah-ree-'ah-bleh)*
void	**nula** *('noo-lah)*
whole life	**de vida completa** *(deh 'vee-dah kohm-'pleh-tah)*

NOTICE!   ¡Fíjese!

Discrimination can be identified in a variety of ways:

It was...   **Fue...** *(foo-'eh)*

age	**la edad** *(lah eh-'dahd)*
disability	**la incapacidad** *(lah een-kah-pah-see-'dahd)*
ethnicity	**la etnia** *(lah 'eht-nee-ah)*
illness	**la enfermedad** *(lah ehn-fehr-meh-'dahd)*
race	**la raza** *(lah 'rah-sah)*
religion	**la religión** *(lah reh-lee-hee-'ohn)*
sex	**el sexo** *(ehl 'sehk-soh)*
sexual orientation	**la orientación sexual**
	(lah oh-ree-ehn-tah-see-'ohn sehk-soo-ahl)
weight	**el peso** *(ehl 'peh-soh)*

PRIVATE PRACTICE   **Práctica privada**

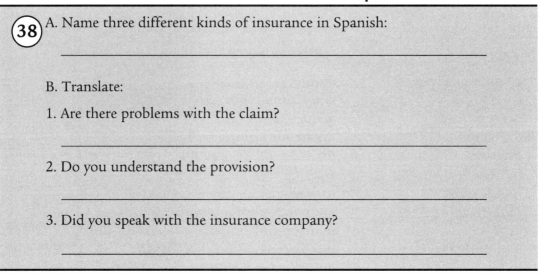

(38) A. Name three different kinds of insurance in Spanish:

_____

B. Translate:

1. Are there problems with the claim?

_____

2. Do you understand the provision?

_____

3. Did you speak with the insurance company?

_____

VERBS IN ACTION!   **¡Verbos activos!**

All kinds of new verbs are required when the topic is banking. Many of these look similar to English:

Do you want...?   **¿Quiere...?** *(kee-'eh-reh)*

to accrue	**acumular** *(ah-koo-moo-'lahr)*
to acquire	**adquirir** *(ahd-kee-'reer)*
to add	**añadir** *(ah-nyah-'deer)*
to adjust	**ajustar** *(ah-hoos-'tahr)*

to approve	**aprobar** *(ah-proh-'bahr)*
to authorize	**autorizar** *(aw-toh-ree-'sahr)*
to borrow	**pedir prestado** *(peh-'deer prehs-'tah-doh)*
to buy	**comprar** *(kohm-'prahr)*
to calculate	**calcular** *(kahl-koo-'lahr)*
to cancel	**cancelar** *(kahn-seh-'lahr)*
to charge	**cargar** *(kahr-'gahr)*
to check	**revisar** *(reh-vee-'sahr)*
to claim	**reclamar** *(reh-klah-'mahr)*
to close	**cerrar** *(sehr-'rahr)*
to collect	**cobrar** *(koh-'brahr)*
to contribute	**contribuir** *(kohn-tree-boo-'eer)*
to count	**contar** *(kohn-'tahr)*
to cover	**cubrir** *(koo-'breer)*
to deliver	**entregar** *(ehn-treh-'gahr)*
to deposit	**depositar** *(deh-poh-see-'tahr)*
to distribute	**distribuir** *(dees-tree-boo-'eer)*
to diversify	**diversificar** *(dee-vehr-see-fee-'kahr)*
to earn	**ganar** *(gah-'nahr)*
to enroll	**matricularse** *(mah-tree-koo-'lahr-seh)*
to exchange	**cambiar** *(kahm-bee-'ahr)*
to expire	**vencer** *(vehn-'sehr)*
to grow	**crecer** *(kreh-'sehr)*
to invest	**invertir** *(een-vehr-'teer)*
to join	**juntar** *(hoon-'tahr)*
to lease	**arrendar** *(ahr-rehn-'dahr)*
to loan	**prestar** *(prehs-'tahr)*
to lose	**perder** *(pehr-'dehr)*
to notify	**notificar** *(noh-tee-fee-'kahr)*
to open	**abrir** *(ah-'breer)*
to pay	**pagar** *(pah-'gahr)*
to prepare	**preparar** *(preh-pah-'rahr)*
to put away	**guardar** *(gwahr-'dahr)*
to put in	**meter** *(meh-'tehr)*
to receive	**recibir** *(reh-see-'beer)*
to rent	**alquilar** *(ahl-kee-'lahr)*
to save	**ahorrar** *(ah-ohr-'rahr)*
to sell	**vender** *(vehn-'dehr)*
to share	**compartir** *(kohm-pahr-'teer)*
to spend	**gastar** *(gahs-'tahr)*
to take away	**quitar** *(kee-'tahr)*
to transfer	**transferir** *(trahns-feh-'reer)*
to verify	**verificar** *(veh-ree-fee-'kahr)*
to withdraw	**sacar** *(sah-'kahr)*

VERBS IN ACTION! ¡Verbos activos!

When the action takes place changes the meaning of each sentence:

BASIC VERB: TO WORK   **Trabajar** *(trah-bah-'hahr)*

RIGHT NOW: I'm working.
                   Estoy trabajando. *(eh-'stoh-ee trah-bah-'hahn-doh)*

EVERY DAY: I work.
                   Trabajo. *(trah-'bah-hoh)*

TOMORROW: I'm going to work.
                   Voy a trabajar. *('voh-ee ah trah-bah-'hahr)*

Now let's take a look at ways to express past actions in Spanish. The two primary tenses are called the *preterit* and the *imperfect*. Read the following examples of the *preterit* tense and, just as you did previously, make the changes to your verbs:

I worked with the client.
Trabajé con el cliente. *(trah-bah-'heh kohn ehl klee-'ehn-teh)*

You (sing.), He, She worked a lot.
Trabajó mucho. *(trah-bah-'hoh 'moo-choh)*

You (pl.), They worked here.
Trabajaron aquí. *(trah-bah-'hah-rohn ah-'kee)*

We worked all day.
Trabajamos todo el día. *(trah-bah-'hah-mohs 'toh-doh ehl 'dee-ah)*

And here's what happens to regular verbs ending in **-er** or **-ir** (e.g., **SALIR**):

I left at 5:00.   **Salí a las cinco.** *(sah-'lee ah lahs 'seen-koh)*
You (sing.), He, She left late.   **Salió tarde.** *(sah-lee-'oh 'tahr-deh)*
You (pl.), They left early.   **Salieron temprano.**
                                    (sah-lee-'eh-rohn tehm-'prah-noh)
We left on Friday.   **Salimos el viernes.**
                                    (sah-'lee-mohs ehl vee-'ehr-nehs)

Unfortunately, some verbs have irregular past tenses in the *preterit*. These three are pretty common and should be practiced first:

TO GO	**Ir** *(eer)*	
I went	**Fui** *(foo-'ee)*	**Fui a la oficina.**
You (sing.), He, She went	**Fue** *(foo-'eh)*	_____
You (pl.), They went	**Fueron** *(foo-'eh-rohn)*	_____
We went	**Fuimos** *(foo-'ee-mohs)*	_____

TO HAVE	**Tener** *(teh-'nehr)*	
I had	**Tuve** *('too-veh)*	**Tuve un problema.**
You (sing.), He, She had	**Tuvo** *('too-voh)*	_____
You (pl.), They had	**Tuvieron** *(too-vee-'eh-rohn)*	_____
We had	**Tuvimos** *(too-'vee-mohs)*	_____

TO SAY	**Decir** *(deh-'seer)*	
I said	**Dije** *('dee-heh)*	**Dije la verdad.**
You (sing.), He, She said	**Dijo** *('dee-hoh)*	_____
You (pl.), They said	**Dijeron** *(dee-'heh-rohn)*	_____
We said	**Dijimos** *(dee-'hee-mohs)*	_____

However, the *imperfect* tense is very common also. Notice how it generally implies that someone *was doing* or *used to do* an action:

-AR verbs	
TO BUY	**Comprar** *(kohm-'prahr)*
I, You (sing.), He, She used to buy	**compraba** *(kohm-'prah-bah)*
You (pl.), They used to buy	**compraban** *(kohm-'prah-bahn)*
We used to buy	**comprábamos** *(kohm-'prah-bah-mohs)*

We used to buy stocks.
Comprábamos las acciones. *(kohm-'prah-bah-mohs lahs ahk-see-'oh-nehs)*

-ER and -IR verbs

TO SELL	Vender *(vehn-'dehr)*
I, You (sing.), He, She was selling	vendía *(vehn-'dee-ah)*
You (pl.), They were selling	vendían *(vehn-'dee-ahn)*
We were selling	vendíamos *(vehn-'dee-ah-mohs)*

She was selling her house.
Vendía su casa. *(vehn-'dee-ah soo 'kah-sah)*

NOTICE! ¡Fíjese!

There are only three irregular verbs in the *imperfect* tense: **SER** (*to be*), **VER** (*to see*), and **IR** (*to go*):

TO BE	Ser *(sehr)*
I was, You (sing.) were, He, She was	era *('eh-rah)*
You (pl.), They were	eran *('eh-rahn)*
We were	éramos *('eh-rah-mohs)*

TO SEE	Ver *(vehr)*
I, You (sing.), He, She saw	veía *(veh-'ee-ah)*
You (pl.), They saw	veían *(veh-'ee-ahn)*
We saw	veíamos *(veh-'ee-ah-mohs)*

TO GO	Ir *(eer)*
I, You (sing.), He, She went	iba *('ee-bah)*
You (pl.), They went	iban *('ee-bahn)*
We went	íbamos *('ee-bah-mohs)*

PRIVATE PRACTICE **Práctica privada**

39 A. Answer these questions in the affirmative. The first one is done for you:

1. ¿Lo sacó?   **Sí, lo saqué.**

2. ¿Lo prestó?   _____

3. ¿Lo gastó?   _____

4. ¿Lo canceló?   _____

5. ¿Lo cambió?   _____

B. Change these sentences from the Present tense to the Imperfect tense:

1.
I have credit cards.   **Tengo tarjetas de crédito.**
I used to have credit cards. **Tenía tarjetas de crédito.**

2.
He speaks with the bank.   **Habla con el banco.**

He was speaking with the bank. _____

3.
They sell car insurance.   **Venden el seguro de carro.**

They were selling auto insurance. _____

Chapter Six

Criminal Law
La ley penal
(lah 'leh-ee peh-'nahl)

To guide the Spanish-speaking client through each phase of the case will require an interpreter, but the following words and phrases will help you set up meetings and start communicating:

Come on this date.
Venga en esta fecha. *('vehn-gah ehn 'ehs-tah 'feh-chah)*

It's a very important meeting.
Es una reunión muy importante.
(ehs 'oo-nah reh-oo-nee-'ohn 'moo-ee eem-pohr-'tahn-teh)

You must be there.
Tiene que asistir. *(tee-'eh-neh keh ah-sees-'teer)*

Take a seat.
Tome asiento. *('toh-meh ah-see-'ehn-toh)*

Thank you for coming.
Gracias por venir. *('grah-see-ahs pohr veh-'neer)*

Pay close attention.
Preste mucha atención. *(prehs-teh 'moo-cha ah-tehn-see-'ohn)*

This is the latest information.
Esta es la información más reciente.
(ehs-tah ehs lah een-foh-mah-see-'ohn mahs reh-see-'ehn-teh)

Please read the report.
Lea el informe, por favor. *('leh-ah ehl een-'fohr-meh pohr fah-'vohr)*

Do you have any questions?
¿Tiene alguna pregunta? *(tee-'eh-neh ahl-'goo-nah preh-'goon-tah)*

Choose what you need from these key phrases:

Have you seen (the) ...?	¿Ha visto ...? *(ah 'vees-toh)*
announcement	**el anuncio** *(ehl ah-'noon-see-oh)*
changes	**los cambios** *(lohs 'kahm-bee-ohs)*
data	**los datos** *(lohs 'dah-tohs)*
disk	**el disco** *(ehl 'dees-koh)*
document	**el documento** *(ehl doh-koo-'mehn-toh)*
e-mail	**el correo electrónico** *(ehl kohr-'reh-oh eh-lehk-'troh-nee-koh)*
facts	**los hechos** *(lohs 'eh-chohs)*
figures	**las cifras** *(lahs 'see-frahs)*
letter	**la carta** *(lah 'kahr-tah)*
list	**la lista** *(lah 'lees-tah)*
mail	**el correo** *(ehl kohr-'reh-oh)*
memo	**el memorándum** *(ehl meh-moh-'rahn-doom)*
message	**el mensaje** *(ehl mehn-'sah-heh)*
notice	**la noticia** *(lah noh-'tee-see-ah)*
page	**la página** *(lah 'pah-hee-nah)*
pamphlet	**el folleto** *(ehl foh-'yeh-toh)*
photo	**la foto** *(lah 'foh-toh)*
report	**el informe** *(ehl een-'fohr-meh)*
results	**los resultados** *(lohs reh-sool-'tah-dohs)*
schedule	**el horario** *(ehl oh-'rah-ree-oh)*
sheet	**la hoja** *(lah 'oh-hah)*
sign	**el letrero** *(ehl leh-'treh-roh)*
text	**el texto** *(ehl 'tehks-toh)*

I'm going to...	Voy a... *('voh-ee ah)*
analyze	**analizar** *(ah-nah-lee-'sahr)*
clarify	**aclarar** *(ah-klah-'rahr)*
confirm	**confirmar** *(kohn-feer-'mahr)*
evaluate	**evaluar** *(eh-vah-loo-'ahr)*
explain	**explicar** *(ex-plee-'kahr)*
identify	**identificar** *(ee-dehn-tee-fee-'kahr)*
respond	**contestar** *(kohn-tehs-'tahr)*
suggest	**sugerir** *(soo-heh-'reer)*

Now use the following words to share your thoughts about the latest information:

I think it's...	Pienso que es... *(pee-'ehn-soh keh ehs)*
acceptable	**aceptable** *(ah-sehp-'tah-bleh)*
appropriate	**apropiado** *(ah-proh-pee-'ah-doh)*
better	**mejor** *(meh-'hohr)*
correct	**correcto** *(kohr-'rehk-toh)*
normal	**normal** *(nohr-'mahl)*
typical	**típico** *('tee-pee-koh)*

I don't believe it's...   **No creo que es...** *(noh 'kreh-oh keh ehs)*

    incorrect   **incorrecto** *(een-kohr-'reh-ktoh)*

    rare   **raro** *('rah-roh)*

    terrible   **terrible** *(tehr-'ree-bleh)*

    unacceptable   **inaceptable** *(ee-nah-sehp-'tah-bleh)*

    worse   **peor** *(peh-'ohr)*

    wrong   **mal** *(mahl)*

I'd like to hear (the)...   **Quisiera escuchar...** *(kee-see-'eh-rah ehs-koo-'chahr)*

    comment   **el comentario** *(ehl koh-mehn-'tah-ree-oh)*

    idea   **la idea** *(lah ee-'deh-ah)*

    interpretation   **la intrepetación** *(lah een-tehr-preh-tah-see-'ohn)*

    opinion   **la opinión** *(lah oh-pee-nee-'ohn)*

    question   **la pregunta** *(lah preh-'goon-tah)*

    reaction   **la reacción** *(lah reh-ahk-see-'ohn)*

    response   **la respuesta** *(lah rehs-'pwehs-tah)*

    thought   **el pensamiento** *(ehl pehn-sah-mee-'ehn-toh)*

This is (the)...   **Esta es...** *('ehs-tah ehs)*

    best way   **la mejor manera** *(lah meh-'hohr mah-'neh-rah)*

    final decision   **la decisión final** *(lah deh-see-see-'ohn fee-'nahl)*

    last opportunity   **la última oportunidad**
                           (lah 'ool-tee-mah oh-pohr-too-nee-'dahd)

    next step   **la etapa siguiente** *(lah eh-'tah-pah see-ghee-'ehn-teh)*

    top priority   **la prioridad más alta**
                           (lah pree-oh-ree-'dahd mahs 'ahl-tah)

Talk to me if you have a problem.
Hábleme si tiene un problema. *('ah-bleh-meh see tee-'eh-neh oon proh-'bleh-mah)*

Everything is confidential.
Todo es confidencial. *('toh-doh ehs kohn-fee-dehn-see-'ahl)*

It will be OK.
Va a salir bien. *(vah ah sah-'leer bee-'ehn)*

THE CRIMINAL CASE
El caso penal
(ehl 'kah-soh peh-'nahl)

Here's an overview of typical words and phrases used during a criminal case:

Felony or misdemeanor?
¿El delito mayor o el delito menor?
(ehl deh-'lee-toh mah-'yohr oh ehl deh-'lee-toh meh-'nohr)

Prosecution or defense?
¿El enjuiciamiento o la defensa?
(ehl ehn-hoo-ee-see-ah-mee-'ehn-toh oh lah deh-'fehn-sah)

Guilty or innocent?
¿Culpable o inocente? *(kool-'pah-bleh oh ee-noh-'sehn-teh)*

Are you (the)...?	**¿Es usted...?** *(ehs oos-'tehd)*
accessory	**el/la cómplice** *(ehl/lah 'kohm-plee-seh)*
defendant	**el acusado/la acusada** *(ehl ah-koo-'sah-doh/lah ah-koo-'sah-dah)*
friend	**el amigo/la amiga** *(ehl ah-'mee-goh/lah ah-'mee-gah)*
inmate	**el preso/la presa** *(ehl 'preh-soh/lah 'preh-sah)*
neighbor	**el vecino/la vecina** *(ehl veh-'see-noh/lah veh-'see-nah)*
owner	**el dueño/la dueña** *(ehl 'dwehn-yoh/lah 'dwehn-yah)*
trustee	**el preso/la presa de confianza** *(ehl 'preh-soh/lah 'preh-sah deh kohn-fee-'ahn-sah)*
relative	**el/la pariente** *(ehl/lah pah-ree-'ehn-teh)*
roommate	**el compañero/la compañera de cuarto** *(ehl kohm-pahn-'yeh-roh/lah kohm-pahn-'yeh-rah deh 'kwahr-toh)*
suspect	**el sospechoso/la sospechosa** *(ehl sohs-peh-'choh-soh/lah sohs-peh-'choh-sah)*
victim	**la víctima** *(lah 'veek-tee-mah)*
witness	**el/la testigo** *(ehl/lah tehs-'tee-goh)*

Did you contact (the)...?	**¿Se comunicó con...?** *(seh koh-moo-nee-'koh kohn)*
bailiff	**el/la alguacil** *(ehl/lah ahl-gwah-'seel)*
defense attorney	**el abogado/la abogada de la defensa** *(ehl ah-boh-'gah-doh/lah ah-boh-'gah-dah deh lah deh-'fehn-sah)*
detective	**el/la detective** *(ehl/lah deh-tehk-'tee-veh)*
district attorney	**el/la fiscal del distrito** *(ehl/lah fees-'kahl dehl dees-'tree-toh)*
investigator	**el investigador/la investigadora** *(ehl een-vehs-tee-gah-'dohr/lah een-vehs-tee-gah-'doh-rah)*
jury	**el jurado** *(ehl hoo-'rah-doh)*
prosecuting attorney	**el abogado acusador/la abogada acusadora** *(ehl ah-boh-'gah-doh ah-koo-sah-'dohr/lah ah-boh-gah-dah ah-koo-sah-'doh-rah)*
public defender	**el defensor/la defensora de oficio** *(ehl deh-fehn-'sohr/lah deh-fehn-'soh-rah deh oh-'fee-see-oh)*

Have you been...?	¿Ha sido...? *(ah 'see-doh)*
accused	**acusado/acusada** *(ah-koo-'sah-doh/ah-koo-'sah-dah)*
arrested	**arrestado/arrestada** *(ahr-rehs-'tah-doh/ahr-rehs-'tah-dah)*
in custody	**detenido/detenida** *(deh-teh-'nee-doh/deh-teh-'nee-dah)*
incarcerated	**encarcelado/encarcelada** *(ehn-kahr-seh-'lah-doh/ehn-kahr-seh-'lah-dah)*
indicted	**condenado/condenada** *(kohn-deh-'nah-doh/kohn-deh-'nah-dah)*
interrogated	**interrogado/interrogada** *(een-tehr-roh-'gah-doh/een-tehr-roh-'gah-dah)*
searched	**registrado/registrada** *(reh-hees-'trah-doh/reh-hees-'trah-dah)*
served a subpoena	**citado/citada** *(see-'tah-doh/see-'tah-dah)*

Do you have (the)...?	¿Tiene...? *(tee-'eh-neh)*
affidavit	**la declaración jurada** *(lah deh-klah-rah-see-'ohn hoo-'rah-dah)*
alibi	**la coartada** *(lah koh-ahr-'tah-dah)*
bail bond	**la escritura de fianza** *(lah ehs-kree-'too-rah deh fee-'ahn-sah)*
brief	**el sumario** *(ehl soo-'mah-ree-oh)*
complaint	**la queja** *(lah 'keh-hah)*
consent	**el permiso** *(ehl pehr-'mee-soh)*
court order	**la orden de la corte** *(lah 'ohr-dehn deh lah 'kohr-teh)*
criminal record	**los antecedentes penales** *(lohs ahn-teh-seh-'dehn-tehs peh-'nah-lehs)*
deposition	**la deposición** *(lah deh-poh-see-see-'ohn)*
evidence	**las pruebas** *(lahs proo-'eh-bahs)*
exhibit	**la prueba instrumental** *(lah proo-'eh-bah eens-troo-mehn-'tahl)*
form	**el formulario** *(ehl fohr-moo-'lah-ree-oh)*
motive	**el motivo** *(ehl moh-'tee-voh)*
proof	**la prueba** *(lah proo-'eh-bah)*
report	**el informe** *(ehl een-'fohr-meh)*
restraining order	**la orden de protección** *(lah 'ohr-dehn deh proh-tehk-see-'ohn)*
search warrant	**la orden de registro** *(lah 'ohr-dehn deh reh-'hees-troh)*
subpoena	**la citación** *(lah see-tah-see-'ohn)*
warrant	**la orden** *(lah 'ohr-dehn)*

Do you understand (the)...?	¿Entiende...? *(ehn-tee-'ehn-deh)*
acquittal	**la absolución** *(lah ahb-soh-loo-see-'ohn)*
allegation	**el alegato** *(ehl ah-leh-'gah-toh)*
appeal	**la apelación** *(lah ah-peh-lah-see-'ohn)*

arrest warrant	**la orden de arresto** *(lah 'ohr-dehn deh ahr-'rehs-toh)*
bail	**la fianza** *(lah fee-'ahn-sah)*
case	**el caso** *(ehl 'kah-soh)*
charge	**la acusación** *(lah ah-koo-sah-see-'ohn)*
claim	**el reclamo** *(ehl reh-'klah-moh)*
continuance	**el aplazamiento** *(ehl ah-plah-sah-mee-'ehn-toh)*
decision	**la decision** *(lah deh-see-see-'ohn)*
deliberation	**la deliberación** *(lah deh-lee-beh-rah-see-'ohn)*
fine	**la multa** *(lah 'mool-tah)*
indictment	**la acusación** *(lah ah-koo-sah-see-'ohn)*
information	**la información** *(lah een-fohr-mah-see-'ohn)*
injunction	**el entredicho** *(ehl ehn-treh-'dee-choh)*
judgment	**el fallo** *(ehl 'fah-yoh)*
jury selection	**la selección del jurado** *(lah seh-lehk-see-'ohn dehl hoo-'rah-doh)*
lawsuit	**el pleito** *(ehl 'pleh-ee-toh)*
litigation process	**el proceso de litigio** *(ehl proh-'seh-soh deh lee-'tee-hee-oh)*
motion	**la moción** *(lah moh-see-'ohn)*
oath	**el juramento** *(ehl hoo-rah-'mehn-toh)*
offense	**la ofensa** *(lah oh-'fehn-sah)*
plea	**el alegato** *(ehl ah-leh-'gah-toh)*
preliminary proceedings	**las diligencias preliminares** *(lahs dee-lee-'hehn-see-ahs 'preh-lee-mee-'nah-rehs)*
punishment	**la pena** *(lah 'peh-nah)*
request	**la petición** *(lah peh-tee-see-'ohn)*
right	**el derecho** *(ehl deh-'reh-choh)*
ruling	**la resolución** *(lah reh-soh-loo-see-'ohn)*
sentence	**la sentencia** *(lah sehn-'tehn-see-ah)*
statute of limitations	**la ley de prescripción** *(lah 'leh-ee deh prehs-kreep-see-'ohn)*
summary proceedings	**la vía sumaria** *(lah 'vee-ah soo-'mah-ree-ah)*
surveillance	**la vigilancia** *(lah vee-hee-'lahn-see-ah)*
verdict	**el veredicto** *(ehl veh-reh-'deek-toh)*

Is it...?	**¿Está...?** *(ehs-'tah)*
accepted	**aceptado** *(ah-sehp-'tah-doh)*
added	**agregado** *(ahg-reh-'gah-doh)*
changed	**cambiado** *(kahm-bee-'ah-doh)*
faulty	**erróneo** *(ehr-'roh-neh-oh)*
reduced	**reducido** *(reh-doo-'see-doh)*
rejected	**rechazado** *(reh-chah-'sah-doh)*
removed	**quitado** *(kee-'tah-doh)*
revised	**revisado** *(reh-vee-'sah-doh)*
well-founded	**fundado** *(foon-'dah-doh)*
dismissed	**rechazado** *(reh-chah-'sah-doh)*

Again, bear in mind that Spanish is learned best when a few related words are grouped:

Let's talk about the...	**Conversemos de...** *(kohn-vehr-'seh-mohs deh)*
arraignment	**el emplazamiento** *(ehl ehm-plah-sah-mee-'ehn-toh)*
hearing	**la audencia** *(lah aw-dee-'ehn-see-ah)*
trial	**el juicio** *(ehl hoo-'ee-see-oh)*
prison	**la prisión** *(lah pree-see-'ohn)*
cell	**la celda** *(lah 'sehl-dah)*
jail	**la cárcel** *(lah 'kahr-sehl)*
arrest	**el arresto** *(ehl ahr-'rehs-toh)*
raid	**la incursión** *(lah een-koor-see-'ohn)*
riot	**el tumulto** *(ehl too-'mool-toh)*
tracks	**los rastros** *(lohs 'rahs-trohs)*
fingerprints	**las huellas digitales** *(lahs 'hweh-yahs dee-hee-'tah-lehs)*
clues	**las pistas** *(lahs 'pees-tahs)*
deliberation	**la deliberación** *(lah deh-lee-beh-rah-see-'ohn)*
argument	**la discusión** *(lah dees-koo-see-'ohn)*
debate	**el debate** *(ehl deh-'bah-teh)*
freedom	**la libertad** *(lah lee-behr-'tahd)*
parole, probation	**la libertad provisional**
	(lah lee-behr-'tahd proh-vee-see-oh-'nahl)
release	**la liberación** *(lah lee-beh-rah-see-'ohn)*
guilty party	**el/la culpable** *(ehl/lah kool-'pah-bleh)*
suspect	**el sospechoso/la sospechosa**
	(ehl sohs-peh-'choh-soh/lah sohs-peh-'choh-sah)
perpetrator	**el/la responsable** *(ehl/lah rehs-pohn-'sah-bleh)*
clemency	**la clemencia** *(lah kleh-'mehn-see-ah)*
pardon	**el indulto** *(ehl een-'dool-toh)*
dismissal	**la desolución** *(lah deh-soh-loo-see-'ohn)*

THE SENTENCE! ¡La frase!

Use these whenever there are questions about a case report:

Do you have the case report number?
¿Tiene usted el número de su caso?
(tee-'eh-neh oos-'tehd ehl 'noo-meh-roh deh soo 'kah-soh)

Would you like a copy of the report?
¿Quisiera una copia del reporte? *(kee-see-'eh-rah 'oo-nah 'koh-pee-ah dehl reh-'pohr-teh)*

We cannot release the report.
No podemos darle el reporte. *(noh poh-'deh-mohs 'dahr-leh ehl reh-'pohr-teh)*

PRIVATE PRACTICE   **Práctica privada**

(40) A. Connect the words that are close in meaning:

1. **la acusación**	**el informe**
2. **el sumario**	**el prisionero**
3. **el preso**	**la evidencia**
4. **la prueba**	**el detective**
5. **el investigador**	**el cargo**

B. Translate—they're easy:

1. **la jurisdicción** _____

2. **la confesión** _____

3. **la infracción** _____

4. **la investigación** _____

5. **el testimonio** _____

CRIMINAL ACTIVITY
La actividad criminal
(lah ahk-tee-vee-'dahd kree-mee-'nahl)

This is a list of common crimes. Work on the most common ones first:

The crime is (the)...   **El crimen es...** *(ehl 'kree-mehn ehs)*

armed robbery	**el atraco a mano armada** *(ehl ah-'trah-koh ah 'mah-noh ahr-'mah-dah)*
arson	**el incendio premeditado** *(ehl een-'sehn-dee-oh preh-meh-dee-'tah-doh)*
assault	**el asalto** *(ehl ah-'sahl-toh)*
battery	**la agresión** *(lah ah-greh-see-'ohn)*
domestic violence	**la violencia doméstica** *(lah vee-oh-'lehn-see-ah doh-'mehs-tee-kah)*
embezzling	**el desfalco** *(ehl dehs-'fahl-koh)*
extortion	**la extorsión** *(lah ex-tohr-see-'ohn)*
forgery	**la falsificación** *(lah fahl-see-fee-kah-see-'ohn)*
fraud	**el fraude** *(ehl 'frah-oo-deh)*

grand theft	**el robo de mayor cuantía**
	(ehl 'roh-boh deh mah-'yohr kwahn-'tee-ah)
identity theft	**el robo de identidad**
	(ehl 'roh-boh deh ee-dehn-tee-'dahd)
kidnapping	**el secuestro** *(ehl seh-'kwehs-troh)*
larceny	**el hurto** *(ehl 'oor-toh)*
libel	**el libelo** *(ehl lee-'beh-loh)*
looting	**el saqueo** *(ehl sah-'keh-oh)*
manslaughter	**el homicidio involuntario**
	(ehl oh-mee-'see-dee-oh een-voh-loon-'tah-ree-oh)
murder	**el asesinato** *(ehl ah-seh-see-'nah-toh)*
perjury	**el perjurio** *(ehl pehr-'hoo-ree-oh)*
rape	**la violación** *(lah vee-oh-lah-see-'ohn)*
robbery	**el robo** *(ehl 'roh-boh)*
smuggling	**el contrabando** *(ehl kohn-trah-'bahn-doh)*
stabbing	**la puñalada** *(lah poon-yah-'lah-dah)*
terrorism	**el terrorismo** *(ehl tehr-roh-'rees-moh)*

It's (the) _____ charge.	**Es la acusación de _____.** *(ehs lah ah-koo-sah-see-'ohn deh)*
animal cruelty	**crueldad a los animales**
	(kroo-ehl-'dahd ah lohs ah-nee-'mah-lehs)
bribery	**soborno** *(soh-'bohr-noh)*
gambling	**juego de apuestas** *('hweh-goh deh ah-poo-'ehs-tahs)*
graffiti	**grafiti** *(grah-'fee-tee)*
harassment	**acosamiento** *(ah-koh-sah-mee-'ehn-toh)*
littering	**tirar basura** *(tee-'rahr bah-'soo-rah)*
loitering	**merodeo** *(meh-roh-'deh-oh)*
trespassing	**intrusión** *(een-troo-see-'ohn)*
vagrancy	**vagancia** *(vah-'gahn-see-ah)*
vandalism	**vandalismo** *(vahn-dah-'lees-moh)*

You are accused of being the	**Se le acusa de ser...** *(seh leh ah-'koo-sah deh sehr)*
bookie	**el corredor de apuestas**
	(ehl kohr-reh-'dohr deh ah-'pwehs-tahs)
drug dealer	**el vendedor de drogas**
	(ehl vehn-deh-'dohr deh 'droh-gahs)
forger	**el falsificador** *(ehl fahl-see-fee-kah-'dohr)*
gang member	**el pandillero** *(ehl pahn-dee-'yeh-roh)*
intruder	**el intruso** *(ehl een-'troo-soh)*
loiterer	**el merodeador** *(ehl meh-roh-deh-ah-'dohr)*
murderer	**el asesino** *(ehl ah-seh-'see-noh)*
pickpocket	**el carterista** *(ehl kahr-teh-'rees-tah)*
pimp	**el alcahuete** *(ehl ahl-kah-oo-'eh-teh)*
racketeer	**el extorsionista** *(ehl ex-tohr-see-oh-'nees-tah)*

rapist	**el violador** *(ehl vee-oh-lah-'dohr)*
smuggler	**el contrabandista** *(ehl kohn-trah-bahn-'dees-tah)*
swindler	**el estafador** *(ehl ehs-tah-fah-'dohr)*
thief	**el ladrón** *(ehl lah-'drohn)*
vagrant	**el vagabundo** *(ehl vah-gah-'boon-doh)*

Was it...?	**¿Fue...?** *(foo-'eh)*
child pornography	**la pornografía de menores** *(lah pohr-noh-grah-'fee-ah deh meh-'noh-rehs)*
indecent exposure	**el exhibicionismo** *(ehl ex-ee-bee-see-oh-'nees-moh)*
lewd behavior	**el comportamiento indecente** *(ehl kohm-pohr-tah-mee-'ehn-toh een-deh-'sehn-teh)*
obscene phone call	**la llamada obscena** *(lah yah-'mah-dah ohb-'seh-nah)*
prostitution	**la prostitución** *(lah prohs-tee-too-see-'ohn)*
sexual molestation	**el abuso sexual** *(ehl ah-'boo-soh sehk-soo-'ahl)*
solicitation	**la incitación** *(lah een-see-tah-see-'ohn)*

NOTICE!   ¡Fíjese!

Discuss sexual issues using the appropriate terminology:

He's...	**Es...** *(ehs)*
bisexual	**bisexual** *(bee-sehk-soo-'ahl)*
homosexual	**homosexual** *(oh-moh-sehk-soo-'ahl)*
transsexual	**transexual** *(trahn-sehk-soo-'ahl)*

There was...	**Había...** *(ah-'bee-ah)*
intercourse	**coito** *('koh-ee-toh)*
masturbation	**masturbación** *(mahs-toor-bah-see-'ohn)*
nudity	**desnudez** *(dehs-noo-'dehs)*
sodomy	**sodomía** *(soh-doh-'mee-ah)*

CRIMINAL BEHAVIOR
El comportamento criminal
(ehl kohm-pohr-tah-mee-'ehn-toh kree-mee-'nahl)

Sometimes you will have to consider the mental or physical state of the people involved in the criminal case. These words should cover some of your concerns:

Is he/she...?	**¿Es una persona...?** *(ehs 'oo-nah pehr-'soh-nah)*
antisocial	**antisocial** *(ahn-tee-soh-see-'ahl)*
disorganized	**desorganizada** *(dehs-ohr-gah-nee-'sah-dah)*
emotional	**emocional** *(eh-moh-see-oh-'nahl)*
irrational	**irracional** *(eer-rah-see-oh-'nahl)*
irritable	**irritable** *(eer-ree-'tah-bleh)*

negative	**negativa** *(neh-gah-'tee-vah)*
pessimistic	**pesimista** *(peh-see-'mees-tah)*
psychotic	**psicótica** *(see-'koh-tee-kah)*
Has he/she seen (the)...?	**¿Ha visto al/a la...?** *(ah 'vees-toh ahl/ah lah)*
neurologist	**neurólogo/neuróloga**
	(neh-oo-'roh-loh-goh/neh-oo-'roh-loh-gah)
psychiatrist	**psiquiatra** *(see-kee-'ah-trah)*
psychologist	**psicólogo/psicóloga** *(see-'koh-loh-goh/see-'koh-loh-gah)*
social worker	**trabajador/trabajadora social**
	(trah-bah-hah-'dohr/trah-bah-hah-'doh-rah soh-see-'ahl)
specialist	**especialista** *(ehs-peh-see-ah-'lees-tah)*
therapist	**terapeuta** *(teh-rah-'peh-oo-tah)*
Is it...?	**¿Es...?** *(ehs)*
Alzheimer's	**enfermedad de Alzheimer**
	(ehn-fehr-meh-'dahd deh ahl-zah-ee-mehr)
anorexia	**anorexia nervosa** *(ah-noh-'rehk-see-ah nehr-vee-'oh-sah)*
Asperger's Syndrome	**síndrome de Asperger**
	('seen-droh-meh deh ahs-'pehr-gehr)
autism	**autismo** *(aw-'tees-moh)*
bulimia	**bulimia nervosa** *(boo-'lee-mee-ah nehr-vee-'oh-sah)*
clinical depression	**depresión clínica** *(deh-preh-see-'ohn 'klee-nee-kah)*
dementia	**demencia** *(deh-'mehn-see-ah)*
Down's Syndrome	**síndrome de Down** *('seen-droh-meh deh 'dah-oon)*
epilepsy	**epilepsia** *(eh-pee-'lehp-see-ah)*
menopause	**menopausia** *(meh-noh-'pah-oo-see-ah)*
paranoia	**paranoia** *(pah-rah-'noh-ee-ah)*
Parkinson's	**enfermedad de Parkinson**
	(ehn-fehr-meh-'dahd deh 'pahr-keen-sohn)
retardation	**retraso mental** *(reh-'trah-soh mehn-'tahl)*
schizophrenia	**esquizofrenia** *(ehs-kee-soh-'freh-nee-ah)*
Tourette's	**síndrome de Tourette** *('seen-droh-meh deh toor-'eht)*
Is it a/an _____ disorder?	**¿Es un trastorno _____?** *(ehs oon trahs-'tohr-noh)*
ADHD	**de hiperactividad con déficit de atención**
	(deh ee-pehr-ahk-tee-vee-'dahd kohn 'deh-fee-seet deh
	ah-tehn-see-'ohn)
anxiety	**de ansiedad** *(deh ahn-see-eh-'dahd)*
bipolar	**maníaco depresivo** *(mah-'nee-ah-koh deh-preh-'see-voh)*
congenital	**congénito** *(kohn-'heh-nee-toh)*
learning	**del aprendizaje** *(dehl ah-prehn-dee-'sah-heh)*
nervous	**nervioso** *(nehr-vee-'oh-soh)*
OCD	**obsesivo compulsivo**
	(ohb-seh-'see-voh kohm-pool-'see-voh)
PTSD	**postraumático** *(pohs-trah-oo-'mah-tee-koh)*

Does he/she need...?	¿Necesita...? *(neh-seh-'see-tah)*
AA	**Alcohólicos Anónimos** *(ahl-koh-'oh-lee-kohs ah-'noh-nee-mohs)*
family therapy	**terapia familiar** *(teh-'rah-pee-ah fah-mee-lee-'ahr)*
continuous care	**cuidado continuo** *(kwee-'dah-doh kohn-'tee-noo-oh)*
counseling	**asesoramiento** *(ah-seh-soh-rah-mee-'ehn-toh)*
group therapy	**terapia en grupo** *(teh-'rah-pee-ah ehn 'groo-poh)*
intensive therapy	**terapia intensiva** *(teh-'rah-pee-ah een-tehn-'see-vah)*
medical supervision	**supervisión médica** *(soo-pehr-vee-see-'ohn 'meh-dee-kah)*
more treatment	**más tratamiento** *(mahs trah-tah-mee-'ehn-toh)*
NA	**Narcóticos Anónimos** *(nahr-'koh-tee-kohs ah-'noh-nee-mohs)*
physical therapy	**fisioterapia** *(fee-see-oh-teh-'rah-pee-ah)*
psychotherapy	**psicoterapia** *(see-koh-teh-'rah-pee-ah)*
recovery	**recuperación** *(reh-koo-peh-rah-see-'ohn)*
rehabilitation	**rehabilitación** *(reh-ah-bee-lee-tah-see-'ohn)*
support group	**un grupo de apoyo** *(oon 'groo-poh deh ah-'poh-yoh)*
12-step program	**el programa de doce pasos** *(ehl proh-'grah-mah deh 'doh-seh 'pah-sohs)*
Is he/she taking...?	¿Toma....? *('toh-mah)*
antidepressants	**antidepresivos** *(ahn-tee-deh-preh-'see-vohs)*
antihypertension	**antihipertensivos** *(ahn-tee-ee-pehr-tehn-'see-vohs)*
antipsychotics	**antisicóticos** *(ahn-tee-see-'koh-tee-kohs)*
dopamine	**dopamina** *(doh-pah-'mee-nah)*
Ritalin®	**Ritalin®** *(ree-tah-'leen)*
sedatives	**calmantes** *(kahl-'mahn-tehs)*
serotonin	**serotonina** *(seh-roh-toh-'nee-nah)*
stimulants	**estimulantes** *(ehs-tee-moo-'lahn-tehs)*
therapeutic drugs	**medicamentos terapeúticos** *(meh-dee-kah-'mehn-tohs teh-rah-'peh-oo-tee-kohs)*

 CULTURAL COMMENT **Comentario cultural**

Lost children, child abuse, and domestic violence are common themes nowadays, and lawyers often find themselves caught up in cases involving very sensitive issues. Serious problems could result if complex messages are communicated inaccurately. Be on the safe side—when situations get touchy, ask for a qualified bilingual translator and interpreter.

THE INVESTIGATION
La investigación
(lah een-vehs-tee-gah-see-'ohn)

Questions related to criminal investigation include a wide variety of vocabulary:

Was he/she...?	**¿Fue...?** *(foo-'eh)*

aggressive	**agresivo/agresiva** *(ah-greh-'see-voh/ah-greh-'see-vah)*
brutal	**brutal** *(broo-'tahl)*
crazy	**loco/loca** *('loh-koh/'loh-kah)*
furious	**furioso/furiosa** *(foo-ree-'oh-soh/foo-ree-'oh-sah)*
vicious	**malsano/malsana** *(mahl-'sah-noh/mahl-'sah-nah)*

Did he/she look...?	**¿Se veía...?** *(seh veh-'ee-ah)*

angry	**enojado/enojada** *(eh-noh-'hah-doh/eh-noh-'hah-dah)*
anxious	**ansioso/ansiosa** *(ahn-see-'oh-soh/ahn-see-'oh-sah)*
bored	**aburrido/aburrida** *(ah-boor-'ree-doh/ah-boor-'ree-dah)*
calm	**tranquilo/tranquila** *(trahn-'kee-loh/trahn-'kee-lah)*
confident	**seguro/segura** *(seh-'goo-roh/seh-'goo-rah)*
confused	**confundido/confundida** *(kohn-foon-'dee-doh/kohn-foon-'dee-dah)*
determined	**decidido/decidida** *(deh-see-'dee-doh/deh-see-'dee-dah)*
excited	**emocionado/emocionada** *(eh-moh-see-oh-'nah-doh/eh-moh-see-oh-'nah-dah)*
indecisive	**indeciso/indecisa** *(een-deh-'see-soh/een-deh-'see-sah)*
nervous	**nervioso/nerviosa** *(nehr-vee-'oh-soh/nehr-vee-'oh-sah)*
scared	**asustado/asustada** *(ah-soos-'tah-doh/ah-soos-'tah-dah)*
surprised	**sorprendido/sorprendida** *(sohr-prehn-'dee-doh/sohr-prehn-'dee-dah)*
uncomfortable	**incómodo/incómoda** *(een-'koh-moh-doh/een-'koh-moh-dah)*
unsure	**inseguro/insegura** *(een-seh-'goo-roh/een-seh-'goo-rah)*
worried	**preocupado/preocupada** *(preh-oh-koo-'pah-doh/preh-oh-koo-'pah-dah)*

Did they give you (the)...?	**¿Le dieron...?** *(leh dee-'eh-rohn)*

AIDS test	**la prueba de SIDA** *(lah proo-'eh-bah deh 'see-dah)*
breath test	**la prueba de aliento** *(lah proo-'eh-bah deh ah-lee-'ehn-toh)*
drug test	**la prueba de drogas** *(lah proo-'eh-bah deh 'droh-gahs)*
eye exam	**la prueba de la vista** *(lah proo-'eh-bah deh lah 'vees-tah)*
medical exam	**el examen médico** *(ehl ex-'ah-mehn 'meh-dee-koh)*
polygraph	**el detector de mentiras** *(ehl deh-tehk-'tohr deh mehn-'tee-rahs)*

Did they...?	¿Le...? *(leh)*
ask you to sign	**pidieron su firma** *(pee-dee-'eh-rohn soo 'feer-mah)*
fingerprint you	**tomaron las huellas digitales** *(toh-'mah-rohn lahs 'hweh-yahs dee-hee-'tah-lehs)*
give you a copy	**dieron una copia** *(de-'eh-rohn 'oo-nah 'koh-pee-ah)*
give you a date	**dieron una fecha** *(dee-'eh-rohn 'oo-nah 'feh-chah)*
explain your rights	**explicaron sus derechos** *(ex-plee-'kah-rohn soos deh-'reh-chohs)*
handcuff you	**pusieron las esposas** *(poo-see-'eh-rohn lahs ehs-'poh-sahs)*
hurt you	**hicieron daño** *(ee-see-'eh-rohn 'dahn-yoh)*
keep your belongings	**retiraron sus pertenencias** *(reh-tee-'rah-rohn soos pehr-teh-'nehn-see-ahs)*
let you make a call	**dejaron hacer una llamada** *(deh-'hah-rohn ah-'sehr 'oo-nah yah-'mah-dah)*
mention bail	**mencionaron la fianza** *(mehn-see-oh-'nah-rohn lah fee-'ahn-sah)*
put you in a cell	**metieron en una celda** *(meh-tee-'eh-rohn ehn 'oo-nah 'sehl-dah)*
release you	**liberaron** *(lee-beh-'rah-rohn)*
remove your clothing	**quitaron su ropa** *(kee-'tah-rohn soo 'roh-pah)*
search you	**registraron** *(reh-hees-'trah-rohn)*
take your picture	**tomaron foto** *(toh-'mah-rohn 'foh-toh)*
tell you why	**dijeron por qué** *(dee-'heh-rohn pohr keh)*

PRIVATE PRACTICE   **Práctica privada**

(41) A. Translate these questions:

1. **¿Estaba actuando brutalmente el sospechoso?**
2. **¿Le dieron la prueba de aliento y le explicaron sus derechos?**
3. **¿Se veía nerviosa y asustada?**

B.

1. Name three felonies and three misdemeanors in Spanish.
2. Name three mental health problems and three mental health treatments in Spanish.

DESCRIBING THE PERSON
Describir a la persona
(dehs-kree-'beer ah lah pehr-'soh-nah)

When describing someone, shoot for both general information as well as specific details:

Was it a child, teen, or adult?
¿Fue un niño, adolescente o adulto?
(foo-'eh oon 'neen-yoh, ah-doh-lehs-'sehn-teh oh ah-'dool-toh)

Was it a man or a woman?
¿Fue hombre o mujer? *(foo-'eh 'ohm-breh oh moo-'hehr)*

Was he/she older or younger?
¿Fue más joven o viejo? *(foo-'eh mahs 'hoh-vehn oh vee-'eh-hoh)*

Can you tell me (the)...?	**¿Puede decirme...?** *(poo-'eh-deh deh-'seer-meh)*
age	**la edad** *(lah eh-'dahd)*
eye color	**el color de los ojos** *(ehl koh-'lohr deh lohs 'oh-hohs)*
hair color	**el color de pelo** *(ehl koh-'lohr deh 'peh-loh)*
height	**la estatura** *(lah ehs-tah-'too-rah)*
race	**la raza** *(lah 'rah-sah)*
size	**el tamaño** *(ehl tah-'mahn-yoh)*
skin color	**el color de piel** *(ehl koh-'lohr deh pee-'ehl)*
weight	**el peso** *(ehl 'peh-soh)*
Was he...?	**¿Era...él?** *('eh-rah ehl)*
bald	**calvo** *('kahl-voh)*
blonde	**rubio** *('roo-bee-oh)*
brunette	**moreno** *(moh-'reh-noh)*
gray-haired	**canoso** *(kah-'noh-soh)*
left-handed	**zurdo** *('soor-doh)*
light-skinned	**de piel clara** *(deh pee-'ehl 'klah-rah)*
red-haired	**pelirojo** *(peh-leer-'roh-hoh)*
right-handed	**diestro** *(dee-'ehs-troh)*
Was she...?	**¿Era...ella?** *('eh-rah 'eh-yah)*
friendly	**amistosa** *(ah-mees-'toh-sah)*
impatient	**impaciente** *(eem-pah-see-'ehn-teh)*
loud	**ruidosa** *(roo-ee-'doh-sah)*
polite	**cortés** *(kohr-'tehs)*
quiet	**quieta** *(kee-'eh-tah)*
rude	**ruda** *('roo-dah)*
shy	**tímida** *('tee-mee-dah)*
strange	**rara** *('rah-rah)*
well-mannered	**bien educada** *(bee-'ehn eh-doo-'kah-dah)*

Be sure to request a good description:

Can you draw it?	**¿Puede dibujarlo?** *('pweh-deh dee-boo-'hahr-loh)*
Can you identify it?	**¿Puede identificarlo?** *('pweh-deh ee-dehn-tee-fee-'kahr-loh)*
Can you remember it?	**¿Puede recordarlo?** *('pweh-deh reh-kohr-'dahr-loh)*

Every detail will be necessary:

What was he/she like?	**¿Cómo era?** *('koh-moh 'eh-rah)*
Did he/she have...?	**¿Tenía...?** *(teh-'nee-ah)*

an accent	**acento** *(ah-'sehn-toh)*
baggy pants	**pantalones anchos** *(pahn-tah-'loh-nehs 'ahn-chohs)*
a beard	**barba** *('bahr-bah)*
braids	**trenzas** *('trehn-sahs)*
crooked teeth	**dientes torcidos** *(dee-'ehn-tehs tohr-'see-dohs)*
a deep voice	**la voz baja** *(lah vohs 'bah-hah)*
dentures	**dentadura postiza** *(dehn-tah-'doo-rah pohs-'tee-sah)*
freckles	**pecas** *('peh-kahs)*
glasses	**anteojos** *(ahn-teh-'oh-hohs)*
high cheekbones	**mejillas altas** *(meh-'ee-yahs 'ahl-tahs)*
a hooked nose	**nariz aguileña** *(nah-'rees ah-ghee-'lehn-yah)*
a mole	**un lunar** *(oon loo-'nahr)*
a moustache	**bigote** *(bee-'goh-teh)*
pockmarks	**marcas de viruela** *('mahr-kahs deh vee-roo-'eh-lah)*
a pony tail	**una coleta** *('oo-nah koh-'leh-tah)*
a round face	**la cara redonda** *(lah 'kah-rah reh-'dohn-dah)*
a scar	**una cicatriz** *('oo-nah see-kah-'trees)*
tatoos	**tatuajes** *(tah-too-'ah-hehs)*
a thin face	**la cara delgada** *(lah 'kah-rah dehl-'gah-dah)*
a wart	**una verruga** *('oo-nah vehr-'roo-gah)*
a wig	**una peluca** *('oo-nah peh-'loo-kah)*
wrinkles	**arrugas** *(ahr-'roo-gahs)*

NOTICE!   **¡Fíjese!**

Use *very* or *a little* to clarify each description:

Era muy alto. *('eh-rah 'moo-ee 'ahl-toh)*
Era un poquito bajo. *('eh-rah oon poh-'kee-toh 'bah-hoh)*

PRIVATE PRACTICE   **Práctica privada**

(42) Answer these questions about yourself:

1. ¿Cuál es su color de pelo?

_____

2. ¿Es Ud. zurdo/zurda?

_____

3. ¿Es Ud. bien educado/educada?

_____

4. ¿Tiene Ud. pecas?

_____

5. ¿Tiene Ud. tatuajes?

_____

THE ROBBERY
El robo
(ehl 'roh-boh)

If the case invoves stolen property, plenty can be said with only a few Spanish words.

Was it your...?	**¿Fue su...?** *(foo-'eh soo)*
business	**negocio** *(neh-'goh-see-oh)*
car	**carro** *('kahr-roh)*
home	**casa** *('kah-sah)*
What did they...?	**¿Qué...?** *(keh)*
break	**quebraron** *(keh-'brah-rohn)*
do	**hicieron** *(ee-see-'eh-rohn)*
move	**movieron** *(moh-vee-'eh-rohn)*
open	**abrieron** *(ah-bree-'eh-rohn)*
remove	**sacaron** *(sah-'kah-rohn)*
steal	**robaron** *(roh-'bah-rohn)*
take	**llevaron** *(yeh-'vah-rohn)*
use	**usaron** *(oo-'sah-rohn)*

Where did they...?	**¿Por dónde...?** *(pohr 'dohn-deh)*
break in	**forzaron** *(fohr-'sah-rohn)*
enter	**entraron** *(ehn-'trah-rohn)*
exit	**escaparon** *(ehs-kah-'pah-rohn)*

Did they take (the)...?	**¿Se llevaron...?** *(seh yeh-'vah-rohn)*
audio system	**el sistema de audio** *(ehl sees-'teh-mah deh 'aw-dee-oh)*
phone	**el teléfono** *(ehl teh-'leh-foh-noh)*
camera	**la cámara** *(lah 'kah-mah-rah)*
electronic equipment	**el equipo electrónico** *(ehl eh-'kee-poh eh-lehk-'troh-nee-koh)*
home theater	**el cine familiar** *(ehl 'see-neh fah-mee-lee-'ahr)*
laptop	**la computadora portátil** *(lah kohm-poo-tah-'doh-rah pohr-'tah-teel)*
monitor	**el monitor** *(ehl moh-nee-'tohr)*
player	**el tocador** *(ehl toh-kah-'dohr)*
printer	**la impresora** *(lah eem-preh-'soh-rah)*
receiver	**el receptor** *(ehl reh-sehp-'tohr)*
recorder	**la grabadora** *(lah grah-bah-'doh-rah)*
scanner	**el escáner** *(ehl ehs-'kah-nehr)*
TV	**el televisor** *(ehl teh-leh-vee-'sohr)*

Did they steal (the)...?	**¿Le robaron...?** *(leh roh-'bah-rohn)*
jewelry	**las joyas** *(lahs 'hoh-yahs)*
cash	**el efectivo** *(ehl eh-fehk-'tee-voh)*
credit card	**la tarjeta de crédito** *(lah tahr-'heh-tah deh 'kreh-dee-toh)*
document	**el documento** *(ehl doh-koo-'mehn-toh)*
furniture	**los muebles** *(lohs moo-'eh-blehs)*

There are also cases involving auto theft:

Who is the legal owner?
¿Quién es el dueño legal? *(kee-'ehn ehs ehl 'dwehn-yoh leh-'gahl)*

Where did you park the vehicle?
¿Dónde estacionó el vehículo? *('dohn-deh ehs-tah-see-oh-'noh ehl veh-'ee-koo-loh)*

What is the license plate number?
¿Cuál es el número de la placa? *(kwahl ehs ehl 'noo-meh-roh deh lah 'plah-kah)*

From what state?
¿De qué estado? *(deh keh ehs-'tah-doh)*

What is the make and model?
¿Cuál is la marca y el modelo? *(kwahl ehs lah 'mahr-kah ee ehl moh-'deh-loh)*

What year is it?
¿De qué año? *(deh keh 'ahn-yoh)*

Did you lock the vehicle?
¿Cerró con llave el vehículo? *(sehr-'roh kohn 'yah-veh ehl veh-'ee-koo-loh)*

Does it have a security system?
¿Tiene un sistema de seguridad? *(tee-'eh-neh oon sees-'teh-mah deh seh-goo-ree-'dahd)*

Are your payments current?
¿Están los pagos al día? *(ehs-'than lohs 'pah-gohs ahl 'dee-ah)*

What color is the vehicle?
¿Cuál es el color del vehículo? *(kwahl ehs ehl koh-'lohr dehl veh-'ee-koo-loh)*

Do you know the VIN number?
¿Sabe el número de identificación?
('sah-beh ehl 'noo-meh-roh deh ee-dehn-tee-fee-kah-see-'ohn)

What is the value of the vehicle?
¿Cuánto vale el vehículo? *('kwahn-toh 'vah-leh ehl veh-'ee-koo-loh)*

Are you offering a reward?
¿Está ofreciendo una recompensa?
(ehs-'tah oh-freh-see-'ehn-doh 'oo-nah reh-kohm-'pehn-sah)

NOTICE!   ¡Fíjese!

Occasionally, you'll get some false information:

It was...	**Fue...** *(foo-'eh)*
a false alarm	**una alarma falsa** *('oo-nah ah-'lahr-mah 'fahl-sah)*
a hoax	**un engaño** *(oon ehn-'gahn-yoh)*
a joke	**un chiste** *(oon 'chees-teh)*
a lie	**una mentira** *('oo-nah mehn-'tee-rah)*
a prank	**una travesura** *('oo-nah trah-veh-'soo-rah)*
a fake	**una falsificación** *('oo-nah fahl-see-fee-kah-see-'ohn)*

HOME BURGLARY
El robo casero
(ehl 'roh-boh kah-'seh-roh)

You may need to rehearse some questions and answers with your client before you enter the courtroom. Begin with these examples:

Tell what...	**Diga lo que...** *('dee-gah loh keh)*
you heard	**escuchó** *(ehs-koo-'choh)*
you saw	**vió** *(vee-'oh)*
you know	**sabe** *('sah-beh)*
you think	**piensa** *(pee-'ehn-sah)*
you believe	**cree** *('kreh-eh)*

Did you lock the front door?
¿Cerró la puerta de entrada con llave?
(sehr-'roh lah 'pwehr-tah deh ehn-'trah-dah kohn 'yah-veh)

Were the windows closed?
¿Estaban cerradas las ventanas? *(ehs-'tah-bahn sehr-'rah-dahs lahs vehn-'tah-nahs)*

Were the lights on?
¿Estaban prendidas las luces? *(ehs-'tah-bahn prehn-'dee-dahs lahs 'loo-sehs)*

Were you asleep?
¿Estaba dormido/dormida? *(ehs-'tah-bah dohr-'mee-doh/dohr-'mee-dah)*

Were you out of town?
¿Estaba de viaje? *(ehs-'tah-bah deh vee-'ah-heh)*

Who has the key?
¿Quién tiene la llave? *(kee-'ehn tee-'eh-neh lah 'yah-veh)*

Did you touch anything?
¿Tocó algo? *(toh-'koh 'ahl-goh)*

Was anyone with you?
¿Había otra persona con usted? *(ah-'bee-ah 'oh-trah pehr-'soh-nah kohn oos-'tehd)*

Did you see the suspect?
¿Lo/la vió al sospechoso? *(loh/lah vee-'oh ahl sohs-peh-'choh-soh)*

Did you see anything strange?
¿Vió algo raro? *(vee-'oh 'ahl-goh 'rah-roh)*

Where were you?
¿Dónde estaba usted? *('dohn-deh ehs-'tah-bah oos-'tehd)*

When did it happen?
¿Cuándo ocurrió? *('kwahn-doh oh-koor-ree-'oh)*

Between what hours?
¿Entre qué horas? *(ehn-treh keh 'oh-rahs)*

Do you have insurance?
¿Tiene seguro? *(tee-'eh-neh seh-'goo-roh)*

What's the estimated loss?
¿Cuál es la pérdida estimada? *(kwahl ehs lah 'pehr-dee-dah ehs-tee-'mah-dah)*

How long did you have it?
¿Por cuánto tiempo lo tenía? *(pohr 'kwahn-toh tee-'ehm-poh loh teh-'nee-ah)*

Note how the following patterns are made of different verb forms:

Was it...?	¿Fue/Estaba...? *(foo-'eh ehs-'tah-bah)*
bought	**comprado** *(kohm-'prah-doh)*
broken	**roto** *('roh-toh)*
burned	**quemado** *(keh-'mah-doh)*
changed	**cambiado** *(kahm-bee-'ah-doh)*
cut	**cortado** *(kohr-'tah-doh)*
destroyed	**destruído** *(dehs-troo-'ee-doh)*
disassembled	**desarmado** *(deh-sahr-'mah-doh)*
identified	**identificado** *(ee-dehn-tee-fee-'kah-doh)*
lost	**perdido** *(pehr-'dee-doh)*
marked	**marcado** *(mahr-'kah-doh)*
modified	**modificado** *(moh-dee-fee-'kah-doh)*
transferred	**transferido** *(trahns-feh-'ree-doh)*
recorded	**grabado** *(grah-'bah-doh)*
recovered	**recuperado** *(reh-koo-peh-'rah-doh)*
ruined	**arruinado** *(ahr-roo-ee-'nah-doh)*
sold	**vendido** *(vehn-'dee-doh)*
stolen	**robado** *(roh-'bah-doh)*
stripped	**despojado** *(dehs-poh-'hah-doh)*

Have you identified the stolen property?
¿Ha identificado la propiedad robada?
(ah ee-dehn-tee-fee-'kah-doh lah proh-pee-eh-'dahd roh-'bah-dah)

Have you made a list?
¿Ha hecho una lista? *(ah 'eh-choh 'oo-nah 'lees-tah)*

Have you indicated the make and model?
¿Ha indicado la marca y el modelo?
(ah een-dee-'kah-doh lah 'mahr-kah ee ehl moh-'deh-loh)

Have you recorded the serial number?
¿Ha escrito el número de serie? *(ah ehs-'kree-toh ehl 'noo-meh-roh deh 'seh-ree-eh)*

Have you found the receipt?
¿Ha encontrado el recibo? *(ah ehn-kohn-'trah-doh ehl reh-'see-boh)*

Can you...?	**¿Puede...?** *(poo-'eh-deh)*
prove that you bought it	**probar que usted lo compró** *(proh-'bahr keh oos-'tehd loh kohm-'proh)*
give a description	**dar una descripción** *(dahr 'oo-nah dehs-kreep-see-'ohn)*
tell me the year	**decirme el año** *(deh-'seer-meh ehl 'ahn-yoh)*
recognize the label	**reconocer la etiqueta** *(reh-koh-noh-'sehr lah eh-tee-'keh-tah)*
Do you know who..?	**¿Sabe quién...?** *('sah-beh kee-'ehn)*
did it	**lo hizo** *(loh 'ee-soh)*
the person was	**fue la persona** *(foo-'eh lah pehr-'soh-nah)*
was there	**estaba allí** *(ehs-'tah-bah ah-'yee)*
said that	**dijo eso** *('dee-hoh 'eh-soh)*
the suspect is	**es el sospechoso** *(ehs ehl sohs-peh-'choh-soh)*
lives here	**vive aquí** *('vee-veh ah-'kee)*
saw what happened	**vió qué pasó** *(vee-'oh keh pah-'soh)*

NOTICE! ¡Fíjese!

Get the names and addresses of everyone! Use *who* and *whose*:

Whose is it?	**¿De quién es?** *(deh kee-'ehn ehs)*
With whom?	**¿Con quién?** *(kohn kee-'ehn)*
To whom?	**¿A quién?** *(ah kee-'ehn)*
From whom?	**¿De quién?** *(deh kee-'ehn)*
For whom?	**¿Para quién?** *('pah-rah kee-'ehn)*

PRIVATE PRACTICE Práctica privada

(43) A. Delete the word in each group that doesn't belong with the others:

1. grabadora, estafador, cámara, impresora
2. abrigo, reloj, pulsera, anillo
3. quemado, cortado, quebrado, preocupado

B. Put the words in order to create investigation questions:

1. lo usted ¿ probar compró puede que ?
2. ? robada identificado la ha propiedad ¿
3. la ¿ cuál ? estimada es pérdida

VIOLENT CRIME
El crimen violento
(ehl 'kree-mehn vee-oh-'lehn-toh)

Piece together what transpired between the two parties. Take note of any new Spanish verbs:

How did it start?	**¿Cómo empezó?** *('koh-moh ehm-peh-'soh)*
Who was involved?	**¿Quién participó?** *(kee-'ehn pahr-tee-see-'poh)*
What were you guys doing?	**¿Qué estaban haciendo ustedes?**
	(keh ehs-'tah-bahn oos-'teh-dehs ah-see-'ehn-doh)

Did they ___ you?	**¿Lo/la ___?** *(loh/lah)*
attack	**atacaron** *(ah-tah-'kah-rohn)*
bite	**mordieron** *(mohr-dee-'eh-rohn)*
chase	**persiguieron** *(pehr-see-ghee-'eh-rohn)*
cut	**cortaron** *(kohr-'tah-rohn)*
follow	**siguieron** *(see-ghee-'eh-rohn)*
grab	**agarraron** *(ah-gahr-'rah-rohn)*
hit	**golpearon** *(gohl-peh-'ah-rohn)*
hurt	**lastimaron** *(lahs-tee-'mah-rohn)*
insult	**insultaron** *(een-sool-'tah-rohn)*
intimidate	**intimidaron** *(een-tee-mee-'dah-rohn)*
kick	**patearon** *(pah-teh-'ah-rohn)*
knock down	**tumbaron** *(toom-'bah-rohn)*
pull	**jalaron** *(hah-'lah-rohn)*
push	**empujaron** *(ehm-poo-'hah-rohn)*
rape	**violaron** *(vee-oh-'lah-rohn)*
rob	**robaron** *(roh-'bah-rohn)*
scratch	**rasguñaron** *(rahs-goon-'yah-rohn)*
shoot	**dispararon** *(dees-pah-'rah-rohn)*
stab	**apuñalaron** *(ah-poon-yah-'lah-rohn)*
threaten	**amenazaron** *(ah-meh-nah-'sah-rohn)*

Were you...?	**¿Estaban...?** *(ehs-'tah-bahn)*
arguing	**discutiendo** *(dees-koo-tee-'ehn-doh)*
doing drugs	**tomando drogas** *(toh-'mahn-doh 'droh-gahs)*
drinking	**tomando alcohol** *(toh-'mahn-doh ahl-koh-'ohl)*
fighting	**peleando** *(peh-leh-'ahn-doh)*
yelling	**gritando** *(gree-'tahn-doh)*

Were they...?	**¿Estaban...?** *(ehs-'tah-bahn)*
armed	**armados** *(ahr-'mah-dohs)*
intoxicated	**intoxicados** *(een-tohk-see-'kah-dohs)*
out of control	**fuera de control** *(foo-'eh-rah deh kohn-'trohl)*

Listen carefully to the responses as you ask each set of questions:

How many were there?
¿Cuántos habían? *('kwahn-tohs ah-'bee-ahn)*

Have you seen them before?
¿Los ha visto antes? *(lohs ah 'vees-toh 'ahn-tehs)*

Were there any witnesses?
¿Habían algunos testigos? *(ah-'bee-ahn ahl-'goo-nohs tehs-'tee-gohs)*

Did you call for help?
¿Pidió ayuda? *(pee-dee-'oh ah-'yoo-dah)*

Did you need an ambulance?
¿Necesitaba una ambulancia? *(neh-seh-see-'tah-bah 'oo-nah ahm-boo-'lahn-see-ah)*

Are you still receiving treatment?
¿Todavía está en tratamiento? *(toh-dah-'vee-ah ehs-'tah ehn trah-tah-mee-'ehn-toh)*

Do you have photos?
¿Tiene fotos? *(tee-'eh-neh 'foh-tohs)*

Did you document everything?
¿Documentó todo? *(doh-koo-mehn-'toh 'toh-doh)*

Do you have proof?
¿Tiene pruebas? *(tee-'eh-neh proo-'eh-bahs)*

Had they been drinking?
¿Habían estado tomando licor? *(ah-'bee-ahn ehs-'tah-doh toh-'mahn-doh lee-'kohr)*

What did they drink?
¿Qué tomó? *(keh toh-'moh)*

¿How much had they drunk?
¿Cuánto habían tomado? *('kwahn-toh ah-'bee-ahn toh-'mah-doh)*

Did it take place at (the)...?	**¿Ocurrió en...?** *(oh-koor-ree-'oh ehn)*
bar	**el bar** *(ehl bahr)*
brothel	**el burdel** *(ehl boor-'dehl)*
casino	**el casino** *(ehl kah-'see-noh)*
concert	**el concierto** *(ehl kohn-see-'ehr-toh)*
dance	**el baile** *(ehl 'bah-ee-leh)*
fair	**la feria** *(lah 'feh-ree-ah)*

festival	**el festival** *(ehl fehs-tee-'vahl)*
game	**el juego** *(ehl 'hweh-goh)*
horse race	**la carrera de caballos**
	(lah kahr-'reh-rah deh kah-'bah-yohs)
massage parlor	**la sala de masajes** *(lah 'sah-lah deh mah-'sah-hehs)*
nightclub	**el club nocturno** *(ehl kloob nohk-'toor-noh)*
park	**el parque** *(ehl 'pahr-keh)*
party	**la fiesta** *(lah fee-'ehs-tah)*
pool hall	**la sala de billar** *(lah 'sah-lah deh bee-'yahr)*
show	**el espectáculo** *(ehl ehs-pehk-'tah-koo-loh)*
stadium	**el estadio** *(ehl ehs-'tah-dee-oh)*
Was there...?	**¿Había...?** *(ah-'bee-ah)*
alcohol	**alcohol** *(ahl-koh-'ohl)*
beer	**cerveza** *(sehr-'veh-sah)*
liquor	**licor** *(lee-'kohr)*
marijuana	**marijuana** *(mah-ree-'hwah-nah)*
narcotics	**narcóticos** *(nahr-'koh-tee-kohs)*
wine	**vino** *('vee-noh)*

NOTICE! ¡Fíjese!

Learn the names for all violent activity:

Did you see (the)...?	**¿Vió...?** *(vee-'oh)*
abuse	**el abuso** *(ehl ah-'boo-soh)*
assault	**el asalto** *(ehl ah-'sahl-toh)*
battery	**la agresión** *(lah ah-greh-see-'ohn)*
beating	**la golpiza** *(lah gohl-'pee-sah)*
manslaughter	**el homicidio involuntario**
	(ehl oh-mee-'see-dee-oh een-voh-loon-'tah-ree-oh)
mugging	**el atraco** *(ehl ah-'trah-koh)*
murder	**el asesinato** *(ehl ah-seh-see-'nah-toh)*
poisoning	**el envenenamiento** *(ehl ehn-veh-neh-nah-mee-'ehn-toh)*
rape	**la violación** *(lah vee-oh-lah-see-'ohn)*
shooting	**los disparos** *(lohs dees-'pah-rohs)*
stabbing	**la puñalada** *(lah poon-yah-'lah-dah)*

THE WEAPONS
Las armas
(lahs 'ahr-mahs)

Crime reports indicate that the following words pop up when weapons are at the scene:

Did you/he/she use the...?	**¿Usó usted/él/ella...?** *(oo-'soh oos-'tehd/ehl/'eh-yah)*
bat	**el bate de béisbol** *(ehl 'bah-teh deh 'beh-ees-bohl)*
belt	**el cinturón** *(ehl seen-too-'rohn)*
billy club	**el garrote** *(ehl gahr-'roh-teh)*
blade	**la navaja** *(lah nah-'vah-hah)*
bomb	**la bomba** *(lah 'bohm-bah)*
bottle	**la botella** *(lah boh-'teh-yah)*
brass knuckles	**las manoplas** *(lahs mah-'noh-plahs)*
chain	**la cadena** *(lah kah-'deh-nah)*
dynamite	**la dinamita** *(lah dee-nah-'mee-tah)*
explosive	**el explosivo** *(ehl ex-ploh-'see-voh)*
firearm	**el arma de fuego** *(ehl 'ahr-mah deh 'fweh-goh)*
fist	**el puño** *(ehl 'poon-yoh)*
hammer	**el martillo** *(ehl mahr-'tee-yoh)*
hatchet	**el hacha** *(ehl 'ah-chah)*
knife	**el cuchillo** *(ehl koo-'chee-yoh)*
pipe	**el tubo** *(ehl 'too-boh)*
pistol	**la pistola** *(lah pees-'toh-lah)*
poison	**el veneno** *(ehl veh-'neh-noh)*
revolver	**el revólver** *(ehl reh-'vohl-vehr)*
rifle	**el rifle** *(ehl 'reef-leh)*
rock	**la piedra** *(lah pee-'eh-drah)*
rope	**la soga** *(lah 'soh-gah)*
scissors	**las tijeras** *(lahs tee-'heh-rahs)*
screwdriver	**el destornillador** *(ehl dehs-tohr-nee-yah-'dohr)*
shotgun	**la escopeta** *(lah ehs-koh-'peh-tah)*
shovel	**la pala** *(lah 'pah-lah)*
stick	**el palo** *(ehl 'pah-loh)*
wire	**el alambre** *(ehl ah-'lahm-breh)*

Now, specifically ask about the firearms:

Do you have a concealed firearm?
¿Tiene un arma de fuego escondida?
(tee-'eh-neh oon 'ahr-mah deh 'fweh-goh ehs-kohn-'dee-dah)

Where did you get the firearm?
¿Dónde consiguió el arma de fuego?
('dohn-deh kohn-see-ghee-'oh ehl 'ahr-mah deh 'fweh-goh)

Are you the owner of the firearm?
¿Es el dueño del arma de fuego? *(ehs ehl 'dwehn-yoh dehl 'ahr-mah deh 'fweh-goh)*

Do you have a license for the firearm?
¿Tiene una licencia para el arma de fuego?
(tee-'eh-neh 'oo-nah lee-'sehn-see-ah 'pah-rah ehl 'ahr-mah deh 'fweh-goh)

Was the firearm loaded?
¿Estaba cargada el arma de fuego?
(ehs-'tah-bah kahr-'gah-dah ehl 'ahr-mah deh 'fweh-goh)

THE SENTENCE!   ¡La frase!

Use these lines to confirm the facts:

Is this correct?	**¿Es correcto esto?** *(ehs kohr-'rehk-toh 'ehs-toh)*
Do you have a doubt?	**¿Tiene una duda?** *(tee-'eh-neh 'oo-nah 'doo-dah)*
Are you sure?	**¿Está seguro?** *(ehs-'tah seh-'goo-roh)*

And use commands when you think it's necessary:

Deny it.	**Niéguelo** *(nee-'eh-gheh-loh)*
Don't deny it.	**No lo niegue.** *(noh loh nee-'eh-gheh)*
Sign the confession.	**Firme la confesión.** *('feer-meh lah kohn-feh-see-'ohn)*
Don't sign the confession.	**No firme la confesión.** *(noh 'feer-meh lah kohn-feh-see-'ohn)*
Tell the truth.	**Diga la verdad.** *(dee-gah lah vehr-'dahd)*

PRIVATE PRACTICE   Práctica privada

(44) A. List three different weapons in Spanish:

_____   _____

B. List three physically violent actions in Spanish:

_____   _____   _____

C. List three places where violent crimes often occur in Spanish:

_____   _____

DETECTIVE WORK
El trabajo de detective
(ehl trah-'bah-hoh deh deh-tehk-'tee-veh)

Lawyers must do a lot of research; focus on every detail:

Was it...?	**¿Fue...?** *(foo-'eh)*
a drive-by	**un disparo de un carro** *(oon dees-'pah-roh deh oon 'kahr-roh)*
a single shot	**un solo balazo** *(oon 'soh-loh bah-'lah-soh)*
a suicide	**un suicidio** *(oon soo-ee-'see-dee-oh)*
an accident	**un accidente** *(oon ahk-see-'dehn-teh)*
in cold blood	**a sangre fría** *(ah 'sahn-greh 'free-ah)*
involuntary	**involuntario** *(een-voh-loon-'tah-ree-oh)*
premeditated	**premeditado** *(pre-meh-dee-'tah-doh)*

Did it involve...?	**¿Tuvo que ver con...?** *('too-voh keh vehr kohn)*
hate	**el odio** *(ehl 'oh-dee-oh)*
insanity	**la locura** *(lah loh-'koo-rah)*
jealousy	**el celos** *(lohs 'seh-lohs)*
love	**el amor** *(ehl ah-'mohr)*
passion	**la pasión** *(lah pah-see-'ohn)*
racism	**el racismo** *(ehl rah-'sees-moh)*
revenge	**la venganza** *(lah vehn-'gahn-sah)*

Do you know (the)...?	**¿Sabe...?** *('sah-beh)*
cause	**la causa** *(lah 'kah-oo-sah)*
exact time	**la hora exacta** *(lah 'oh-rah ex-'ahk-tah)*
motive	**el motivo** *(ehl moh-'tee-voh)*
place	**el sitio** *(ehl 'see-tee-oh)*
purpose	**el propósito** *(ehl proh-'poh-see-toh)*
reason	**la razón** *(lah rah-'sohn)*

Was there a strange _____?	**¿Había _____ raro/rara?** *(ah-'bee-ah ___ 'rah-roh/'rah-rah)*
object	**un objeto** *(oon ohb-'heh-toh)*
package	**un paquete** *(oon pah-'keh-teh)*
person	**una persona** *('oo-nah pehr-'soh-nah)*
smell	**un olor** *(oon oh-'lohr)*
sound	**un sonido** *(oon soh-'nee-doh)*

Now explain to the client how the police are handling the case:

They're going to...	**Van a...** *(vahn ah)*
gather evidence	**recoger evidencia** *(reh-koh-'hehr eh-vee-'dehn-see-ah)*
look for clues	**buscar indicios** *(boos-'kahr een-'dee-see-ohs)*
take pictures	**tomar fotos** *(toh-'mahr 'foh-tohs)*

They use (the)...	**Usan...** *('oo-sahn)*
drops	**las gotas** *(lahs 'goh-tahs)*
plastic bag	**la bolsa de plástico** *(lah 'bohl-sah deh 'plahs-tee-koh)*
powder	**el polvo** *(ehl 'pohl-voh)*
spray	**el aerosol** *(ehl ah-eh-roh-'sohl)*
sticky disk	**el disco pegajoso** *(ehl 'dees-koh peh-gah-'hoh-soh)*

They checked (the)...	**Analizaron...** *(ah-nah-lee-'sah-rohn)*
ashes	**las cenizas** *(lahs seh-'nee-sahs)*
blood	**la sangre** *(lah 'sahn-greh)*
hair	**el pelo** *(ehl 'peh-loh)*
print	**la huella** *(lah 'hweh-yah)*
stain	**la mancha** *(lah 'mahn-chah)*
track	**la pista** *(lah 'pees-tah)*

NOTICE!   ¡Fíjese!

Use these other Spanish words to talk about incarceration:

fugitive	**el fugitivo** *(ehl foo-hee-'tee-voh)*
guard	**el guardia** *(ehl 'gwahr-dee-ah)*
inmate	**el preso** *(ehl 'preh-soh)*
prison	**la prisión** *(lah pree-see-'ohn)*
prisoner	**el prisionero** *(ehl pree-see-oh-'neh-roh)*
probation officer	**el oficial de libertad provisional** *(ehl oh-fee-see-'ahl deh lee-behr-'tahd proh-vee-see-oh-'nahl)*
trustee	**el prisionero con privilegios** *(ehl pree-see-oh-'neh-roh kohn pree-vee-'leh-hee-ohs)*
visiting room	**el salón de visitantes** *(ehl sah-'lohn deh vee-see-'tahn-tehs)*
warden	**el carcelero** *(ehl kahr-seh-'leh-roh)*

ILLEGAL DRUGS
Las drogas ilegales
(lahs 'droh-gahs ee-leh-'gah-lehs)

If the criminal activity involves drugs, these terms will help to communicate your messages:

Was he/she arrested for...?	**¿Fue arrestado por...?** *(foo-'eh ahr-rehs-'tah-doh pohr)*
possession	**la posesión** *(lah poh-seh-see-'ohn)*
producing	**la producción** *(lah proh-dook-see-'ohn)*
selling	**la venta** *(lah 'vehn-tah)*
transporting	**el transporte** *(ehl trahns-'pohr-teh)*
using	**el consumo** *(ehl kohn-'soo-moh)*
Did they find (the)...?	**¿Encontraron...?** *(ehn-kohn-'trah-rohn)*
bag	**la bolsa** *(lah 'bohl-sah)*
balloon	**el globo** *(ehl 'gloh-boh)*
brick	**el ladrillo** *(ehl lah-'dree-yoh)*
capsule	**la cápsula** *(lah 'kahp-soo-lah)*
chemical	**la sustancia química** *(lah soos-'tahn-see-ah 'kee-mee-kah)*
cigarette	**el cigarrillo** *(ehl see-gahr-'ree-yoh)*
kit	**el estuche** *(ehl ehs-'too-cheh)*
liquid	**el líquido** *(ehl 'lee-kee-doh)*
needle	**la aguja** *(lah ah-'goo-hah)*
piece	**el pedazo** *(ehl peh-'dah-soh)*
pill	**la píldora** *(lah 'peel-doh-rah)*
pipe	**la pipa** *(lah 'pee-pah)*
plant	**la planta** *(lah 'plahn-tah)*
powder	**el polvo** *(ehl 'pohl-voh)*
razor	**la navaja** *(lah nah-'vah-hah)*
residue	**el residuo** *(ehl reh-'see-doo-oh)*
rock	**la piedra** *(lah pee-'eh-drah)*
spoon	**la cuchara** *(lah koo-'chah-rah)*
syringe	**la jeringa** *(lah heh-'reen-gah)*
tablet	**la tableta** *(lah tah-'bleh-tah)*
vial	**el frasco** *(ehl 'frahs-koh)*

Get right to the point:

Do you have a prescription?
¿Tiene una receta? *(tee-'eh-neh 'oo-nah reh-'seh-tah)*

Have you been arrested before?
¿Ha sido arrestado antes? *(ah 'see-doh ahr-rehs-'tah-doh 'ahn-tehs)*

How long have you been using?
¿Por cuánto tiempo ha estado usando?
(pohr 'kwahn-toh tee-'ehm-poh ah ehs-'tah-doh oo-'sahn-doh)

What's the name of your contact?
¿Cuál es el nombre de su conexión?
(kwahl ehs ehl 'nohm-breh deh soo koh-nehk-see-'ohn)

How much did it cost you?
¿Cuánto le costó? *('kwahn-toh leh kohs-'toh)*

Where did you buy it?
¿Dónde lo compró? *('dohn-deh loh kohm-'proh)*

When did you start using drugs?
¿Cuándo comenzó a tomar drogas? *('kwahn-doh koh-mehn-'soh ah toh-'mahr 'droh-gahs)*

Here's another common pattern in Spanish:

What did you/he/she swallow?	**¿Qué tragó?** *(keh trah-'goh)*
What did you/he/she eat?	**¿Qué comió?** *(keh koh-mee-'oh)*
What did you/he/she inject?	**¿Qué inyectó?** *(keh een-yehk-'toh)*
What did you/he/she take?	**¿Qué tomó?** *(keh toh-'moh)*
What did you/he/she buy?	**¿Qué compró?** *(keh kohm-'proh)*
What did you/he/she sell?	**¿Qué vendió?** *(keh vehn-dee-'oh)*

Were you...?	**¿Estaba usted...?** *(ehs-'tah-bah oos-'tehd)*
Was he/she...?	**¿Estaba él/ella...?** *(ehs-'tah-bah ehl/'eh-yah)*

    disoriented   **desorientado/desorientada**
                            (deh-soh-ree-ehn-'tah-doh/deh-soh-ree-ehn-'tah-dah)
    asleep   **dormido/dormida** *(dohr-'mee-doh/dohr-'mee-dah)*
    awake   **despierto/despierta** *(dehs-pee-'ehr-toh/dehs-pee-'ehr-tah)*
    dizzy   **mareado/mareada** *(mah-reh-'ah-doh/mah-reh-'ah-dah)*
    drugged   **drogado/drogada** *(droh-'gah-doh/drog-'gah-dah)*
    unconscious   **inconsciente** *(een-kohn-see-'ehn-teh)*

Fortunately, many of the Spanish and English words related to drugs are spelled about the same:

Did you/he/she have (the)...?	**¿Tenía usted/él/ella...?** *(teh-'nee-ah oos-'tehd/ehl/'eh-yah)*

    acid   **el ácido** *(ehl 'ah-see-doh)*
    amphetamine   **la anfetamina** *(lah ahn-feh-tah-'mee-nah)*
    barbiturate   **el barbitúrico** *(ehl bahr-bee-'too-ree-koh)*
    cocaine   **la cocaine** *(lah koh-kah-'ee-nah)*
    crack   **el crack** *(ehl krahk)*
    ecstasy   **el éxtasis** *(ehl 'ex-tah-sees)*

hallucinogens	**los alucinógenos** *(lohs ah-loo-see-'noh-heh-nohs)*
hashish	**el hachís** *(ehl ah-'chees)*
heroin	**la heroína** *(lah eh-roh-'ee-nah)*
inhalants	**los inhaladores** *(lohs een-ah-lah-'doh-rehs)*
marijuana	**la marijuana** *(lah mah-ree-'hwah-nah)*
mescaline	**la mescalina** *(lah mehs-kah-'lee-nah)*
methamphetamine	**la metanfetamina** *(lah meh-tahn-feh-tah-'mee-nah)*
morphine	**la morfina** *(lah mohr-'fee-nah)*
narcotics	**los narcóticos** *(lohs nahr-'koh-tee-kohs)*
opium	**el opio** *(ehl 'oh-pee-oh)*
psilocybin	**la silocibina** *(lah see-loh-see-'bee-nah)*
sedative	**el sedante** *(ehl seh-'dahn-teh)*
steroids	**los esteroides** *(lohs ehs-teh-'roh-ee-dehs)*
stimulants	**los estimulantes** *(lohs ehs-tee-moo-'lahn-tehs)*
tranquilizer	**el tranquilizante** *(ehl trahn-kee-lee-'sahn-teh)*

NOTICE!   ¡Fíjese!

Conversations about drugs often include simple measurements:

gram	**el gramo** *(ehl 'grah-moh)*
half	**la mitad** *(lah mee-'tahd)*
kilogram	**el kilogramo** *(ehl kee-loh-'grah-moh)*
milligram	**el milígramo** *(ehl mee-'lee-grah-moh)*
ounce	**la onza** *(lah 'ohn-sah)*
pound	**la libra** *(lah 'lee-brah)*
quarter	**el cuarto** *(ehl 'kwahr-toh)*
tablespoon	**la cucharada** *(lah koo-chah-'rah-dah)*
teaspoon	**la cucharadita** *(lah koo-chah-rah-'dee-tah)*

PRIVATE PRACTICE   Práctica privada

(45) Connect the words that belong together best:

1. huellas	venganza
2. píldora	despierto
3. opio	evidencia
4. odio	heroína
5. dormido	cápsula

VERBS IN ACTION!   ¡Verbos activos!

Add more actions that relate to criminal law:

to abuse	**abusar** *(ah-boo-'sahr)*
to accept	**aceptar** *(ah-sehp-'tahr)*
to accuse	**acusar** *(ah-koo-'sahr)*
to admit	**admitir** *(ahd-mee-'teer)*
to analyze	**analizar** *(ah-nah-lee-'sahr)*
to appeal	**apelar** *(ah-peh-'lahr)*
to arrest	**arrestar** *(ahr-rehs-'tahr)*
to authorize	**autorizar** *(aw-toh-ree-'sahr)*
to belong to	**pertenecer** *(pehr-teh-neh-'sehr)*
to break in	**forzar** *(fohr-'sahr)*
to break	**quebrar** *(keh-'brahr)*
to chase	**perseguir** *(pehr-seh-'gheer)*
to check	**revisar** *(reh-vee-'sahr)*
to fight	**pelear** *(peh-leh-'ahr)*
to hit	**golpear** *(gohl-peh-'ahr)*
to investigate	**investigar** *(een-vehs-tee-'gahr)*
to kill	**matar** *(mah-'tahr)*
to look for	**buscar** *(boos-'kahr)*
to maim	**lisiar** *(lee-see-'ahr)*
to mutilate	**mutilar** *(moo-tee-'lahr)*
to obtain	**obtener** *(ohb-teh-'nehr)*
to paralyze	**paralizar** *(pah-rah-lee-'sahr)*
to promise	**prometer** *(proh-meh-'tehr)*
to prosecute	**acusar** *(ah-koo-'sahr)*
to prove	**probar** *(proh-'bahr)*
to refuse	**rehusar** *(reh-oo-'sahr)*
to search	**registrar** *(reh-ees-'trahr)*
to share	**compartir** *(kohm-pahr-'teer)*
to shoot	**disparar** *(dees-pah-'rahr)*
to stab	**apuñalar** *(ah-poon-yah-'lahr)*
to steal	**robar** *(roh-'bahr)*
to submit	**presentar** *(preh-sehn-'tahr)*
to support	**apoyar** *(ah-poh-'yahr)*
to suppose	**suponer** *(soo-poh-'nehr)*
to take drugs	**tomar drogas** *(toh-'mahr 'droh-gahs)*
to testify	**testificar** *(tehs-tee-fee-'kahr)*
to threaten	**amenazar** *(ah-meh-nah-'sahr)*

NOTICE! ¡Fíjese!

Feel free to add a few time-referenced expressions:

periodically	**de vez en cuando** *(deh vehs ehn 'kwahn-doh)*

Toma drogas de vez en cuando.

in advance	**con anticipación** *(kohn ahn-tee-see-pah-see-'ohn)*

_____

beforehand	**de antemano** *(deh ahn-teh-'mah-noh)*

_____

THE SENTENCE! ¡La frase!

Review the verb forms we've studied so far in this guidebook. Note the spelling and pronunciation changes that take place when you shift from one time reference to the next:

I'm working there now.
Estoy trabajando ahí ahora.
(ehs-'toh-ee trah-bah-'hahn-doh ah-'ee ah-'oh-rah)

I work there every day.
Trabajo ahí todos los días.
(trah-'bah-hoh ah-'ee 'toh-dohs lohs 'dee-ahs)

I will work there tomorrow.
Voy a trabajar ahí mañana.
('voh-ee ah trah-bah-'hahr ah-'ee mahn-'yah-nah)

I worked there yesterday.
Trabajé ahí ayer. *(trah-bah-'heh ah-'ee ah-'yehr)*

I worked there a long time ago.
Trabajaba ahí hace muchos años.
(trah-bah-'hah-bah ah-'ee ah-'seh 'moo-chohs 'ahn-yohs)

Now, look at this next two-part verb form, which refers to actions that have already taken place. The first part consists of forms of the verb *to have*—**haber** *(ah-'behr)*, while the second part consists of the past participle of abother verb. Both parts must be used together:

	HABER	PAST PARTICIPLE	
I've	**He**	left	**salido** *(sah-'lee-doh)*
		eaten	**comido** *(koh-'mee-doh)*
You've (sing.), She's, He's	**Ha**	arrived	**llegado** *(yeh-'gah-doh)*
		called	**llamado** *(yah-'mah-doh)*
You've (pl.), They've	**Han**	worked	**trabajado** *(trah-bah-'hah-doh)*
		driven	**manejado** *(mah-neh-'hah-doh)*
We've	**Hemos**	learned	**aprendido** *(ah-prehn-'dee-doh)*

Here are some examples:

I've called here many times.
He llamado aquí muchas veces. *(eh yah-'mah-doh ah-'kee 'moo-chahs 'veh-sehs)*

She's taken drugs.
Ella ha tomado drogas. *('eh-yah ah toh-'mah-doh 'droh-gahs)*

We've testified before.
Hemos testificado antes. *('eh-mohs tehs-tee-fee-'kah-doh 'ahn-tehs)*

 VERBS IN ACTION!   ¡Verbos activos!

Many past participles in Spanish can be used as descriptive words. Notice how they generally end in the letters **-ado** or **-ido**:

They are stolen cars.
Son carros robados. *(sohn 'kahr-rohs roh-'bah-dohs)*

The doors are destroyed.
Las puertas están destruidas. *(lahs 'pwehr-tahs ehs-'tahn dehs-troo-'ee-dahs)*

He was stabbed.
Estaba apuñalado. *(ehs-'tah-bah ah-poon-yah-'lah-doh)*

Unfortunately, a handful of past participles are considered irregular. Here are three examples:

(Hacer:) I've done the job.
He hecho el trabajo. *(eh 'eh-choh ehl trah-'bah-hoh)*
(Poner:) He's put the pistol here.
Ha puesto la pistola aquí. *(ah 'pwehs-toh lah pees-'toh-lah ah-'kee)*
(Ver:) We've seen the man.
Hemos visto al hombre. *('eh-mohs 'vees-toh ahl 'ohm-breh)*

PRIVATE PRACTICE   **Práctica privada**

46 Here's more verb review. Fill in the blanks with the correct forms. The first one is done for you:

TO CHECK	**Revisar**
I'm checking	**Estoy revisando**
I check	**Reviso**
I'm going to check	**Voy a revisar**
I checked	**Revisé**
I used to check	**Revisaba**
I have checked	**He revisado**

1. TO FIGHT   **Pelear**

I'm fighting   _____

I fight   _____

I'm going to fight   _____

I fought   _____

I used to fight   _____

I have fought   _____

2. TO HELP   **Ayudar**

I'm helping   _____

I help   _____

I'm going to help   _____

I helped   _____

I used to help   _____

I have helped   _____

CULTURAL COMMENT   **Comentario cultural**

Mirroring a universal characteristic, once Hispanics establish friendly relationships, it's not uncommon for them to use nicknames when referring to others. It is meant to show intimacy, and not disrespect, so don't be surprised if you are given a new name. Besides, it might be fun to look up the translations for any terms of endearment that you hear.

WE'RE DONE! CONGRATULATIONS!
¡Hemos terminado!¡Felicitaciones!
('eh-mohs tehr-mee-'nah-doh, feh-lee-see-tah-see-'oh-nehs)

¡Buen trabajo! We've come to the end of our Spanish training in this guidebook. Hopefully, much of what you've read has already been put into practice, and you're excited about learning more. The vocabulary and grammar presentations, along with the language and culture tips, were specifically designed to get you started. So now, **mis amigos**, the rest is up to you.

Adiós y muy buena suerte,

Bill Harvey

ENGLISH–SPANISH GLOSSARY

VOCABULARY

Spanish nouns, adjectives, and articles may be feminine or masculine. That is why nouns are preceded by the feminine **la** or the masculine **el**, and the adjectives are listed in both masculine and feminine form (e.g., **enojado/enojada**). When there is an exception and the noun is either masculine or feminine (**artista**), then the articles are shown together (**el/la artista**).

A

a	**un/una** *(oon/ˈoo-nah)*
ability	**la habilidad** *(lah ah-bee-lee-ˈdahd)*
above	**encima** *(ehn-ˈsee-mah)*
abuse	**el abuso** *(ehl ah-ˈboo-soh)*
abused	**abusado/abusada** *(ah-boo-ˈsah-doh/ah-boo-ˈsah-dah)*
accent	**el acento** *(ehl ah-ˈsehn-toh)*
accessory	**el/la cómplice** *(ehl/lah ˈkohm-plee-seh)*
accident	**el accidente** *(ehl ahk-see-ˈdehn-teh)*
account	**la cuenta** *(lah ˈkwehn-tah)*
accountant	**el contador/la contadora** *(ehl kohn-tah-ˈdohr/lah kohn-tah-ˈdoh-rah)*
accounting	**la contabilidad** *(lah kohn-tah-bee-lee-ˈdahd)*
accrued	**acumulado/acumulada** *(ah-koo-moo-ˈlah-doh/ah-koo-moo-ˈlah-dah)*
accusation	**la acusación** *(lah ah-koo-sah-see-ˈohn)*
accused	**el acusado/la acusada** *(ah-koo-ˈsah-doh/ah-koo-ˈsah-dah)*
acid	**el ácido** *(ehl ˈah-see-doh)*
acquital	**la absolución** *(lah ahb-soh-loo-see-ˈohn)*
active	**activo/activa** *(ahk-ˈtee-voh/ahk-ˈtee-vah)*
address	**la dirección** *(lah dee-rehk-see-ˈohn)*
adjustment	**el ajuste** *(ehl ah-ˈhoos-teh)*
administrator	**el administrador/la administradora** *(ehl ahd-mee-nees-trah-ˈdohr/lah ahd-mee-nees-trah-ˈdoh-rah)*
adolescent	**el/la adolescente** *(ehl/lah ah-doh-lehs-ˈsehn-teh)*
adoption	**la adopción** *(lah ah-dohp-see-ˈohn)*
advertising	**la publicidad** *(lah poo-blee-see-ˈdahd)*
advice	**el consejo** *(ehl kohn-ˈseh-hoh)*
advisor	**el consejero** *(ehl kohn-seh-ˈheh-roh)*
affidavit	**la declaración jurada** *(lah deh-klah-rah-see-ˈohn hoo-ˈrah-dah)*
afraid	**asustado/asustada** *(ah-soos-ˈtah-doh/ah-soos-ˈtah-dah)*

after	**después**	*(dehs-'pwehs)*
age	**la edad**	*(lah eh-'dahd)*
agency	**la agencia**	*(lah ah-'hehn-see-ah)*
agenda	**el orden del día**	*(ehl 'ohr-dehn dehl 'dee-ah)*
agent	**el/la agente**	*(ehl/lah ah-'hehn-teh)*
aggressive	**agresivo/agresiva**	*(ah-greh-'see-voh/ah-greh-'see-vah)*
agreement	**el acuerdo**	*(ehl ah-'kwehr-doh)*
AIDS	**el SIDA**	*(ehl 'see-dah)*
AIDS test	**la prueba de SIDA**	*(lah proo-'eh-bah deh 'see-dah)*

air conditioning   **el aire acondicionado**
(ehl 'ah-ee-reh ah-kohn-dee-see-oh-'nah-doh)

airline	**la aerolínea**	*(lah ah-eh-roh-'lee-neh-ah)*
airport	**el aeropuerto**	*(ehl ah-eh-roh-'pwehr-toh)*
aisle	**el pasillo**	*(ehl pah-'see-yoh)*
alcohol	**el alcohol**	*(ehl ahl-koh-'ohl)*
alibi	**la coartada**	*(lah koh-ahr-'tah-dah)*

alimony   **la manutención conyugal**
(lah mah-noo-tehn-see-'ohn kohn-yoo-'gahl)

allegation	**el alegato**	*(ehl ah-leh-'gah-toh)*
allergies	**las alergias**	*(lahs ah-'lehr-hee-ahs)*
allocation	**la asignación**	*(lah ah-seeg-nah-see-'ohn)*
almost	**casi**	*(kah-see)*
alone	**solo/sola**	*('soh-loh/'soh-lah)*
along	**a lo largo**	*(ah loh 'lahr-goh)*
already	**ya**	*(yah)*
always	**siempre**	*(see-'ehm-preh)*
A.M.	**de la mañana**	*(deh lah mahn-'yah-nah)*
ambulance	**la ambulancia**	*(la ahm-boo-'lahn-see-ah)*
amendment	**la enmienda**	*(lah ehn-mee-'ehn-dah)*

American   **el norteamericano/la norteamericana**
(ehl nohr-teh-ah-meh-ree-'kah-noh/lah nohr-teh-ah-meh-ree-'kah-nah)

amortization	**la amortización**	*(lah ah-mohr-tee-sah-see-'ohn)*
amount	**el monto**	*(ehl 'mohn-toh)*
amphetamine	**la anfetamina**	*(lah ahn-feh-tah-'mee-nah)*
analyst	**el/la analista**	*(ehl/lah ah-nah-'lees-tah)*
and	**y**	*(ee)*
anesthetist	**el/la anestesista**	*(ehl/lah ah-nehs-teh-'sees-tah)*
angry	**enojado/enojada**	*(eh-noh-'hah-doh/eh-noh-'hah-dah)*
animal	**el animal**	*(ehl ah-nee-'mahl)*
ankle	**el tobillo**	*(ehl toh-'bee-yoh)*
announcement	**el anuncio**	*(ehl ah-'noon-see-oh)*
annuity	**la anualidad**	*(lah ah-'nwah-lee-dahd)*

annulled	**anulado/anulada** *(ah-noo-'lah-doh/ah-noo-'lah-dah)*
annulment	**la anulación** *(lah ah-noo-lah-see-'ohn)*
anxious	**ansioso/ansiosa** *(ahn-see-'oh-soh/ahn-see-'oh-sah)*
anyone	**cualquiera** *(kwahl-kee-'eh-rah)*
anything	**cualquier cosa** *(kwahl-kee-'ehr 'koh-sah)*
anywhere	**en cualquier sitio** *(ehn kwahl-kee-'ehr 'see-tee-oh)*
apartment	**el apartamento** *(ehl ah-pahr-tah-'mehn-toh)*
apathetic	**apático/apática** *(ah-'pah-tee-koh/ah-'pah-tee-kah)*
apology	**la disculpa** *(lah dees-'kool-pah)*
appeal	**la apelación** *(lah ah-peh-lah-see-'ohn)*
appendix	**el apéndice** *(ehl ah-'pehn-dee-seh)*
applicant	**el/la solicitante** *(ehl/lah soh-lee-see-'tahn-teh)*
application	**la solicitud** *(lah soh-lee-see-'tood)*
appointment	**la cita** *(lah 'see-tah)*
appraisal	**el avalúo** *(ehl ah-vah-'loo-oh)*
appraiser	**el tasador/la tasadora** *(ehl tah-sah-'dohr/lah tah-sah-'doh-rah)*
appreciation	**la revalorización** *(lah reh-vah-loh-ree-sah-see-'ohn)*
approval	**la aprobación** *(lah ah-proh-bah-see-'ohn)*
approved	**aprobado/aprobada** *(ah-proh-'bah-doh/ah-proh-'bah-dah)*
APR	**la tasa de interés anual** *(lah 'tah-sah deh een-teh-'rehs ah-noo-'ahl)*
April	**abril** *(ah-'breel)*
architect	**el arquitecto/la arquitecta** *(ehl ahr-kee-'tehk-toh/lah ahr-kee-'tehk-tah)*
area code	**el código de area** *(ehl 'koh-dee-goh deh 'ah-reh-ah)*
argument	**la discusión** *(lah dees-koo-see-'ohn)*
arm	**el brazo** *(ehl 'brah-soh)*
armchair	**el sillón** *(ehl see-'yohn)*
armed	**armado/armada** *(ahr-'mah-doh/ahr-'mah-dah)*
armed robbery	**el atraco a mano armada** *(ehl ah-'trah-koh ah 'mah-noh ahr-'mah-dah)*
around	**alrededor** *(ahl-reh-deh-'dohr)*
arraignment	**el emplazamiento** *(ehl ehm-plah-sah-mee-'ehn-toh)*
arrangement	**el arreglo** *(ehl ahr-'reh-gloh)*
arrest	**el arresto** *(ehl ahr-'rehs-toh)*
arrest warrant	**la orden de detención** *(lah 'ohr-dehn deh deh-tehn-see-'ohn)*
arrested	**arrestado/arrestada** *(ahr-rehs-'tah-doh/ahr-rehs-'tah-dah)*
arson	**el incendio premeditado** *(ehl een-'sehn-dee-oh preh-meh-dee-'tah-doh)*
artist	**el/la artista** *(ehl/lah ahr-'tees-tah)*
asbestos	**el asbesto** *(ehl ahs-'behs-toh)*
ashes	**las cenizas** *(lahs seh-'nee-sahs)*
asleep	**dormido/dormida** *(dohr-'mee-doh/dohr-'mee-dah)*

assault	**el asalto** *(ehl ah-'sahl-toh)*
assessment	**la tasación fiscal** *(lah tah-sah-see-'ohn fees-'kahl)*
assets	**los bienes** *(lohs bee-'eh-nehs)*
assignor	**el/la cedente** *(ehl/lah seh-'dehn-teh)*
assistant	**el/ la asistente** *(ehl/lah ah-sees-'tehn-teh)*
associate	**el asociado/la asociada** *(ehl ah-soh-see-'ah-doh/lah ah-soh-see-'ah-dah)*
asylum	**el asilo** *(ehl ah-'see-loh)*
at	**en** *(ehn)*
athlete	**el/la atleta** *(ehl/lah aht-'leh-tah)*
ATM	**el cajero automático** *(ehl kah-'heh-roh aw-toh-'mah-tee-koh)*
attachment	**el adjunto** *(ehl ahd-'hoon-toh)*
attorney	**el abogado/la abogada** *(ehl ah-boh-'gah-doh/lah ah-boh-'gah-dah)*
attorney general	**el procurador general** *(ehl proh-koo-rah-'dohr heh-neh-'rahl)*
audit	**la auditoria** *(lah aw-dee-toh-'ree-ah)*
auditor	**el auditor/la auditora** *(ehl aw-dee-'tohr/lah aw-dee-'toh-rah)*
August	**agosto** *(ah-'gohs-toh)*
aunt	**la tía** *(lah 'tee-ah)*
author	**el autor/la autora** *(ehl aw-'tohr/lah aw-'toh-rah)*
auto loan	**el préstamo de carro** *(ehl 'prehs-tah-moh deh 'kahr-roh)*
autopsy	**la autopsia** *(lah aw-'tohp-see-ah)*
available	**disponible** *(dees-poh-'nee-bleh)*
avenue	**la avenida** *(lah ah-veh-'nee-dah)*
average	**el promedio** *(ehl proh-'meh-dee-oh)*
awake	**despierto/despierta** *(dehs-pee-'ehr-toh/dehs-pee-'ehr-tah)*
ax	**el hacha** *(ehl 'ah-chah)*

B

baby	**el/la bebé** *(ehl/lah beh-'beh)*
back	**atrás** *(ah-'trahs)*
back (body)	**la espalda** *(lah ehs-'pahl-dah)*
back taxes	**los impuestos atrasados** *(lohs eem-'pwehs-tohs ah-trah-'sah-dohs)*
backpack	**la mochila** *(lah moh-'chee-lah)*
bad	**malo/mala** *('mah-loh/'mah-lah)*
bag	**la bolsa** *(lah 'bohl-sah)*
bail	**la fianza** *(lah fee-'ahn-sah)*
bail bond	**la escritura de fianza** *(lah ehs-kree-'too-rah deh fee-'ahn-sah)*
bailiff	**el/la alguacil** *(ehl/lah ahl-gwah-'seel)*
balance	**el saldo** *(ehl 'sahl-doh)*
bald	**calvo/calva** *('kahl-voh/'kahl-vah)*
bank	**el banco** *(ehl 'bahn-koh)*

bank account	**la cuenta bancaria** *(lah 'kwehn-tah bahn-'kah-ree-ah)*
banker	**el banquero/la banquera** *(ehl bahn-'keh-roh/lah bahn-'keh-rah)*
bankruptcy	**la bancarrota** *(lah bahn-kahr-'roh-tah)*
bar exam	**el examen de abogacía** *(ehl ex-'ah-mehn deh ah-boh-gah-'see-ah)*
bar	**el bar** *(ehl bahr)*
barbiturate	**el barbitúrico** *(ehl bahr-bee-'too-ree-koh)*
barefoot	**descalzo/descalza** *(dehs-'kahl-soh/dehs-'kahl-sah)*
bargain	**la ganga** *(lah 'gahn-gah)*
bartender	**el cantinero/la cantinera** *(ehl kahn-tee-'neh-roh/lah kahn-tee-'neh-rah)*
baseball bat	**el bate de béisbol** *(ehl 'bah-teh deh 'beh-ees-bohl)*
bathing suit	**el traje de baño** *(ehl 'trah-heh deh 'bahn-yoh)*
battery	**la agresión** *(lah ah-greh-see-'ohn)*
beard	**la barba** *(lah 'bahr-bah)*
beating	**la paliza** *(lah pah-'lee-sah)*
because	**porque** *('pohr-keh)*
beer	**la cerveza** *(lah sehr-'veh-sah)*
before	**antes** *('ahn-tehs)*
behavior	**el comportamiento** *(ehl kohm-pohr-tah-mee-'ehn-toh)*
behind	**detrás** *(deh-'trahs)*
belt	**el cinturón** *(ehl seen-too-'rohn)*
bench	**el banco** *(ehl 'bahn-koh)*
bench (seat)	**la banca** *(lah 'bahn-kah)*
beneficiary	**el beneficiario/la beneficiaria** *(ehl beh-neh-fee-see-'ah-ree-oh/lah beh-neh-fee-see-'ah-ree-ah)*
benefits	**los beneficios** *(lohs beh-neh-'fee-see-ohs)*
beside	**al lado** *(ahl 'lah-doh)*
better	**mejor** *(meh-'hohr)*
between	**entre** *('ehn-treh)*
bicycle	**la bicicleta** *(lah bee-see-'kleh-tah)*
big	**grande** *('grahn-deh)*
bill	**la cuenta** *(lah 'kwehn-tah)*
billy club	**el garrote** *(ehl gahr-'roh-teh)*
binder	**la cobertura provisional** *(lah koh-behr-'too-rah proh-vee-see-oh-'nahl)*
biological	**biológico/biológica** *(bee-oh-'loh-hee-koh/bee-oh-'loh-hee-kah)*
birth	**el nacimiento** *(ehl nah-see-mee-'ehn-toh)*
birth certificate	**el certificado de nacimiento** *(ehl sehr-tee-fee-'kah-doh deh nah-see-mee-'ehn-toh)*
birth date	**la fecha de nacimiento** *(lah 'feh-chah deh nah-see-mee-'ehn-toh)*
birth defect	**el defecto natal** *(ehl deh-'fehk-toh nah-'tahl)*
bitter	**amargo/amarga** *(ah-'mahr-goh/ah-'mahr-gah)*
black	**negro/negra** *('neh-groh/'neh-grah)*

bladder	**la vejiga** *(lah veh-'hee-gah)*
blade	**la navaja** *(lah nah-'vah-hah)*
blind	**ciego/ciega** *(see-'eh-goh/see-'eh-gah)*
blonde	**rubio/rubia** *('roo-bee-oh/'roo-bee-ah)*
blood	**la sangre** *(lah 'sahn-greh)*
blood type	**el tipo de sangre** *(ehl 'tee-poh deh 'sahn-greh)*
blouse	**la blusa** *(lah 'bloo-sah)*
blue	**azul** *(ah-'sool)*
board	**la tabla** *(lah 'tah-blah)*
boat	**el bote** *(ehl 'boh-teh)*
bodily injury	**la lesión corporal** *(lah leh-see-'ohn kohr-poh-'rahl)*
bomb	**la bomba** *(lah 'bohm-bah)*
bond	**el bono** *(ehl 'boh-noh)*
bone	**el hueso** *(ehl 'hweh-soh)*
book	**el libro** *(ehl 'lee-broh)*
bookie	**el corredor de apuestas** *(ehl kohr-reh-'dohr deh ah-'pwehs-tahs)*
bookkeeper	**el contable** *(ehl kohn-'tah-bleh)*
bookshelf	**el librero** *(ehl lee-'breh-roh)*
boots	**las botas** *(lahs 'boh-tahs)*
border control	**el control de la frontera** *(ehl kohn-'trohl deh lah frohn-'teh-rah)*
bored	**aburrido/aburrida** *(ah-boor-'ree-doh/ah-boor-'ree-dah)*
borrower	**el prestatario/la prestataria** *(ehl prehs-tah-'tah-ree-oh/lah prehs-tah-'tah-ree-ah)*
both	**ambos/ambas** *('ahm-bohs/'ahm-bahs)*
bothered	**molesto/molesta** *(moh-'lehs-toh/moh-'lehs-tah)*
bottle	**la botella** *(lah boh-'teh-yah)*
bottom	**el fondo** *(ehl 'fohn-doh)*
boy	**el niño** *(ehl 'neen-yoh)*
boyfriend	**el novio** *(ehl 'noh-vee-oh)*
bracelet	**la pulsera** *(lah pool-'seh-rah)*
braids	**las trenzas** *(lahs 'trehn-sahs)*
brain	**el cerebro** *(ehl seh-'reh-broh)*
brakes	**los frenos** *(lohs 'freh-nohs)*
branch office	**la sucursal** *(lah soo-koor-'sahl)*
brand	**la marca** *(lah 'mahr-kah)*
brave	**valiente** *(vah-lee-'ehn-teh)*
breakfast	**el desayuno** *(ehl deh-sah-'yoo-noh)*
breast	**el seno** *(ehl 'seh-noh)*
breath test	**la prueba de aliento** *(lah proo-'eh-bah deh ah-lee-'ehn-toh)*
bribery	**el soborno** *(ehl soh-'bohr-noh)*
brick	**el ladrillo** *(ehl lah-'dree-yoh)*
bride	**la novia** *(lah 'noh-vee-ah)*

bridegroom	**el novio** *(ehl 'noh-vee-oh)*
bridge	**el puente** *(ehl 'pwehn-teh)*
brief	**el sumario** *(ehl soo-'mah-ree-oh)*
briefcase	**el maletín** *(ehl mah-lee-'teen)*
bright	**brillante** *(bree-'yahn-teh)*
broken	**roto/rota** *('roh-toh/'roh-tah)*
broker	**el corredor** *(ehl kohr-reh-'dohr)*
brooch	**el broche** *(ehl 'broh-cheh)*
brothel	**el burdel** *(ehl boor-'dehl)*
brother	**el hermano** *(ehl ehr-'mah-noh)*
brother-in-law	**el cuñado** *(ehl koon-'yah-doh)*
brown	**café** *(kah-'feh)*
bruise	**la contusión** *(lah kohn-too-see-'ohn)*
brunette	**moreno/morena** *(moh-'reh-noh/moh-'reh-nah)*
budget	**el presupuesto** *(ehl preh-soo-'pwehs-toh)*
building code	**las normas de construcción**
	(lahs 'nohr-mahs deh kohns-trook-see-'ohn)
building	**el edificio** *(ehl eh-dee-'fee-see-oh)*
bullet	**la bala** *(lah 'bah-lah)*
bump	**el rompemuelle** *(ehl rohm-peh-'mweh-yeh)*
bureau	**el departamento** *(ehl deh-pahr-tah-'mehn-toh)*
burial	**el entierro** *(ehl ehn-tee-'ehr-roh)*
burn	**la quemadura** *(lah keh-mah-'doo-rah)*
bus	**el autobús** *(ehl aw-toh-'boos)*
bus stop	**la parada de autobús** *(lah pah-'rah-dah deh aw-toh-'boos)*
business	**el negocio** *(ehl neh-'goh-see-oh)*
business card	**la tarjeta comercial** *(lah tahr-'heh-tah koh-mehr-see-'ahl)*
busy	**ocupado/ocupada** *(oh-koo-'pah-doh/oh-koo-'pah-dah)*
but	**pero** *('peh-roh)*
buttock	**la nalga** *(lah 'nahl-gah)*
buyer	**el comprador** *(ehl kohm-prah-'dohr)*

C

cabinet	**el gabinete** *(ehl gah-bee-'neh-teh)*
cadaver	**el cadáver** *(ehl kah-'dah-vehr)*
cafeteria	**la cafetería** *(lah kah-feh-teh-'ree-ah)*
calculator	**la calculadora** *(lah kahl-koo-lah-'doh-rah)*
calendar	**el calendario** *(ehl kah-lehn-'dah-ree-oh)*
caliber	**el calibre** *(ehl kah-'lee-breh)*
call	**la llamada** *(lah yah-'mah-dah)*
calm	**tranquilo/tranquila** *(trahn-'kee-loh/trahn-'kee-lah)*
camcorder	**la filmadora** *(lah feel-mah-'doh-rah)*

camera	**la cámara** *(lah 'kah-mah-rah)*
cancellation	**la cancelación** *(lah kahn-seh-lah-see-'ohn)*
cancer	**el cáncer** *(ehl 'kahn-sehr)*
cap	**la gorra** *(lah 'gohr-rah)*
capable	**capaz** *(kah-'pahs)*
capital	**el capital** *(ehl kah-pee-'tahl)*
capital gains	**la ganancia de capital** *(lah gah-'nahn-see-ah deh kah-pee-'tahl)*
capsule	**la cápsula** *(lah 'kahp-soo-lah)*
car	**el carro** *(ehl 'kahr-roh)*
car accident	**el accidente de carro** *(ehl ahk-see-'dehn-teh deh 'kahr-roh)*
car jack	**la gata de carro** *(lah 'gah-tah deh 'kahr-roh)*
car lot	**el lote de carros** *(ehl 'loh-teh deh 'kahr-rohs)*
card	**la tarjeta** *(lah tahr-'heh-tah)*
cardiologist	**el cardiólogo/la cardióloga** *(ehl kahr-dee-'oh-loh-goh/lah kahr-dee-'oh-loh-gah)*
care	**el cuidado** *(ehl koo-ee-'dah-doh)*
careless	**descuidado/descuidada** *(dehs-koo-ee-'dah-doh/dehs-koo-ee-'dah-dah)*
carpenter	**el carpintero/la carpintera** *(ehl kahr-peen-'teh-roh/lah kahr-peen-'teh-rah)*
carpet	**la alfombra** *(lah ahl-'fohm-brah)*
cartridge	**el cartucho** *(ehl kahr-'too-choh)*
case	**el caso** *(ehl 'kah-soh)*
case number	**el número del caso** *(ehl 'noo-meh-roh dehl 'kah-soh)*
cash	**el efectivo** *(ehl eh-fehk-'tee-voh)*
cash flow	**el flujo de efectivo** *(ehl 'floo-hoh deh eh-fehk-'tee-voh)*
cashier	**el cajero/la cajera** *(ehl kah-'heh-roh/lah kah-'heh-rah)*
cashier's check	**el cheque de caja** *(ehl 'cheh-keh deh 'kah-hah)*
casino	**el casino** *(ehl kah-'see-noh)*
cause	**la causa** *(lah 'kah-oo-sah)*
ceiling	**el techo** *(ehl 'teh-choh)*
cell (jail)	**la celda** *(lah 'sehl-dah)*
cell phone	**el celular** *(ehl seh-loo-'lahr)*
cemetery	**el cementerio** *(ehl seh-mehn-'teh-ree-oh)*
cent	**el centavo** *(ehl sehn-'tah-voh)*
center	**el centro** *(ehl 'sehn-troh)*
ceremony	**la ceremonia** *(lah seh-reh-'moh-nee-ah)*
certificate	**el certificado** *(ehl sehr-tee-fee-'kah-doh)*
certification	**la certificación** *(lah sehr-tee-fee-kah-see-'ohn)*
chain	**la cadena** *(lah kah-'deh-nah)*
chair	**la silla** *(lah 'see-yah)*
challenged	**retrasado/retrasada** *(reh-trah-'sah-doh/reh-trah-'sah-dah)*

change	**el cambio** *(ehl 'kahm-bee-oh)*
charge	**la acusación** *(lah ah-koo-sah-see-'ohn)*
charged	**acusado/acusada** *(ah-koo-'sah-doh/ah-koo-'sah-dah)*
charity	**la caridad** *(lah kah-ree-'dahd)*
check	**el cheque** *(ehl 'cheh-keh)*
checkbook	**la chequera** *(lah cheh-'keh-rah)*
checking account	**la cuenta de cheques** *(lah 'kwehn-tah deh 'cheh-kehs)*
chemicals	**los químicos** *(lohs 'kee-mee-kohs)*
chest	**el pecho** *(ehl 'peh-choh)*
child	**el niño** *(ehl 'neen-yoh)*
child support	**la manutención infantil** *(lah mah-noo-tehn-see-'ohn een-fahn-'teel)*
child welfare	**el bienestar infantil** *(ehl bee-eh-nehs-'tahr een-fahn-'teel)*
childhood	**la niñez** *(lah neen-'yehs)*
chiropractor	**el quiropráctico/la quiropráctica** *(ehl kee-roh-'prahk-tee-koh/lah kee-roh-'prahk-tee-kah)*
church	**la iglesia** *(lah eeg-'leh-see-ah)*
cigarette	**el cigarrillo** *(ehl see-gahr-'ree-yoh)*
circuit court	**el tribunal del circuito** *(ehl tree-boo-'nahl dehl seer-koo-'ee-toh)*
citizen	**el ciudadano/la ciudadana** *(ehl see-oo-dah-'dah-noh/lah see-oo-dah-'dah-nah)*
citizenship	**la ciudadanía** *(lah see-oo-dah-dah-'nee-ah)*
city	**la ciudad** *(lah see-oo-'dahd)*
city hall	**el municipio** *(ehl moo-nee-'see-pee-oh)*
city manager	**el gerente municipal** *(ehl heh-'rehn-teh moo-nee-see-'pahl)*
civil	**civil** *(see-'veel)*
civil court	**el tribunal civil** *(ehl tree-boo-'nahl see-'veel)*
civil rights	**los derechos civiles** *(lohs deh-'reh-chohs see-'vee-lehs)*
civil suit	**la demanda civil** *(lah deh-'mahn-dah see-'veel)*
civil union	**la unión civil** *(lah oo-nee-'ohn see-'veel)*
claim	**el reclamo, la demanda** *(ehl reh-'klah-moh, lah deh-'mahn-dah)*
claimant	**el/la reclamante** *(ehl/lah reh-klah-'mahn-teh)*
class	**la clase** *(lah 'klah-seh)*
clause	**la cláusula** *(lah 'klah-oo-soo-lah)*
clean	**limpio/limpia** *('leem-pee-oh/'leem-pee-ah)*
cleaning	**la limpieza** *(lah leem-pee-'eh-sah)*
clear	**claro/clara** *('klah-roh/'klah-rah)*
clearance	**la aprobación** *(lah ah-proh-bah-see-'ohn)*
clemency	**la clemencia** *(lah kleh-'mehn-see-ah)*
clergy	**el clérigo/la clériga** *(ehl 'kleh-ree-goh/lah 'kleh-ree-gah)*
clerk	**el/la oficinista** *(ehl/lah oh-fee-see-'nees-tah)*
clerk's desk	**el escritorio del escribano** *(ehl ehs-kree-'toh-ree-oh dehl ehs-kree-'bah-noh)*

clever	**hábil** *('ah-beel)*
client	**el cliente/la clienta** *(ehl klee-'ehn-teh/lah klee-'ehn-tah)*
clinic	**la clínica** *(lah 'klee-nee-kah)*
clock	**el reloj** *(ehl reh-'loh)*
close	**cerca** *('sehr-kah)*
closing	**el cierre** *(ehl see-'ehr-reh)*
clothing	**la ropa** *(lah 'roh-pah)*
clue	**el indicio** *(ehl een-'dee-see-'oh)*
cocaine	**la cocaína** *(lah koh-kah-'ee-nah)*
code	**el código** *(ehl 'koh-dee-goh)*
code enforcement	**el cumplimiento de códigos** *(ehl koom-plee-mee-'ehn-toh deh 'koh-dee-gohs)*
coffin	**el ataúd** *(ehl ah-tah-'ood)*
coin	**la moneda** *(lah moh-'neh-dah)*
cold	**frío/fría** *('free-oh/'free-ah)*
collaboration	**la colaboración** *(lah koh-lah-boh-rah-see-'ohn)*
collateral	**colateral** *(koh-lah-teh-'rahl)*
collection	**el cobro** *(ehl 'koh-broh)*
collection agency	**la agencia de cobros** *(lah ah-'hehn-see-ah deh 'koh-brohs)*
collision	**el choque** *(ehl 'choh-keh)*
colon	**el colon** *(ehl 'koh-lohn)*
color	**el color** *(ehl koh-'lohr)*
comment	**el comentario** *(ehl koh-mehn-'tah-ree-oh)*
commerce	**el comercio** *(ehl koh-'mehr-see-oh)*
commitment	**el compromiso** *(ehl kohm-proh-'mee-soh)*
commodities	**las mercancías** *(lahs mehr-kahn-'see-ahs)*
communication	**la comunicación** *(lah koh-moo-nee-kah-see-'ohn)*
community	**la comunidad** *(lah koh-moo-nee-'dahd)*
company	**la compañía** *(lah kohm-pah-'nee-ah)*
comparison	**la comparación** *(lah kohm-pah-rah-see-'ohn)*
compensation	**la compensación** *(lah kohm-pehn-sah-see-'ohn)*
competitor	**el competidor/la competidora** *(ehl kohm-peh-tee-'dohr/lah kohm-peh-tee-'doh-rah)*
complaint	**la queja** *(lah 'keh-hah)*
complex	**el complejo** *(ehl kohm-'pleh-hoh)*
complication	**la complicación** *(lah kohm-plee-kah-see-'ohn)*
compound	**compuesto/compuesta** *(kohm-'pwehs-toh/kohm-'pwehs-tah)*
comprehensive	**amplio/amplia** *('ahm-plee-oh/'ahm-plee-ah)*
computer	**la computadora** *(lah kohm-poo-tah-'doh-rah)*
concealed	**escondido/escondida** *(ehs-kohn-'dee-doh/ehs-kohn-'dee-dah)*
concert	**el concierto** *(ehl kohn-see-'ehr-toh)*
concise	**conciso/concisa** *(kohn-'see-soh/kohn-'see-sah)*

concussion	**la conmoción** *(lah kohn-moh-see-'ohn)*
condition	**la condición** *(lah kohn-dee-see-'ohn)*
condominium	**el condominio** *(ehl kohn-doh-'mee-nee-oh)*
conduct	**la conducta** *(lah kohn-'dook-tah)*
conference	**la conferencia** *(lah kohn-feh-'rehn-see-ah)*
conference room	**la sala de conferencias** *(lah 'sah-lah deh kohn-feh-'rehn-see-ahs)*
confidence	**la confianza** *(lah kohn-fee-'ahn-sah)*
confident	**seguro/segura** *(seh-'goo-roh/seh-'goo-rah)*
confidential	**confidencial** *(kohn-fee-dehn-see-'ahl)*
conflict	**el conflicto** *(ehl kohn-'fleek-toh)*
confused	**confundido/confundida** *(kohn-foon-'dee-doh/kohn-foon-'dee-dah)*
congress	**el congreso** *(ehl kohn-'greh-soh)*
connection	**la conexión** *(lah kohn-ex-see-'ohn)*
consciousness	**el conocimiento** *(ehl koh-noh-see-mee-'ehn-toh)*
consent	**el permiso** *(ehl pehr-'mee-soh)*
consequence	**la consecuencia** *(lah kohn-she-'kwehn-see-ah)*
consolidation	**la consolidación** *(lah kohn-soh-lee-dah-see-'ohn)*
constitutional	**constitucional** *(kohns-tee-too-see-oh-'nahl)*
construction	**la construcción** *(lah kohns-trook-see-'ohn)*
consulate	**el consulado** *(ehl kohn-soo-'lah-doh)*
consultant	**el consultor/la consultora** *(ehl kohn-sool-'tohr/lah kohn-sool-'toh-rah)*
consultation	**la consulta** *(lah kohn-'sool-tah)*
consumer	**el consumidor/la consumidora** *(ehl kohn-soo-mee-'dohr/lah kohn-soo-mee-'doh-rah)*
consumption	**el consumo** *(ehl kohn-'soo-moh)*
continuance	**el aplazamiento** *(ehl ah-plah-sah-mee-'ehn-toh)*
contract	**el contrato** *(ehl kohn-'trah-toh)*
contractor	**el/la contratista** *(ehl/lah kohn-trah-'tees-tah)*
contribution	**la contribución** *(lah kohn-tree-boo-see-'ohn)*
conventional	**convencional** *(kohn-vehn-see-oh-'nahl)*
conversation	**la conversación** *(lah kohn-vehr-sah-see-'ohn)*
cook	**el cocinero/la cocinera** *(ehl koh-see-'neh-roh/lah koh-see-'neh-rah)*
cooperation	**la cooperación** *(lah koh-oh-peh-rah-see-'ohn)*
copier	**la copiadora** *(lah koh-pee-ah-'doh-rah)*
copy	**la copia** *(lah 'koh-pee-ah)*
corner	**la esquina** *(lah ehs-'kee-nah)*
coroner	**el médico/la médica legista** *(ehl 'meh-dee-koh/lah 'meh-dee-kah leh-'hees-tah)*
corporation	**la corporación** *(lah kohr-poh-rah-see-'ohn)*
corpse	**el cadáver** *(ehl kah-'dah-vehr)*

correction	**la corrección** *(lah kohr-rehk-see-'ohn)*
cost	**el costo** *(ehl 'kohs-toh)*
couch	**el sofá** *(ehl soh-'fah)*
counsel	**el abogado consultor** *(ehl ah-boh-'gah-doh kohn-sool-'tohr)*
counseling	**el asesoramiento** *(ehl ah-seh-soh-rah-mee-'ehn-toh)*
counter	**el mostrador** *(ehl mohs-trah-'dohr)*
counteroffer	**la contraoferta** *(lah kohn-trah-oh-'fehr-tah)*
countersuit	**la contrademanda** *(lah kohn-trah-deh-'mahn-dah)*
country	**el país** *(ehl pah-'ees)*
country of birth	**el país natal** *(ehl pah-'ees nah-'tahl)*
county	**el condado** *(ehl kohn-'dah-doh)*
county court	**el tribunal del condado** *(ehl tree-boo-'nahl dehl kohn-'dah-doh)*
courier	**el mensajero/la mensajera** *(ehl mehn-sah-'heh-roh/lah mehn-sah-'heh-rah)*
court	**el tribunal, la corte** *(ehl tree-boo-'nahl, lah 'kohr-teh)*
court clerk	**el actuario/la actuaria** *(ehl ahk-too-'ah-ree-oh/lah ahk-too-'ah-ree-ah)*
court date	**la fecha de la audiencia** *(lah 'feh-chah deh lah aw-dee-'ehn-see-ah)*
court of appeals	**el tribunal de apelaciones** *(ehl tree-boo-'nahl deh ah-peh-lah-see-'oh-nehs)*
court order	**la orden de la corte** *(lah 'ohr-dehn deh lah 'kohr-teh)*
court recorder	**el estenógrafo/la estenógrafa** *(ehl ehs-the-'noh-grah-foh/lah ehs-teh-'noh-grah-fah)*
court referee	**el árbitro del tribunal** *(ehl 'ahr-bee-troh dehl tree-boo-'nahl)*
courtroom	**la sala de tribunal** *(lah 'sah-lah deh tree-boo-'nahl)*
courtyard	**el patio** *(ehl 'pah-tee-oh)*
cousin	**la prima/el primo** *(lah 'pree-mah/ehl 'pree-moh)*
coverage	**la cobertura** *(lah koh-behr-'too-rah)*
coworker	**el compañero/la compañera de trabajo** *(ehl kohm-pahn-'yeh-roh/lah kohm-pahn-'yeh-rah deh trah-'bah-hoh)*
CPA	**el contador público/la contadora pública** *(ehl kohn-tah-'dohr 'poo-blee-koh/lah kohn-tah-'doh-rah 'poo-blee-kah)*
crane	**la grúa** *(lah 'groo-ah)*
crazy	**loco/loca** *('loh-koh/'loh-kah)*
credit	**el crédito** *(ehl 'kreh-dee-toh)*
credit card	**la tarjeta de crédito** *(lah tahr-'heh-tah deh 'kreh-dee-toh)*
credit company	**la compañía crediticia** *(lah kohm-pah-'nee-ah kreh-dee-'tee-see-ah)*
credit rating	**la clasificación de crédito** *(lah klah-see-fee-kah-see-'ohn deh 'kreh-dee-toh)*
credit report	**el informe de crédito** *(ehl een-'fohr-meh deh 'kreh-dee-toh)*
credit score	**el puntaje de crédito** *(ehl poon-'tah-heh deh 'kreh-dee-toh)*

credit union	**el banco cooperativo** *(ehl 'bahn-koh koh-oh-peh-rah-'tee-voh)*
creditor	**el acreedor/la acreedora** *(ehl ah-kreh-eh-'dohr/lah ah-kreh-eh-'doh-rah)*
crime	**el crimen** *(ehl 'kree-mehn)*
criminal	**criminal** *(kree-mee-'nahl)*
criminal activity	**la actividad criminal** *(lah ahk-tee-vee-'dahd kree-mee-'nahl)*
criminal court	**el tribunal penal** *(ehl tree-boo-'nahl peh-'nahl)*
criminal record	**los antecedentes penales** *(lohs ahn-teh-seh-'dehn-tehs peh-'nah-lehs)*
criminal trial	**el juicio penal** *(ehl hoo-'ee-see-oh peh-'nahl)*
crisis	**la crisis** *(lah 'kree-sees)*
crosswalk	**el cruce de peatones** *(ehl 'kroo-seh deh peh-ah-'toh-nehs)*
cruelty	**la crueldad** *(lah kroo-ehl-'dahd)*
current	**actual** *(ahk-too-'ahl)*
custodian	**el guardián/la guardiana** *(ehl gwahr-dee-'ahn/lah gwahr-dee-'ah-nah)*
customer	**el cliente/la clienta** *(ehl klee-'ehn-teh/lah klee-'ehn-tah)*
customer service	**el servicio para los clientes** *(ehl sehr-'vee-see-oh 'pah-rah lohs klee-'ehn-tehs)*
customs	**la aduana** *(lah ah-'dwah-nah)*
cycle	**el ciclo** *(ehl 'see-kloh)*

D

dagger	**la daga** *(lah 'dah-gah)*
damage	**los perjuicios** *(lohs pehr-hoo-'ee-see-ohs)*
dance	**el baile** *(ehl 'bah-ee-leh)*
danger	**el peligro** *(ehl peh-'lee-groh)*
dangerous	**peligroso/peligrosa** *(peh-lee-'groh-soh/peh-lee-'groh-sah)*
dark-skinned	**de tez oscura** *(deh tehs ohs-'koo-rah)*
data	**los datos** *(lohs 'dah-tohs)*
database	**la base de datos** *(lah 'bah-seh deh 'dah-tohs)*
date	**la fecha** *(lah 'feh-chah)*
date of birth	**la fecha de nacimiento** *(lah 'feh-chah deh nah-see-mee-'ehn-toh)*
daughter	**la hija** *(lah 'ee-hah)*
daughter-in-law	**la nuera** *(lah 'nweh-rah)*
day	**el día** *(ehl 'dee-ah)*
dead	**muerto/muerta** *('mwehr-toh/'mwehr-tah)*
deaf	**sordo/sorda** *('sohr-doh/'sohr-dah)*
dealer	**el concesionario/la concesionaria** *(ehl kohn-seh-see-oh-'nah-ree-oh/lah kohn-seh-see-oh-'nah-ree-ah)*
death	**la muerte** *(lah 'mwehr-teh)*
death certificate	**el certificado de defunción** *(eh sehr-tee-fee-'kah-doh deh deh-foon-see-'ohn)*

debate	**el debate** *(ehl deh-'bah-teh)*
debt	**la deuda** *(lah 'deh-oo-dah)*
deceased	**el difunto/la difunta** *(ehl dee-'foon-toh/lah dee-'foon-tah)*
deceitful	**engañoso/engañosa** *(ehn-gahn-'yoh-soh/ehn-gahn-'yoh-sah)*
December	**diciembre** *(dee-see-'ehm-breh)*
decision	**la decisión** *(lah deh-see-see-'ohn)*
declaration	**la declaración** *(lah deh-klah-rah-see-'ohn)*
deductible	**deducible** *(deh-doo-'seeb-leh)*
deduction	**la deducción** *(lah deh-dook-see-'ohn)*
deed	**la escritura** *(lah ehs-kree-'too-rah)*
default	**el incumplimiento** *(ehl een-koom-plee-mee-'ehn-toh)*
defective product	**el producto defectuoso** *(ehl proh-'dook-toh deh-fehk-too-'oh-soh)*
defendant (civil)	**el demandado/la demandada** *(ehl deh-mahn-'dah-doh/lah deh-mahn-'dah-dah)*
defendant (crim.)	**el acusado/la acusada** *(ehl ah-koo-'sah-doh/lah ah-koo-'sah-dah)*
defense	**la defensa** *(lah deh-'fehn-sah)*
defense attorney	**el abogado defensor/la abogada defensora** *(ehl ah-boh-'gah-doh deh-fehn-'sohr/lah ah-boh-'gah-dah deh-fehn-'soh-rah)*
deferred	**diferido/diferida** *(dee-feh-'ree-doh/dee-feh-'ree-dah)*
delay	**el retraso** *(ehl reh-'trah-soh)*
delayed	**retrasado/retrasada** *(reh-trah-'sah-doh/reh-trah-'sah-dah)*
deliberation	**la deliberación** *(lah deh-lee-beh-rah-see-'ohn)*
delivery	**la entrega** *(lah ehn-'treh-gah)*
dentist	**el/la dentista** *(ehl/lah dehn-'tees-tah)*
department	**el departamento** *(ehl deh-pahr-tah-'mehn-toh)*
department of justice	**el ministerio de justicia** *(ehl mee-nees-'teh-ree-oh deh hoos-'tee-see-ah)*
dependent	**el dependiente/la dependienta** *(ehl deh-pehn-dee-'ehn-teh/lah deh-pehn-dee-'ehn-tah)*
deportation	**la deportación** *(lash deh-pohr-tah-see-'ohn)*
deposit	**el depósito** *(ehl deh-'poh-see-toh)*
deposition	**la deposición** *(lah deh-poh-see-see-'ohn)*
depreciation	**la depreciación** *(lah deh-preh-see-ah-see-'ohn)*
depression	**la depresión** *(lah deh-preh-see-'ohn)*
descendent	**el/la descendiente** *(ehl/lah dehs-sehn-dee-'ehn-teh)*
design	**el diseño** *(ehl dee-'sehn-yoh)*
desire	**el deseo** *(ehl deh-'seh-oh)*
desk	**el escritorio** *(ehl ehs-kree-'toh-ree-oh)*
desperate	**desesperado/deseperada** *(deh-sehs-peh-'rah-doh/deh-sehs-peh-'rah-dah)*
destroyed	**destruido/destruida** *(dehs-troo-'ee-doh/dehs-troo-'ee-dah)*
detailed	**detallado/detallada** *(deh-tah-'yah-doh/deh-tah-'yah-dah)*

detail	**el detalle** *(ehl deh-'tah-yeh)*
detective	**el/la detective** *(ehl/lah deh-tehk-'tee-veh)*
detention	**la detención** *(lah deh-tehn-see-'ohn)*
deterioration	**el deterioro** *(ehl deh-teh-ree-'oh-roh)*
determined	**decidido/decidida** *(deh-see-'dee-doh/deh-see-'dee-dah)*
detour	**el desvío** *(ehl dehs-'vee-oh)*
developer	**el urbanizador/la urbanizadora** *(ehl oor-bah-nee-sah-'dohr/lah oor-bah-nee-sah-'doh-rah)*
development	**el desarrollo** *(ehl deh-sahr-'roh-yoh)*
difference	**la diferencia** *(lah dee-feh-'rehn-see-ah)*
difficult	**difícil** *(dee-'fee-seel)*
dinner	**la cena** *(lah 'seh-nah)*
director	**el director/la directora** *(ehl dee-rehk-'tohr/lah dee-rehk-'toh-rah)*
dirty	**sucio/sucia** *('soo-see-oh/'soo-see-ah)*
disability	**la incapacidad** *(lah een-kah-pah-see-'dahd)*
disability (insur.)	**el subsidio por incapacidad laboral** *(ehl soob-'see-dee-oh pohr een-kah-pah-see-'dahd lah-boh-'rahl)*
disabled	**incapacitado/incapacitada** *(een-kah-pah-see-'tah-doh/een-kah-pah-see-'tah-dah)*
disagreement	**el desacuerdo** *(ehl deh-sah-'kwehr-doh)*
disclosure	**la revelación** *(lah reh-veh-lah-see-'ohn)*
discount	**el descuento** *(ehl dehs-'kwehn-toh)*
discrepancy	**la discrepancia** *(lah dees-kreh-'pahn-see-ah)*
discrimination	**la discriminación** *(lah dees-kree-mee-nah-see-'ohn)*
dishwasher	**el/la lavaplatos** *(ehl/lah lah-vah-'plah-tohs)*
disk	**el disco** *(ehl 'dees-koh)*
dismissal	**la desolución** *(lah deh-soh-loo-see-'ohn)*
dismissed	**rechazado/rechazada** *(reh-chah-'sah-doh/reh-chah-'sah-dah)*
disparity	**la disparidad** *(lah dees-pah-ree-'dahd)*
dispute	**la disputa** *(lah dees-'poo-tah)*
dissolution	**la disolución** *(lah dee-soh-loo-see-'ohn)*
distracted	**distraído/distraída** *(dees-trah-'ee-doh/dees-trah-'ee-dah)*
distribution	**la distribución** *(lah dees-tree-boo-see-'ohn)*
district	**el distrito** *(ehl dees-'tree-toh)*
district attorney	**el/la fiscal de distrito** *(ehl/lah fees-'kahl deh dees-'tree-toh)*
district court	**el tribunal de distrito** *(ehl tree-boo-'nahl deh dees-'tree-toh)*
divided	**dividido/dividida** *(dee-vee-'dee-doh/dee-vee-dee-'dah)*
dividend	**el dividendo** *(ehl dee-vee-'dehn-doh)*
division	**la división** *(lah dee-vee-see-'ohn)*
divorce	**el divorcio** *(ehl dee-'vohr-see-oh)*
divorced	**divorciado/divorciada** *(dee-vohr-see-'ah-doh/dee-vohr-see-'ah-dah)*
dizziness	**el mareo** *(ehl mah-'reh-oh)*

DNA testing	**la prueba de ADN**	*(lah proo-'eh-bah deh ah-deh-'eh-neh)*
docket	**el horario de juicios**	*(ehl oh-'rah-ree-oh deh hoo-'ee-see-ohs)*
doctor	**el médico/la médica**	*(ehl 'meh-dee-koh/lah 'meh-dee-kah)*
document	**el documento**	*(ehl doh-koo-'mehn-toh)*
dog	**el perro**	*(ehl 'pehr-roh)*
dog bite	**la mordida de perro**	*(lah mohr-'dee-dah deh 'pehr-roh)*
dollar	**el dólar**	*(ehl 'doh-lahr)*
domestic	**doméstico/doméstica**	*(doh-'mehs-tee-koh/doh-'mehs-tee-kah)*
domestic violence	**la violencia doméstica**	*(lah vee-oh-'lehn-see-ah doh-'mehs-tee-kah)*
donation	**la donación**	*(lah doh-nah-see-'ohn)*
door	**la puerta**	*(lah 'pwehr-tah)*
doubtful	**dudoso/dudosa**	*(doo-'doh-soh/doo-'doh-sah)*
down	**abajo**	*(ah-'bah-hoh)*
down payment	**el pago inicial**	*(ehl 'pah-goh ee-nee-see-'ahl)*
downtown	**el centro**	*(ehl 'sehn-troh)*
drawer	**el cajón**	*(ehl kah-'hohn)*
dress	**el vestido**	*(ehl vehs-'tee-doh)*
drink	**la bebida**	*(lah beh-'bee-dah)*
drive-by	**el disparo de un carro**	*(ehl dees-'pah-roh deh oon 'kahr-roh)*
driver	**el/la chofer**	*(ehl/lah choh-'fehr)*
driver's license	**la licencia de manejar**	*(lah lee-'sehn-see-ah deh mah-neh-'hahr)*
drop	**la gota**	*(lah 'goh-tah)*
drowning	**el ahogamiento**	*(ehl ah-oh-gah-mee-'ehn-toh)*
drug	**la droga**	*(lah 'droh-gah)*
drug addict	**el drogadicto/la drogadicta**	*(ehl droh-gah-'deek-toh/lah droh-gah-'deek-tah)*
drug addiction	**la drogadicción**	*(lah droh-gah-deek-see-'ohn)*
drug court	**el tribunal de drogas ilegales**	*(ehl tree-boo-'nahl deh 'droh-gahs ee-leh-'gah-lehs)*
drug dealer	**el vendedor de drogas**	*(ehl vehn-deh-'dohr deh 'droh-gahs)*
drug test	**la prueba de drogas**	*(lah proo-'eh-bah deh 'droh-gahs)*
drug traffic	**el narcotráfico**	*(ehl nahr-koh-'trah-fee-koh)*
drugged	**drogado/drogada**	*(droh-'gah-doh/droh-'gah-dah)*
drunk	**el borracho/la borracha**	*(ehl bohr-'rah-choh/lah bohr-'rah-chah)*
drunk driving	**la conducción en estado de embriaguez**	*(lah kohn-dook-see-'ohn ehn ehs-'tah-doh deh ehm-bree-ah-'ghez)*
due date	**la fecha de vencimiento**	*(lah 'feh-chah deh vehn-see-mee-'ehn-toh)*
duration	**la duración**	*(lah doo-rah-see-'ohn)*
during	**durante**	*(doo-'rahn-teh)*
duty free	**libre de derechos**	*('lee-breh deh deh-'reh-chohs)*
dynamite	**la dinamita**	*(lah dee-nah-'mee-tah)*

E

ear	**la oreja** *(lah oh-'reh-hah)*
early	**temprano** *(tehm-'prah-noh)*
earnings	**los ingresos** *(lohs een-'greh-sohs)*
earphones	**los audífonos** *(lohs aw-'dee-foh-nohs)*
earplugs	**los tapones de oído** *(lohs tah-'poh-nehs deh oh-'ee-doh)*
earring	**el arete** *(ehl ah-'reh-teh)*
easement	**el derecho de vía** *(ehl deh-'reh-choh deh 'vee-ah)*
east	**el este** *(ehl 'ehs-teh)*
easy	**fácil** *('fah-seel)*
economy	**la economía** *(lah eh-koh-noh-'mee-ah)*
economic	**económico/económica** *(eh-koh-'noh-mee-koh/eh-koh-'noh-mee-kah)*
ecstasy (drug)	**el éxtasis** *(ehl 'ex-tah-sees)*
education	**la educación** *(lah eh-doo-kah-see-'ohn)*
eighth	**octavo/octava** *(ohk-'tah-voh/ohk-'tah-vah)*
elbow	**el codo** *(ehl 'koh-doh)*
elder abuse	**el abuso de ancianos** *(ehl ah-'boo-soh deh ahn-see-'ah-nohs)*
elderly person	**el anciano/la anciana** *(ehl ahn-see-'ah-noh/lah ahn-see-'ah-nah)*
electricity	**la electricidad** *(lah eh-lehk-tree-see-'dahd)*
elevator	**el ascensor** *(ehl ahs-sehn-'sohr)*
eligible	**elegible** *(eh-leh-'hee-bleh)*
e-mail	**el correo electrónico** *(ehl kohr-'reh-oh eh-lehk-'troh-nee-koh)*
embarrassed	**turbado/turbada** *(toor-'bah-doh/toor-'bah-dah)*
embezzling	**el desfalco** *(ehl dehs-'fahl-koh)*
emergency	**la emergencia** *(lah eh-mehr-'hehn-see-ah)*
emigrant	**el/la emigrante** *(ehl/lah eh-mee-'grahn-teh)*
eminent domain	**el dominio eminente** *(ehl doh-'mee-nee-oh eh-mee-'nehn-teh)*
emotional	**emocional** *(eh-moh-see-'oh-nahl)*
employed	**empleado/empleada** *(ehm-pleh-'ah-doh/ehm-pleh-'ah-dah)*
employee	**el empleado/la empleada** *(ehl ehm-pleh-'ah-doh/lah ehm-pleh-'ah-dah)*
employer	**el empresario/la empresaria** *(ehl ehm-preh-'sah-ree-oh/lah ehm-preh-'sah-ree-ah)*
employment	**el empleo** *(ehl ehm-'pleh-oh)*
endowment	**la dotación** *(lah doh-tah-see-'ohn)*
endownment insurance	**el seguro de póliza dotal** *(ehl seh-'goo-roh deh 'poh-lee-sah doh-'tahl)*
engagement	**el compromiso** *(ehl kohm-proh-'mee-soh)*
engine	**el motor** *(ehl moh-'tohr)*
engineer	**el ingeniero/la ingeniera** *(ehl een-heh-nee-'eh-roh/lah een-heh-nee-'eh-rah)*
English	**el inglés** *(ehl een-'glehs)*

enough	**suficiente** *(soo-fee-see-'ehn-teh)*
entertainment	**la diversión** *(lah dee-vehr-see-'ohn)*
entrance	**la entrada** *(lah ehn-'trah-dah)*
envelope	**el sobre** *(ehl 'soh-breh)*
environment	**el medio ambiente** *(ehl 'meh-dee-oh ahm-bee-'ehn-teh)*
equal	**igual** *(ee-'gwahl)*
equipment	**el equipo** *(ehl eh-'kee-poh)*
equity	**la equidad** *(lah eh-kee-'dahd)*
equity loan	**el préstamo de valor líquido** *(ehl 'prehs-tah-moh deh vah-'lohr 'lee-kee-doh)*
error	**el error** *(ehl ehr-'rohr)*
escalator	**la escalera mecánica** *(lah ehs-kah-'leh-rah meh-'kah-nee-kah)*
escrow	**la plica** *(lah 'plee-kah)*
estate planning	**la planificación de bienes** *(lah plah-nee-fee-kah-see-'ohn deh bee-'eh-nehs)*
estimate	**el estimado** *(ehl ehs-tee-'mah-doh)*
ethical	**ético** *('eh-tee-koh)*
ethnicity	**la etnia** *(lah 'eht-nee-ah)*
European	**europeo/europea** *(eh-oo-roh-'peh-oh/eh-oo-roh-'peh-ah)*
everyone	**todos** *('toh-dohs)*
everything	**todo** *('toh-doh)*
everywhere	**por todas partes** *(pohr 'toh-dahs 'pahr-tehs)*
eviction	**el desalojo** *(ehl deh-sah-'loh-hoh)*
eviction notice	**el aviso de desalojo** *(ehl ah-'vee-soh deh deh-sah-'loh-hoh)*
evidence	**la evidencia** *(lah eh-vee-'dehn-see-ah)*
exam	**el examen** *(ehl ex-'ah-mehn)*
examination	**el reconocimiento** *(ehl reh-koh-noh-see-mee-'ehn-toh)*
examiner	**el examinador/la examinadora** *(ehl ex-ah-mee-nah-'dohr/lah ex-ah-mee-nah-'doh-rah)*
excited	**emocionado/emocionada** *(eh-moh-see-'oh-nah-doh/eh-moh-see-oh-'nah-dah)*
exclusion	**la exclusión** *(lah ex-kloo-see-'ohn)*
exclusive	**exclusivo/exclusiva** *(ex-kloo-'see-voh/ex-kloo-'see-vah)*
executor	**el/la albacea** *(ehl/lah ahl-bah-'seh-ah)*
exhausted	**agotado/agotada** *(ah/goh-'tah-doh/ah-goh-'tah-dah)*
exhibit	**la prueba instrumental** *(lah proo-'eh-bah eens-troo-mehn-'tahl)*
exhibit area	**el área de pruebas instrumentales** *(ehl 'ah-reh-ah deh proo-'eh-bahs eens-troo-mehn-'tah-lehs)*
existing	**existente** *(ex-ees-'tehn-teh)*
exit	**la salida** *(lah sah-'lee-dah)*
expense	**el gasto** *(ehl 'gahs-toh)*
expensive	**caro/cara** *('kah-roh/'kah-rah)*
experience	**la experiencia** *(lah ex-peh-ree-'ehn-see-ah)*

expert	**el experto** *(ehl ex-'pehr-toh)*
expert witness	**el testigo pericial** *(ehl tehs-'tee-goh peh-ree-see-'ahl)*
expertise	**la competencia** *(lah kohm-peh-'tehn-see-ah)*
expiration	**el vencimiento** *(ehl vehn-see-mee-'ehn-toh)*
expiration date	**la fecha de vencimiento** *(lah 'feh-chah deh vehn-see-mee-'ehn-toh)*
expired	**vencido/vencida** *(vehn-'see-doh/vehn-'see-dah)*
explanation	**la explicación** *(lah ex-plee-kah-see-'ohn)*
explosive	**el explosivo** *(ehl ex-ploh-'see-voh)*
express mail	**el correo expreso** *(ehl kohr-'reh-oh ex-'preh-soh)*
ex-spouse	**el ex-esposo** *(ehl ex-ehs-'poh-soh)*
extension	**la extensión** *(lah ex-tehn-see-'ohn)*
extortion	**la extorsión** *(lah ex-tohr-see-'ohn)*
eye	**el ojo** *(ehl 'oh-hoh)*
eye color	**el color de los ojos** *(ehl koh-'lohr deh lohs 'oh-hohs)*
eye exam	**la prueba de la vista** *(lah proo-'eh-bah deh lah 'vees-tah)*

F

face	**la cara** *(lah 'kah-rah)*
factory	**la fábrica** *(lah 'fah-bree-kah)*
fact	**el hecho** *(ehl 'eh-choh)*
faint	**desfallecido/desfallecida** *(dehs-fah-yeh-'see-doh/dehs-fah-yeh-'see-dah)*
fair	**justo/justa** *('hoos-toh/'hoos-tah)*
fake	**falsificado/falsificada** *(fahl-see-fee-'kah-doh/fahl-see-fee-'kah-dah)*
fall	**el otoño** *(ehl oh-'tohn-yoh)*
fall equipment	**la protección contra caídas** *(lah proh-tehk-see-'ohn 'kohn-trah kah-'ee-dahs)*
false alarm	**la falsa alarma** *(lah 'fahl-sah ah-'lahr-mah)*
family	**la familia** *(lah fah-'mee-lee-ah)*
family business	**la empresa familiar** *(lah ehm-'preh-sah fah-mee-lee-'ahr)*
family court	**el tribunal de asuntos familiares** *(ehl tree-boo-'nahl deh ah-'soon-tohs fah-mee-lee-'ah-rehs)*
family law court	**el tribunal de derecho familiar** *(ehl tree-boo-'nahl deh deh-'reh-choh fah-mee-lee-'ahr)*
family member	**el/la pariente** *(ehl/lah pah-ree-'ehn-teh)*
family physician	**el médico de familia** *(ehl 'meh-dee-koh deh fah-'mee-lee-ah)*
fan	**el ventilador** *(ehl vehn-tee-lah-'dohr)*
far	**lejos** *('leh-hohs)*
farm	**la granja** *(lah 'grahn-hah)*
farmer	**el granjero/la granjera** *(ehl grahn-'heh-roh/lah grahn-'heh-rah)*
fast	**rápido/rápida** *('rah-pee-doh/'rah-pee-dah)*
fat	**gordo/gorda** *('gohr-doh/'gohr-dah)*

father	**el padre** *(ehl 'pah-dreh)*
father-in-law	**el suegro** *(ehl 'sweh-groh)*
fault	**la culpa** *(lah 'kool-pah)*
fax machine	**el fax** *(ehl faks)*
FDA	**la Dirección de Alimentos y Medicinas** *(lah dee-rehk-see-'ohn deh ah-lee-'mehn-tohs ee meh-dee-'see-nahs)*
February	**febrero** *(feh-'breh-roh)*
federal	**federal** *(feh-deh-'rahl)*
federal court	**el tribunal federal** *(ehl tree-boo-'nahl feh-deh-'rahl)*
federal income tax	**el impuesto de ingresos federal** *(ehl eem-'pwehs-toh deh een-'greh-sohs feh-deh-'rahl)*
fee	**el honorario** *(ehl oh-noh-'rah-ree-oh)*
feeling	**el sentimiento** *(ehl sehn-tee-mee-'ehn-toh)*
felony	**el delito mayor** *(ehl deh-'lee-toh mah-'yohr)*
fever	**la fiebre** *(lah fee-'eh-breh)*
fiancé	**el novio comprometido** *(ehl 'noh-vee-oh kohm-proh-meh-'tee-doh)*
fiancée	**la novia comprometida** *(lah 'noh-vee-ah kohm-proh-meh-'tee-dah)*
fiduciary	**el fiduciario/la fiduciaria** *(ehl fee-doo-see-'ah-ree-oh/lah fee-doo-see-'ah-ree-ah)*
field	**el campo de trabajo** *(ehl 'kahm-poh deh trah-'bah-hoh)*
fifth	**quinto/quinta** *('keen-toh/'keen-tah)*
fight	**la pelea** *(lah peh-'leh-ah)*
figure	**la cifra** *(lah 'see-frah)*
file	**el fichero** *(ehl fee-'cheh-roh)*
file cabinet	**el archivo** *(ehl ahr-'chee-voh)*
filing	**la clasificación** *(lah klah-see-fee-kah-see-'ohn)*
filing clerk	**el secretario/la secretaria de actas** *(ehl seh-kreh-'tah-ree-oh/lah seh-kreh-'tah-ree-ah deh 'ahk-tahs)*
final	**final** *(fee-'nahl)*
finance	**las finanzas** *(lahs fee-'nahn-sahs)*
financial trouble	**el problema financiero** *(ehl proh-'bleh-mah fee-nahn-see-'eh-roh)*
financing	**la financiación** *(lah fee-nahn-see-ah-see-'ohn)*
fines	**las multas** *(lahs 'mool-tahs)*
finger	**el dedo** *(ehl 'deh-doh)*
fingernails	**las uñas** *(lahs 'oon-yahs)*
fingerprints	**las huellas digitales** *(lahs 'hweh-yahs dee-hee-'tah-lehs)*
fire	**el incendio** *(ehl een-'sehn-dee-oh)*
fire department	**el departamento de bomberos** *(ehl deh-pahr-tah-'mehn-toh deh bohm-'beh-rohs)*
firearm	**el arma de fuego** *(ehl 'ahr-mah deh foo-'eh-goh)*
firefighter	**el bombero/la bombera** *(elh bohm-'beh-roh/lah bohm-'beh-rah)*

first	**primero/primera** *(pree-'meh-roh/pree-'meh-rah)*
first language	**el primer lenguaje** *(ehl pree-'mehr lehn-'gwah-heh)*
fist	**el puño** *(ehl 'poon-yoh)*
fixed	**fijo/fija** *(fee-hoh/'fee-hah)*
flag	**la bandera** *(lah bahn-'deh-rah)*
floor	**el piso** *(ehl 'pee-soh)*
folder	**la carpeta** *(lah kahr-'peh-tah)*
food	**la comida** *(lah koh-'mee-dah)*
food stamp	**el cupón de alimentos** *(ehl koo-'pohn deh ah-lee-'mehn-tohs)*
foot	**el pie** *(ehl pee-'eh)*
foreclosure	**el juicio hipotecario** *(ehl hoo-'ee-see-oh ee-poh-teh-'kah-ree-oh)*
foreign	**extranjero/extranjera** *(ex-trahn-'heh-roh/ex-trahn-'heh-rah)*
foreign national	**el extranjero/la extranjera** *(ehl ex-trahn-'heh-roh/lah ex-trahn-'heh-rah)*
forged	**falsificado/falsificada** *(fahl-see-fee-'kah-doh/fahl-see-fee-'kah-dah)*
forger	**el falsificador/la falsificadora** *(ehl fahl-see-fee-kah-'dohr/lah fahl-see-fee-kah-'doh-rah)*
forgery	**la falsificación** *(lah fahl-see-fee-kah-see-'ohn)*
fork	**el tenedor** *(ehl teh-neh-'dohr)*
form	**el formulario** *(ehl fohr-moo-'lah-ree-oh)*
formal	**formal** *(fohr-'mahl)*
forward	**adelante** *(ah-deh-'lahn-teh)*
foster care	**la crianza de niños ajenos** *(lah kree-'ahn-sah deh 'neen-yohs ah-'heh-nohs)*
foundation	**los cimientos** *(lohs see-mee-'ehn-tohs)*
fountain	**la fuente** *(lah foo-'ehn-teh)*
fourth	**cuarto/cuarta** *('kwahr-toh/'kwahr-tah)*
fraud	**el fraude** *(ehl frah-oo-deh)*
free (no cost)	**gratis** *('grah-tees)*
free (unconstrained)	**libre** *('lee-breh)*
Friday	**viernes** *(vee-'ehr-nehs)*
friend	**el amigo/la amiga** *(ehl ah-'mee-goh/lah ah-'mee-gah)*
friendly	**amistoso/amistosa** *(ah-mees-'toh-soh/ah-mees-'toh-sah)*
friendship	**el compañerismo** *(ehl kohm-pahn-yeh-'rees-moh)*
front desk	**el escritorio principal** *(ehl ehs-kree-'toh-ree-oh preen-see-'pahl)*
fugitive	**el fugitivo/la fugitiva** *(ehl foo-hee-'tee-voh/lah foo-hee-'tee-vah)*
full name	**el nombre completo** *(ehl 'nohm-breh kohm-'pleh-toh)*
funded	**financiado/financiada** *(fee-nahn-see-'ah-doh/fee-nahn-see-'ah-dah)*
fundraising	**la recaudación de fondos** *(lah reh-kah-oo-dah-see-'ohn deh 'fohn-dohs)*
funds	**los fondos** *(lohs 'fohn-dohs)*

funeral	**el funeral** *(ehl foo-neh-'rahl)*
funny	**chistoso/chistosa** *(chees-'toh-soh/chees-'toh-sah)*
furious	**furioso/furiosa** *(foo-ree-'oh-soh/foo-ree-'oh-sah)*
furniture	**los muebles** *(lohs 'mweh-blehs)*

G

gallbladder	**la vesícula** *(lah veh-'see-koo-lah)*
gambling	**el juego de apuesta** *(ehl 'hweh-goh deh ah-'pwehs-tah)*
game	**el juego** *(ehl 'hweh-goh)*
gang	**la pandilla** *(lah pahn-'dee-yah)*
gang member	**el pandillero/la pandillera** *(ehl pahn-dee-'yeh-roh/lah pahn-dee-'yeh-rah)*
garage	**el garaje** *(ehl gah-'rah-heh)*
gardener	**el jardinero/la jardinera** *(ehl hahr-dee-'neh-roh/lah hahr-dee-'neh-rah)*
garnishment	**el embargo de salario** *(ehl ehm-'bahr-goh deh sah-'lah-ree-oh)*
gas (gasoline)	**la bencina** *(lah behn-'see-nah)*
gas station	**la gasolinera** *(lah gah-soh-lee-'neh-rah)*
gate	**el portón** *(ehl pohr-'tohn)*
gavel	**el mazo** *(ehl 'mah-soh)*
gay	**homosexual** *(oh-moh-sehk-soo-'ahl)*
genitals	**los genitales** *(lohs heh-nee-'tah-lehs)*
gift	**el regalo** *(ehl reh-'gah-loh)*
girl	**la niña** *(lah 'neen-yah)*
girlfriend	**la novia** *(lah 'noh-vee-ah)*
glass (drinking)	**el vaso** *(ehl 'vah-soh)*
glass (material)	**el vidrio** *(ehl 'vee-dree-oh)*
glasses	**los anteojos** *(lohs ahn-teh-'oh-hohs)*
global	**mundial** *(moon-dee-'ahl)*
gloves	**los guantes** *(lohs 'gwahn-tehs)*
glue	**el pegamento** *(ehl peh-gah-'mehn-toh)*
goggles	**las gafas** *(lahs 'gah-fahs)*
good	**bueno/buena** *(boo-'eh-noh/boo-'eh-nah)*
goods	**los bienes** *(lohs bee-'eh-nehs)*
government	**el gobierno** *(ehl goh-bee-'ehr-noh)*
governor	**el gobernador/la gobernadora** *(ehl goh-behr-nah-'dohr/lah goh-behr-nah-'doh-rah)*
grace period	**el período de gracia** *(ehl peh-'ree-oh-doh deh 'grah-see-ah)*
graffiti	**el grafiti** *(ehl grah-'fee-tee)*
gram	**el gramo** *(ehl 'grah-moh)*
grand theft	**el robo de mayor cuantía** *(ehl 'roh-boh deh mah-'yohr kwahn-'tee-ah)*

granddaughter	**la nieta** *(lah nee-'eh-tah)*
grandfather	**el abuelo** *(ehl ah-'bweh-loh)*
grandmother	**la abuela** *(lah ah-'bweh-lah)*
grandson	**el nieto** *(ehl nee-'eh-toh)*
grant	**la beca** *(lah 'beh-kah)*
gray	**gris** *(grees)*
green	**verde** *('vehr-deh)*
green card	**la tarjeta verde** *(lah tahr-'heh-tah 'vehr-deh)*
gross income	**el ingreso bruto** *(ehl een-'greh-soh 'broo-toh)*
group	**el grupo** *(ehl 'groo-poh)*
group number	**el número de grupo** *(ehl 'noo-meh-roh deh 'groo-poh)*
growth	**el crecimiento** *(ehl kreh-see-mee-'ehn-toh)*
guarantee	**la garantía** *(lah gah-rahn-'tee-ah)*
guaranteed	**garantizado/garantizada** *(gah-rahn-tee-'sah-doh/gah-rahn-tee-'sah-dah)*
guard	**el/la guardia** *(ehl/lah 'gwahr-dee-ah)*
guardian	**el guardián/la guardiana** *(ehl gwahr-dee-'ahn/lah gwahr-dee-'ah-nah)*
guardianship	**la tutela** *(lah too-'teh-lah)*
guardrail	**la baranda** *(lah bah-'rahn-dah)*
guide	**el guía/la guía** *(ehl 'ghee-ah/lah 'ghee-ah)*
guidelines	**las pautas** *(lahs 'pah-oo-tahs)*
guilty	**culpable** *(kool-'pah-bleh)*
gun	**el arma de fuego** *(ehl 'ahr-mah deh 'fweh-goh)*
gunshot wound	**la herida de bala** *(lah eh-'ree-dah deh 'bah-lah)*
gym	**el gimnasio** *(ehl heem-'nah-see-oh)*
gynecologist	**el ginecólogo/la ginecóloga** *(ehl hee-neh-'koh-loh-goh/lah hee-neh-'koh-loh-gah)*

H

hair	**el cabello** *(ehl kah-'beh-yoh)*
half	**la mitad** *(lah mee-'tahd)*
hallway	**el corredor** *(ehl kohr-reh-'dohr)*
hammer	**el martillo** *(ehl mahr-'tee-yoh)*
hand	**la mano** *(lah 'mah-noh)*
handicap	**la incapacidad** *(lah een-kah-pah-see-'dahd)*
handkerchief	**el pañuelo** *(ehl pahn-yoo-'eh-loh)*
handle	**el mango** *(ehl 'mahn-goh)*
handling	**los gastos de tramitación** *(lohs 'gahs-tohs deh trah-mee-tah-see-'ohn)*
handsome	**guapo/guapa** *('gwah-poh/'gwah-pah)*
harassment	**el acosamiento** *(ehl ah-koh-sah-mee-'ehn-toh)*
hard hat	**el casco duro** *(ehl 'kahs-koh 'doo-roh)*

harm	**el perjuicio** *(ehl pehr-hoo-'ee-see-oh)*
hat	**el sombrero** *(ehl sohm-'breh-roh)*
hate	**el odio** *(ehl 'oh-dee-oh)*
hazard	**el peligro** *(ehl peh-'lee-groh)*
he	**él** *(ehl)*
head	**la cabeza** *(lah kah-'beh-sah)*
headache	**el dolor de cabeza** *(ehl doh-'lohr deh kah-'beh-sah)*
health	**la salud** *(lah sah-'lood)*
health care	**el cuidado médico** *(ehl kwee-'dah-doh 'meh-dee-koh)*
healthy	**saludable** *(sah-loo-'dah-bleh)*
hearing	**la audencia** *(lah ah-oo-dee-'ehn-see-ah)*
heart	**el corazón** *(ehl koh-rah-'sohn)*
heart attack	**el ataque cardíaco** *(ehl ah-'tah-keh kahr-'dee-ah-koh)*
heart trouble	**los problemas cardíacos** *(lohs proh-'bleh-mahs kahr-'dee-ah-kohs)*
heat	**el calor** *(ehl kah-'lohr)*
heatstroke	**la insolación** *(lah een-soh-lah-see-'ohn)*
heater	**el calentador** *(ehl kah-lehn-tah-'dohr)*
heating	**la calefacción** *(lah kah-leh-fahk-see-'ohn)*
height	**la estatura** *(lah ehs-tah-'too-rah)*
heir	**el heredero/la heredera** *(ehl eh-reh-'deh-roh/lah eh-reh-'deh-rah)*
help	**la ayuda** *(lah ah-'yoo-dah)*
helper	**el ayudante/la ayudanta** *(ehl ah-yoo-'dahn-teh/lah ah-yoo-'dahn-tah)*
her	**su** *(soo)*
here	**aquí** *(ah-'kee)*
heroin	**la heroína** *(lah eh-roh-'ee-nah)*
higher court	**el juzgado de primera instancia** *(ehl hoos-'gah-doh deh pree-'meh-rah eens-'tahn-see-ah)*
highway	**la carretera** *(lah kahr-reh-'teh-rah)*
hijacking	**el robo en tránsito** *(ehl 'roh-boh ehn 'trahn-see-toh)*
hip	**la cadera** *(lah kah-'deh-rah)*
his	**su** *(soo)*
hoax	**el engaño** *(ehl ehn-'gahn-yoh)*
hole	**el hoyo** *(ehl 'oh-yoh)*
holster	**la funda** *(lah 'foon-dah)*
home	**el hogar** *(ehl oh-'gahr)*
home equity loan	**el préstamo sobre la equidad de una vivienda** *(ehl 'prehs-tah-moh 'soh-breh lah eh-kee-'dahd deh 'oo-nah vee-vee-'ehn-dah)*
home loan	**el préstamo para comprar casa** *(ehl 'prehs-tah-moh 'pah-rah kohm-'prahr 'kah-sah)*
home page	**la página inicial** *(lah 'pah-hee-nah ee-nee-see-'ahl)*

homeland security	**la seguridad nacional** *(lah seh-goo-ree-'dahd nah-see-oh-'nahl)*
homeowner	**el propietario de la vivienda** *(ehl proh-pee-eh-'tah-ree-oh deh lah vee-vee-'ehn-dah)*
homicide	**el homicidio** *(ehl oh-mee-'see-dee-oh)*
homosexual	**el/la homosexual** *(ehl/lah oh-moh-sek-soo-'ahl)*
honest	**honesto/honesta** *(oh-'nehs-toh/oh-'nehs-tah)*
honeymoon	**la luna de miel** *(lah 'loo-nah deh mee-'ehl)*
honorable	**honorable** *(oh-noh-'rah-bleh)*
horse	**el caballo** *(ehl kah-'bah-yoh)*
hospital	**el hospital** *(ehl ohs-pee-'tahl)*
hostile	**hostil** *(ohs-'teel)*
hot	**caliente** *(kah-lee-'ehn-teh)*
hotel	**el hotel** *(ehl oh-'tehl)*
house	**la casa** *(lah 'kah-sah)*
house pet	**el animal doméstico** *(ehl ah-nee-'mahl doh-'mehs-tee-koh)*
housekeeper	**el casero/la casera** *(ehl kah-'seh-roh/lah kah-'seh-rah)*
housing	**la vivienda** *(lah vee-vee-'ehn-dah)*
human body	**el cuerpo humano** *(ehl 'kwehr-poh oo-'mah-noh)*
human resources	**los recursos humanos** *(lohs reh-'koor-sohs oo-'mah-nohs)*
hurtful	**ofensivo/ofensiva** *(oh-fehn-'see-voh/oh-fehn-'see-vah)*
husband	**el esposo** *(ehl ehs-'poh-soh)*

I

I	**yo** *(yoh)*
I-94 number	**el número de residente** *(ehl 'noo-meh-roh deh reh-see-'dehn-teh)*
ice	**el hielo** *(ehl ee-'eh-loh)*
ice pick	**el picahielo** *(ehl pee-kah-ee-'eh-loh)*
idea	**la idea** *(lah ee-'deh-ah)*
identification	**la identificación** *(lah ee-dehn-tee-fee-kah-see-'ohn)*
identified	**identificado/identificada** *(ee-dehn-tee-fee-'kah-doh/ee-dehn-tee-fee-'kah-dah)*
identity theft	**el robo de identidad** *(ehl 'roh-boh deh ee-dehn-tee-'dahd)*
illegal	**ilegal** *(ee-leh-'gahl)*
illegal status	**el estado ilegal** *(ehl ehs-'tah-doh ee-leh-'gahl)*
illness	**la enfermedad** *(lah ehn-fehr-meh-'dahd)*
immediate	**inmediato/inmediata** *(een-meh-dee-'ah-toh/een-meh-dee-'ah-tah)*
immigrant	**el/la inmigrante** *(ehl/la een-mee-'grahn-teh)*
immigration	**la inmigración** *(lah een-mee-grah-see-'ohn)*
immigration laws	**las leyes inmigratorias** *(lahs 'leh-yehs een-mee-grah-'toh-ree-ahs)*
immunity	**la inmunidad** *(lah een-moo-nee-'dahd)*
impatient	**impaciente** *(eem-pah-see-'ehn-teh)*
important	**importante** *(eem-pohr-'tahn-teh)*

imposter	**el impostor/la impostora** (*ehl eem-pohs-'tohr/lah eem-pohs-'toh-rah*)
improvement	**la mejora** (*lah meh-'hoh-rah*)
in	**en** (*ehn*)
in custody	**detenido/detenida** (*deh-teh-'nee-doh/deh-teh-'nee-dah*)
in force	**en vigencia** (*ehn vee-'hehn-see-ah*)
in front	**enfrente** (*ehn-'frehn-teh*)
in person	**en persona** (*ehn pehr-'soh-nah*)
incarcerated	**encarcelado/encarcelada** (*ehn-kahr-seh-'lah-doh/ehn-kahr-seh-'lah-dah*)
incarceration	**el encarcelamiento** (*ehl ehn-kahr-seh-lah-mee-'ehn-toh*)
incest	**el incesto** (*ehl een-'sehs-toh*)
included	**incluido/incluida** (*een-kloo-'ee-doh/een-kloo-'ee-dah*)
inconvenient	**inconveniente** (*enn-kohn-veh-nee-'ehn-teh*)
indemnization	**la indemnización** (*lah een-dehm-nee-sah-see-'ohn*)
index	**el índice** (*ehl 'een-dee-seh*)
indicted	**acusado/acusada** (*ah-koo-'sah-doh/ah-koo-'sah-dah*)
indictment	**la acusación** (*lah ah-koo-sah-see-'ohn*)
inexpensive	**barato/barata** (*bah-'rah-toh/bah-'rah-tah*)
inferior	**inferior** (*een-feh-ree-'ohr*)
informal	**informal** (*een-fohr-'mahl*)
information	**la información** (*lah een-fohr-mah-see-'ohn*)
inheritance	**la herencia** (*lah eh-'rehn-see-ah*)
injection	**la inyección** (*lah een-yehk-see-'ohn*)
injunction	**el entredicho** (*ehl ehn-treh-'dee-choh*)
injured	**lastimado/lastimada** (*lahs-tee-'mah-doh/lahs-tee-'mah-dah*)
injury	**la lesión** (*lah leh-see-'ohn*)
inmate	**el preso/la presa** (*ehl 'preh-soh/lah 'preh-sah*)
innocent	**inocente** (*ee-noh-'sehn-teh*)
insanity	**la locura** (*lah loh-'koo-rah*)
inside	**adentro** (*ah-'dehn-troh*)
inspection	**la inspección** (*lah eens-pehk-see'ohn*)
inspector	**el inspector/la inspectora** (*ehl eens-pehk-'tohr/lah eens-pehk-'toh-rah*)
installment	**la cuota** (*lah koo-'oh-tah*)
instructions	**las instrucciones** (*lahs eens-trook-see-'oh-nehs*)
insufficient funds	**los fondos insuficientes** (*lohs 'fohn-dohs een-soo-fee-see-'ehn-tehs*)
insurance	**el seguro** (*ehl seh-'goo-roh*)
insurance company	**la compañía de seguros** (*lah kohm-pah-'nee-ah deh seh-'goo-rohs*)
insurer	**el asegurador/la aseguradora** (*ehl ah-seh-goo-rah-'dohr/lah ah-seh-goo-rah-'doh-rah*)

intelligent	**inteligente** *(een-teh-lee-'hehn-teh)*
interest	**el interés** *(ehl een-teh-'rehs)*
interest rate	**la tasa de interés** *(lah 'tah-sah deh een-teh-'rehs)*
international	**internacional** *(een-tehr-nah-see-oh-'nahl)*
Internet	**el internet** *(ehl een-tehr-'neht)*
interpretation	**la intrepretación** *(lah een-tehr-preh-tah-see-'ohn)*
interpreter	**el/la intérprete** *(ehl/lah een-'tehr-preh-teh)*
interrogation	**la interrogación** *(lah een-tehr-roh-gah-see-'ohn)*
interview	**la entrevista** *(lah ehn-treh-'vees-tah)*
intruder	**el intruso/la intrusa** *(ehl een-'troo-soh/lah een-'troo-sah)*
invalid	**inválido/inválida** *(een-'vah-lee-doh/een-'vah-lee-dah)*
inventory	**las existencias** *(lahs ex-ees-'tehn-see-ahs)*
investigator	**el investigador/la investigadora** *(ehl een-vehs-tee-gah-'dohr/lah een-vehs-tee-gah-'doh-rah)*
investment	**la inversión** *(lah een-vehr-see-'ohn)*
investor	**el/la inversionista** *(ehl/lah een-vehr-see-oh-'nees-tah)*
invoice	**la factura** *(lah fahk-'too-rah)*
involuntary	**involuntario/involuntaria** *(een-voh-loon-'tah-ree-oh/een-voh-loon-'tah-ree-ah)*
IRA	**la cuenta de jubilación individual** *(lah 'kwehn-tah deh hoo-bee-lah-see-'ohn een-dee-vee-doo-'ahl)*
irresponsible	**irresponsable** *(eer-rehs-pohn-'sah-bleh)*
irrevocable	**irrevocable** *(eer-reh-voh-'kah-bleh)*
itemized	**detallado/detallada** *(deh-tah-'yah-doh/deh-tah-'yah-dah)*
IV	**intravenoso/intravenosa** *(een-trah-veh-'noh-soh/een-trah-veh-'noh-sah)*

J

jacket	**la chaqueta** *(lah chah-'keh-tah)*
jail	**la cárcel** *(lah 'kahr-sehl)*
janitor	**el/la conserje** *(ehl/lah kohn-'sehr-heh)*
January	**enero** *(eh-'neh-roh)*
jealous	**celoso/celosa** *(seh-'loh-soh/seh-'loh-sah)*
jealousy	**los celos** *(lohs 'seh-lohs)*
jewelry	**las joyas** *(lahs 'hoh-yahs)*
job	**el trabajo** *(ehl trah-'bah-hoh)*
joint	**mancomunado/mancomunada** *(mahn-koh-moo-'nah-doh/mahn-koh-moo-'nah-dah)*
joint account	**la cuenta conjunta** *(lah 'kwehn-tah kohn-'hoon-tah)*
joint agreement	**el acuerdo mutuo** *(ehl ah-'kwehr-doh 'moo-too-oh)*
joint custody	**la custodia en común** *(laj koos-'toh-dee-ah ehn koh-'moon)*
joint property	**la propiedad conjunta** *(lah proh-pee-eh-'dahd kohn-'hoo-tah)*
joke	**el chiste** *(ehl 'chees-teh)*

judge	**el juez/la jueza** *(ehl hoo-'ehs/lah hoo-'eh-sah)*
judge's bench	**la banca del juez** *(lah 'bahn-kah dehl hoo-'ehs)*
judgment	**el fallo** *(ehl 'fah-yoh)*
judicial process	**el proceso judicial** *(ehl proh-'seh-soh hoo-dee-see-'ahl)*
July	**julio** *('hoo-lee-oh)*
June	**junio** *('hoo-nee-oh)*
jurisdiction	**la jurisdicción** *(lah hoo-rees-deek-see-'ohn)*
jury	**el jurado** *(ehl hoo-'rah-doh)*
jury box	**la tribuna del jurado** *(lah tree-'boo-nah dehl hoo-'rah-doh)*
jury member	**el/la miembro del jurado** *(ehl/lah mee-'ehm-broh dehl hoo-'rah-doh)*
jury trial	**el juicio con jurado** *(ehl hoo-'ee-see-oh kohn hoo-'rah-doh)*
justice	**la justicia** *(lah hoos-'tee-see-ah)*
justification	**la justificación** *(lah hoos-tee-fee-kah-see-'ohn)*
juvenile court	**el tribunal de menores** *(ehl tree-boo-'nahl deh meh-'noh-rehs)*
juvenile law	**la ley de menores** *(lah 'leh-ee deh meh-'noh-rehs)*

K

kidnapping	**el secuestro** *(ehl seh-'kwehs-troh)*
kidney	**el riñón** *(ehl reen-'yohn)*
kilogram	**el kilogramo** *(ehl kee-loh-'grah-moh)*
kind	**amable** *(ah-'mah-bleh)*
kit	**el estuche** *(ehl ehs-'too-cheh)*
knee	**la rodilla** *(lah roh-'dee-yah)*
knife	**el cuchillo** *(ehl koo-'chee-yoh)*

L

label	**la etiqueta** *(lah eh-tee-'keh-tah)*
laborer	**el obrero** *(ehl oh-'breh-roh)*
lamp	**la lámpara** *(lah 'lahm-pah-rah)*
land	**el terreno** *(ehl tehr-'reh-noh)*
landlord	**el propietario/la propietaria** *(ehl proh-pee-eh-'tah-ree-oh/lah proh-pee-eh-'tah-ree-ah)*
laptop	**la computadora portátil** *(lah kohm-poo-tah-'doh-rah pohr-'tah-teel)*
larceny	**el hurto** *(ehl 'oor-toh)*
last name	**el apellido** *(ehl ah-peh-'yee-doh)*
late	**tarde** *('tahr-deh)*
later	**luego** *(loo-'eh-goh)*
Latin American	**el latinoamericano/la latinoamericana** *(ehl lah-tee-noh-ah-meh-ree-'kah-noh/lah lah-tee-noh-ah-meh-ree-* *'kah-nah)*
Latino assistance	**la ayuda para latinos** *(lah ah-'yoo-dah 'pah-rah lah-'tee-nohs)*

laundering	**el blanqueo de dinero** *(ehl blahn-'keh-oh deh dee-'neh-roh)*
law	**la ley** *(lah 'leh-ee)*
law firm	**el bufete** *(ehl boo-'feh-teh)*
lawsuit	**el pleito** *(ehl 'pleh-ee-toh)*
lawyer	**el abogado/la abogada** *(ehl ah-boh-'gah-doh/lah ah-boh-'gah-dah)*
lease	**el arriendo** *(ehl ahr-ree-'ehn-doh)*
left	**izquierdo/izquierda** *(ees-kee-'ehr-doh/ees-kee-'ehr-dah)*
leg	**la pierna** *(lah pee-'ehr-nah)*
legal	**legal** *(leh-'gahl)*
legal action	**la demanda judicial** *(lah deh-'mahn-dah hoo-dee-see-'ahl)*
legal advisor	**el asesor jurídico/la asesora jurídica** *(ehl ah-seh-'sohr hoo-'ree-dee-koh/lah ah-seh-'soh-rah hoo-'ree-dee-kah)*
legal aid	**la ayuda para asuntos jurídicos** *(lah ah-'yoo-dah 'pah-rah ah-'soon-tohs hoo-'ree-de-kohs)*
legal counsel	**el asesoramiento jurídico** *(ehl ah-seh-soh-rah-mee-'ehn-toh hoo-'ree-dee-koh)*
legal custody	**la custodia jurídica** *(lah koos-'toh-dee-ah hoo-'ree-dee-kah)*
legal defense	**la defensa juridica** *(lah deh-'fehn-sah hoo-'ree-dee-kah)*
legal practice	**el bufete** *(ehl boo-'feh-teh)*
legal protection	**la protección jurídica** *(lah proh-tehk-see-'ohn hoo-'ree-dee-kah)*
legal resources	**los recursos jurídicos** *(lohs reh-'koor-sohs hoo-'ree-dee-kohs)*
legal separation	**la separación legal** *(lah seh-pah-rah-see-'ohn leh-'gahl)*
legal services	**los servicios jurídicos** *(lohs sehr-'vee-see-ohs hoo-'ree-dee-kohs)*
legal support	**el apoyo jurídico** *(ehl ah-'poh-yoh hoo-'ree-dee-koh)*
legalization	**la legalización** *(lah leh-gah-lee-sah-see-'ohn)*
legitimate	**legítimo/legítima** *(leh-'hee-tee-moh/leh-'hee-tee-mah)*
lender	**el/la prestamista** *(ehl/lah prehs-tah-'mees-tah)*
lesbian	**la lesbiana** *(lah lehs-bee-'ah-nah)*
less	**menos** *('meh-nohs)*
lessee	**el arrendatario/la arrendataria** *(ehl ahr-rehn-dah-'tah-ree-oh/lah ahr-rehn-dah-'tah-ree-ah)*
lessor	**el arrendador/la arrendadora** *(ehl ahr-rehn-dah-'dohr/lah ahr-rehn-dah-'doh-rah)*
letter (mail)	**la carta** *(lah 'kahr-tah)*
level	**el nivel** *(ehl nee-'vehl)*
liability	**la obligación** *(lah oh-blee-gah-see-'ohn)*
liability insurance	**el seguro de responsabilidad civil** *(ehl seh-'goo-roh deh rehs-pohn-sah-bee-lee-'dahd see-'veel)*
libel	**el libelo** *(ehl lee-'beh-loh)*
librarian	**el bibliotecario/la bibliotecaria** *(ehl bee-blee-oh-teh-'kah-ree-oh/lah bee-blee-oh-teh-'kah-ree-ah)*
library	**la biblioteca** *(lah bee-blee-oh-'teh-kah)*
license	**la licencia** *(lah lee-'sehn-see-ah)*

license plate	**la placa** *(lah 'plah-kah)*
lie	**la mentira** *(lah mehn-'tee-rah)*
lien	**el embargo preventivo** *(ehl ehm-'bahr-goh preh-vehn-'tee-voh)*
life	**la vida** *(lah 'vee-dah)*
life support	**el mantenimiento de vida** *(ehl mahn-teh-nee-mee-'ehn-toh deh 'vee-dah)*
light	**la luz** *(lah loos)*
limit	**el límite** *(ehl 'lee-mee-teh)*
limited liability corporation	**la sociedad de responsabilidad limitada** *(lah soh-see-eh-'dahd deh rehs-pohn-sah-bee-lee-'dahd lee-mee-'tah-dah)*
line	**la línea** *(lah 'lee-neh-ah)*
liquidity	**la liquidez** *(lah lee-kee-'dehs)*
liquor	**el licor** *(ehl lee-'kohr)*
list	**la lista** *(lah 'lees-tah)*
litigation	**la litigación** *(lah lee-tee-gah-see-'ohn)*
littering	**el arrojo de basura** *(ehl ahr-'roh-hoh deh bah-'soo-rah)*
liver	**el hígado** *(ehl 'ee-gah-doh)*
living trust	**el fideicomiso activo** *(ehl fee-deh-ee-koh-'mee-soh ahk-'tee-voh)*
living will	**el testamento en vida** *(ehl tehs-tah-'mehn-toh ehn 'vee-dah)*
loan	**el préstamo** *(ehl 'prehs-tah-moh)*
loan officer	**el/la agente de préstamos** *(ehl/lah ah-'hehn-teh deh 'prehs-tah-mohs)*
lobby	**el vestíbulo** *(ehl vehs-'tee-boo-loh)*
location	**la ubicación** *(lah oo-bee-kah-see-'ohn)*
loitering	**el merodeo** *(ehl meh-roh-'deh-oh)*
long	**largo/larga** *('lahr-goh/'lahr-gah)*
long-term	**a largo plazo** *(ah 'lahr-goh 'plah-soh)*
looting	**el saqueo** *(ehl sah-'keh-oh)*
loss	**la pérdida** *(lah 'pehr-dee-dah)*
loss of income	**la pérdida de ingresos** *(lah 'pehr-dee-dah deh een-'greh-sohs)*
lost	**perdido/perdida** *(pehr-'dee-doh/pehr-'dee-dah)*
lottery	**la lotería** *(lah loh-teh-'ree-ah)*
loud	**ruidoso/ruidosa** *(roo-ee-'doh-soh/roo-ee-'doh-sah)*
love	**el amor** *(ehl ah-'mohr)*
low-cost	**de bajo costo** *(deh 'bah-hoh 'kohs-toh)*
lower court	**el juzgado menor** *(ehl hoos-'gah-doh meh-'nohr)*
lunch	**el almuerzo** *(ehl ahl-moo-'ehr-soh)*
lungs	**los pulmones** *(lohs pool-'moh-nehs)*

M

machinist	**el operario de máquina** *(ehl oh-peh-'rah-ree-oh deh 'mah-kee-nah)*
magazine	**la revista** *(lah reh-'vees-tah)*
maiden name	**el nombre de soltera** *(ehl 'nohm-breh deh sohl-'teh-rah)*

mail	**el correo** *(ehl kohr-'reh-oh)*
mail carrier	**el cartero/la cartera** *(ehl kahr-'teh-roh/lah kahr-'teh-rah)*
mailbox	**el buzón** *(ehl boo-'sohn)*
main office	**la oficina principal** *(lah oh-fee-'see-nah preen-see-'pahl)*
maintenance	**el mantenimiento** *(ehl mahn-teh-nee-mee-'ehn-toh)*
make	**la marca** *(lah 'mahr-kah)*
malpractice	**la negligencia profesional** *(lah neh-ghlee-'hehn-see-ah proh-feh-see-oh-'nahl)*
man	**el hombre** *(ehl 'ohm-breh)*
management	**la administración** *(lah ahd-mee-nees-trah-see-'ohn)*
manager	**el gerente/la gerenta** *(ehl heh-'rehn-teh/lah he-'rehn-tah)*
mandated	**ordenado/ordenada** *(ohr-deh-'nah-doh/ohr-deh-'nah-dah)*
manslaughter	**el homicidio involuntario** *(ehl oh-mee-'see-dee-oh een-voh-loon-'tah-ree-oh)*
manufacturer	**el/la fabricante** *(ehl/lah fah-bree-'kahn-teh)*
map	**el mapa** *(ehl 'mah-pah)*
March	**marzo** *('mahr-soh)*
margin	**el margen** *(ehl 'mahr-hehn)*
marijuana	**la marijuana** *(lah mah-ree-'hwah-nah)*
marital status	**el estado civil** *(ehl ehs-'tah-doh see-'veel)*
maritime	**marítimo/maritima** *(mah-'ree-tee-moh/mah-'ree-tee-mah)*
market	**el mercado** *(ehl mehr-'kah-doh)*
marriage	**el matrimonio** *(ehl mah-tree-'moh-nee-oh)*
married couple	**los cónyuges** *(lohs 'kohn-yoo-ghehs)*
married	**casado/casada** *(kah-'sah-doh/kah-'sah-dah)*
mask	**la máscara** *(lah 'mahs-kah-rah)*
matches	**los fósforos** *(lohs 'fohs-foh-rohs)*
matter	**el asunto** *(ehl ah-'soon-toh)*
mature	**maduro/madura** *(mah-'doo-roh/mah-'doo-rah)*
matured	**pagadero** *(pah-gah-'deh-roh)*
maximal	**máximo/máxima** *('mahk-see-moh/'mahk-see-mah)*
May	**mayo** *('mah-yoh)*
mayor	**el alcalde/la alcaldesa** *(ehl ahl-'kahl-deh/lah ahl-kahl-'deh-sah)*
mean	**cruel** *(kroo-'ehl)*
mechanic	**el mecánico/la mecánica** *(ehl meh-'kah-nee-koh/lah meh-'kah-nee-kah)*
media coverage	**la cobertura informativa** *(lah koh-behr-'too-rah een-fohr-mah-'tee-vah)*
mediation	**la mediación** *(lah meh-dee-ah-see-'ohn)*
mediator	**el mediador/la mediadora** *(ehl meh-dee-ah-'dohr/lah meh-dee-ah-'doh-rah)*
medical care	**el cuidado médico** *(ehl koo-ee-'dah-doh 'meh-dee-koh)*
medical charges	**los cargos médicos** *(lohs 'kahr-gohs 'meh-dee-kohs)*

medical exam	**el examen médico** *(ehl ex-ʻah-mehn ʻmeh-dee-koh)*
medical history	**la historia médica** *(lah ees-ʻtoh-ree-ah ʻmeh-dee-kah)*
medicine	**la medicina** *(lah meh-dee-ʻsee-nah)*
meeting	**la reunión** *(lah reh-oo-nee-ʻohn)*
member	**el miembro/la miembra** *(ehl mee-ʻehm-broh/lah mee-ʻehm-brah)*
memo	**el memorándum** *(ehl meh-moh-ʻrahn-doom)*
mental health	**la salud mental** *(lah sah-ʻlood mehn-ʻtahl)*
menu	**el menú** *(ehl meh-ʻnoo)*
merchandise	**las mercancías** *(lahs mehr-kahn-ʻsee-ahs)*
merchant	**el/la comerciante** *(ehl/lah koh-mehr-see-ʻahn-teh)*
message	**el mensaje** *(ehl mehn-ʻsah-heh)*
microphone	**el micrófono** *(ehl mee-ʻkroh-foh-noh)*
middle	**el medio** *(ehl ʻmeh-dee-oh)*
midnight	**la medianoche** *(lah meh-dee-ah-ʻnoh-cheh)*
minimum	**el mínimo/la mínima** *(ehl ʻmee-nee-moh/lah ʻmee-nee-mah)*
minor	**el/la menor de edad** *(ehl/lah meh-ʻnohr deh eh-ʻdahd)*
minute	**el minuto** *(ehl mee-ʻnoo-toh)*
misdemeanor	**el delito menor** *(ehl deh-ʻlee-toh meh-ʻnohr)*
misrepresentation	**la representación fraudulenta** *(lah reh-preh-sehn-tah-see-ʻohn frah-oo-doo-ʻlehn-tah)*
Miss	**la señorita** *(lah sehn-yoh-ʻree-tah)*
mistreatment	**el maltrato** *(ehl mahl-ʻtrah-toh)*
model	**el modelo** *(ehl moh-ʻdeh-loh)*
mold	**el moho** *(ehl ʻmoh-hoh)*
mole	**el lunar** *(ehl loo-ʻnahr)*
Monday	**lunes** *(ʻloo-nehs)*
money	**el dinero** *(ehl dee-ʻneh-roh)*
money market	**el mercado de valores** *(ehl mehr-ʻkah-doh deh vah-ʻloh-rehs)*
money order	**el giro postal** *(ehl ʻhee-roh pohs-ʻtahl)*
monitor	**el monitor** *(ehl moh-nee-ʻtohr)*
month	**el mes** *(ehl mehs)*
more	**más** *(mahs)*
morgue	**la morgue** *(lah ʻmohr-geh)*
mortgage	**la hipoteca** *(lah ee-poh-ʻteh-kah)*
mortician	**el director de pompas fúnebres** *(ehl dee-rehk-ʻtohr deh ʻpohm-pahs ʻfoo-neh-brehs)*
mortuary	**mortuorio/mortuoria** *(mohr-too-ʻoh-ree-oh/mohr-too-ʻoh-ree-ah)*
motel	**el motel** *(ehl moh-ʻtehl)*
mother	**la madre** *(lah ʻmah-dreh)*
mother-in-law	**la suegra** *(lah ʻsweh-grah)*
motion	**la petición** *(lah peh-tee-see-ʻohn)*
motive	**el motivo** *(ehl moh-ʻtee-voh)*

motorcycle	**la moto** *(lah 'moh-toh)*
mouse	**el ratón** *(ehl rah-'tohn)*
mouth	**la boca** *(lah 'boh-kah)*
movie theater	**el cine** *(ehl 'see-neh)*
Mr.	**señor** *(sehn-'yohr)*
Mrs.	**señora** *(sehn-'yoh-rah)*
mugging	**el atraco** *(ehl ah-'trah-koh)*
municipal court	**el tribunal municipal** *(ehl tree-boo-'nahl moo-nee-see-'pahl)*
murder	**el asesinato** *(ahl ah-seh-see-'nah-toh)*
murderer	**el asesino/la asesina** *(ehl ah-seh-'see-noh/lah ah-seh-'see-nah)*
muscle	**el músculo** *(ehl 'moos-koo-loh)*
museum	**el museo** *(ehl moo-'seh-oh)*
musician	**el músico/la música** *(ehl 'moo-see-koh/lah 'moo-see-kah)*
mutual	**mutuo/mutua** *('moo-too-oh/'moo-too-ah)*
mutual fund	**el fondo mutualista** *(ehl 'fohn-doh moo-too-ah-'lees-tah)*
my	**mi** *(mee)*

N

narcotic	**el narcótico** *(ehl nahr-'koh-tee-koh)*
national	**nacional** *(nah-see-oh-'nahl)*
nationality	**la nacionalidad** *(lah nah-see-oh-nah-lee-'dahd)*
native language	**la lengua maternal** *(lah 'lehn-gwah mah-'tehr-nah)*
natural causes	**las causas naturales** *(lahs 'kah-oo-sahs nah-too-'rah-lehs)*
naturalization	**la naturalización** *(lah nah-too-rah-lee-sah-see-'ohn)*
near	**cerca** *('sehr-kah)*
necessary	**necesario/necesaria** *(neh-seh-'sah-ree-oh/neh-seh-'sah-ree-ah)*
neck	**el cuello** *(ehl 'kweh-yoh)*
necklace	**el collar** *(ehl koh-'yahr)*
need	**la necesidad** *(lah neh-seh-see-'dahd)*
needle	**la aguja** *(lah ah-'goo-hah)*
neglect, negligence	**la negligencia** *(lah neh-glee-'hehn-see-ah)*
negociation	**la negociación** *(lah neh-goh-see-ah-see-'ohn)*
neighbor	**el vecino/la vecina** *(ehl veh-'see-noh/lah veh-'see-nah)*
neighborhood	**el barrio** *(ehl 'bahr-ree-oh)*
nephew	**el sobrino** *(ehl soh-'bree-noh)*
nerve	**el nervio** *(ehl 'nehr-vee-oh)*
nervous	**nervioso/nerviosa** *(nehr-vee-'oh-soh/nehr-vee-'oh-sah)*
net income	**el ingreso neto** *(ehl een-'greh-soh 'neh-toh)*
neurologist	**el neurólogo/la neuróloga** *(ehl neh-oo-'roh-loh-goh/lah neh-oo-'roh-loh-gah)*
never	**nunca** *('noon-kah)*
new	**nuevo/nueva** *(noo-'eh-voh/noo-'eh-vah)*

newlywed	**el recién casado/la recién casada** *(ehl reh-see-'ehn kah-'sah-doh/lah reh-see-'ehn kah-'sah-dah)*
newspaper	**el periódico** *(ehl peh-ree-'oh-dee-koh)*
next of kin	**el pariente más cercano** *(ehl pah-ree-'ehn-teh mahs sehr-'kah-noh)*
next to	**al lado** *(ahl 'lah-doh)*
niece	**la sobrina** *(lah soh-'bree-nah)*
nightclub	**el club nocturno** *(ehl kloob nohk-'toor-noh)*
ninth	**noveno/novena** *(noh-'veh-noh/noh-'veh-nah)*
no one	**nadie** *('nah-dee-eh)*
nowhere	**en ningún sitio** *(ehn neen-'goon 'see-tee-oh)*
noise	**el ruido** *(ehl roo-'ee-doh)*
none	**ninguno** *(neen-'goo-noh)*
nonprofit	**sin fines lucrativos** *(seen 'fee-nehs loo-krah-'tee-vohs)*
noon	**el mediodía** *(ehl meh-dee-oh-'dee-ah)*
north	**el norte** *(ehl 'nohr-teh)*
nose	**la naríz** *(lah nah-'rees)*
notarized	**notarizado/notarizada** *(noh-tah-ree-'sah-doh/noh-tah-ree-'sah-dah)*
notary	**el notario/la notaria** *(ehl noh-'tah-ree-oh/lah noh-'tah-ree-ah)*
notary public	**el notario público/la notaria pública** *(ehl noh-'tah-ree-oh 'poo-blee-koh/lah noh-'tah-ree-ah 'poo-blee-kah)*
nothing	**nada** *('nah-dah)*
notice	**el aviso** *(ehl ah-'vee-soh)*
November	**noviembre** *(noh-vee-'ehm-breh)*
null and void	**nulo y sin efecto** *('noo-loh ee seen eh-'fehk-toh)*
number	**el número** *(ehl 'noo-meh-roh)*
nurse	**el enfermero/la enfermera** *(ehl ehn-fehr-'meh-roh/lah ehn-fehr-'meh-rah)*

O

oath	**el juramento** *(ehl hoo-rah-'mehn-toh)*
object	**el objeto** *(ehl ohb-'heh-toh)*
obligatory	**obligatorio/obligatoria** *(oh-blee-gah-'toh-ree-oh/oh-blee-gah-'toh-ree-ah)*
obscene	**obsceno/obscena** *(ohb-'seh-noh/ohb-'seh-nah)*
obstetrician	**el/la obstetra** *(ehl/lah ohbs-'teh-trah)*
occupation	**la ocupación** *(lah oh-koo-pah-see-'ohn)*
October	**octubre** *(ohk-'too-breh)*
offense	**la ofensa** *(lah oh-'fehn-sah)*
offer	**la oferta** *(lah oh-'fehr-tah)*
office	**la oficina** *(lah oh-fee-'see-nah)*
office building	**el edificio de oficinas** *(ehl eh-dee-'fee-see-oh deh oh-fee-'see-nahs)*

office clerk	**el oficinista/la oficinista** *(ehl oh-fee-see-ˈnees-tah/lah oh-fee-see-ˈnees-tah)*
officer	**el funcionario/la funcionaria** *(ehl foon-see-oh-ˈnah-ree-oh/lah foon-see-oh-ˈnah-ree-ah)*
official	**oficial** *(oh-fee-see-ˈahl)*
old	**viejo/vieja** *(vee-ˈeh-hoh/vee-ˈeh-hah)*
older	**mayor** *(mah-ˈyohr)*
on	**en** *(ehn)*
on-line	**en línea** *(ehn ˈlee-neh-ah)*
only	**solamente** *(soh-lah-ˈmehn-teh)*
opinion	**la opinión** *(lah oh-pee-nee-ˈohn)*
opportunity	**la oportunidad** *(lah oh-pohr-too-nee-ˈdahd)*
option	**la opción** *(lah ohp-see-ˈohn)*
or	**o** *(oh)*
orange	**anaranjado/anaranjada** *(ah-nah-rahn-ˈhah-doh/ah-nah-rahn-ˈhah-dah)*
order (arrangement)	**el orden** *(ehl ˈohr-dehn)*
order (command)	**la orden** *(lah ˈohr-dehn)*
order (commercial)	**el pedido** *(ehl peh-ˈdee-doh)*
organization	**la organización** *(lah ohr-gah-nee-sah-see-ˈohn)*
orientation	**la orientación** *(lah oh-ree-ehn-tah-see-ˈohn)*
original	**el original** *(ehl oh-ree-hee-ˈnahl)*
orphan	**el huérfano/la huérfana** *(ehl oo-ˈehr-fah-noh/lah oo-ˈehr-fah-nah)*
other	**otro/otra** *(ˈoh-troh/ˈoh-trah)*
other party	**la otra parte** *(lah ˈoh-trah ˈpahr-teh)*
ounce	**la onza** *(lah ˈohn-sah)*
our	**nuestro/nuestra** *(noo-ˈehs-troh/noo-ˈehs-trah)*
outside	**afuera** *(ah-foo-ˈeh-rah)*
over	**sobre** *(ˈsoh-breh)*
overcoat	**el abrigo** *(ehl ah-ˈbree-goh)*
overdose	**la sobredosis** *(lah soh-breh-ˈdoh-sees)*
overdraft	**el sobregiro** *(ehl soh-breh-ˈhee-roh)*
overdue	**vencido/vencida** *(vehn-ˈsee-doh/vehn-ˈsee-dah)*
owner	**el dueño/la dueña** *(ehl doo-ˈehn-yoh/lah doo-ˈehn-yah)*
oxygen	**el oxígeno** *(ehl ohk-ˈsee-heh-noh)*

P

package	**el paquete** *(ehl pah-ˈkeh-teh)*
packaging	**el empaque** *(ehl ehm-ˈpah-keh)*
page	**la página** *(lah ˈpah-hee-nah)*
paid	**pagado/pagada** *(pah-ˈgah-doh/pah-ˈgah-dah)*

pain	**el dolor** *(ehl doh-'lohr)*
pain and suffering	**el dolor y sufrimiento** *(ehl doh-'lohr ee soo-free-mee-'ehn-toh)*
paint	**la pintura** *(lah peen-'too-rah)*
painter	**el pintor/la pintora** *(ehl peen-'tohr/lah peen-'toh-rah)*
pamphlet	**el folleto** *(ehl foh-'yeh-toh)*
pants	**los pantalones** *(lohs pahn-tah-'loh-nehs)*
paper	**el papel** *(ehl pah-'pehl)*
paper clip	**el sujetapapeles** *(elh soo-heh-tah-pah-'peh-lehs)*
paperwork	**el papeleo** *(ehl pah-peh-'leh-oh)*
paralegal	**el asistente/la asistenta legal** *(ehl ah-sees-'tehn-teh/lah ah-sees-'tehn-tah leh-'gahl)*
pardon	**el indulto** *(ehl een-'dool-toh)*
parenthood	**la paternidad** *(lah pah-tehr-nee-'dahd)*
parents	**los padres** *(lohs 'pah-drehs)*
park	**el parque** *(ehl 'pahr-keh)*
parking	**el estacionamiento** *(ehl ehs-tah-see-oh-nah-mee-'ehn-toh)*
parking area	**la zona de estacionamiento** *(lah 'soh-nah deh ehs-tah-see-oh-nah-mee-'ehn-toh)*
parking meter	**el parquímetro** *(ehl pahr-'kee-meh-troh)*
parking ticket	**la boleta de estacionamiento** *(lah boh-'leh-tah deh ehs-tah-see-oh-nah-mee-'ehn-toh)*
parole	**la libertad provisional** *(lah lee-behr-'tahd proh-vee-see-oh-'nahl)*
partial	**parcial** *(pahr-see-'ahl)*
participation	**la participación** *(lah pahr-tee-see-pah-see-'ohn)*
partition	**el tabique** *(ehl tah-'bee-keh)*
partner	**el socio/la socia** *(ehl 'soh-see-oh/lah 'soh-see-ah)*
partnership	**la asociación** *(lah ah-soh-see-ah-see-'ohn)*
party	**la fiesta** *(lah fee-'ehs-tah)*
passenger	**el pasajero/la pasajera** *(ehl pah-sah-'heh-roh/lah pah-sah-'heh-rah)*
passion	**la pasión** *(lah pah-see-'ohn)*
passport	**el pasaporte** *(ehl pah-sah-'pohr-teh)*
password	**la contraseña** *(lah kohn-trah-'sehn-yah)*
patent	**la patente** *(lah pah-'tehn-teh)*
paternity	**la paternidad** *(lah pah-tehr-nee-'dahd)*
patient	**el/la paciente** *(ehl/lah pah-see-'ehn-teh)*
paycheck	**el cheque de sueldo** *(ehl 'cheh-keh deh 'swehl-doh)*
payment	**el pago** *(ehl 'pah-goh)*
payor	**el pagador/la pagadora** *(ehl pah-gah-'dohr/lah pah-gah-'doh-rah)*
payroll deduction	**la deducción de nómina** *(lah deh-dook-see-'ohn deh 'noh-mee-nah)*
PDA	**la computadora de bolsillo** *(lah kohm-poo-tah-'doh-rah deh bohl-'see-yoh)*

pedestrian	**el/la peatón** *(ehl/lah peh-ah-ʿtohn)*
pediatrician	**el/la pediatra** *(ehl/lah peh-dee-ʿah-trah)*
pen	**el lapicero** *(ehl lah-pee-ʿseh-roh)*
penalty	**la multa** *(lah ʿmool-tah)*
pencil	**el lápiz** *(ehl ʿlah-pees)*
pendant	**el pendiente** *(ehl pehn-dee-ʿehn-teh)*
pension	**la pensión** *(lah pehn-see-ʿohn)*
people	**la gente** *(lah ʿhehn-teh)*
percentage	**el porcentaje** *(ehl pohr-sehn-ʿtah-heh)*
periodically	**periódicamente** *(peh-ree-oh-dee-kah-ʿmehn-teh)*
perjury	**el perjurio** *(ehl pehr-ʿhoo-ree-oh)*
permit	**el permiso** *(ehl pehr-ʿmee-soh)*
perpetrator	**el/la responsable** *(ehl/lah rehs-pohn-ʿsah-bleh)*
person	**la persona** *(lah pehr-ʿsoh-nah)*
personal injury	**la lesión corporal** *(lah leh-see-ʿohn kohr-poh-ʿrahl)*
personal property	**los bienes muebles** *(lohs bee-ʿeh-nehs moo-ʿeh-blehs)*
pests	**las plagas** *(lahs ʿplah-gahs)*
petition	**la petición** *(lah peh-tee-see-ʿohn)*
petitioners	**los peticionarios/las peticionarias** *(lohs peh-tee-see-oh-ʿnah-ree-ohs/lahs peh-tee-see-oh-ʿnah-ree-ahs)*
pets	**los animales domésticos** *(lohs ah-nee-ʿmah-lehs doh-ʿmehs-tee-kohs)*
pharmaceutical	**farmacéutico/farmacéutica** *(fahr-mah-ʿseh-oo-tee-koh/fahr-mah-ʿseh-oo-tee-kah)*
pharmacist	**el farmacéutico/la farmacéutica** *(ehl fahr-mah-ʿseh-oo-tee-koh/lah fahr-mah-ʿseh-oo-tee-kah)*
phone	**el teléfono** *(ehl teh-ʿleh-foh-noh)*
phone number	**el número de teléfono** *(ehl ʿnoo-meh-roh deh teh-ʿleh-foh-noh)*
photo	**la foto** *(lah ʿfoh-toh)*
physical	**físico/física** *(ʿfee-see-koh/ʿfee-see-kah)*
physical custody	**la custodia física** *(lah koos-ʿtoh-dee-ah ʿfee-see-kah)*
physical injury	**el trauma físico** *(ehl ʿtrah-oo-mah ʿfee-see-koh)*
physical therapy	**la terapia física** *(lah teh-ʿrah-pee-ah ʿfee-see-kah)*
pickpocket	**el/la carterista** *(ehl/lah kahr-teh-ʿrees-tah)*
picture ID	**la identificación con foto** *(lah ee-dehn-tee-fee-kah-see-ʿohn kohn ʿfoh-toh)*
piece	**el pedazo** *(ehl peh-ʿdah-soh)*
pill	**la píldora** *(lah ʿpeel-doh-rah)*
pilot	**el/la piloto** *(ehl/lah pee-ʿloh-toh)*
pimp	**el alcahuete/la alcahueta** *(ehl ahl-kah-oo-ʿeh-teh/lah ahl-kah-oo-ʿeh-tah)*
pin number	**el número de identificación personal** *(ehl ʿnoo-meh-roh deh ee-dehn-tee-fee-kah-see-ʿohn pehr-soh-ʿnahl)*

pink	**rosado/rosada** *(roh-'sah-doh/roh-'sah-dah)*
pipe	**el tubo** *(ehl 'too-boh)*
pistol	**la pistola** *(lah pees-'toh-lah)*
place	**el lugar** *(ehl loo-'gahr)*
plaintiff	**el/la demandante** *(ehl/lah deh-mahn-'dahn-teh)*
plan	**el plan** *(ehl plahn)*
planning	**la planificación** *(lah plah-nee-fee-kah-see-'ohn)*
plant	**la planta** *(lah 'plahn-tah)*
plastic bag	**la bolsa de plástico** *(lah 'bohl-sah deh 'plahs-tee-koh)*
plate number	**el número de placa** *(ehl 'noo-meh-roh deh 'plah-kah)*
player	**el tocador** *(ehl toh-kah-'dohr)*
playground	**el campo de recreo** *(ehl 'kahm-poh deh reh-'kreh-oh)*
plea	**el alegato** *(ehl ah-leh-'gah-toh)*
plumber	**el plomero/la plomera** *(ehl ploh-'meh-roh/lah ploh-'meh-rah)*
plumbing	**la tubería** *(lah too-beh-'ree-ah)*
P.M.	**de la tarde/de la noche** *(deh lah 'tahr-deh/deh lah 'noh-cheh)*
points	**los puntos hipotecarios** *(lohs 'poon-tohs ee-poh-teh-'kah-ree-ohs)*
poison	**el veneno** *(ehl veh-'neh-noh)*
poisoning	**el envenenamiento** *(ehl ehn-veh-neh-nah-mee-'ehn-toh)*
police	**la policía** *(lah poh-lee-'see-ah)*
police chief	**el jefe/la jefa de policía** *(ehl 'heh-feh/lah 'heh-fah deh poh-lee-'see-ah)*
police department	**el departamento de policía** *(ehl deh-pahr-tah-'mehn-toh deh poh-lee-'see-ah)*
police officer	**el/la policía** *(ehl/lah poh-lee-'see-ah)*
police station	**la estación de policía** *(lah ehs-tah-see-'ohn deh poh-lee-'see-ah)*
policy	**la póliza** *(lah 'poh-lee-sah)*
policy number	**el número de póliza** *(ehl 'noo-meh-roh deh 'poh-lee-sah)*
polite	**cortés** *(kohr-'tehs)*
polygraph	**el detector de mentiras** *(ehl deh-tehk-'tohr deh mehn-'tee-rahs)*
pool hall	**la sala de billar** *(lah 'sah-lah deh bee-'yahr)*
poor	**pobre** *('poh-breh)*
poorly	**mal** *(mahl)*
pornography	**la pornografía** *(lah pohr-noh-grah-'fee-ah)*
portfolio	**los valores en cartera** *(lohs vah-'loh-rehs ehn kahr-'teh-rah)*
possession	**la posesión** *(lah poh-seh-see-'ohn)*
post office	**el correo** *(ehl kohr-'reh-oh)*
poster	**el cartel** *(ehl kahr-'tehl)*
postponed	**aplazado/aplazada** *(ah-plah-'sah-doh/ah-plah-'sah-dah)*
post-traumatic	**postraumático/postraumática** *(pohs-trah-oo-'mah-tee-koh/pohs-trah-oo-'mah-tee-kah)*
pothole	**el bache** *(ehl 'bah-cheh)*

pound	**la libra** *(lah 'lee-brah)*
powder	**el polvo** *(ehl 'pohl-voh)*
power of attorney	**la poder notarial** *(ehl poh-'dehr noh-tah-ree-'ahl)*
prank	**la travesura** *(lah trah-veh-'soo-rah)*
preference	**la preferencia** *(lah preh-feh-'rehn-see-ah)*
pregnant	**embarazada** *(ehm-bah-rah-'sah-dah)*
preliminary	**preliminario/preliminaria** *(preh-lee-mee-'nah-ree-oh/preh-lee-mee-'nah-ree-ah)*
premeditated	**premeditado/premeditada** *(preh-meh-dee-'tah-doh/preh-meh-dee-'tah-dah)*
premium	**la prima** *(lah 'pree-mah)*
prenuptial	**prematrimonial** *(preh-mah-tree-moh-nee-'ahl)*
prepaid	**prepagado/prepagada** *(preh-pah-'gah-doh/preh-pah-'gah-dah)*
prescription	**la receta médica** *(lah reh-'seh-tah 'meh-dee-kah)*
president	**el presidente/la presidenta** *(ehl preh-see-'dehn-teh/lah preh-see-'dehn-tah)*
pretty	**bonito/bonita** *(boh-'nee-toh/boh-'nee-tah)*
prevention	**la prevención** *(lah preh-vehn-see-'ohn)*
previous	**previo/previa** *('preh-vee-oh/'preh-vee-ah)*
price	**el precio** *(ehl 'preh-see-oh)*
price-fixing	**la fijación de precios** *(lah fee-hah-see-'ohn deh 'preh-see-ohs)*
prime rate	**la tasa de interés preferencial** *(lah 'tah-sah deh een-teh-'rehs preh-feh-rehn-see-'ahl)*
printer	**la impresora** *(lah eem-preh-'soh-rah)*
prior	**anterior** *(ahn-teh-ree-'ohr)*
priority	**la prioridad** *(lah pree-oh-ree-'dahd)*
prison	**la prisión** *(lah pree-see-'ohn)*
prisoner	**el prisionero/la prisionera** *(ehl pree-see-oh-'neh-roh/lah pree-see-oh-'neh-rah)*
privacy	**la privacidad** *(lah pree-vah-see-'dahd)*
private	**privado/privada** *(pree-'vah-doh/pree-'vah-dah)*
private property	**la propiedad privada** *(lah proh-pee-eh-'dahd pree-'vah-dah)*
probate	**la validación testamentaria** *(lah vah-lee-dah-see-'ohn tehs-tah-mehn-'tah-ree-ah)*
probate court	**el tribunal testamentario** *(ehl tree-boo-'nahl tehs-tah-mehn-'tah-ree-oh)*
probation	**la libertad provisional** *(lah lee-behr-'tahd proh-vee-see-oh-'nahl)*
probation officer	**el oficial de libertad provisional** *(ehl oh-fee-see-'ahl deh lee-behr-'tahd proh-vee-see-oh-'nahl)*
problem	**el problema** *(ehl proh-'bleh-mah)*
procedure	**el procedimiento** *(ehl proh-seh-dee-mee-'ehn-toh)*
proceedings	**los trámites** *(lohs 'trah-mee-tehs)*
process	**el proceso** *(ehl proh-'seh-soh)*

product	**el producto** (*ehl proh-'dook-toh*)
production	**la producción** (*lah proh-dook-see-'ohn*)
professional	**professional** (*proh-feh-see-oh-'nahl*)
profit	**la ganancia** (*lah gah-'nahn-see-ah*)
program	**el programa** (*ehl proh-'grah-mah*)
projector	**el proyector** (*ehl proh-yehk-'tohr*)
promissory note	**el pagaré** (*ehl pah-gah-'reh*)
proof	**la prueba** (*lah proo-'eh-bah*)
property	**la propiedad** (*lah proh-pee-eh-'dahd*)
proposal	**la propuesta** (*lah proh-poo-'ehs-tah*)
proposition	**la proposición** (*lah proh-poh-see-see-'ohn*)
prosecution	**el enjuiciamiento** (*ehl ehn-hoo-ee-see-ah-mee-'ehn-toh*)
prosecution attorney	**el abogado acusador** (*ehl ah-boh-'gah-doh ah-koo-sah-'dohr*)
prosecutor	**el/la fiscal** (*ehl/lah fees-'kahl*)
prostitution	**la prostitución** (*lah prohs-tee-too-see-'ohn*)
protection	**la protección** (*lah proh-tehk-see-'ohn*)
protection order	**la orden de protección** (*lah 'ohr-dehn deh proh-tehk-see-'ohn*)
provider	**el proveedor/la proveedora** (*ehl proh-veh-eh-'dohr/lah proh-veh-eh-'doh-rah*)
provision	**la estipulación** (*lah ehs-tee-poo-lah-see-'ohn*)
provisional	**provisional** (*proh-vee-see-oh-'nahl*)
psychiatrist	**el/la psiquiatra** (*ehl/lah see-kee-'ah-trah*)
psychological	**psicológico/psicológica** (*see-koh-'loh-ee-koh/see-koh-'loh-ee-kah*)
psychologist	**el psicólogo/la psicóloga** (*ehl see-'koh-loh-goh/lah see-'koh-loh-gah*)
public	**público/pública** (*'poo-blee-koh/'poo-blee-kah*)
public defender	**el defensor público** (*ehl deh-fehn-'sohr 'poo-blee-koh*)
public records	**los archivos públicos** (*lohs ahr-'chee-vohs 'poo-blee-kohs*)
published	**publicado/publicada** (*poo-blee-'kah-doh/poo-blee-'kah-dah*)
punctual	**puntual** (*poon-too-'ahl*)
punishment	**la pena** (*lah 'peh-nah*)
purple	**morado/morada** (*moh-'rah-doh/moh-'rah-dah*)
purpose	**el propósito** (*ehl proh-'poh-see-toh*)
purse	**la cartera** (*lah kahr-'teh-rah*)

Q

qualified	**calificado/calificada** (*kah-lee-fee-'kah-doh/lah-lee-fee-'kah-dah*)
quality	**la calidad** (*lah kah-lee-'dahd*)
quarrel	**la discusión** (*lah dees-koo-see-'ohn*)
quarterly	**trimestral** (*tree-mehs-'trahl*)
question	**la pregunta** (*lah preh-'goon-tah*)
quiet	**quieto/quieta** (*kee-'eh-toh/kee-'eh-tah*)
quota	**la cuota** (*lah koo-'oh-tah*)

R

race	**la raza** *(lah 'rah-sah)*
racism	**el racismo** *(ehl rah-'sees-moh)*
racketeer	**el/la extorsionista** *(ehl/lah ex-tohr-see-oh-'nees-tah)*
radiologist	**el radiólogo/la radióloga** *(ehl rah-dee-'oh-loh-goh/lah rah-dee-'oh-loh-gah)*
raid	**la incursión** *(lah een-koor-see-'ohn)*
rain	**la lluvia** *(lah 'yoo-vee-ah)*
raincoat	**el impermeable** *(ehl eem-pehr-meh-'ah-bleh)*
ranch	**el rancho** *(ehl 'rahn-choh)*
rape	**la violación** *(lah vee-oh-lah-see-'ohn)*
rapist	**el violador/la violadora** *(ehl vee-oh-lah-'dohr/lah vee-oh-lah-'doh-rah)*
rat	**la rata** *(lah 'rah-tah)*
rate (cost)	**la tarifa** *(lah tah-'ree-fah)*
rate (ratio)	**la tasa** *(lah 'tah-sah)*
rating	**la clasificación** *(lah klah-see-fee-kah-see-'ohn)*
ratio	**la proporción** *(lah proh-pohr-see-'ohn)*
razor	**la navaja** *(lah nah-'vah-hah)*
reaction	**la reacción** *(lah reh-ahk-see-'ohn)*
ready	**listo/lista** *('lees-toh/'lees-tah)*
real estate	**los bienes raíces** *(lohs bee-'eh-nehs rah-'ee-sehs)*
reason	**la razón** *(lah rah-'sohn)*
rebate	**la rebaja** *(lah reh-'bah-hah)*
recall	**el retiro** *(ehl reh-'tee-roh)*
receipt	**el recibo** *(ehl reh-'see-boh)*
receiver	**el receptor** *(ehl reh-sehp-'tohr)*
reception	**la recepción** *(lah reh-sehp-see-'ohn)*
reception desk	**la recepción** *(lah reh-sehp-see-'ohn)*
receptionist	**el/la receptionista** *(ehl/lah reh-sehp-see-oh-'nees-tah)*
recommendation	**la recomendación** *(lah reh-koh-mehn-dah-see-'ohn)*
records	**los archivos** *(lohs ahr-'chee-vohs)*
recorded	**grabado/grabada** *(grah-'bah-doh/grah-'bah-dah)*
recorder	**la grabadora** *(lah grah-bah-'doh-rah)*
recording	**el registro** *(ehl reh-'hees-troh)*
red	**rojo/roja** *('roh-hoh/'roh-hah)*
reduction	**la dismunición** *(lah dees-mee-noo-see-'ohn)*
references	**las referencias** *(lahs reh-feh-'rehn-see-ahs)*
referral services	**los servicios de referencia** *(lohs sehr-'vee-see-ohs deh reh-feh-'rehn-see-ah)*
refinance	**el refinanciamiento** *(ehl reh-fee-nahn-see-ah-mee-'ehn-toh)*
refugee	**el refugiado/la refugiada** *(ehl reh-foo-hee-'ah-doh/lah reh-foo-hee-'ah-dah)*

refund	**el reembolso** *(ehl reh-ehm-'bohl-soh)*
region	**la región** *(lah reh-hee-'ohn)*
registration	**el registro** *(ehl reh-'hees-troh)*
regulation	**la regulación** *(lah reh-goo-lah-see-'ohn)*
regulations	**los reglamentos** *(lohs reh-glah-'mehn-tohs)*
reimbursement	**el reembolso** *(ehl reh-ehm-'bohl-soh)*
rejected	**rechazado/rechazada** *(reh-chah-'sah-doh/reh-chah-'sah-dah)*
relationship	**la relación** *(lah reh-lah-see-'ohn)*
relatives	**los parientes** *(lohs pah-ree-'ehn-tehs)*
release	**la liberación** *(lah lee-beh-rah-see-'ohn)*
religion	**la religión** *(lah reh-lee-hee-'ohn)*
religious	**religioso/religiosa** *(reh-lee-hee-'oh-soh/reh-lee-hee-'oh-sah)*
remote control	**el control remoto** *(ehl kohn-'trohl reh-'moh-toh)*
renewable	**renovable** *(reh-noh-'vah-bleh)*
renewal	**la renovación** *(lah reh-noh-vah-see-'ohn)*
rent	**el alquiler** *(ehl ahl-kee-'lehr)*
rental car	**el carro de alquiler** *(ehl 'kahr-roh deh ahl-kee-'lehr)*
repair	**la reparación** *(lah reh-pah-rah-see-'ohn)*
replacement	**el reemplazo** *(ehl reh-ehm-'plah-soh)*
report	**el reporte** *(ehl reh-'pohr-teh)*
reporter	**el reportero/la reportera** *(ehl reh-pohr-'teh-roh/lah reh-pohr-'teh-rah)*
repossessed	**recobrado/recobrada** *(reh-koh-'brah-doh/reh-'koh-'brah-dah)*
representation	**la representación** *(lah reh-preh-sehn-tah-see-'ohn)*
representative	**el/la representante** *(ehl/lah reh-preh-sehn-'tahn-teh)*
request	**la petición** *(lah peh-tee-see-'ohn)*
requirement	**el requisito** *(ehl reh-kee-'see-toh)*
research	**la investigación** *(lah een-vehs-tee-gah-see-'ohn)*
resentful	**resentido/resentida** *(reh-sehn-'tee-doh/reh-sehn-'tee-dah)*
residence	**el domicilio** *(ehl doh-mee-'see-lee-oh)*
residence card	**la tarjeta de residencia** *(lah tahr-'heh-tah deh reh-see-'dehn-see-ah)*
resident	**el/la residente** *(ehl/lah reh-see-'dehn-teh)*
resolved	**resuelto/resuelta** *(reh-soo-'ehl-toh/reh-soo-'ehl-tah)*
resources	**los recursos** *(lohs reh-'koor-sohs)*
respirator	**el respirador** *(ehl rehs-pee-rah-'dohr)*
response	**la respuesta** *(lah rehs-'pwehs-tah)*
responsibility	**la responsabilidad** *(lah rehs-pohn-sah-bee-lee-'dahd)*
rest home	**el sanatorio** *(ehl sah-nah-'toh-ree-oh)*
restaurant	**el restaurante** *(ehl rehs-tah-oo-'rahn-teh)*
restless	**inquieto/inquieta** *(een-kee-'eh-toh/een-kee-'eh-tah)*
restraining order	**la orden de protección** *(lah 'ohr-dehn deh proh-tehk-see-'ohn)*

restriction	**la restricción** (*lah rehs-treek-see-'ohn*)
restroom	**el baño** (*ehl 'bahn-yoh*)
result	**el resultado** (*ehl reh-sool-'tah-doh*)
retail price	**el precio al por menor** (*ehl 'preh-see-oh ahl pohr meh-'nohr*)
retirement plan	**el plan de jubilación** (*ehl plahn deh hoo-bee-lah-see-'ohn*)
return	**la devolución** (*lah deh-voh-loo-see-'ohn*)
revenge	**la venganza** (*lah vehn-'gahn-sah*)
revolver	**el revólver** (*ehl reh-'vohl-vehr*)
reward	**la recompensa** (*lah reh-kohm-'pehn-sah*)
rib	**la costilla** (*lah kohs-'tee-yah*)
rich	**rico/rica** (*'ree-koh/'ree-kah*)
rider	**la cláusula adicional** (*lah 'klah-oo-soo-lah ah-dee-see-oh-'nahl*)
rifle	**el rifle** (*ehl 'ree-fleh*)
right	**la derecha** (*lah deh-'reh-chah*)
rights	**los derechos** (*lohs deh-'reh-chohs*)
ring	**el anillo** (*ehl ah-'nee-yoh*)
riot	**el tumulto** (*ehl too-'mool-toh*)
risk	**el riesgo** (*ehl ree-'ehs-goh*)
road	**el camino** (*ehl kah-'mee-noh*)
robbery	**el robo** (*ehl 'roh-boh*)
rock	**la roca** (*lah 'roh-kah*)
roof	**el tejado** (*ehl teh-'hah-doh*)
room	**el cuarto** (*ehl 'kwahr-toh*)
roommate	**el compañero/la compañera de cuarto** (*ehl kohm-pahn-'yeh-roh/lah kohm-pahn'yeh-rah deh 'kwahr-toh*)
rope	**la soga** (*lah 'soh-gah*)
rough	**tosco/tosca** (*'tohs-koh/'tohs-kah*)
rounds	**las visitas de rutina** (*lahs vee-'see-tahs deh roo-'tee-nah*)
row	**la fila** (*lah 'fee-lah*)
rubber bands	**las ligas de goma** (*lahs 'lee-gahs deh 'goh-mah*)
rude	**grosero/grosera** (*groh-'seh-roh/groh-'seh-rah*)
rule	**la regla** (*lah 'reh-glah*)
rules	**los reglamentos** (*lohs reh-glah-'mehn-tohs*)
ruling	**la resolución** (*lah reh-soh-loo-see-'ohn*)
runaway child	**el niño fugitivo** (*ehl 'neen-yoh foo-hee-'tee-voh*)

S

sad	**triste** (*'trees-teh*)
safe	**seguro/segura** (*seh-'goo-roh/seh-'goo-rah*)
safe (box)	**la caja fuerte** (*lah 'kah-hah foo-'ehr-teh*)
safety	**la seguridad** (*lah seh-goo-ree-'dahd*)
safety glasses	**los lentes de protección** (*lohs 'lehn-tehs deh proh-tehk-see-'ohn*)

safety line	**la cuerda de seguridad** *(lah 'kwehr-dah deh seh-goo-ree-'dahd)*
salary	**el salario** *(ehl sah-'lah-ree-oh)*
sale	**la venta** *(lah 'vehn-tah)*
salesperson	**el vendedor/la vendedora** *(ehl vehn-deh-'dohr/lah vehn-deh-'doh-rah)*
sandals	**las sandalias** *(lahs sahn-'dah-lee-ahs)*
sanitary	**sanitario/sanitaria** *(sah-nee-'tah-ree-oh/sah-nee-'tah-ree-ah)*
Saturday	**sábado** *('sah-bah-doh)*
savings	**los ahorros** *(lohs ah-'ohr-rohs)*
savings account	**la cuenta de ahorros** *(lah 'kwehn-tah deh ah-'ohr-rohs)*
scanner	**el escáner** *(ehl ehs-'kah-nehr)*
scar	**la cicatriz** *(lah see-kah-'trees)*
scared	**asustado/asustada** *(ah-soos-'tah-doh/ah-soos-'tah-dah)*
schedule	**el horario** *(ehl oh-'rah-ree-oh)*
scholarship	**la beca** *(lah 'beh-kah)*
school	**la escuela** *(lah ehs-'kweh-lah)*
scissors	**las tijeras** *(lahs tee-'heh-rahs)*
scratch	**el rasguño** *(ehl rahs-'goon-yoh)*
screen	**la pantalla** *(lah pahn-'tah-yah)*
screwdriver	**el destornillador** *(ehl dehs-tohr-nee-yah-'dohr)*
seal	**el sello** *(ehl 'seh-yoh)*
sealed	**sellado/sellada** *(seh-'yah-doh/seh-'yah-dah)*
search	**el registro** *(ehl reh-'hees-troh)*
search warrant	**la orden de registro** *(lah 'ohr-dehn deh reh-'hees-troh)*
searched	**registrado/registrada** *(reh-hees-'trah-doh/reh-hees-'trah-dah)*
seat	**el asiento** *(ehl ah-see-'ehn-toh)*
seat belt	**el cinturón de seguridad** *(ehl seen-too-'rohn deh seh-goo-ree-'dahd)*
second	**segundo/segunda** *(seh-'goon-doh/seh-'goon-dah)*
second (time)	**el segundo** *(ehl seh-'goon-doh)*
secretary	**el secretario/la secretaria** *(ehl seh-kreh-'tah-ree-oh/lah seh-kreh-'tah-ree-ah)*
secure	**seguro/segura** *(seh-'goo-roh/seh-'goo-rah)*
securities	**los valores** *(lohs vah-'loh-rehs)*
security	**la seguridad** *(lah seh-goo-ree-'dahd)*
security area	**la zona de seguridad** *(lah 'soh-nah deh seh-goo-ree-'dahd)*
security deposit	**el depósito de garantía** *(ehl deh-'poh-see-toh deh gah-rahn-'tee-ah)*
security system	**el sistema de seguridad** *(ehl sees-'teh-mah deh seh-goo-ree-'dahd)*
sedative	**el sedante** *(ehl seh-'dahn-teh)*
seizure	**el ataque** *(ehl ah-'tah-keh)*
semiautomatic	**semiautomático/semiautomática** *(seh-mee-aw-toh-'mah-tee-koh/seh-mee-aw-toh-'mah-tee-kah)*

sensitive	**sensible** *(sehn-'see-bleh)*
sentence	**la sentencia** *(lah sehn-'tehn-see-ah)*
September	**septiembre** *(sehp-tee-'ehm-breh)*
serious	**serio/seria** *('seh-ree-oh/'seh-ree-ah)*
served	**citado/citada** *(see-'tah-doh/see-'tah-dah)*
service	**el servicio** *(ehl sehr-'vee-see-oh)*
session	**la sesión** *(lah seh-see-'ohn)*
settlement	**el convenio** *(ehl kohn-'veh-nee-oh)*
seventh	**séptimo/séptima** *('sehp-tee-moh/'sehp-tee-mah)*
sewage	**las aguas cloacales** *(lahs 'ah-gwahs kloh-ah-'kah-lehs)*
sex	**el sexo** *(ehl sehk-soh)*
sex crimes	**los delitos sexuales** *(lohs deh-'lee-tohs sehk-soo-'ah-lehs)*
sexual orientation	**la orientación sexual** *(lah oh-ree-ehn-tah-see-'ohn sehk-soo-'ahl)*
shared	**compartido/compartida** *(kohm-pahr-'tee-doh/kohm-pahr-'tee-dah)*
she	**ella** *('eh-yah)*
sheet	**la hoja** *(lah 'oh-hah)*
shipment	**el envío** *(ehl ehn-'vee-oh)*
shipper	**el fletador/la fletadora** *(ehl fleh-tah-'dohr/lah fleh-tah-'doh-rah)*
shipping	**el envío** *(ehl ehn-'vee-oh)*
shirt	**la camisa** *(lah kah-'mee-sah)*
shock	**la postración nerviosa** *(lah pohs-trah-see-'ohn nehr-vee-'oh-sah)*
shoes	**las zapatos** *(lohs sah-'pah-tohs)*
shooting	**los disparos** *(lohs dees-'pah-rohs)*
shopping	**las compras** *(lahs 'kohm-prahs)*
shopping center	**el centro comercial** *(ehl 'sehn-troh koh-mehr-see-'ahl)*
short (in height)	**bajo/baja** *('bah-hoh/'bah-hah)*
short (in length)	**corto/corta** *('kohr-toh/'kohr-tah)*
shorts	**los calzoncillos** *(lohs kahl-sohn-'see-yohs)*
short-term	**a corto plazo** *(ah 'kohr-toh 'plah-soh)*
shotgun	**la escopeta** *(lah ehs-koh-'peh-tah)*
shoulder	**el hombro** *(ehl 'ohm-broh)*
shovel	**la pala** *(lah 'pah-lah)*
show	**el espectáculo** *(ehl ehs-pehk-'tah-koo-loh)*
shredder	**la trituradora** *(lah tree-too-rah-'doh-rah)*
shy	**tímido/tímida** *('tee-mee-doh/'tee-mee-dah)*
sibling	**el hermano/la hermana** *(ehl ehr-'mah-noh/lah ehr-'mah-nah)*
side	**el lado** *(ehl 'lah-doh)*
sidewalk	**la acera** *(lah ah-'seh-rah)*
signal	**la señal** *(lah sehn-'yahl)*
signature	**la firma** *(lah 'feer-mah)*
signed	**firmado/firmada** *(feer-'mah-doh/feer-'mah-dah)*

simple	**simple** *('seem-pleh)*
since	**desde** *('dehs-deh)*
single	**soltero/soltera** *(sohl-'teh-roh/sohl-'teh-rah)*
sister	**la hermana** *(lah ehr-'mah-nah)*
sister-in-law	**la cuñada** *(lah koon-'yah-dah)*
sixth	**sexto/sexta** *('sehks-toh/'sehks-tah)*
size	**el tamaño** *(ehl tah-'mahn-yoh)*
skin	**la piel** *(lah pee-'ehl)*
skirt	**la falda** *(lah 'fahl-dah)*
skyscraper	**el rascacielos** *(ehl rahs-kah-see-'eh-lohs)*
slip and fall	**el resbalón y la caída** *(ehl rehs-bah-'lohn ee lah kah-'ee-dah)*
slippery	**resbaladizo/resbaladiza** *(rehs-bah-lah-'dee-soh/rehs-bah-lah-'dee-sah)*
sloppy	**desaliñado/desaliñada** *(deh-sah-leen-'yah-doh/deh-sah-leen-'yah-dah)*
slow	**lento/lenta** *('lehn-toh/'lehn-tah)*
slowly	**lentamente** *(lehn-tah-'mehn-teh)*
small	**chico/chica** *('chee-koh/'chee-kah)*
small business	**la pequeña empresa** *(lah peh-'kehn-yah ehm-'preh-sah)*
small claims	**los reclamos menores** *(lohs reh-'klah-mohs meh-'noh-rehs)*
smell	**el olor** *(ehl oh-'lohr)*
smuggling	**el contrabando** *(ehl kohn-trah-'bahn-doh)*
snow	**la nieve** *(lah nee-'eh-veh)*
social security	**el seguro social** *(ehl seh-'goo-roh soh-see-'ahl)*
social services	**los servicios sociales** *(lohs sehr-'vee-see-ohs soh-see'ah-lehs)*
socks	**los calcetines** *(lohs kahl-seh-'tee-nehs)*
sofa	**el sofá** *(ehl soh-'fah)*
sold	**vendido/vendida** *(vehn-'dee-doh/vehn-'dee-dah)*
sole proprietorship	**la empresa de propiedad individual** *(lah ehm-'preh-sah deh proh-pee-eh-'dahd een-dee-vee-doo-'ahl)*
solicitation	**la incitación** *(lah enn-see-tah-see'ohn)*
some	**unos/unas** *('oo-nohs/'oo-nahs)*
someone	**alguien** *('ahl-ghee-ehn)*
something	**algo** *('ahl-goh)*
sometimes	**a veces** *(ah 'veh-sehs)*
somewhere	**en algún sitio** *(ehn ahl-'goon 'see-tee-oh)*
son	**el hijo** *(ehl 'ee-hoh)*
son-in-law	**el yerno** *(ehl 'yehr-noh)*
soon	**pronto** *('prohn-toh)*
sore	**dolorido/dolorida** *(doh-loh-'ree-doh/doh-loh-'ree-dah)*
sound	**el sonido** *(ehl soh-'nee-doh)*
south	**el sur** *(ehl soor)*

South American	**el sudamericano/la sudamericana** *(ehl soo-dah-meh-ree-'kah-noh/lah soo-dah-meh-ree-'kah-nah)*
Spanish	**el español/la española** *(ehl ehs-pahn-'yohl/lah ehs-pahn-'yoh-lah)*
speaker (device)	**el altavoz** *(ehl ahl-tah-'vohs)*
specialist	**el/la especialista** *(ehl/lah ehs-peh-see-ah-'lees-tah)*
spinal cord	**la médula espinal** *(lah 'meh-doo-lah ehs-pee-'nahl)*
sponsor	**el patrocinador/la patrocinadora** *(ehl pah-troh-see-nah-'dohr/lah pah-troh-see-nah-'doh-rah)*
sponsorship	**el patrocinio** *(ehl pah-troh-'see-nee-oh)*
spoon	**la cuchara** *(lah koo-'chah-rah)*
sport	**el deporte** *(ehl deh-'pohr-teh)*
sportcoat	**el saco** *(ehl 'sah-koh)*
spousal	**conyugal** *(kohn-yoo-'gahl)*
spouse	**el cónyugue** *(ehl 'kohn-yoo-gheh)*
sprained	**dislocado/dislocada** *(dees-loh-'kah-doh/dees-loh-'kah-dah)*
spray	**el aerosol** *(ehl ah-eh-roh-'sohl)*
spring	**la primavera** *(lah pree-mah-'veh-rah)*
stabbing	**la puñalada** *(lah poon-yah-'lah-dah)*
stage	**la etapa** *(lah eh-'tah-pah)*
stain	**la mancha** *(lah 'mahn-chah)*
stairs	**la escalera** *(lah ehs-kah-'leh-rah)*
stamp	**el sello** *(ehl 'seh-yoh)*
stand	**el estrado de testigos** *(ehl ehs-'trah-doh deh tehs-'tee-gohs)*
standards	**las normas** *(lahs 'nohr-mahs)*
stapler	**la engrapadora** *(lah ehn-grah-pah-'doh-rah)*
state	**el estado** *(ehl ehs-'tah-doh)*
state court	**el tribunal estatal** *(ehl tree-boo-'nahl ehs-tah-'tahl)*
state income tax	**el impuesto de ingresos estatal** *(ehl eem-'pwehs-toh deh een-'greh-sohs ehs-tah-'tahl)*
state law	**la ley estatal** *(lah 'leh-ee ehs-tah-'tahl)*
statement	**la declaración** *(lah deh-klah-rah-see-'ohn)*
statue	**la estatua** *(lah ehs-'tah-too-ah)*
steering wheel	**el volante** *(ehl voh-'lahn-teh)*
stenographer	**el taquígrafo/la taquígrafa** *(ehl tah-'kee-grah-foh/lah tah-'kee-grah-fah)*
step	**el paso** *(ehl 'pah-soh)*
stepdaughter	**la hijastra** *(lah ee-'hahs-trah)*
stepfather	**el padrastro** *(ehl pah-'drahs-troh)*
stepmother	**la madrastra** *(lah mah-'drahs-trah)*
steps (stages)	**los pasos** *(lohs 'pah-sohs)*
steps (stairs)	**los escalones** *(lohs ehs-kah-'loh-nehs)*
stepson	**el hijastro** *(ehl ee-'hahs-troh)*
steroid	**el esteroide** *(ehl ehs-teh-'roh-ee-deh)*

stick	**el palo** *(ehl 'pah-loh)*
stitch	**la puntada** *(lah poon-'tah-dah)*
stockings	**las medias** *(lahs 'meh-dee-ahs)*
stocks	**las acciones** *(lahs ahk-see-'oh-nehs)*
stolen	**robado/robada** *(roh-'bah-doh/roh-'bah-dah)*
stolen property	**la propiedad robada** *(lah proh-pee-eh-'dahd roh-'bah-dah)*
stomach	**el estómago** *(ehl ehs-'toh-mah-goh)*
stool	**el banquillo** *(ehl bahn-'kee-yoh)*
stop sign	**el señal de parada** *(lah sehn-'yahl deh pah-'rah-dah)*
store	**la tienda** *(lah tee-'ehn-dah)*
storeroom	**el depósito** *(ehl deh-'poh-see-toh)*
storm	**la tormenta** *(lah tohr-'mehn-tah)*
straight	**recto/recta** *('rehk-toh/'rehk-tah)*
strange	**raro/rara** *('rah-roh/'rah-rah)*
strategy	**la estrategia** *(lah ehs-trah-'teh-ee-ah)*
street	**la calle** *(lah 'kah-yeh)*
stress	**el estrés** *(ehl ehs-'trehs)*
stroke	**el derrame cerebral** *(ehl dehr-'rah-meh seh-reh-'brahl)*
strong	**fuerte** *(foo-'ehr-teh)*
student	**el/la estudiante** *(ehl/lah ehs-too-dee-'ahn-teh)*
subpoena	**la citación** *(lah see-tah-see-'ohn)*
subway	**el metro** *(ehl 'meh-troh)*
success	**el éxito** *(ehl 'ex-ee-toh)*
suffering	**el sufrimiento** *(eh soo-free-mee-'ehn-toh)*
suicide	**el suicidio** *(ehl soo-ee-'see-dee-oh)*
suit	**el traje** *(ehl 'trah-heh)*
sum	**la suma** *(lah 'soo-mah)*
summary proceedings	**la vía sumaria** *(lah 'vee-ah soo-'mah-ree-ah)*
summer	**el verano** *(ehl veh-'rah-noh)*
sun	**el sol** *(ehl sohl)*
Sunday	**el domingo** *(ehl doh-'meen-goh)*
sunglasses	**los lentes de sol** *(lohs 'lehn-tehs deh sohl)*
superior court	**el tribunal superior** *(ehl tree-boo-'nahl soo-peh-ree-'ohr)*
supermarket	**el supermercado** *(ehl soo-pehr-mehr-'kah-doh)*
supervisor	**el supervisor/la supervisora** *(ehl soo-pehr-vee-'sohr/lah soo-pehr-vee-'soh-rah)*
supplies	**los suministros** *(lohs soo-mee-'nees-trohs)*
support	**el apoyo** *(ehl ah-'poh-yoh)*
supreme court	**el tribunal supremo** *(ehl tree-boo-'nahl soo-'preh-moh)*
surgeon	**el cirujano/la cirujana** *(ehl see-roo-'hah-noh/lah see-roo-'hah-nah)*
surgery	**la cirugía** *(lah see-roo-'hee-ah)*

surprised	**sorprendido/sorprendida** *(sohr-prehn-'dee-doh/sohr-prehn-'dee-dah)*
surveillance	**la vigilancia** *(lah vee-hee-'lahn-see-ah)*
surviving	**sobreviviente** *(soh-breh-vee-vee-'ehn-teh)*
suspect	**el sospechoso/la sospechosa** *(ehl sohs-peh-'choh-soh/lah sohs-peh-'choh-sah)*
suspicious	**suspicaz** *(soos-pee-'kahs)*
sweater	**el suéter** *(ehl soo-'eh-tehr)*
swimming pool	**la piscina** *(lah pee-'see-nah)*
swindler	**el estafador/la estafadora** *(ehl ehs-tah-fah-'dohr/lah ehs-tah-fah-'doh-rah)*
syringe	**la jeringa** *(lah heh-'reen-gah)*
system	**el sistema** *(ehl sees-'teh-mah)*

T

table	**la mesa** *(lah 'meh-sah)*
tablespoon	**la cucharada** *(lah koo-chah-'rah-dah)*
tablet	**la tableta** *(lah tah-'bleh-tah)*
tailor	**el/la sastre** *(ehl/lah 'sahs-treh)*
tall	**alto/alta** *('ahl-toh/'ahl-tah)*
tattoo	**el tatuaje** *(ehl tah-too-'ah-heh)*
tax	**el impuesto** *(ehl eem-'pwehs-toh)*
tax allowance	**el descuento impositivo** *(ehl dehs-koo-'ehn-toh eem-poh-see-'tee-voh)*
tax bracket	**el grupo impositivo** *(ehl 'groo-poh eem-poh-see-'tee-voh)*
tax code	**el código impositivo** *(ehl 'koh-dee-goh eem-poh-see-'tee-voh)*
tax collection	**la recaudación de impuestos** *(lah reh-kah-oo-dah-see-'ohn deh eem-'pwehs-tohs)*
tax evasion	**la evasión fiscal** *(lah eh-vah-see-'ohn fees-'kahl)*
tax exemption	**la exención de impuestos** *(lah ex-ehn-see-'ohn deh eem-'pwehs-tohs)*
tax return (check)	**la devolución de impuestos** *(lah deh-voh-loo-see-'ohn deh eem-'pwehs-tohs)*
tax return (forms)	**la declaración de ingresos** *(lah deh-klah-rah-see-'ohn deh een-'greh-sohs)*
teacher	**el maestro/la maestra** *(ehl mah-'ehs-troh/lah mah-'ehs-trah)*
teaspoon	**la cucharadita** *(lah koo-chah-rah-'dee-tah)*
technician	**el técnico/la técnica** *(ehl 'tehk-nee-koh/lah 'tehk-nee-kah)*
teeth	**los dientes** *(lohs dee-'ehn-tehs)*
telephone	**el teléfono** *(ehl teh-'leh-foh-noh)*
television (medium)	**la televisión** *(lah teh-leh-vee-see-'ohn)*
television (set)	**el televisor** *(ehl teh-leh-vee-'sohr)*
teller	**el cajero/la cajera** *(ehl kah-'heh-roh/lah kah-'heh-rah)*

tenant	**el inquilino/la inquilina** *(ehl een-kee-'lee-noh/lah een-kee-'lee-nah)*
tenth	**décimo/décima** *('deh-see-moh/'deh-see-mah)*
term	**el término** *(ehl 'tehr-mee-noh)*
territory	**el territorio** *(ehl tehr-ree-'toh-ree-oh)*
terrorism	**el terrorismo** *(ehl tehr-roh-'rees-moh)*
testate	**el testador/la testadora** *(ehl tehs-tah-'dohr/lah tehs-tah-'doh-rah)*
testimony	**el testimonio** *(ehl tehs-tee-'moh-nee-oh)*
text	**el texto** *(ehl 'tehks-toh)*
the	**el/la/los/las** *(ehl/lah/lohs/lahs)*
their	**su** *(soo)*
then	**entonces** *(ehn-'tohn-sehs)*
therapist	**el/la terapeuta** *(ehl/lah teh-rah-'peh-oo-tah)*
there	**allí** *(ah-'yee)*
there is/are	**hay** *('ah-ee)*
they	**ellos/ellas** *('eh-yohs/'eh-yahs)*
thief	**el ladrón/la ladrona** *(ehl lah-'drohn/lah lah-'droh-nah)*
thin	**delgado/delgada** *(dehl-'gah-doh/dehl-'gah-dah)*
thing	**la cosa** *(lah 'koh-sah)*
third	**tercero/tercera** *(tehr-'seh-roh/tehr-'seh-rah)*
third party	**la tercera persona** *(lah tehr-'seh-rah pehr-'soh-nah)*
thought	**el pensamiento** *(ehl pehn-sah-mee-'ehn-toh)*
threat	**la amenaza** *(lah ah-meh-'nah-sah)*
throat	**la garganta** *(lah gahr-'gahn-tah)*
Thursday	**el jueves** *(ehl hoo-'eh-vehs)*
ticket	**la boleta** *(lah boh-'leh-tah)*
tie	**la corbata** *(lah kohr-'bah-tah)*
time	**el tiempo** *(ehl tee-'ehm-poh)*
time (hour)	**la hora** *(lah 'oh-rah)*
times	**las veces** *(lahs 'veh-sehs)*
tire	**el neumático** *(ehl neh-oo-'mah-tee-koh)*
title	**el título** *(ehl 'tee-too-loh)*
title insurance	**el seguro contra defectos en títulos de propiedad** *(ehl seh-'goo-roh 'kohn-trah deh-'fehk-tohs ehn 'tee-too-lohs deh proh-pee-eh-'dahd)*
to	**a** *(ah)*
to be	**estar/ser** *(ehs-'tahr/sehr)*
today	**hoy** *('oh-ee)*
toe	**el dedo del pie** *(ehl 'deh-doh dehl pee-'eh)*
together	**juntos** *('hoon-tohs)*
toll booth	**la caseta de peaje** *(lah kah-'seh-tah deh peh-'ah-heh)*
tomorrow	**mañana** *(mahn-'yah-nah)*

too much	**demasiado** *(deh-mah-see-'ah-doh)*
tool	**la herramienta** *(lah ehr-rah-mee-'ehn-tah)*
total	**el total** *(ehl toh-'tahl)*
tourist	**el/la turista** *(ehl/lah too-'rees-tah)*
tow truck	**la grúa** *(lah 'groo-ah)*
toward	**hacia** *('ah-see-ah)*
towing company	**la compañía de remolque** *(lah kohm-pah-'nee-ah deh reh-'mohl-keh)*
town	**el pueblo** *(ehl poo-'eh-bloh)*
toxic material	**la sustancia tóxica** *(lah soos-'tahn-see-ah 'tohk-see-kah)*
track	**el rastro** *(ehl 'rahs-troh)*
trademark	**la marca registrada** *(lah 'mahr-kah reh-hees-'trah-dah)*
traditional	**tradicional** *(trah-dee-see-oh-'nahl)*
traffic	**el tráfico** *(ehl 'trah-fee-koh)*
traffic court	**el juzgado de tráfico** *(ehl hoos-'gah-doh deh 'trah-fee-koh)*
traffic school	**la escuela de tráfico** *(lah ehs-koo-'eh-lah deh 'trah-fee-koh)*
traffic signal	**el semáforo** *(ehl seh-'mah-foh-roh)*
tragedy	**la tragedia** *(lah trah-'heh-dee-ah)*
tragic	**trágico/trágica** *('trah-ee-koh/'trah-ee-kah)*
train	**el tren** *(ehl trehn)*
training	**el entrenamiento** *(ehl ehn-treh-nah-mee-'ehn-toh)*
tranquilizer	**el tranquilizante** *(ehl trahn-kee-lee-'sahn-teh)*
transaction	**la transacción** *(lah trahn-sahk-see-'ohn)*
transfer	**la transferencia** *(lah trahns-feh-'rehn-see-ah)*
transgendered	**transexual** *(trahn-sehk-soo-'ahl)*
translator	**el traductor/la traductora** *(ehl trah-dook-'tohr/lah trah-dook-'toh-rah)*
transportation	**el transporte** *(ehl trahns-'pohr-teh)*
trap	**la trampa** *(lah 'trahm-pah)*
trash	**la basura** *(lah bah-'soo-rah)*
trash container	**el basurero** *(ehl bah-soo-'reh-roh)*
trauma	**el trauma** *(ehl 'trah-oo-mah)*
treatment	**el tratamiento** *(ehl trah-tah-mee-'ehn-toh)*
trespassing	**la intrusión** *(lah een-troo-see-'ohn)*
trial	**el juicio** *(ehl hoo-'ee-see-oh)*
trouble	**el problema** *(ehl proh-'bleh-mah)*
truck	**el camión** *(ehl kah-mee-'ohn)*
truck driver	**el camionero/la camionera** *(ehl kah-mee-oh-'neh-roh/lah kah-mee-oh-'neh-rah)*
trust	**el fideicomiso** *(ehl fee-deh-ee-koh-'mee-soh)*
trust funds	**los fondos fiduciarios** *(lohs 'fohn-dohs fee-doo-see-'ah-ree-ohs)*

trustee (finance)	**el fideicomisario/la fideicomisaria** *(ehl fee-deh-ee-koh-mee-'sah-ree-oh/lah fee-deh-ee-koh-mee-'sah-ree-ah)*
trustee (prison)	**el preso de confianza** *(ehl 'preh-soh deh kohn-fee-'ahn-sah)*
T-shirt	**la camiseta** *(lah kah-mee-'seh-tah)*
Tuesday	**el martes** *(ehl 'mahr-tehs)*
tunnel	**el túnel** *(ehl 'too-nehl)*
tutorage	**la tutoría** *(lah too-toh-'ree-ah)*
twin	**el gemelo/la gemela** *(ehl heh-'meh-loh/lah heh-'meh-lah)*
type	**el tipo** *(ehl 'tee-poh)*
typical	**típico/típica** *('tee-pee-koh/'tee-pee-kah)*

U

U.S. citizen	**el ciudadano/la ciudadana estadounidense** *(ehl see-oo-dah-'dah-noh/lah see-oo-dah-'dah-nah ehs-tah-doh-oo-nee-'dehn-seh)*
ugly	**feo/fea** *('feh-oh/'feh-ah)*
uncle	**el tío** *(ehl 'tee-oh)*
uncomfortable	**incómodo/incómoda** *(enn-'koh-moh-doh/een-'koh-moh-dah)*
unconscious	**inconsciente** *(enn-kohn-see-'ehn-teh)*
under	**debajo** *(deh-'bah-hoh)*
understanding	**el entendimiento** *(ehl ehn-tehn-dee-mee-'ehn-toh)*
underwear	**la ropa interior** *(lah 'roh-pah een-teh-ree-'ohr)*
unemployment	**el desempleo** *(ehl deh-sehm-'pleh-oh)*
unfair	**injusto/injusta** *(een-'hoos-toh/eehn-'hoos-tah)*
unhappy	**descontento/descontenta** *(dehs-kohn-'tehn-toh/dehs-kohn-'tehn-tah)*
uniform	**el uniforme** *(ehl oo-nee-'fohr-meh)*
union	**el sindicato** *(ehl seen-dee-'kah-toh)*
unit	**la unidad** *(lah oo-nee-'dahd)*
united	**unido/unida** *(oo-'nee-doh/oo-'nee-dah)*
university	**la universidad** *(lah oo-nee-vehr-see-'dahd)*
unsafe	**peligroso/peligrosa** *(peh-lee-'groh-soh/peh-lee-'groh-sah)*
unsigned	**sin firma** *(seen 'feer-mah)*
unsure	**inseguro/insegura** *(een-seh'goo-roh/een-seh'goo-rah)*
until	**hasta** *('ahs-tah)*
up	**arriba** *(ahr-'ree-bah)*
upbringing	**la crianza** *(lah kree-'ahn-sah)*
USA	**Estados Unidos** *(ehs-'tah-dohs oo-'nee-dohs)*
use	**el uso** *(ehl 'oo-soh)*
utilities	**los servicios públicos** *(lohs sehr-'vee-see-ohs 'poo-blee-kohs)*
utilities department	**el departamento de servicios públicos** *(ehl deh-pahr-tah-'mehn-toh deh sehr-'vee-see-ohs 'poo-blee-kohs)*

V

VA benefits	**los beneficios de veterano** *(lohs beh-neh-'fee-see-ohs deh veh-teh-'rah-noh)*
vagrancy	**la vagancia** *(lah vah-'gahn-see-ah)*
valid	**válido/válida** *('vah-lee-doh/'vah-lee-dah)*
valuation	**la tasación** *(lah tah-sah-see-'ohn)*
value	**el valor** *(ehl vah-'lohr)*
vandalism	**el vandalismo** *(ehl vahn-dah-'lees-moh)*
variable	**variable** *(vah-ree-'ah-bleh)*
variance	**la variación** *(lah vah-ree-ah-see-'ohn)*
vehicle	**el vehículo** *(ehl veh-'ee-koo-loh)*
vending machine	**la máquina vendedora** *(lah 'mah-kee-nah vehn-deh-'doh-rah)*
ventilation	**la ventilación** *(lah vehn-tee-lah-see'ohn)*
verbal	**verbal** *(vehr-'bahl)*
verdict	**el veredicto** *(ehl veh-reh-'deek-toh)*
verification	**la verificación** *(lah veh-ree-fee-kah-see-'ohn)*
vest	**el chaleco** *(ehl chah-'leh-koh)*
veteran	**el veterano** *(ehl veh-teh-'rah-noh)*
vial	**el frasco** *(ehl 'frahs-koh)*
vice-president	**el vicepresidente/la vicepresidenta** *(ehl vee-seh-preh-see-'dehn-teh/lah vee-seh-preh-see-'dehn-tah)*
vicious	**malsano/malsana** *(mahl-'sah-noh/mahl-'sah-nah)*
victim	**la víctima** *(lah 'veek-tee-mah)*
videocamera	**la videocámara** *(lah vee-deh-oh-'kah-mah-rah)*
view	**la vista** *(lah 'vees-tah)*
viewer	**el espectador/la espectadora** *(ehl ehs-pehk-tah-'dohr/lah ehs-pehk-tah-'doh-rah)*
viewing window	**la ventana de observación** *(lah vehn-'tah-nah deh ohb-sehr-vah-see-'ohn)*
VIN number	**el número de identificación del vehículo** *(ehl 'noo-meh-roh deh ee-dehn-tee-fee-kah-see-'ohn dehl veh-'ee-koo-loh)*
violence	**la violencia** *(lah vee-oh-'lehn-see-ah)*
violent	**violento/violenta** *(vee-oh-'lehn-toh/vee-oh-'lehn-tah)*
visa	**la visa** *(lah 'vee-sah)*
vision	**la vista** *(lah 'vees-tah)*
visitation	**la visita** *(lah vee-'see-tah)*
visitation rights	**el derecho de visita** *(ehl deh-'reh-choh deh vee-'see-tah)*
visiting room	**el salón de visitantes** *(ehl sah-'lohn deh vee-see-'tahn-tehs)*
visitor	**el/la visitante** *(ehl/lah vee-see-'tahn-teh)*
voice mail	**la contestadora telefónica** *(lah kohn-tehs-tah-'doh-rah teh-leh-'foh-nee-kah)*
voided	**cancelado/cancelada** *(kahn-seh-'lah-doh/kahn-seh-'lah-dah)*

W

W-2 forms	**los formularios W-2** *(lohs fohr-moo-'lah-ree-ohs 'doh-bleh veh dohs)*
waiter	**el mesero/la mesera** *(ehl meh-'seh-roh/lah meh-'seh-rah)*
waiting period	**el período de espera** *(ehl peh-'ree-oh-doh deh ehs-'peh-rah)*
waiting room	**la sala de espera** *(lah 'sah-lah deh ehs-'peh-rah)*
waiver	**la renuncia** *(lah reh-'noon-see-ah)*
walkway	**el pasillo** *(ehl pah-'see-yoh)*
wall	**la pared** *(lah pah-'rehd)*
wallet	**la billetera** *(lah bee-yeh-'teh-rah)*
warden	**el carcelero/la carcelera** *(ehl kahr-seh-'leh-roh/lah kahr-seh-'leh-rah)*
warning	**la advertencia** *(lah ahd-vehr-'tehn-see-ah)*
warrant	**la orden** *(lah 'ohr-dehn)*
water	**el agua** *(ehl 'ah-gwah)*
water fountain	**el surtidor de agua** *(ehl soor-tee-'dohr deh 'ah-gwah)*
we	**nosotros/nosotras** *(noh-'soh-trohs/noh-'soh-trahs)*
weak	**débil** *('deh-beel)*
wealth	**el patrimonio** *(ehl pah-tree-'moh-nee-oh)*
weapon	**el arma** *(ehl 'ahr-mah)*
weather	**el clima** *(ehl 'klee-mah)*
website	**la página de web** *(lah 'pah-hee-nah deh oo-'ehb)*
wedding	**la boda** *(lah 'boh-dah)*
Wednesday	**el miércoles** *(ehl mee-'ehr-koh-lehs)*
week	**la semana** *(lah seh-'mah-nah)*
weight	**el peso** *(ehl 'peh-soh)*
well-being	**el bienestar** *(ehl bee-eh-nehs-'tahr)*
well-mannered	**de buenos modales** *(deh boo-'eh-nohs moh-'dah-lehs)*
west	**el oeste** *(ehl oh-'ehs-teh)*
while	**mientras** *(mee-'ehn-trahs)*
white	**blanco/blanca** *('blahn-koh/'blahn-kah)*
White House	**la Casa Blanca** *(lah 'kah-sah 'blahn-kah)*
wholesale	**el precio al por mayor** *(ehl 'preh-see-oh ahl pohr mah-'yohr)*
widowed	**viudo/viuda** *(vee-'oo-doh/vee-'oo-dah)*
wife	**la esposa** *(lah ehs-'poh-sah)*
wig	**la peluca** *(lah peh-'loo-kah)*
will	**el testamento** *(ehl tehs-tah-'mehn-toh)*
wind	**el viento** *(ehl vee-'ehn-toh)*
window	**la ventana** *(lah vehn-'tah-nah)*
wine	**el vino** *(ehl 'vee-noh)*
winter	**el invierno** *(ehl een-vee-'ehr-noh)*
wire	**el alambre** *(ehl ah-'lahm-breh)*

wire transfer	**la transferencia electrónica** *(lah trahns-feh-'rehn-see-ah eh-lehk-'troh-nee-kah)*
with	**con** *(kohn)*
witness	**el/la testigo** *(ehl/lah tehs-'tee-goh)*
woman	**la mujer** *(lah moo-'hehr)*
work	**el trabajo** *(ehl trah-'bah-hoh)*
worker	**el obrero** *(ehl oh-'breh-roh)*
workers' compensation	**la compensación laboral** *(lah kohm-pehn-sah-see-'ohn lah-boh-'rahl)*
worksite	**el lugar de trabajo** *(ehl loo-'gahr deh trah-'bah-hoh)*
worried	**preocupado/preocupada** *(preh-oh-koo-'pah-doh/preh-oh-koo-'pah-dah)*
worse	**peor** *(peh-'ohr)*
wristwatch	**el reloj de pulsera** *(ehl reh-'loh deh pool-'seh-rah)*
wrist	**la muñeca** *(lah moon-'yeh-kah)*
written	**escrito/escrita** *(ehs-'kree-toh/ehs-'kree-tah)*
wrong	**equivocado/equivocada** *(eh-kee-voh-'kah-doh/eh-kee-voh-'kah-dah)*
wrongful death	**la muerte por negligencia** *(lah moo-'ehr-teh pohr neh-glee-'hehn-see-ah)*

X

X-rays	**los rayos equis** *(lohs 'rah-yohs 'eh-kees)*

Y

year	**el año** *(ehl 'ahn-yoh)*
yellow	**amarillo** *(ah-mah-'ree-yoh)*
yesterday	**ayer** *(ah-'yehr)*
yield	**el rédito** *(ehl 'reh-dee-toh)*
you (sing.)	**usted** *(oos-'tehd)*
you (pl.)	**ustedes** *(oos-'teh-dehs)*
young	**joven** *('hoh-vehn)*
young person	**el/la joven** *(ehl/lah 'hoh-vehn)*
younger	**menor** *(meh-'nohr)*
your	**su** *(soo)*
youth	**la juventud** *(lah hoo-vehn-'tood)*

Z

zip code	**la zona postal** *(lah 'soh-nah pohs-'tahl)*

VERB INFINITIVES

A

to abuse	**abusar** *(ah-boo-'sahr)*
to accept	**aceptar** *(ah-sehp-'tahr)*
to accrue	**acumular** *(ah-koo-moo-'lahr)*
to accuse	**acusar** *(ah-koo-'sahr)*
to acquire	**adquirir** *(ahd-kee-'reer)*
to add	**añadir** *(ahn-yah-'deer)*
to adjust	**ajustar** *(ah-hoos-'tahr)*
to admit	**admitir** *(ahd-mee-'teer)*
to admonish	**amonestar** *(ah-moh-nehs-'tahr)*
to advise	**aconsejar** *(ah-kohn-she-'hahr)*
to affirm	**afirmar** *(ah-feer-'mahr)*
to allege	**alegar** *(ah-leh-'gahr)*
to allow	**permitir** *(pehr-mee-'teer)*
to amend	**enmendar** *(ehn-mehn-'dahr)*
to analyze	**analizar** *(ah-nah-see-'sahr)*
to announce	**anunciar** *(ah-noon-see-'ahr)*
to answer	**contestar** *(kohn-tehs-'tahr)*
to antagonize	**antagonizar** *(ahn-tah-goh-nee-'sahr)*
to appeal	**apelar** *(ah-peh-'lahr)*
to approve	**aprobar** *(ah-proh-'bahr)*
to argue	**arguir** *(ahr-goo-'eer)*
to arrange	**arreglar** *(ahr-reh-'glahr)*
to arrest	**arrestar** *(ahr-rehs-'tahr)*
to ask	**preguntar** *(preh-goon-'tahr)*
to ask for	**pedir** *(peh-'deer)*
to attack	**atacar** *(ah-tah-'kahr)*
to attend	**asistir** *(ah-sees-'teer)*
to authorize	**autorizar** *(aw-toh-ree-'sahr)*
to avoid	**evitar** *(eh-vee-'tahr)*

B

to beat	**golpear** *(gohl-peh-'ahr)*
to begin	**empezar** *(ehm-peh-'sahr)*
to believe	**creer** *(kreh-'ehr)*
to belong to	**pertenecer** *(pehr-teh-neh-'sehr)*
to bind	**compeler** *(kohm-peh-'lehr)*
to bind over	**conminar** *(kohn-mee-'nahr)*

to borrow	**pedir prestado** *(peh-'deer prehs-'tah-doh)*
to bother	**molestar** *(moh-lehs-'tahr)*
to break	**romper** *(rohm-'pehr)*
to break in	**forzar** *(fohr-'sahr)*
to bring	**traer** *(trah-'ehr)*
to build	**construir** *(kohns-troo-'eer)*
to buy	**comprar** *(kohm-'prahr)*

C

to calculate	**calcular** *(kahl-koo-'lahr)*
to call	**llamar** *(yah-'mahr)*
to calm down	**calmarse** *(kahl-'mahr-seh)*
to cancel	**cancelar** *(kahn-seh-'lahr)*
to challenge	**recusar** *(reh-koo-'sahr)*
to change	**cambiar** *(kahm-bee-'ahr)*
to charge	**cargar** *(kahr-'gahr)*
to chase	**perseguir** *(pehr-seh-'gheer)*
to check	**revisar** *(reh-vee-'sahr)*
to claim	**reclamar** *(reh-klah-'mahr)*
to clarify	**aclarar** *(ah-klah-'rahr)*
to click	**hacer clic** *(ah-'sehr kleek)*
to close	**cerrar** *(sehr-'rahr)*
to collect	**cobrar** *(koh-'brahr)*
to come	**venir** *(veh-'neer)*
to commit	**cometer** *(koh-meh-'tehr)*
to complain	**quejarse** *(keh-'hahr-seh)*
to comply	**cumplir** *(koom-'pleer)*
to confirm	**confirmar** *(kohn-feer-'mahr)*
to confiscate	**confiscar** *(kohn-fees-'kahr)*
to confront	**confrontar** *(kohn-frohn-'tahr)*
to connect	**conectar** *(koh-nehk-'tahr)*
to continue	**continuar** *(kohn-tee-'nwahr)*
to contribute	**contribuir** *(kohn-tree-boo-'eer)*
to convey	**transmitir** *(trahns-mee-'teer)*
to copy	**copiar** *(koh-pee-'ahr)*
to counsel	**aconsejar** *(ah-kohn-she-'hahr)*
to count	**contar** *(kohn-'tahr)*
to cover	**cubrir** *(koo-'breer)*
to crash	**chocar** *(choh-'kahr)*
to cry	**llorar** *(yoh-'rahr)*
to curse	**maldecir** *(mahl-deh-'seer)*
to cut	**cortar** *(kohr-'tahr)*

D

to deal with	**atender** *(ah-tehn-'dehr)*
to deem	**estimar** *(ehs-tee-'mahr)*
to defend	**defender** *(deh-fehn-'dehr)*
to delete	**eliminar** *(eh-lee-mee-'nahr)*
to deliberate	**deliberar** *(deh-lee-beh-'rahr)*
to deliver	**entregar** *(ehn-treh-'gahr)*
to demand	**exigir** *(ex-ee-'heer)*
to demonstrate	**demostrar** *(deh-mohs-'trahr)*
to deposit	**depositar** *(deh-poh-see-'tahr)*
to describe	**describir** *(dehs-kree-'beer)*
to deserve	**merecer** *(meh-reh-'sehr)*
to destroy	**destruir** *(dehs-troo-'eer)*
to develop	**desarrollar** *(deh-sahr-roh-'yahr)*
to discriminate	**discriminar** *(dees-kree-mee-'nahr)*
to dismiss	**despedir** *(dehs-peh-'deer)*
to dispute	**disputar** *(dees-poo-'tahr)*
to distribute	**distribuir** *(dees-tree-boo-'eer)*
to diversify	**diversificar** *(dee-vehr-see-fee-'kahr)*
to divide	**dividir** *(dee-vee-'deer)*
to divorce	**divorciarse** *(dee-vohr-see-'ahr-seh)*
to do	**hacer** *(ah-'sehr)*
to document	**documentar** *(doh-koo-mehn-'tahr)*
to download	**bajar** *(bah-'hahr)*
to drag	**mover** *(moh-'vehr)*
to drink	**beber** *(beh-'behr)*
to drive	**manejar** *(mah-neh-'hahr)*
to drown	**ahogarse** *(ah-oh-'gahr-seh)*

E

to earn	**ganar** *(gah-'nahr)*
to eat	**comer** *(koh-'mehr)*
to endorse	**endosar** *(ehn-doh-'sahr)*
to enforce	**hacer cumplir** *(ah-sehr koom-'pleer)*
to enjoin	**prohibir** *(proh-ee-'beer)*
to enroll	**matricularse** *(mah-tree-koo-'lahr-seh)*
to enter	**entrar** *(ehn-'trahr)*
to establish	**establecer** *(ehs-tah-bleh-'sehr)*
to evaluate	**evaluar** *(eh-vah-loo-'ahr)*
to evict	**desahuciar** *(deh-sah-oo-see-'ahr)*
to examine	**examinar** *(ex-ah-mee-'nahr)*

to exchange	**cambiar** *(kahm-bee-'ahr)*
to execute	**ejecutar** *(eh-heh-koo-'tahr)*
to exercise	**ejercitarse** *(eh-hehr-see-'tahr-seh)*
to exonerate	**exonerar** *(ex-oh-neh-'rahr)*
to expire	**vencer** *(vehn-'sehr)*
to explain	**explicar** *(ex-plee-'kahr)*
to expunge	**erradicar** *(her-rah-dee-'kahr)*

F

to fight	**luchar** *(loo-'chahr)*
to file	**archivar** *(ahr-chee-'vahr)*
to file for	**reclamar** *(reh-klah-'mahr)*
to finalize	**finalizar** *(fee-nah-lee-'sahr)*
to find	**encontrar** *(ehn-kohn-'trahr)*
to fix	**reparar** *(reh-pah-'rahr)*
to follow	**seguir** *(she-'gheer)*
to forget	**olvidar** *(ohl-vee-'dahr)*
to formulate	**formalizar** *(fohr-mah-lee-'sahr)*
to forward	**reenviar** *(reh-ehn-vee-'ahr)*

G

to gain	**ganar** *(gah-'nahr)*
to get	**conseguir** *(kohn-she-'gheer)*
to get married	**casarse** *(kah-'sahr-seh)*
to get sick	**enfermarse** *(ehn-fehr-'mahr-seh)*
to give	**dar** *(dahr)*
to go	**ir** *(eer)*
to gossip	**chismear** *(chees-meh-'ahr)*
to grab	**agarrar** *(ah-gahr-'rahr)*
to grow	**crecer** *(kreh-'sehr)*

H

to happen	**ocurrir** *(oh-koor-'reer)*
to harass	**acosar** *(ah-koh-'sahr)*
to have	**tener** *(teh-'nehr)*
to heal	**sanar** *(sah-'nahr)*
to hear	**oír** *(oh-'eer)*
to hire	**contratar** *(kohn-trah-'tahr)*
to hit	**pegar** *(peh-'gahr)*
to humiliate	**humillar** *(hoo-mee-'yahr)*
to hurt	**lastimar** *(lahs-tee-'mahr)*

I

to identify	**identificar** *(ee-dehn-tee-fee-'kahr)*
to immigrate	**inmigrar** *(een-mee-'grahr)*
to impound	**embargar** *(ehm-bahr-'gahr)*
to improve	**mejorar** *(meh-hoh-'rahr)*
to include	**incluir** *(een-kloo-'eer)*
to increase	**aumentar** *(ah-oo-mehn-'tahr)*
to incriminate	**incriminar** *(een-kree-mee-'nahr)*
to injure	**herir** *(eh-'reer)*
to install	**instalar** *(eens-tah-'lahr)*
to insult	**insultar** *(een-sool-'tahr)*
to intimidate	**intimidar** *(een-tee-mee-'dahr)*
to invest	**invertir** *(een-vehr-'teer)*
to investigate	**investigar** *(een-vehs-tee-'gahr)*
to issue	**emitir** *(eh-mee-'teer)*

J

to join	**juntar** *(hoon-'tahr)*
to joke	**bromear** *(broh-meh-'ahr)*

K

to keep	**mantener** *(mahn-teh-'nehr)*
to kill	**matar** *(mah-'tahr)*
to knock down	**derribar** *(dehr-ree-'bahr)*
to know	**saber** *(sah-'behr)*
to know someone	**conocer** *(koh-noh-'sehr)*

L

to learn	**aprender** *(ah-prehn-'dehr)*
to lease	**arrendar** *(ahr-rehn-'dahr)*
to leave	**salir** *(sah-'leer)*
to leave (behind)	**dejar** *(deh-'hahr)*
to limit	**limitar** *(lee-mee-'tahr)*
to listen	**escuchar** *(ehs-koo-'chahr)*
to litigate	**litigar** *(lee-tee-'gahr)*
to live	**vivir** *(vee-'veer)*
to loan	**prestar** *(prehs-'tahr)*
to log in	**conectarse** *(koh-nehk-'tahr-seh)*
to look	**mirar** *(mee-'rahr)*
to look for	**buscar** *(boos-'kahr)*
to lose	**perder** *(pehr-'dehr)*

M

to maim	**lisiar** *(lee-see-'ahr)*
to maintain	**mantener** *(mahn-teh-'nehr)*
to make	**hacer** *(ah-'sehr)*
to manage	**administrar** *(ahd-mee-nees-'trahr)*
to meet	**reunirse** *(reh-oo-'neer-seh)*
to move	**mover** *(moh-'vehr)*
to move away	**mudarse** *(moo-'dahr-seh)*
to murder	**asesinar** *(ah-seh-see-'nahr)*
to mutilate	**mutilar** *(moo-tee-'lahr)*

N

to negociate	**negociar** *(neh-goh-see-'ahr)*
to notify	**notificar** *(noh-tee-fee-'kahr)*

O

to obtain	**obtener** *(ohb-teh-'nehr)*
to offer	**ofrecer** *(oh-freh-'sehr)*
to open	**abrir** *(ah-'breer)*

P

to paralyze	**paralizar** *(pah-rah-lee-'sahr)*
to pay	**pagar** *(pah-'gahr)*
to plead	**abogar** *(ah-boh-'gahr)*
to possess	**poseer** *(poh-seh-'her)*
to post	**dar aviso** *(dahr ah-'vee-soh)*
to postpose	**posponer** *(pohs-poh-'nehr)*
to prepare	**preparar** *(preh-pah-'rahr)*
to present	**presentar** *(preh-sehn-'tahr)*
to press	**oprimir** *(oh-pree-'meer)*
to pressure	**presionar** *(preh-see-oh-'nahr)*
to print	**imprimir** *(eem-pree-'meer)*
to process	**tramitar** *(trah-mee-'tahr)*
to produce	**producir** *(proh-doo-'seer)*
to promise	**prometer** *(proh-meh-'tehr)*
to prosecute	**enjuiciar** *(ehn-hoo-ee-see-'ahr)*
to protect	**proteger** *(proh-teh-'hehr)*
to prove	**probar** *(proh-'bahr)*
to provide	**proveer** *(proh-veh-'ehr)*
to pull	**jalar** *(hah-'lahr)*
to punch	**golpear** *(gohl-peh-'ahr)*
to punish	**castigar** *(kahs-tee-'gahr)*

to push	**empujar** *(ehm-poo-ʿhahr)*
to put away	**guardar** *(gwahr-ʿdahr)*
to put in	**meter** *(meh-ʿtehr)*

R

to rape	**violar** *(vee-oh-ʿlahr)*
to read	**leer** *(leh-ʿehr)*
to receive	**recibir** *(reh-see-ʿbeer)*
to recommend	**recomendar** *(reh-koh-mehn-ʿdahr)*
to recover	**recuperarse** *(reh-koo-peh-ʿrahr-seh)*
to reduce	**reducir** *(reh-doo-ʿseer)*
to refuse	**rehusar** *(reh-oo-ʿsahr)*
to relax	**relajarse** *(reh-lah-ʿhahr-seh)*
to release	**liberar** *(lee-beh-ʿrahr)*
to remove	**sacar** *(sah-ʿkahr)*
to renovate	**renovar** *(reh-noh-ʿvahr)*
to rent	**alquilar** *(ahl-kee-ʿlahr)*
to repair	**reparar** *(reh-pah-ʿrahr)*
to reply	**responder** *(rehs-pohn-ʿdehr)*
to report	**reportar** *(reh-pohr-ʿtahr)*
to request	**solicitar** *(soh-lee-see-ʿtahr)*
to respect	**respetar** *(rehs-peh-ʿtahr)*
to respond	**contestar** *(kohn-tehs-ʿtahr)*
to rest	**descansar** *(dehs-kahn-ʿsahr)*
to return	**regresar** *(reh-greh-ʿsahr)*
to reverse	**anular el fallo** *(ah-noo-ʿlahr ehl ʿfah-yoh)*

S

to save	**guardar** *(gwahr-ʿdahr)*
to say	**decir** *(deh-ʿseer)*
to seal	**sellar** *(seh-ʿyahr)*
to search	**registrar** *(reh-hees-ʿtrahr)*
to see	**ver** *(vehr)*
to select	**escoger** *(ehs-koh-ʿhehr)*
to sell	**vender** *(vehn-ʿdehr)*
to send	**enviar** *(ehn-vee-ʿahr)*
to separate	**separar** *(she-pah-ʿrahr)*
to serve	**servir** *(sehr-ʿveer)*
to share	**compartir** *(kohm-pahr-ʿteer)*
to shoot	**disparar** *(dees-pah-ʿrahr)*
to shout	**gritar** *(gree-ʿtahr)*
to show	**mostrar** *(mohs-ʿtrahr)*

to sit	**sentarse** *(sehn-'tahr-seh)*
to slap	**abofetear** *(ah-boh-feh-teh-'ahr)*
to sleep	**dormir** *(dohr-'meer)*
to smoke	**fumar** *(foo-'mahr)*
to speak	**hablar** *(ah-'blahr)*
to spend	**gastar** *(gahs-'tahr)*
to stab	**apuñalar** *(ah-poon-yah-'lahr)*
to stand	**pararse** *(pah-'rahr-seh)*
to start	**iniciar** *(ee-nee-see-'ahr)*
to steal	**robar** *(roh-'bahr)*
to strangle	**estrangular** *(ehs-trahn-goo-'ahr)*
to strike	**golpear** *(gohl-peh-'ahr)*
to study	**estudiar** *(ehs-too-dee-'ahr)*
to submit	**presentar** *(preh-sehn-'tahr)*
to subrogate	**subrogar** *(soob-roh-'gahr)*
to sue	**demandar** *(deh-mahn-'dahr)*
to suffer	**sufrir** *(soo-'freer)*
to suggest	**sugerir** *(soo-heh-'reer)*
to support	**apoyar** *(ah-poh-'yahr)*
to suppose	**suponer** *(soo-poh-'nehr)*
to suppress	**suprimir** *(soo-pree-'meer)*
to surrender	**entregarse** *(ehn-treh-'gahr-seh)*
to suspend	**suspender** *(soos-pehn-'dehr)*

T

to take	**tomar** *(toh-'mahr)*
to take care of	**cuidar** *(koo-ee-'dahr)*
to take drugs	**tomar drogas** *(toh-'mahr 'droh-gahs)*
to take pictures	**tomar fotos** *(toh-'mahr 'foh-tohs)*
to tease	**burlarse** *(boor-'lahr-seh)*
to tell	**decir** *(deh-'seer)*
to testify	**atestiguar** *(ah-tehs-tee-'gwahr)*
to think	**pensar** *(pehn-'sahr)*
to threaten	**amenazar** *(ah-meh-nah-'sahr)*
to transfer	**transferir** *(trahns-feh-'reer)*
to try	**probar** *(proh-'bahr)*
to turn in	**entregar** *(ehn-treh-'gahr)*

U

to understand	**entender** *(ehn-tehn-'dehr)*
to uphold	**sustentar** *(soos-tehn-'tahr)*
to use	**usar** *(oo-'sahr)*

V

to verify	**verificar** *(veh-ree-fee-'kahr)*
to visit	**visitar** *(vee-see-'tahr)*

W

to wait	**esperar** *(ehs-peh-'rahr)*
to walk	**caminar** *(kah-mee-'nahr)*
to warn	**conminar** *(kohn-mee-'nahr)*
to win	**ganar** *(gah-'nahr)*
to withdraw	**retirar** *(reh-tee-'rahr)*
to withhold	**rehusar** *(reh-oo-'sahr)*
to work	**trabajar** *(trah-bah-'hahr)*
to write	**escribir** *(ehs-kree-'beer)*

Y

to yell	**gritar** *(gree-'tahr)*

EXPRESSIONS

Again, please.	**Otra vez, por favor.** *('oh-trah vehs pohr fah-'vohr)*
All the better!	**¡Tanto mejor!** *('tahn-toh meh-'hohr)*
And this, too.	**Y este, también.** *(ee 'ehs-teh tahm-bee-'ehn)*
And you?	**¿Y usted?** *(ee oos-'tehd)*
Be careful!	**¡Tenga cuidado!** *('tehn-gah koo-ee-'dah-doh)*
Cheers!	**¡Salud!** *(sah-'lood)*
Come in!	**¡Adelante!** *(ah-deh-'lahn-teh)*
Congratulations!	**¡Felicitaciones!** *(feh-lee-see-tah-see-'oh-nehs)*
Do not do it.	**No lo haga.** *(noh loh 'ah-gah)*
Do you need an interpreter?	**¿Necesita un intérprete?**
	(neh-seh-'see-tah oon een-'tehr-preh-teh)
Do you remember?	**¿Se acuerda?** *(seh ah-'kwehr-dah)*
Do you understand?	**¿Entiende usted?** *(ehn-tee-'ehn-deh oos-'tehd)*
Don't be late!	**¡No llegue tarde!** *(noh 'yeh-geh 'tahr-deh)*
Don't worry.	**No se preocupe.** *(noh seh preh-oh-'koo-peh)*
Everything's OK.	**Todo está bien.** *('toh-doh ehs-'tah bee-'ehn)*
Excuse me.	**Con permiso.** *(kohn pehr-'mee-soh)*
Give my regards to...	**Me saluda a...** *(meh sah-'loo-dah ah)*
Go ahead!	**¡Pase!** *('pah-seh)*
God willing!	**¡Si Dios quiere!** *(see dee-'ohs kee-'eh-reh)*
Good afternoon.	**Buenas tardes.** *('bweh-nahs 'tahr-dehs)*
Good evening.	**Buenas noches.** *('bweh-nahs 'noh-chehs)*
Good idea!	**¡Buena idea!** *('bweh-nah ee-'deh-ah)*
Good luck!	**¡Buena suerte!** *('bweh-nah 'swehr-teh)*
Good morning.	**Buenos días.** *('bweh-nohs 'dee-ahs)*
Good job!	**¡Bien hecho!** *(bee-'ehn 'eh-choh)*
Good-bye!	**¡Adiós!** *(ah-dee-'ohs)*
Great!	**¡Muy bien!** *('moo-ee bee-'ehn)*
Happy anniversary!	**¡Feliz aniversario!** *(feh-'lees ah-nee-vehr-'sah-ree-oh)*
Happy birthday!	**¡Feliz cumpleaños!** *(feh-'lees koom-pleh-'ahn-yohs)*
Happy Easter!	**¡Feliz Pascua!** *(feh-'lees 'pahs-kwah)*
Happy holidays!	**¡Felices fiestas!** *(feh-'lee-sehs fee-'ehs-tahs)*
Happy New Year!	**¡Feliz año nuevo!** *(feh-'lees 'ahn-yoh 'nweh-voh)*
Have a good time!	**¡Que disfrute!** *(keh dees-'froo-teh)*
Have a nice day!	**¡Que le vaya bien!** *(keh leh 'vah-yah bee-'ehn)*
Have a nice trip!	**¡Buen viaje!** *('bwehn vee-'ah-heh)*
Hi!	**¡Hola!** *('oh-lah)*
How are you?	**¿Cómo está?** *('koh-moh ehs-'tah)*
How do you say it?	**¿Cómo se dice?** *('koh-moh seh 'dee-seh)*
How do you spell it?	**¿Cómo se deletrea?** *('koh-moh seh deh-leh-'treh-ah)*
How may I help you?	**¿En qué puedo servirle?** *(ehn keh 'pweh-doh sehr-'veer-leh)*

How much does it cost?	**¿Cuánto cuesta?** *('kwahn-toh 'kwehs-tah)*
How old are you?	**¿Cuántos años tiene usted?** *('kwahn-tohs 'ahn-yohs tee-'eh-neh oos-'tehd)*
How sad!	**¡Qué triste!** *(keh 'trees-teh)*
How's it going!	**¡Qué tal!** *(keh tahl)*
How's the weather?	**¿Qué tiempo hace?** *(keh tee-'ehm-poh 'ah-seh)*
I agree!	**¡De acuerdo!** *(deh ah-'kwehr-doh)*
I don't know.	**No sé.** *(noh seh)*
I don't understand.	**No entiendo.** *(noh ehn-tee-'ehn-doh)*
I hope so!	**¡Ojalá!** *(oh-hah-'lah)*
I remember!	**¡Yo recuerdo!** *(yoh reh-'kwehr-doh)*
I see!	**¡Ya veo!** *(yah 'veh-oh)*
I speak a little Spanish.	**Hablo poquito español.** *('ah-bloh poh-'kee-toh ehs-pahn-'yohl)*
I think so!	**¡Creo que sí!** *('kreh-oh keh see)*
I'm learning Spanish.	**Estoy aprendiendo español.** *(ehs-'toh-ee ah-prehn-dee-'ehn-doh ehs-pahn-'yohl)*
I'm so glad!	**¡Me alegro!** *(meh ah-'leh-groh)*
I'm sorry.	**Lo siento.** *(loh see-'ehn-toh)*
It doesn't matter!	**¡No importa!** *(noh eem-'pohr-tah)*
Just a moment.	**Un momento.** *(oon moh-'mehn-toh)*
Keep going.	**Siga.** *('see-gah)*
Let's go!	**¡Vamos!** *('vah-mohs)*
Letter by letter.	**Letra por letra.** *('leh-trah pohr 'leh-trah)*
May I come in?	**¿Se puede?** *(seh 'pweh-deh)*
Maybe!	**¡Quizás!** *(kee-'sahs)*
Me, neither!	**¡Yo tampoco!** *(yoh tahm-'poh-koh)*
Me, too!	**¡Yo también!** *(yoh tahm-bee-'ehn)*
Merry Christmas!	**¡Feliz Navidad!** *(feh-'lees nah-vee-'dahd)*
More or less!	**¡Más o menos!** *(mahs oh 'meh-nohs)*
More slowly.	**Más despacio.** *(mahs dehs-'pah-see-oh)*
My name is...	**Me llamo...** *(meh 'yah-moh)*
Nice to meet you!	**¡Mucho gusto!** *('moo-choh 'goos-toh)*
No problem!	**¡No hay problema!** *(noh 'ah-ee proh-'bleh-mah)*
No smoking, please.	**Favor de no fumar.** *(fah-'vohr deh noh foo-'mahr)*
No wonder!	**¡Con razón!** *(kohn rah-'sohn)*
Not like that.	**Así no.** *(ah-'see noh)*
Not yet.	**Todavía no.** *(toh-dah-'vee-ah noh)*
Nothing much!	**¡Sin novedad!** *(seen noh-veh-'dahd)*
Number by number.	**Número por número.** *('noo-meh-roh pohr 'noo-meh-roh)*
Of course!	**¡Por supuesto!** *(pohr soo-'pwehs-toh)*
Oh my gosh!	**¡Dios mío!** *(dee-'ohs 'mee-oh)*
Pardon me.	**Perdón.** *(pehr-'dohn)*
Please.	**Por favor.** *(pohr fah-'vohr)*

Ready?	**¿Listo?** *('lees-toh)*
Really?	**¿Es verdad?** *(ehs vehr-'dahd)*
Right away!	**¡En seguida!** *(ehn seh-'ghee-dah)*
Same to you.	**Igualmente.** *(ee-gwahl-'mehn-teh)*
Say it in English.	**Dígalo en inglés.** *('dee-gah-loh ehn een-'glehs)*
See you later!	**¡Hasta luego!** *('ahs-tah loo-'eh-goh)*
So what!	**¡Qué importa!** *(keh eem-'pohr-tah)*
So-so.	**Así-así.** *(ah-'see ah-'see)*
Sure!	**¡Claro!** *('klah-roh)*
Take a seat.	**Tome asiento.** *('toh-meh ah-see-'ehn-toh)*
Thank goodness!	**¡Gracias a Dios!** *('grah-see-ahs ah dee-'ohs)*
Thank you very much.	**Muchas gracias.** *('moo-chahs 'grah-see-ahs)*
Thanks for your patience.	**Gracias por su paciencia.** *('grah-see-ahs pohr soo pah-see-'ehn-see-ah)*
That depends!	**¡Depende!** *(deh-'pehn-deh)*
That's better.	**Eso está mejor.** *('eh-soh ehs-'tah meh-'hohr)*
That's for sure!	**¡Es cierto!** *(ehs see-'ehr-toh)*
That's great!	**¡Qué bueno!** *(keh 'bweh-noh)*
That's it.	**Eso es.** *('eh-soh ehs)*
That's OK!	**¡Está bien!** *(ehs-'tah bee-'ehn)*
The pleasure is mine.	**El gusto es mío.** *(ehl 'goos-toh ehs 'mee-oh)*
The same thing.	**La misma cosa.** *(lah 'mees-mah 'koh-sah)*
Very well.	**Muy bien.** *('moo-ee bee-'ehn)*
Welcome!	**¡Bienvenidos!** *(bee-ehn-veh-'nee-dohs)*
What a joke!	**¡Qué chiste!** *(keh 'chees-teh)*
What a shame!	**¡Qué lástima!** *(keh 'lahs-tee-mah)*
What does it mean?	**¿Qué significa?** *(keh seeg-nee-'fee-kah)*
What time is it?	**¿Qué hora es?** *(keh 'oh-rah ehs)*
What's going on?	**¿Qué pasa?** *(keh 'pah-sah)*
What's your name?	**¿Cómo se llama?** *('koh-moh seh 'yah-mah)*
Where are you from?	**¿De dónde es?** *(deh 'dohn-deh ehs)*
Word for word.	**Palabra por palabra.** *(pah-'lah-brah pohr pah-'lah-brah)*
Yes!	**¡Sí!** *(see)*
You got it?	**¿Lo entiende?** *(loh ehn-tee-'ehn-deh)*
You're welcome.	**De nada.** *(deh 'nah-dah)*

COMMANDS

Answer!	**¡Conteste!** *(kohn-'tehs-teh)*
Bring...	**Traiga...** *('trah-ee-gah)*
Buy...	**Compre...** *('kohm-preh)*
Call!	**¡Llame!** *('yah-meh)*
Change...	**Cambie...** *('kahm-bee-eh)*

Check!	**¡Revise!** *(reh-'vee-seh)*
Clean...	**Limpie...** *('leem-pee-eh)*
Close...	**Cierre...** *(see-'ehr-reh)*
Come!	**¡Venga!** *('vehn-gah)*
Continue!	**¡Siga!** *('see-gah)*
Drive!	**¡Maneje!** *(mah-'neh-heh)*
Enter!	**¡Entre!** *('ehn-treh)*
Explain!	**¡Explique!** *(ex-'plee-keh)*
Fill out...	**Llene...** *('yeh-neh)*
Finish!	**¡Termine!** *(tehr-'mee-neh)*
Give...	**Dé...** *(deh)*
Go!	**¡Vaya!** *('vah-yah)*
Hurry up!	**¡Apúrese!** *(ah-'poo-reh-seh)*
Leave!	**¡Salga!** *('sahl-gah)*
Listen!	**¡Escuche!** *(ehs-'koo-cheh)*
Look!	**¡Mire!** *('mee-reh)*
Look for...	**Busque...** *('boos-keh)*
Open...	**Abra...** *('ah-brah)*
Park...	**Estacione...** *(ehs-tah-see-'oh-neh)*
Pick up...	**Recoja...** *(reh-'koh-hah)*
Put...	**Ponga...** *('pohn-gah)*
Put inside...	**Meta...** *('meh-tah)*
Read!	**¡Lea!** *('leh-ah)*
Remove...	**Saque...** *('sah-keh)*
Set up...	**Prepare...** *(preh-'pah-reh)*
Sign!	**¡Firme!** *('feer-meh)*
Sit down!	**¡Siéntese!** *(see-'ehn-teh-seh)*
Speak!	**¡Hable!** *('ah-bleh)*
Stand up!	**¡Levántese!** *(leh-'vahn-teh-seh)*
Start!	**¡Comience!** *(koh-mee-'ehn-seh)*
Stay!	**¡Quédese!** *('keh-deh-seh)*
Study!	**¡Estudie!** *(ehs-'too-dee-eh)*
Take...	**Tome...** *('toh-meh)*
Tell...	**Diga...** *('dee-gah)*
Throw out...	**Tire...** *('tee-reh)*
Use...	**Use...** *('oo-seh)*
Wait!	**¡Espere!** *(ehs-'peh-reh)*
Walk!	**¡Camine!** *(kah-'mee-neh)*
Write!	**¡Escriba!** *(ehs-'kree-bah)*

ANSWERS TO
PRIVATE PRACTICE EXERCISES

1   1. los carros rojos
     2. tres casas grandes
     3. las mesas negras

2   A. 1. cinco
          2. ocho
          3. uno
    B. 1. cinco mil
          2. trescientos
          3. sesenta y siete

3   1. ayer   mañana
     2. arriba   abajo
     3. siempre   nunca
     4. enfrente   detrás
     5. tarde   temprano

4   1. *(kee-'ehn trah-'bah-hah ehl doh-'meen-goh? 'nah-dee-eh)*
       Who works on Sunday? No one.
     2. *('kwahn-toh choh-koh-'lah-teh kee-'eh-reh oos-'tehd? Loh deh-'mahs)*
       How much chocolate do you want? The rest.
     3. *('dohn-deh ehs-'tahn lahs kohm-poo-tah-'doh-rahs? Pohr 'toh-dahs 'pahr-tehs)*
       Where are the computers? Everywhere.

5   1. ¿Qué hora es?
     2. A las ocho cuarenta y cinco de la mañana.
     3. Son las nueve.

6   1. lunes, <u>martes</u>, miércoles, jueves, <u>viernes</u> sábado, <u>domingo</u>
     2. <u>enero</u>, febrero, marzo, <u>abril</u>, mayo, <u>junio</u>
     3. julio, agosto, septiembre, <u>octubre</u>, <u>noviembre</u>, diciembre

7   1. Hace frío.
     2. Es verano.
     3. Hay una tormenta.
     4. ¿Qué tiempo hace?
     5. Hace sol y viento.

8   1. viejo   joven
        2. limpio   sucio
        3. malo   bueno
        4. gordo   delgado
        5. difícil   fácil
        6. rico   pobre
        7. grande   chico

9   A.   1. estoy
             2. está
             3. están
        B.   1. somos
             2. soy
             3. es

10 *Answers will vary.*

11 1. There are two men in the house.
        2. There is no water.
        3. Is there a problem?

12 A.   1. to accept
             2. to accuse
             3. to admit
             4. to authorize
             5. to cause
             6. to compensate
             7. to communicate
             8. to confirm
             9. to confiscate
             10. to consult
             11. to cooperate
             12. to determine
        B.   1. Voy a comer.
             2. Favor de no venir mañana.
             3. Quisiera investigar.

13 What can I do for you?
        I need legal help.
        Are you a new client?
        Yes. You are immigration lawyers, right?
        Yes, but I am not a lawyer. I am the receptionist. Take a seat, please.
          Somebody will be with you in a moment.

14 *Answers will vary.*

15 A. *Answers will vary.*
        B.   1. empresario   empleado
             2. disponible   listo
             3. bombero   policía
             4. competencia   experiencia
             5. calendario   horario

16 A. 1. You need the consultation.
      2. Let's talk about the case.
      3. We'll determine the best way.
   B. 1. **archivo**
      2. **condado**
      3. **resultado**

17 A. 1. **ascensor**
      2. **planificador**
      3. **gabinete**
      4. **impresora**
      5. **asiento**
      6. **lápiz**
   B. *Answers will vary.*

18 A. >**¿Aló, está Raul?**
    < **No, lo siento. ¿Quisiera dejar un recado?**
    > **Sí, gracias. Mi nombre es Smith y estoy llamando de la oficina de su abogado.**
   B. 1. **Visite nuestro sitio web.**
      2. **El mensaje no está en el buzón.**
      3. **¿Cuándo necesito abrir el directorio?**

19 1. **Estamos estudiando.**
   2. **Estamos aprendiendo.**
   3. **Estamos observando.**
   4. **Estamos verificando.**
   5. **Estamos saliendo.**

20 A. 1. **el tribunal juvenil**
      2. **la corte, el tribunal**
      3. **el tribunal de divorcio**
   B. 1. criminal court
      2. traffic court
      3. small claims court
   C. 1. **la licencia**   **el registro**
      2. **la multa**   **la boleta**
      3. **el cheque**   **el efectivo**

21 1. **comercio**
   2. **semáforo**
   3. **desarrollo**

22 1. Move back.
   2. Call me tomorrow.
   3. Don't give him/her the number.
   4. Head west.
   5. Bring us the documents.
   6. Don't send them the money.

23 A. 1. doce
        2. detrás
        3. los asientos
    B. 1. arriba   abajo
        2. enfrente   detrás
        3. lejos   cerca
        4. adentro   afuera
        5. derecha   izquierda
    C. 1. el alguacil
        2. el testigo
        3. el estenógrafo

24 A. 1. Preste atención.
        2. Puede(n) sentarse.
        3. Aquí tiene el procedimiento.
    B. 1. alegato
        2. demanda
        3. juicio
    C. 1. contestar
        2. hablar
        3. dar

25 A. *Answers will vary.*
    B. 1. abrigo
        2. pizarra
        3. algo

26 1. trabaja   She works a lot.
    2. mandamos   We send money.
    3. regresan   They return late.
    4. escribo   I write the information.
    5. usa   He uses the pencil.

27 A. *Answers will vary.*
    B. *Answers will vary.*
    C. 1. requisito   ley
        2. asilo   inmunidad
        3. trámite   proceso
        4. difícil   grave
        5. atrasado   aplazado

28 A. 1. ¿Necesita un abogado de lesiones corporales?
        2. ¿Quisiera demandar por daños?
        3. Trabajamos con casos de negligencia médica.
    B. 1. terapeuta
        2. póliza
        3. cuello
        4. advertencia
        5. autobús

29 **A.** *Answers will vary.*
  B. *Answers will vary.*

30 **A.** *Answers will vary.*
  B. 1. oreja
    2. llamada
    3. volante

31 **A.** 1. la orden la demanda
    2. el salario los ingresos
    3. el cónyuge el esposo
    4. el alegato el cargo
    5. el deseo la necesidad
  B. 1. younger child
    2. kidnapping
    3. felony
    4. relationships
    5. mistreatment
    6. meeting
  C. *Answers will vary.*

32 **A.** 1. ofensivo grosero
    2. furioso enojado
    3. burlarse molestar
    4. nervioso ansioso
    5. joven menor
    6. calmarse relajarse
  B. *Answers will vary.*

33 **A.** 1. llamar call Voy a llamar.
    2. descansar rest Voy a descansar.
    3. hacer ejercicio do exercise Voy a hacer ejercicio.
    4. tomar medicina take medication Voy a tomar medicina.
    5. gritar yell Voy a gritar.
  B. 1. llamaré, llamará, llamarán, llamaremos
    2. descansaré, descansará, descansarán, descansaremos
    3. haré, hará, harán, haremos
    4. tomaré, tomará, tomarán, tomaremos
    5. gritaré, gritará, gritarán, gritaremos

34 **A.** *Answers will vary.*
  B. 1. el cambio las monedas
    2. el pedido la factura
    3. la solicitud el formulario
  C. 1. la tasa de interés
    2. la cuenta de ahorros
    3. el pago adelantado
    4. la tarjeta de crédito
    5. los bienes raíces

35 A. 1. la carta
        2. el socio
        3. jurados
    B. 1. los bienes
        2. el fideicomiso
        3. el testamento

36 A. I have a family business. It's a local business and we work with a variety of products and services.
    B. 1. Sí, vendemos.
        2. Sí, instalamos.
        3. Sí, compramos.
        4. Sí, construimos.
        5. Sí, invertimos.
    C. 1. compra   venta
        2. precio   costo
        3. ganga   descuento
        4. proporción   porcentaje
        5. correo   envío

37 A. *Answers will vary.*
    B. 1. propietario   inquilino
        2. ruido   olor
        3. tuberías   electricidad
        4. techo   piso
        5. exclusivo   privado
    C. 1. el aviso de desalojo
        2. el depósito de seguridad
        3. la equidad de una vivienda

38 A. *Answers will vary.*
    B. 1. ¿Hay problemas con el reclamo?
        2. ¿Entiende la estipulación?
        3. ¿Habló con la compañía de seguros?

39 A. 1. Sí, lo saqué.
        2. Sí, lo presté.
        3. Sí, lo gasté.
        4. Sí, lo cancelé.
        5. Sí, lo cambié.
    B. 1. Tenía tarjetas de crédito.
        2. Hablaba con el banco.
        3. Vendían el seguro de carro.

40 A. 1. la acusación   el cargo
        2. el sumario   el informe
        3. el preso   el prisionero
        4. la prueba   la evidencia
        5. el investigador   el detective
    B. 1. jurisdiction
        2. confession
        3. infraction
        4. investigation
        5. testimony

41 A. 1. Was the suspect acting brutally?
        2. Did they give him a breath test and explain his rights to him?
        3. Did she look nervous and scared?
    B. *Answers will vary.*

42 *Answers will vary.*

43 A. 1. estafador
        2. abrigo
        3. preocupado
    B. 1. ¿Puede probar que usted lo compró?
        2. ¿Ha identificado la propiedad robada?
        3. ¿Cuál es la pérdida estimada?

44 A. *Answers will vary.*
    B. *Answers will vary.*
    C. *Answers will vary.*

45 1. huellas   evidencia
    2. píldora   cápsula
    3. opio   heroína
    4. odio   venganza
    5. dormido   despierto

46 1. Pelear, Estoy peleando, Peleo, Voy a pelear, Peleé, Peleaba,
       He peleado
    2. Ayudar, Estoy ayudando, Ayudo, Voy a ayudar, Ayudé, Ayudaba,
       He ayudado

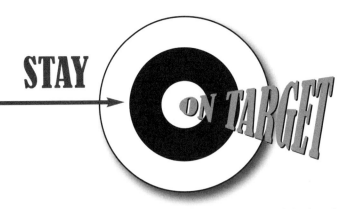

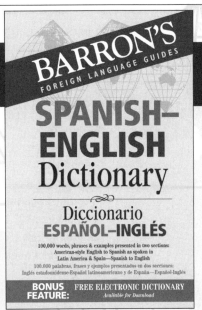

HOW TO USE THE AUDIO CDs

These CDs should be used in conjunction with the book. You may listen to the CDs on a CD player or a computer. To play a CD on your computer, insert it into the CD-ROM drive, and choose an audio media program if one doesn't launch automatically.

CD No.	Track No.	Chapter	Description
1	1		Introduction
	2		Pronunciation
	3		Greetings
	4		Questions
	5		Everyday vocabulary
	6–7		People & family
	8		Singular articles
	9		Colors. Adjectives
	10		Numbers
	11		Plural articles
	12		Word order
	13		Questions
	14		To be (*ser/estar*). Use of *no*
	15		Pronouns. Possession
	16		Commands
	17		Verb infinitives
	18		Verb endings
	19		Prepositions
	20–22		Legal vocabulary. Gender. Questions
	23		What? How much? How many? Who?
	24		Where? Directions. In, on, at
	25		When? Telling time
	26		Days of the week. Months. Dates
	27		To have. Articles

CD No.	Track No.	Chapter	Description
2	1		Present indicative tense
	2		City vocabulary
	3–4		Court vocabulary. Commands
	5		Court professionals. Gender
	6		Future tense
	7		Commands. Vocabulary
	8		Verbs
	9		Telephone. Computers
	10		Requests
	11		Immigration issues
	12		Personal injury law. Verbs
	13		Medical vocabulary. The body
	14		Giving instructions. Accidents & injuries
	15		Safety items
	16		Verb infinitives. Past tense
	17		Family law
	18		Feelings
	19		Commands. There is and there are
	20		Human attributes
	21		Business. Finance. Real estate law
	22		Financial vocabulary
	23		Business law. Questions
	24–25		Insurance law
	26		Finance verbs. Imperfect
	27–29		Criminal law
	30		Compound tenses
	31		Review